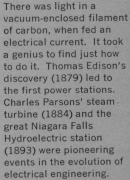

There was light in a vacuum-enclosed filament of carbon, when fed an electrical current. It took a genius to find just how to do it. Thomas Edison's discovery (1879) led to the first power stations. Charles Parsons' steam turbine (1884) and the great Niagara Falls Hydroelectric station (1893) were pioneering events in the evolution of electrical engineering.

Automotive engineering really began to roll about 1885, when Gottlieb Daimler's first internal-combustion car appeared. Henry Ford's genius was to create mass-production —Model T's for the millions. Rudolph Diesel developed his famed work-horse engine in 1892. Civil engineers set out to build roads fast enough to keep up with the drivers. That race isn't over yet.

Dedicated to my mother,
Edna Webb Earle

JAMES H. EARLE, Texas A&M University

descriptive geometry

ADDISON-WESLEY PUBLISHING COMPANY

Reading, Massachusetts

Menlo Park, California · London · Don Mills, Ontario

Chapter opening illustrations are reproduced through the courtesy of the National Aeronautics and Space Administration.

Endpaper drawings are reproduced through the courtesy of Keuffel & Esser Co.

PREFACE

Design is a major function of the engineer and technician, and descriptive geometry and engineering graphics are the fundamental tools of the design process. Descriptive geometry is presented in this textbook as a problem-solving tool and as a means of developing solutions to technical problems. The principles presented in this text are closely related to actual engineering design problems. A generous number of photographs of products and equipment are included to show some of the many applications of descriptive geometry to various projects.

Our treatment of descriptive geometry motivates the student by exposing him to engineering examples taken from real-life situations. Instead of boring the student with synthetic projects, the approach taken in this text has proved to stimulate his interest in engineering and technology as creative professions.

Several techniques of presentation have been used that improve the exposition and help the student to understand the concepts and procedures discussed. Many of these techniques allow the student to grasp principles on his own, thus requiring less of the instructor's time while allowing the average student to cover more material than in the conventional course. For greater clarity, a second color has been introduced to highlight significant steps and notes in the illustrations. The more complex problems are solved by the *step method,* whereby the steps leading to the solution of a problem are presented in sequence, with the instructional text closely related to each step. Since this method of developing a solution by steps shows the actual progression of graphical construction, the student can review the procedure and theory involved in a problem while studying alone without the help of an instructor. To determine the effectiveness of the step method,* it was tested throughout a semester's work and the results were compared with those obtained by conventional textbook methods. A statistical comparison of 2800 experimental samples showed that the step method was 20 percentage points superior to the conventional approach. This result prompted the author to introduce the step method in this volume.

Enough material is included in this text for a course in descriptive geometry for the engineering student or technology student. The design process is mentioned briefly at the beginning of the book and is referred to throughout the remaining chapters. This emphasis on the design process is more useful to industry and the technical professions than is the abstract approach in which drafting skill receives primary emphasis.

The problems at the end of each chapter are structured to be difficult enough to be interesting, but not so difficult as to be beyond the ability of the average student. The text can be used with a number of problem books compiled each semester by the staff of the Department of Engineering Design Graphics at Texas A&M University. The authors of this series of problem books published by Addison-Wesley Publishing Company are James H. Earle, Samuel M. Cleland, Lawrence E. Stark, Paul M. Mason, North B. Bardell, Richard F. Vogel, J. Timothy Coppinger, Michael P. Guerard, and John P. Oliver. At present there are five problem books available in the series Design and Descriptive Geometry Problems (1, 2, 3, 4, and 5). Each of these problem books is completely different from the others in the series. All contain design problems and industrial applications to be solved by graphical methods. Also available are teachers' guides and solution booklets which provide solutions, course outlines, and quizzes. This continuing series provides the instructor with a different set of problems for each semester.

Thanks are due to the hundreds of industries who provided photographs, drawings, and examples included in this book. Appreciation is also due to Professor Michael P. Guerard of Texas A&M University for his assistance in preparing the section on nomography. Credits would not be complete without mentioning the encouragement, confidence, and assistance given to the author by the staff of Addison-Wesley Publishing Company. They have been instrumental in recognizing the need for a book of this type and in expediting its publication.

*James H. Earle, *An Experimental Comparison of Three Self-Instruction Formats for Descriptive Geometry.* Unpublished dissertation, Texas A&M University, College Station, Texas, 1964.

College Station, Texas   J. H. E.
January 1971

CONTENTS

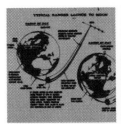

IDENTIFICATION

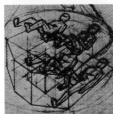

PRELIMINARY IDEAS

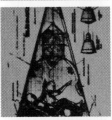

REFINEMENT

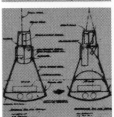

ANALYSIS

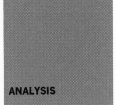

DECISION

IMPLEMENTATION

1

INTRODUCTION TO DESCRIPTIVE GEOMETRY AND GRAPHICS

1-1 INTRODUCTION

Engineering and technology have made significant contributions to the betterment of our living standards. Essentially all of our daily activities are assisted by products, systems, and services made possible by advances in technology. The fact that utilities, heating and cooling equipment, automobiles, machinery, and consumer products have been provided at economical prices to the bulk of our national population is largely due to the technological and engineering professions.

The engineer and technologist must function as a member of a team that includes other related, and sometimes unrelated, disciplines. Many engineers have worked in cooperation with members of the medical profession on innovations in life-saving mechanisms. Other engineers act as technical representatives or salesmen who explain and demonstrate applications of technical products to a specialized segment of the market. Even though there is a wide range of activities within the broad field of engineering, the engineer is basically a designer. This is the activity that most clearly distinguishes him from other associated members of the technological team.

As a member of a team and as a designer, the engineer encounters many problems which require not only unique solutions but also methods of clearly representing these solutions to associates. Graphical methods and descriptive geometry often yield a solution to a problem that

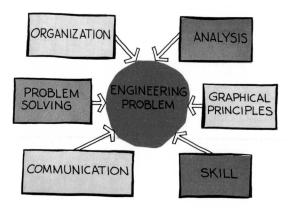

Fig. 1–1. Problems in this text require a total engineering approach with the engineering problem as the central theme.

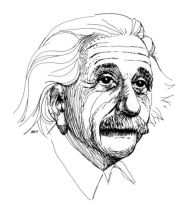

Fig. 1–2. Albert Einstein, the famous physicist, said, "Imagination is more important than knowledge . . ."

may be difficult to solve by other methods. Not only are graphics and descriptive geometry essential in solving problems, but these methods can be used in preparing detailed working drawings from which the project can be built by craftsmen under the supervision of a technician.

This book is extensively illustrated to provide as many practical applications as possible of descriptive geometry to real problems. The examples found here will be helpful in introducing the student to the various fields of technology and in showing the application of graphical principles to a wide range of problems. Descriptive geometry is not an abstract science, but it is a valuable tool for the solution of technical problems.

Creativity and imagination are encouraged by this textbook as essential ingredients of engineering and technology. All descriptive geometry principles are presented as tools of creativity and technological innovation in solving elementary engineering problems, using a systematic approach (Fig. 1–1). Albert Einstein (Fig. 1–2), the famous physicist, said that "Imagination is more important than knowledge, for knowledge is limited, whereas imagination embraces the entire world . . . stimulating progress, giving birth to evolution . . . ."

1–2 ENGINEERING GRAPHICS

Engineering graphics is usually considered to be the total field of graphical problem solving and includes two major areas of specialization, descriptive geometry and working drawings. Other areas that can be utilized for a wide variety of scientific and engineering applications are also included within the field. These are nomography, graphical mathematics, empirical equations, technical illustration, vector analysis, graphical analysis, and other graphical applications associated with each of the different engineering industries. Engineering graphics should not be confused with drafting, since it is considerably more extensive than the communication of an idea in the form of a working drawing. Graphical methods are the primary means of creating a solution to a problem requiring innovations not already available to the designer. Graphics is the designer's method of thinking, solving, and communicating his ideas throughout the design process. Man's progress can be attributed to a great extent to the area of engineering graphics. Even the simplest of structures could not have been designed or built without drawings, diagrams, and details that explained their construction

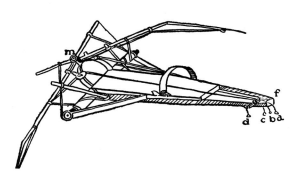

Fig. 1–3. Leonardo da Vinci developed many creative designs through the use of graphical methods.

Fig. 1–4. Gaspard Monge, the "father of descriptive geometry."

(Fig. 1–3). For many years technical drawings, such as they were, were confined to two dimensions, usually a plan view. Supplemental sketches and pictorials were used to explain other dimensions of the project being depicted. Gradually, graphical methods were developed to show three related views of an object to simulate its three-dimensional representation. A most significant development in the engineering graphics area was descriptive geometry as introduced by Gaspard Monge (Fig. 1–4).

1–3 DESCRIPTIVE GEOMETRY

Gaspard Monge (1746–1818) is considered the "father of descriptive geometry." Young Monge used this graphical method of solving design problems related to fortifications and battlements while a military student in France. He was scolded by his headmaster for not solving a problem by the usual, long, tedious mathematical process traditionally used for problems of this type. It was only after long explanations and comparisons of the solutions of both methods that he was able to convince the faculty that his graphical methods could be used to solve the problem in considerably less time.

This was such an improvement over the mathematical solution that it was kept a military secret for 15 years before it was allowed to be taught as part of the technical curriculum. Monge became a scientific and mathematical aid to Napoleon during his reign as general and emperor of France.

Descriptive geometry has been simplified from the "indirect" method introduced by Monge to the "direct" method used today. In the "indirect" method, the first angle of projection is used primarily, with the front view projected above the top view, and the projections are revolved onto the projection planes to obtain the desired relationships (Fig. 1–5). The "direct" method utilizes the third angle, with the top view projected over the front view, and auxiliary views are projected directly to auxiliary planes in succession until the required geometric relationships are found.

Descriptive geometry can be defined as the projection of three-dimensional figures onto a two-dimensional plane of paper in such a manner as to allow geometric manipulations to determine lengths, angles, shapes, and other descriptive information concerning the figures. The type of problems lending themselves to solution by descriptive geometry, although very

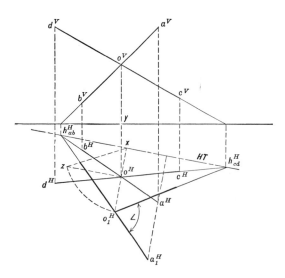

Fig. 1–5. An indirect solution to a descriptive geometry problem utilizing the Mongean method. (Courtesy of C. H. Schumann, Jr., *Descriptive Geometry*, 3rd Edition, Van Nostrand, 1938.)

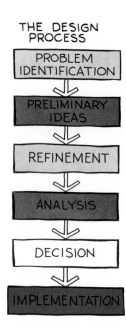

THE DESIGN PROCESS

Fig. 1–6. The steps of the design process.

common, are usually considerably more difficult to solve by mathematics. The simple determination of the angle between planes is a basic descriptive geometry problem, but is difficult to determine mathematically when the plane of the angle does not appear true size in the given views.

1-4 INTRODUCTION TO DESIGN

Engineering graphics in general and descriptive geometry in particular are important in the design of any product or system. These are the methods used by the designer in communicating with himself and with others. He uses these methods to develop and solve many problems that would be difficult to solve by other methods.

The terms "design" and "design process" will be used often in this book to call attention to the application of the principles discussed here to the solution of engineering and technological problems. This is to encourage you to develop your imagination and to become aware of the process used in developing original solutions to problems. Consideration of the role of descrip-

tive geometry in the design process will make the principles more meaningful to you.

The following article will briefly discuss the *design process* to give you an overview of the procedures that are followed. The design process is not a rigid formula but a flexible approach to the solution of a problem. Better results are usually obtained when the designer follows a somewhat disciplined procedure rather than using an unstructured approach.

1-5 THE DESIGN PROCESS

The act of devising a solution to a problem by a combination of principles, resources, and products is design. As we stated at the beginning of this chapter, the design of a product is the most distinguishing responsibility that separates the engineer from the scientist and the technician. His solutions may involve a combination of existing components in a different arrangement to provide a more efficient result or they may involve the development of an entirely new product; but in either case his work is referred to as the act of designing. This

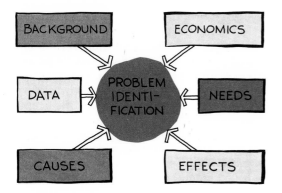

Fig. 1-7. Problem identification requires the accumulation of as much information concerning the problem as possible before a solution is attempted by the designer.

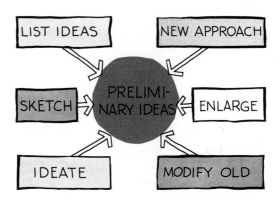

Fig. 1-8. Preliminary ideas are developed after the identification step has been completed. All possibilities should be listed and sketched to give the designer a broad selection of ideas from which to work.

process is not an inspirational phenomenon that is experienced by only a few, but is the result of a systematic, disciplined approach to the needs of the problem.

The design process is the usual pattern of activities that are followed by the designer in arriving at the solution of a technological problem. Many combinations of steps have been suggested to enable one to achieve design objectives. This book emphasizes a six-step design process that is a composite of the sequences most commonly employed in solving problems. The six steps are: (1) Problem identification, (2) Preliminary ideas, (3) Problem refinement, (4) Analysis, (5) Decision, and (6) Implementation (Fig. 1-6).

Engineering graphics and descriptive geometry have been integrated into these steps to stress their role in the creative process of designing. These areas are probably more critical to the design process than any other single field of study. The following articles present the design process while succeeding chapters illustrate the applications of graphics to it.

1-6   PROBLEM IDENTIFICATION

Many engineering problems are not clearly defined nor do they have apparent solutions. As in any problem situation, it is necessary that the

problem be identified and understood before an attempt should be made to solve it (Fig. 1-7). For example, a prominent concern today is air pollution. If you were assigned to find ways of reducing air pollution, you would first have to identify the problem. We know that many impurities are released into the atmosphere that are unhealthy and cause general discomfort. But is the problem the control of the sources of the impurities, their elimination, the control of atmospheric conditions that harbor impurities, or the creation of an artificial atmosphere that is free of the polluted air?

Assume that there is a bad intersection where traffic is unusually congested. What is the problem? Is it too many cars for the capacity of the road, is it poorly synchronized signals, is it poorly routed traffic, or is it visual obstructions resulting in congestion of traffic? The answers to questions such as these would be very helpful in identifying the problem and consequently arriving at a conclusion. Field data gathered at the site can provide valuable information that will serve to identify the problem.

1-7   PRELIMINARY IDEAS

Once the problem has been identified, the next step is to accumulate as many ideas for solution as possible (Fig. 1-8). Preliminary ideas can be

Fig. 1-9. The refinement of the lunar vehicle required that angles, lengths, joints, and clearances be determined through the use of descriptive geometry and other graphical methods before analysis of the structure was possible. (Courtesy of Ryan Aircraft Corporation.)

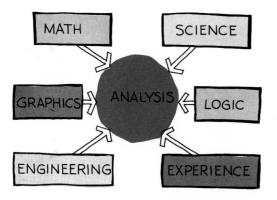

Fig. 1-10. The analysis phase of the design process is the application of all available technological methods from science to graphics in evaluating the refined designs.

gathered by individual or group approaches. Preliminary ideas should be sufficiently broad to allow for unique solutions that could revolutionize present methods. All ideas should be recorded in written form. Many rough sketches of preliminary ideas should be made and retained as a means of generating original ideas and stimulating the design process. Ideas and comments should be noted on the sketches as a basis for further preliminary designs.

Preliminary ideas can be gathered from several commonly used methods, including brainstorming, market analysis, or research of present designs. All work relating to preliminary ideas is most useful if completed in graphical form for easy analysis.

1-8 PROBLEM REFINEMENT

Several of the better preliminary ideas are selected for further refinement to determine their true merits. Rough sketches are converted to scale drawings that will permit space analysis, critical measurements, and the calculation of areas and volumes affecting the design. Consideration must be given to spatial relationships, angles between planes, lengths of structural members, intersections of surfaces and planes. Information of this type is necessary to determine the feasibility of manufacture and the physical characteristics of a design. Descriptive geometry is a very valuable tool for determining information of this type, and it precludes the necessity for tedious mathematical and analytical methods. Engineering graphics is employed to construct the necessary views of the design so that it can be analyzed for its spatial characteristics with descriptive geometry.

An example of a problem of this type is illustrated in the landing gear of the lunar vehicle shown in Fig. 1-9. It was necessary for the designer to make many freehand sketches of the design and finally a scale drawing to establish clearances with the landing surface. The configuration of the landing gear was drawn to scale in the descriptive views of the landing craft. It was necessary, at this point, to determine certain fundamental lengths, angles, and specifications that are related to the fabrication of the gear. The length of each leg of the landing apparatus and the angles between the members at the point of junction had to be found to design a connector, and the angles the legs made with the body of the spacecraft had to be known in order to design these joints. All of this information was easily and quickly determined with the use of descriptive geometry. The employment of descriptive geometry as a preliminary means of determining this information facilitates the application of analytical principles to convert this information into equations for mathematical solutions. Chapters 2 through 8 are devoted to a presentation of graphical methods of problem refinements.

1–9 ANALYSIS

Analysis is the step of the design process where engineering and scientific principles are used most (Fig. 1–10). Analysis involves the study of the best designs to determine the comparative merits of each with respect to cost, strength, function, and market appeal. Graphical principles can also be applied to analysis to a considerable extent. The determination of stress is somewhat simpler with graphical vectors than with the analytical method. Functional relationships between moving parts will also provide data that can be obtained graphically more easily than by analytical methods. Graphical solutions to analytical problems offer a readily available means of checking the solution, therefore reducing checking time. Graphical methods can also be applied to the conversion of functions of mechanisms to a graphical format that will permit the designer to convert this action into an equation form that will be easy to utilize. Data can be gathered and graphically analyzed that would otherwise be difficult to analyze by mathematical means. For instance, empirical curves that do not fit a normal equation are often integrated graphically when the mathematical process would involve unwieldy and complicated equations.

Graphical methods are vital supplements to the engineering sciences when applied to the analysis procedure. These methods should be well understood by the engineer, technician, or designer, to afford him every available aid to effectively solve a problem in the minimum time. Chapters 9 and 10 cover this phase of the design process.

Models constructed at reduced scales are valuable to the analysis of a design to establish relationships of moving parts and outward appearances, and to evaluate other design characteristics. Full-scale prototypes are often constructed after the scale models have been studied for function. This provides a tangible model for further development prior to extensive manufacture on a large volume basis. Graphical methods are applied as tools for modifying designs at each revision.

1–10 DECISION

A decision must be made at this stage to select a single design that will be accepted as the solution of the design problem (Fig. 1–11). Each of the several designs that have been refined and analyzed will offer unique features, and it will probably not be possible to include all of these in a single final solution. In many cases, the final design is a compromise that offers as many of the best features as possible.

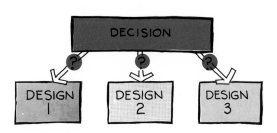

Fig. 1–11. Decision is the selection of the best design or design features to be implemented.

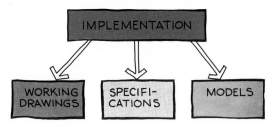

Fig. 1–12. Implementation is the final step of the design process, where drawings and specifications are prepared from which the final product can be constructed.

The decision may be made by the designer on an independent, unassisted basis, or it may be made by a group of associates. Regardless of the size of the group making the decision as to which design will be accepted, graphics is a primary means of presenting the proposed designs for a decision. The outstanding aspects of each design usually lend themselves to presentation in the form of graphs which compare costs of manufacturing, weights, operational characteristics, and other data that would be considered in arriving at the final decision. Pictorial sketches or formal pictorials are excellent methods of graphically studying different designs before arriving at a decision.

When working on a small project, the designer must communicate with himself through these methods if he is to make the decision independently. When the approval of a design is made by a group of associates or people unfamiliar with the technical aspects of his work, different forms of graphics that will satisfy the needs of the audience are used to aid in the decision process. More detailed schematics, graphs, and pictorials are used to communicate the advantages and disadvantages of each design in as clear a format as possible.

1–11   IMPLEMENTATION

The final design concept must be presented in a workable form after the best design has been selected and decided upon. This type of presen-

tation refers primarily to the working drawings and specifications that are used as the actual instruments for the fabrication of the product, whether it is a small piece of hardware or a bridge (Fig. 1–12). Engineering graphics fundamentals must be used to convert all preliminary designs and data into the language of the manufacturer who will be responsible for the conversion of the ideas into a reality. Workmen must have complete detailed instructions for the manufacture of each single part, measured to a thousandth of an inch to facilitate its proper manufacture. Working drawings must be sufficiently detailed and explicit to provide a legal basis for a contract which will be the document for the contractor's bid on the job.

Plans are usually executed by draftsmen and technicians who are specialists in this area. The designer or engineer must be sufficiently knowledgeable in graphical presentation to be able to supervise the preparation of working drawings even though he may not be involved in the mechanics of producing them. He must approve all plans and specifications prior to their release for production. This responsibility necessitates that he be well-rounded in all aspects of graphical techniques to enable him to approve the plans with assurance. This step of the design process is probably less creative than the subsequent steps, but it is no less important than any other step.

1–12   SOLUTION OF PROBLEMS

The problems at the end of each chapter are provided to afford the student an opportunity to test his understanding of the principles covered in the preceding text. Most problems deal with an understanding of the theoretical concepts rather than specific applications. An understanding of theoretical concepts will enable the student to solve comprehensive problems involving engineering applications.

Most problems are to be solved on $8\frac{1}{2}'' \times 11''$ paper, using instruments or drawing freehand as specified. The paper can be printed with a $\frac{1}{4}$-in. grid to assist in laying out the problems, or plain paper can be used with the layout made with a 16 scale (architect's scale). The grid of the given problems in later chapters represents $\frac{1}{4}$-in. intervals that can be counted and transferred to a like grid paper or scaled on plain paper. Each problem sheet should be endorsed as shown in Fig. 1–13. The endorsement should include the student's seat number, and name, the date, and the problem number. Guidelines should be drawn with a straightedge to aid in lettering, using $\frac{1}{8}$-in. letters. All points, lines, and planes should be lettered using $\frac{1}{8}$-in. letters with guidelines in all cases. Reference planes should be noted appropriately when applicable. Most problems have a minimum of lettering and notations given, which requires the student to provide the necessary notations in keeping with the instructions of each chapter.

Problems of an essay type, as in this chapter, should have their answers lettered, using

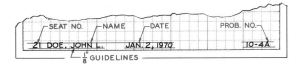

Figure 1–13

approved, single-stroke, Gothic lettering. Guidelines should be used to assist in alignment and uniformity of lettering. Each page should be numbered and stapled in the upper left corner if turned in for review by the instructor. All solved problems should be maintained in the student's notebook for future reference during the course and other courses later in his college curriculum.

PROBLEMS

1. Assume that you are responsible for designing a car jack that would be more serviceable than present models. Review the six steps of the design process given in this chapter and make a brief outline of what you would do to apply these steps to your attempt to design a jack. Write the sequential steps and the methods that would be used to carry out each step. List the subject areas that would be used for each step and indicate the more difficult problems that you would anticipate at each step. Keep your outline brief, but thorough. Freehand letter your paper.

2. As an introductory problem to the steps of the design process, design a door stop that could be used to prevent a door from slamming into a wall. This stop could be attached to the floor or the door and should be as simple as possible. Make sketches and notes as necessary to give tangible evidence that you have proceeded through the six steps and label each

step. Your work should be entirely freehand and rapid. Do not spend longer than 30 minutes on this problem. Indicate any information you would need in a final design approach that may not be accessible to you now.

3. List areas that you must consider during the problem identification phase of a design project for the following products: a new skillet design for the housewife, a lock for a bicycle, a handle for a piece of luggage, an escape from prison, a child's toy, a stadium seat, a desk lamp, an improved umbrella, a hotdog stand.

4. Make a series of rough, freehand sketches to indicate your preliminary ideas for the solution of the following problems: a functional powdered soap dispenser for washing hands, a protector for a football player with an injured elbow, a method of positioning the cross-bar at a pole vault pit, a portable seat for waiting in long lines, a method of protecting windshields of parked cars during freezing weather, a pet-proof garbage can, a bicycle rack, a door knob, a seat to support a small child in a bathtub.

5. Evaluate the sketches made in Exercise 4 above and briefly outline in narrative form the information that would be needed to refine your design into a workable form. Use freehand lettering, striving for a neat, readable paper.

6. Many automobiles are available on the market. Explain your decision for selecting the one that would be most appropriate for the activities listed below: a trip on a sightseeing tour in the mountains, a hunting trip in a wooded area for several days, a trip from coast to coast, the delivering of groceries, a business trip downtown. List the type of vehicle, model, its features and why you made your decision to select it.

IDENTIFICATION

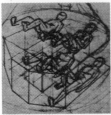
PRELIMINARY IDEAS

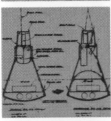
REFINEMENT

ANALYSIS

DECISION

IMPLEMENTATION

2
APPLICATION OF DESCRIPTIVE GEOMETRY

2-1 INTRODUCTION

Descriptive geometry has more applications to *problem refinement* than to any other step of the design process. Once a problem has been defined and a sufficient number of preliminary ideas have been conceived, the designer advances to the refinement step. In design refinement, it is necessary to make instrument drawings that are rendered to scale, to provide an accurate check on critical dimensions and measurements that were sketched during the early stages of the design process. Where clearances or other measurements are important, freehand sketches can be misleading. A scale drawing will give a true picture of the dimensions in question (Fig. 2–1).

A large part of the refinement step is the determination of the physical properties of a design and the comparison of these with the properties of alternative solutions. For example, scale drawings for refinement were made of three proposed configurations of the "Big Joe" spacecraft (Fig. 2–2). Scale drawings of this type are helpful in developing the final shape and dimensions of a design.

The calculation of practically any given physical property begins with basic geometric elements—points, lines, areas, volumes, and angles. The measurements of these elements are determined as a design is refined prior to the preparation of working drawings. The refined design is not necessarily a working drawing, but it is a scale drawing from which an accurate appraisal can be made.

11

Fig. 2-1. The designer's first step in the refinement phase of his preliminary ideas is the preparation of scale drawings. (Courtesy of the Chrysler Corporation.)

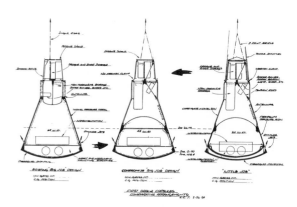

Fig. 2-2. These scale drawings were used to refine the final design of the "Big Joe" spacecraft and to incorporate desirable features from other systems. (Courtesy of the National Aeronautics and Space Administration.)

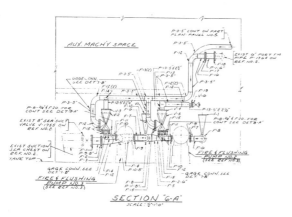

Fig. 2-3. This piping drawing illustrates many applications of descriptive geometry used to communicate a complex system within a naval destroyer. (Courtesy of Boston Naval Shipyard.)

Fig. 2-4. An example of a piping system in a submarine that must be evolved by descriptive geometry methods similar to those used in the plan shown in Fig. 2-3. (Official photograph, U. S. Navy.)

It is in the refinement procedure, where areas, lengths, and angles are determined, that descriptive geometry is used to the greatest extent. Descriptive geometry provides a very accurate and fast method of determining physical relationships and properties with a minimum of difficulty.

2-2 APPLICATION OF DESCRIPTIVE GEOMETRY

Descriptive geometry is the study of points, lines, and surfaces in three-dimensional space. This area of study has many applications to the refinement of a preliminary design and its analysis. Descriptive geometry can be applied

Fig. 2–5. This 10-ft-diameter underwater sphere could not have been designed without descriptive geometry methods. (Official photograph, U. S. Navy.)

Fig. 2–6. The complex joints of the structural members were designed with the use of descriptive geometry. (Official photograph, U. S. Navy.)

to engineering problems that would be difficult to solve by other engineering methods. For example, the piping drawing shown in Fig. 2–3 involved considerable descriptive geometry before the dimensions of the pipes could be determined and specified. A photograph of a section of installed pipes is shown in Fig. 2–4. Descriptive geometry is the primary method used in refining a design of this type. The bend angles were easily calculated and specified by descriptive geometry, whereas the mathematical solution of this problem would be more complex to solve.

Another example of a problem that was refined by descriptive geometry is a structural frame for the 10-ft-diameter underwater sphere (Fig. 2–5). Before working drawings could be made, the physical properties and dimensions of the spherical pentagons had to be determined through a series of auxiliary views. The determination of the angles between the members was necessary before the joints could be detailed to give the snug fit illustrated in Fig. 2–6. A further refinement was the development of the necessary jigs for holding the components during assembly (Fig. 2–7). The solution of this

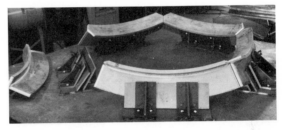

Fig. 2–7. Jigs used to assemble the frame were designed through the use of descriptive geometry. (Official photograph, U. S. Navy.)

problem would be essentially impossible without the principles of descriptive geometry.

Yet another example of the use of descriptive geometry is found in the snow-compaction equipment used for operation in the Antarctic (Fig. 2–8). The gusset plates required for fastening the bracing members, which intersect at oblique angles, were designed and refined with descriptive geometry. The solution of problems of this type is very complex when attempted with mathematics, whereas descriptive geometry principles can be applied with the minimum of difficulty.

Fig. 2–8. The fabrication and design of this snow-compaction equipment used descriptive geometry principles to refine the preliminary ideas. (Official photograph, U. S. Navy.)

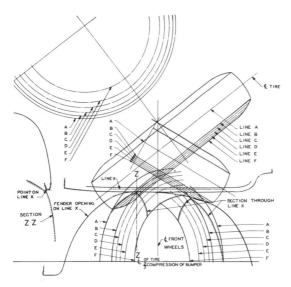

Fig. 2–9. The clearance between a fender and a tire is used to determine the fender opening of an automobile by the application of descriptive geometry and graphical methods. (Courtesy of Chrysler Corporation.)

A layout drawing for refining an automotive design is shown in Fig. 2–9. Here the designer's task was to determine the limitations of the size of the fender opening so as to allow minimum clearance between the wheel and

the fender. The wheel is turned to its maximum steering angles to locate lines of interference, which will determine the minimum opening of the front fender. The left side of the layout shows a section of the fender opening turn-under. Line X in the plan view shows the lowest part of the fender turn-under, which is the potential line of interference. The largest over-size tire is also shown. Section Z–Z is developed from the tire shape when it is in the position previously described. The shaded tire sections through line X indicate the conditions which determine the fender opening.

2–3 PRESENTATION OF DESCRIPTIVE GEOMETRY

The succeeding six chapters are devoted to the introduction of those fundamentals of descriptive geometry that are most commonly applied to the refinement of design problems. Many examples of practical applications will be given in each chapter to illustrate uses of descriptive geometry for common design problems. The principles described can be applied to essentially all three-dimensional problems involving the relationships of points, lines, and surfaces; they thus give the designer access to a valuable problem-solving tool.

The more fundamental principles of descriptive geometry are presented by the step method, in which a problem is separated into successive, sequential steps to enable the student to follow the solution with the minimum of confusion from superfluous lines and construction (Fig. 2–10). Each successive step is printed in color for added emphasis and ease of interpretation. A brief explanation of the steps of solution is given in text directly below each step of construction to afford the maximum association between construction and explanation. Instructions are also given in the body of the regular text material to supplement the step-by-step instructions.

This method of presentation has been tested during a semester project where approximately 3000 samples were taken and used to compare its advantages with the conventional format for descriptive geometry problems, where the prob-

ANGLE BETWEEN TWO OBLIQUE PLANES

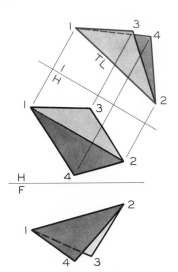

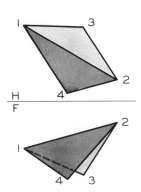

Given: The top and front views of two intersecting planes.
Required: The angle between the two planes.
References: Article 5–4, Article 4–10.

Step 1: The angle between two planes can be seen in a view where the line of intersection appears as a point. First, project a primary auxiliary view perpendicularly from a principal view of the line of intersection. In this case, the view is projected from the top view. Line 1–2 will appear true length in the primary auxiliary view.

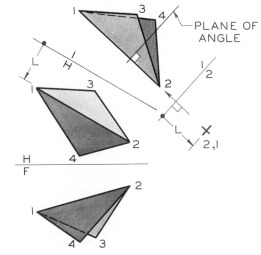

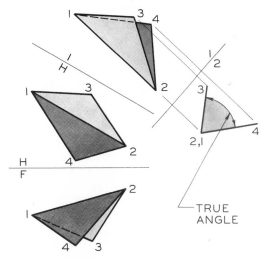

Step 2: The point view of the line of intersection, 1–2, is found in the secondary auxiliary view. Locate this view by transferring the measurement L from the edge view of the primary projection plane, as indicated. The plane of the angle appears as an edge perpendicular to the true-length view of the line of intersection in the primary auxiliary.

Step 3: Complete the edge views of the planes in the secondary auxiliary view by locating points 3 and 4 in the same manner as in Step 2. The angle between the planes can be measured in this view since the line of intersection appears as a point and the planes appear as edges.

Fig. 2–10. An example of the step method of presenting a descriptive geometry problem in sequential steps. An angle is found between two oblique planes in this case; instructions are associated with each step.

lems are given in their entirety with all notes and construction. The step method was found to be superior in all cases, and showed a separation of scores in excess of 20 percentage points on the more difficult problems.* This format is well suited for home study and self-instruction, and can serve as a future reference for solving descriptive geometry problems. Moreover, this improved method of presenting the principles of descriptive geometry shortens the instruction time usually devoted to the introduction of principles, and allows more time for design and application aspects of graphical methods.

Problems have been reduced to the fundamental elements of points, lines, and surfaces for simplification of the basic principles. All actual engineering problems can be reduced to these elements and solved in the same manner as the example problems. Identification of the type of problems encountered is the initial step of problem solution. If the solution desired is the determination of the angle between two planes of a design, the problem can be resolved to the two planes in question and solved as the application of this principle. For example, the angle between two planes of an automobile windshield is found in Fig. 2-11 when two orthographic views have been obtained.

The succeeding chapters should be carefully read and then reviewed in detail, because the principles they present will be employed to a considerable extent to refine preliminary design solutions. Since the refinement phase of the design process provides the transition from a preliminary idea to the necessary specifications and information required for the preparation of working drawings, it is, in essence, the problem-solving portion of a design project. In this phase graphical methods are used extensively, with descriptive geometry being a primary tool for solving many problems that do not lend themselves to mathematical solutions.

* Earle, James H., "An Experimental Comparison of Three Self-Instruction Formats for Descriptive Geometry" (unpublished Ed.D. thesis, Texas A&M University, 1964).

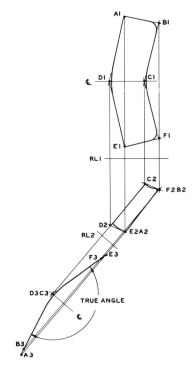

Fig. 2-11. The angle between the planes of a windshield can be determined by simplifying the problem to the fundamental planes involved. (Courtesy of Chrysler Corporation).

2-4 REFINEMENT OF AN ENGINEERING DESIGN

An example design problem encountered in a research and development program was to develop a design for a Mobile Laboratory that would travel on the moon's surface. The vehicle was to provide a 14-day, 250-mile lunar operational range capability for two men. The Bendix Corporation was responsible for the four-wheel traction drive mechanism (TDM) and front-wheel steering drive mechanism (SDM) designs.

Many preliminary sketches were prepared to provide a selection of various possible solutions to this problem. These were evaluated to determine the most appropriate design for the project needs. Figure 2-12 shows the conceptual design layout of the left front wheel TDM and SDM incorporating DC series motors, two-ratio

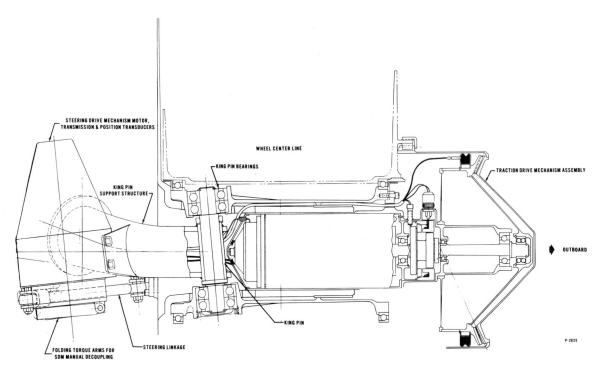

Fig. 2–12. A preliminary refinement drawing of a left front wheel for a vehicle designed to travel on the moon's surface. Dimensions and details of construction can be omitted on refinement drawings. (Courtesy of Bendix Corporation.)

electric clutch systems and final stage hermetically sealed nutator transmission. The TDM units were designed to be mounted within each wheel axle. Although this drawing was drawn to scale, it is not a working drawing, since dimensions and sufficient information to construct the assembly are not given. This is merely a drawing used to refine the preliminary sketches. Note that several oblique angles are incorporated in the design, which will require solution by descriptive geometry.

A pictorial of the refined design introduced in Fig. 2–12 is shown in Fig. 2–13 to better describe the concept to the customer. It is easier to understand the relationships of the parts of the assembly in this partially sectioned pictorial.

This final preliminary concept was accepted and the contract was awarded.

A follow-up contract was awarded for the design and fabrication of a mobility test article (MTA) vehicle intended for earth-testing the MOLAB mobility system. The mobility test article TDM and SDM hardware was to provide the same mobility characteristics as the proposed MOLAB designs within a limited cost and delivery schedule. The final refinement of the design is shown in Fig. 2–14. This drawing shows the MTA hardware design for the left front wheel TDM and SDM systems. Two adjacent orthographic views were drawn to enable the designer to project auxiliary views using descriptive geometry so that the critical dimen-

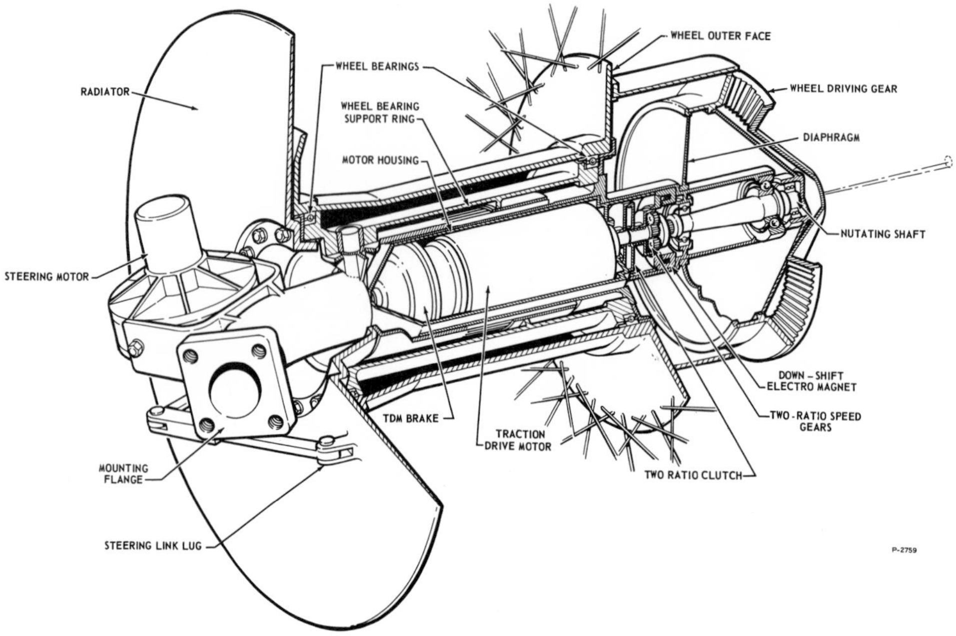

Fig. 2–13. A pictorial of the wheel assembly shown in Fig. 2–12, clarifying its assembly. (Courtesy of Bendix Corporation.)

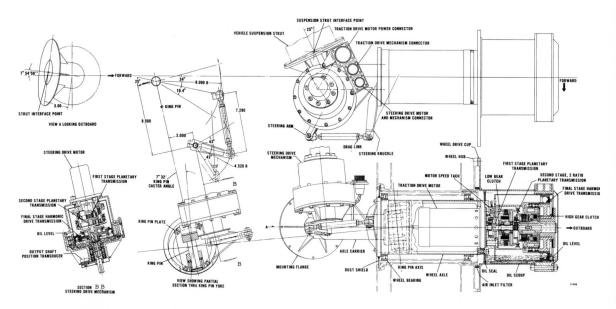

Fig. 2–14. The final refinement of the wheel mechanism is achieved through the application of descriptive geometry to determine physical properties of its linkage system. Additional auxiliary views were also used to finalize the design. Note that this assembly is more complicated than the initial refinement in Fig. 2–12. (Courtesy of Bendix Corporation.)

Fig. 2–15. A photograph of the completed, deliverable wheel assembly. (Courtesy of Bendix Corporation.)

Fig. 2–16. Descriptive geometry principles were utilized in arriving at the final configuration of this heavy-duty truck frame. (Courtesy of LeTourneau-Westinghouse Company.)

sions of the steering linkage could be determined. Descriptive geometry was also used to establish the position of the mounting flange so that it could be attached properly to the vehicle suspension strut. A comparison between this drawing and the initial refinement (Fig. 2–12) indicates the increased complexity of the completed design.

A photograph of the final deliverable hardware is shown in Fig. 2–15. This design problem is typical of those encountered in industry. Regardless of the degree of complexity of the design or the system employed, whether hydraulic, electronic, or mechanical, the final product must be designed to be assembled as a unit. This design of an assembly required the application of spatial relations and descriptive geometry principles to determine critical relationships.

Another problem of this type is the design of a frame for a heavy-duty truck (Fig. 2–16). This frame is composed of intersecting planes and surfaces that must be refined so that they may be analyzed for strength by the application of engineering principles. The true size of oblique surfaces must be found along with the angles between the intersecting planes and flanges. This information must be known before complete working drawings can be made. Again, descriptive geometry is the primary method used to obtain this information.

2-5 A CASE STUDY

The previous example has illustrated the application of graphical methods to the refinement of a preliminary design and the development of final, dimensioned drawings. The following case study of the design of a surgical light is presented to reinforce your understanding of the application of descriptive geometry and graphical methods to the solution of technical problems. This light was designed by the Castle Company, a subsidiary of Sybron Corporation.

The Problem. With advances in medicine and innovations in surgery, a need for improved surgical lighting has emerged. In the average office there may be 100 to 200 footcandles of light falling on desk tops, but a surgical light must provide at least 2500 footcandles. In addition, it is important for the light to be as natural as possible so that the subtle and often critical color variations of tissues and organs during operations can be distinguished. The development of a design for a surgical light is twofold, involving both the illumination system and the geometry of the hardware. A light must be designed to function as required by operating room procedures; it must also be as economical as possible.

Investigation and Problem Identification. Since the light will be used by surgeons, it is necessary to work with members of the medical profession

Fig. 2–17. A well-adapted surgical lamp emits light that passes around the surgeon's shoulders with a minimum of shadow. (Courtesy of Sybron Corporation.)

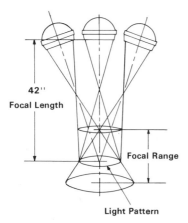

Fig. 2–18. A lighting system that provides a good lighting pattern with a focal range between 30″ and 60″. The prime focus is 42″ below the reflector. (Courtesy of Sybron Corporation.)

Fig. 2–19. Engineers and technicians work cooperatively with medical personnel to establish the needs of an operating room and the factors that affect lighting. (Courtesy of Sybron Corporation; photograph by Brad Bliss.)

to determine their special needs. The first consideration is the need for illumination that can be varied from 2000 to 5000 footcandles. The fixtures must be designed to allow dispersal of heat away from the surgeon; the light should be as "cool" as possible. The light should be as similar to natural daylight as is feasible and should be reflected to provide a shadow-free work surface. All aspects of the system must be adjustable to a number of positions within an eight- to ten-foot circle.

Geometry of the Problem. A major concern of the designer is the positioning of the light sources so that maximum light falls on the work area with the minimum of obstruction. A sketch of a well-adapted lamp is shown in Fig. 2–17. Note that light emitted from specially designed reflectors converges to a small beam at shoulder level to minimize the shadows that are cast by interference of the surgeon's shoulders, arms, and hands. The particular reflector

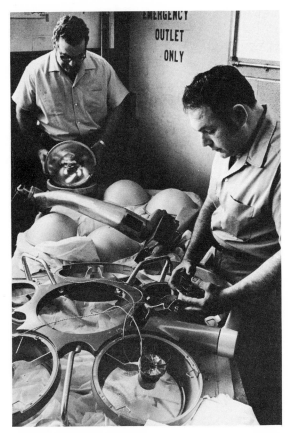

Fig. 2–20. Prototypes of the better designs are constructed for testing and analysis. Note the three-dimensional aspects of this prototype that were designed with the aid of descriptive geometry principles. (Courtesy of Sybron Corporation; photograph by Brad Bliss.)

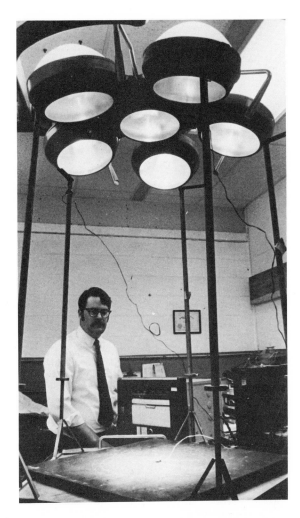

Fig. 2–21. A prototype is tested to determine its effectiveness under conditions simulating the operating room installation. (Courtesy of Sybron Corporation; photograph by Brad Bliss.

design that was developed, with a focal range between 30″ and 60″, is shown in Fig. 2–18. The prime focus is 42″ below the reflector glass. This prime focus provides an illumination pattern about 16″ in diameter.

These geometric parameters required the designer to approach a number of problems involving descriptive geometry and spatial analysis. He had to establish what height would give the optimum light. He used principles of descriptive geometry to determine the best angular position of each light and the number of lights needed to provide an adequate illuminated area. Having made these specifications, he had to design the yoke that supported the lights so that it would properly position the lights and allow the required range of adjustments.

An analysis of the needs of an operating room was made with the assistance of medical personnel (Fig. 2–19). This study provided information concerning ceiling heights, factors affecting

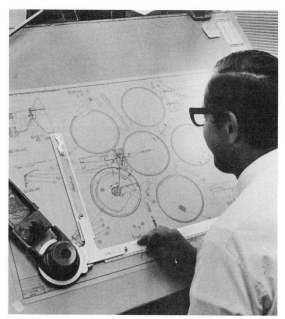

Fig. 2–22. The completed design is presented in the form of a working drawing from which the actual product will be fabricated. (Courtesy of Sybron Corporation; photograph by Brad Bliss.)

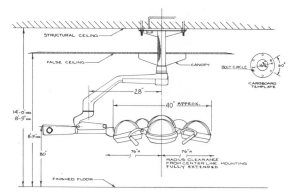

Fig. 2–23. The overall dimensions of the final design are shown in this assembly drawing. (Courtesy of Sybron Corporation.)

Fig. 2–24. A photograph of the final design. (Courtesy of Sybron Corporation.)

eye fatigue, and the range of positions required of the light. This information was used to establish the requirements of the hardware and fixtures to support the light reflectors.

Solution. Teams of specialists worked on various aspects of the problem. Some engineers worked on operating controls and mechanisms that would enable the surgeon to position the light at any desired height or angle. Others worked on intensity controls to provide a choice of several different intensity levels. Hundreds of drawings were prepared to present preliminary design ideas for the solution of various problems. These were studied, refined, and used for the construction of prototypes (Fig. 2–20). These prototypes were tested in the laboratory to determine the design's effectiveness, its geometry, and the light intensity (Fig. 2–21).

After the prototypes were analyzed and modified to give the optimum results, a decision was

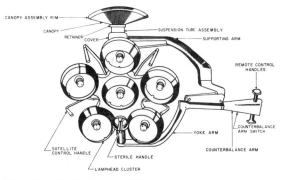

Fig. 2–25. Descriptive geometry principles were used in the design of light positions, the supporting hardware, the handles, and other spatial relationships. (Courtesy of Sybron Corporation.)

Fig. 2–26. The implementation of the completed design involves the assembly of the lighting components. (Courtesy of Sybron Corporation; photograph by Brad Bliss.)

Fig. 2–27. Light clusters are wired in accordance with the designer's drawings. (Courtesy of Sybron Corporation; photograph by Brad Bliss.)

made to proceed with the best design, prepare final drawings, and implement the design. Specific details of the structure and geometrical relationships were drawn in the form of working drawings and assembly drawings from which the technicians could produce the end product (Fig. 2–22).

The Design. A drawing of the finished design is shown in Fig. 2–23, where the critical dimensions are indicated. A photograph of the light (Fig. 2–24) clarifies the assembly of the unit. The various positions into which the light can be revolved were arrived at by the application of descriptive geometry during the refinement stage of the design process. The yoke was designed with the aid of descriptive geometry principles to direct the lights to focus on the work area. The angular measurements and the lengths of the components were also determined by descriptive geometry.

The satellite control handles used for adjusting individual light pods are examples of components that had to be designed by the application of descriptive geometry (Fig. 2–25). The supporting arms that permit the light to be moved to a number of positions were analyzed by the use of graphical principles of revolution and linkage analysis. Each of these problems of geometry was approached with the aid of graphical methods.

Implementation. Once the production details had been solved, the various units of the surgical light were assembled (Fig. 2–26). The light clusters were fabricated and wired in conformance with the designer's drawings (Fig. 2–27).

Technical illustrators were responsible for the preparation of an instruction manual to describe the use and operation of the finished product (Fig. 2–28). Manuals of this type, to be easily

Fig. 2–28. The technical illustrator prepares drawings for operational manuals for the users and installers of the lights. (Courtesy of Sybron Corporation; photograph by Brad Bliss.)

understood with a minimum of study, must use graphical illustrations. An installation manual was also required to describe the details of installation in operating rooms. The technical illustrator must consult with engineers and technicians to make sure that all important details are covered in the manuals.

The final step of the process is the marketing and distribution of the completed product. Packaging must be designed that will meet shipping specifications and provide protection to the light during shipment (Fig. 2–29). Shipping costs must be considered as well as manufacturing costs when the price of a product is established.

Fig. 2–29. The last step for the manufacturer is the packaging and shipping of the lights to customers. (Courtesy of Sybron Corporation; photograph by Brad Bliss.)

2-6 SUMMARY

This chapter has given a number of examples of the application of descriptive geometry to the solution of technical problems. Descriptive geometry is a valuable problem-solving tool that should be used by a designer to refine his ideas and to establish physical properties. Most descriptive geometry principles presented in this textbook are discussed as they apply to actual problems. They are also discussed in the traditional manner, in terms of points, lines, and planes, with each problem reduced to its essential elements to facilitate understanding.

You should observe your surroundings, the products you use and structures that serve you. You will note many aspects of these products and structures that required the application of descriptive geometry principles. This awareness of your surroundings will improve your appreciation of descriptive geometry as a problem-solving tool.

PROBLEMS

Problems should be presented on $8\frac{1}{2}'' \times 11''$ paper, grid or plain, using the format introduced in Article 1-12. Each grid square represents $\frac{1}{4}''$. All notes, sketches, drawings, and graphical work should be neatly prepared in keeping with good practices as covered in this volume. Written matter should be legibly lettered using $\frac{1}{8}''$ guidelines.

1. When refining a design for a folding lawn chair, what physical properties would a designer need to determine? What physical properties would be needed for the following items: A TV-set base, a golf cart, a child's swing set, a portable typewriter, an earthen dam, a shortwave radio, a portable camping tent, a warehouse dolly used for moving heavy boxes?

2. Why should scale drawings be used in the refinement of a design rather than freehand sketches? Explain.

3. List five examples of problems that involve spatial relationships that could be solved by the application of descriptive geometry. Explain your answers.

4. Make a freehand sketch of two oblique planes that intersect. Indicate by notes and algebraic equations how you would determine the angle between these planes mathematically.

5. What is the difference between a working drawing and a refinement drawing? Explain your answer and give examples.

6. How many preliminary designs should be refined when this step of the design process is reached? Explain.

7. Make a list of refinement drawings that would be needed to develop the installation and design of a 100-ft radio antenna. Make rough sketches indicating the type of drawings needed with notes to explain their purposes.

8. After a refinement drawing has been made and the design is found to be lacking in some respects, so that it is eliminated as a possible solution, what should be the designer's next step? Explain.

9. Would a pictorial be helpful as a refinement drawing? Explain your answer.

10. List several design projects that an engineer or technician in your particular field of engineering would probably be responsible for. Outline the type of refinement drawings that would be necessary in projects of this type.

IDENTIFICATION

PRELIMINARY IDEAS

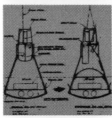

REFINEMENT

ANALYSIS

DECISION

IMPLEMENTATION

3

FUNDAMENTAL SPATIAL RELATIONSHIPS

3-1 ORTHOGRAPHIC PROJECTION

The preparation of engineering drawings that must be used by large numbers of people working on a common project in a variety of geographical locations requires a universal system of presentation. This universal system is *orthographic projection,* which is the basis of standard practices and conventions of engineering drawing. We shall now take a more penetrating look at the underlying theory supporting this standardized form of presentation.

Orthographic projection may be defined as a method of representing three-dimensional objects through the use of views which are projected perpendicularly onto planes of projection with parallel projectors. The three mutually perpendicular projection planes, called principal planes, are shown as they would be positioned in space in Fig. 3–1A. Part B of the figure shows the transformation of the three principal planes into one common plane (part C). This common plane is the sheet of paper on which the engineer, designer, or draftsman must represent a three-dimensional object that may vary in size from a small bolt to a large bridge girder. Since projection planes are infinite in size and therefore have no perimeters, there is no need to indicate their surfaces in the manner shown in part C. However, the intersections of the planes, or fold lines, are usually drawn as shown in part D to aid in the solution of descriptive geometry problems. Note that the three principal planes—*horizontal, frontal,* and *profile*—are represented by means of the single letters H, F, and P placed on their respective sides of the fold lines. This system of notation will be used throughout this book.

Fig. 3–1. The principal projection planes.

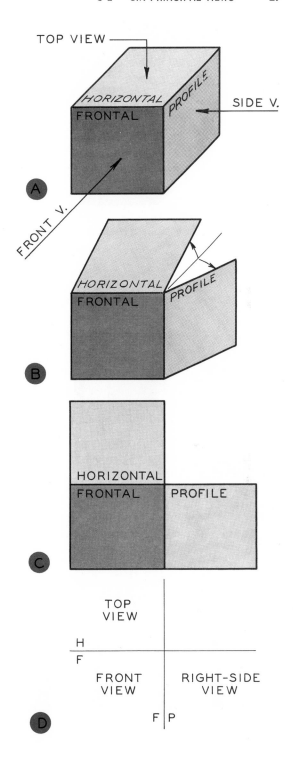

Figure 3–1 illustrates the relationship between the three principal planes pictorially and orthographically. It should be noted that the *front view* is projected onto the *frontal* projection plane; the *side* view onto the *profile* projection plane; and the *top* view onto the *horizontal* projection plane. This system allows three-dimensional objects to be represented by means of related, two-dimensional views in a manner which will be developed in this chapter.

3–2 SIX PRINCIPAL VIEWS

Some objects cannot be fully represented through the three views mentioned in the first article, but require separate views projected from each side. The system of orthographic projection permits six principal views of a given object to be drawn. Figure 3–2A suggests how an imaginary box formed by the six principal planes is opened to form one common plane, as shown in part B of the figure. It should be observed that the top and bottom planes are both horizontal planes and are labeled with the letter H; the front and rear views are both frontal planes and are noted with the letter F, and the left and right side views are both profile planes and are labeled with the letter P.

Only rarely are all six principal projection planes required to describe an object. It is more usual that additional views other than principal views are required to describe certain details of an object. These views are projected onto planes called auxiliary planes, which are not parallel to the three principal planes. Succeeding chapters will develop this concept, while this chapter will be devoted to the review of principal projections.

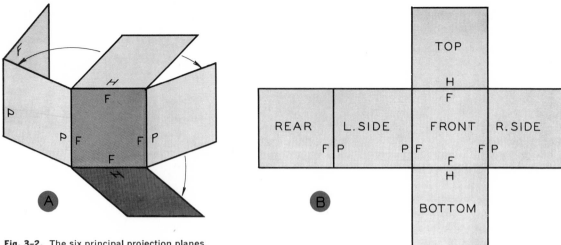

Fig. 3–2. The six principal projection planes.

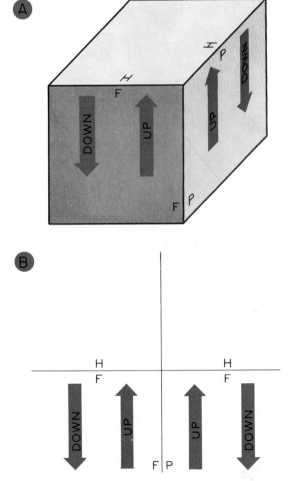

Fig. 3–3. The directions of up and down in orthographic projections.

3–3 DIRECTIONAL RELATIONSHIPS

Certain verbal terms are used to describe spatial relationships both in orthographic projection and in general discussion. The more commonly used terms are forward, back, left, right, up, and down. Combinations of these directions will allow an object to be generally located in space. A knowledge of the relationship of directional terms to orthographic projection is necessary for a thorough understanding of descriptive geometry principles.

The parallel directions of up and down are illustrated in Fig. 3–3A. These directions are perpendicular to the horizontal plane on which the top view is projected. Since the arrows which indicate up and down directions are vertical, they would appear as points on the horizontal plane if shown. Part B of the figure shows how the directional arrows would project in orthographic projection on a single drawing surface. Note that the directions are perpendicular to the horizontal plane and parallel to the frontal and profile planes in the orthographic layout, just as they are in the pictorial. The directional arrows projected onto the frontal and profile planes are the same length since they are vertical.

Left and right directions are shown pictorially in Fig. 3–4A. Both of these parallel directions are perpendicular to the profile plane. If the projection planes were revolved into the conventional position, the directions would project

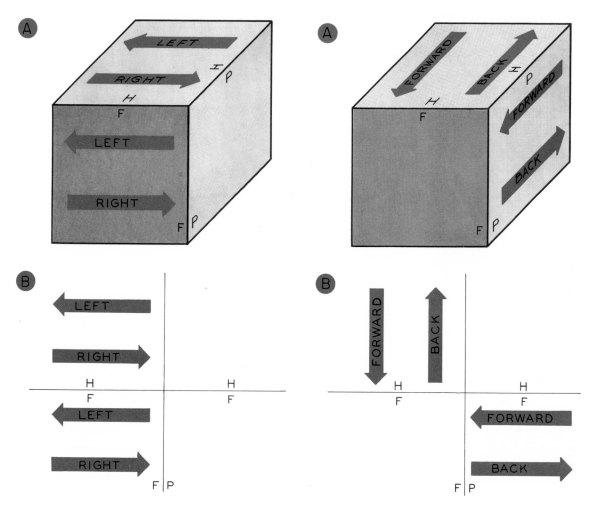

Fig. 3–4. The directions of left and right in orthographic projections.

Fig. 3–5. The directions of backward and forward in orthographic projections.

as shown in part B. The directional arrows are parallel to the horizontal plane and perpendicular to the profile plane. To locate a point that is to the right or left of a given point, we must use the front or top view, since the profile plane cannot reflect this difference in position.

Forward and backward directions are shown pictorially in Fig. 3–5A. The parallel directional arrows are parallel to the horizontal and profile planes. These relationships are also illustrated in the usual three-view arrangement for orthographic projection in part B. Location of a point

in space with respect to forward or backward directions must be established in either the horizontal view or the profile view, since they cannot be established in the front view.

Any two of the three basic groups of directions will establish the location of a point on a principal plane. For example, a point located below the horizontal plane and to the left of the profile would be positioned on the frontal plane. The third basic direction, forward or back of the frontal plane, locates the point with respect to three-dimensional space.

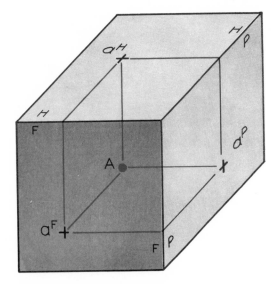

Fig. 3–6. Orthographic projection of a point.

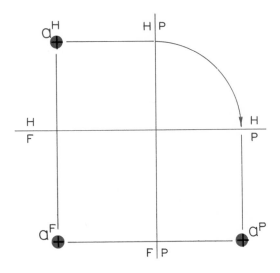

Fig. 3–7. Three views of a point.

3–4 ORTHOGRAPHIC PROJECTION OF A POINT

The point is the basic geometric element that is used to establish all other elements regardless of their degree of complication. A point is a theoretical location in space and has no dimensions. However, a series of points can establish areas, volumes, and lengths, which are the basis of our physical world. An understanding of the orthographic projections of a point will enable the student to project essentially any geometric form onto an orthographic plane and thereby solve a multitude of graphical problems.

A point in space must be projected perpendicularly onto at least two principal planes to establish its true position. Figure 3–6 is a pictorial representation of a point projected onto each of the principal planes. Lower-case letters are sometimes used to distinguish projections of a point from the actual point in space, which is denoted with a capital letter. Superscripts of H, F, or P are used in conjunction with the lower-case letters to indicate the specific projection of the point. Students have found that this system of notation helps them to grasp fundamental principles in the introductory stages of orthographic projection, and it will be applied to projections of points, lines, and planes in this chapter.

The three orthographic projections or views of point A are shown in Fig. 3–7. The point is at the same distance below the horizontal projection plane in the front view as it is in the right side view, and it is located directly below the top view of point A. Similarly, the top and side views of the point are at the same distance from the edge view of the frontal plane. These relationships are shown in pictorial form in Fig. 3–6. Note that the projector lines between a^H, a^P, and a^F are perpendicular to the principal planes (fold lines) in both of these illustrations.

Point A can be located easily from a verbal description which uses units of measurement taken from the fold lines. Assume that the following coordinates were given: (1) 4.6 units left of the profile plane, (2) 5 units below the horizontal plane, and (3) 4 units back of the frontal plane. The measurement of 4.6 units to the left can be established in the top and front views as shown in Fig. 3–8. This procedure locates a projector perpendicular to the H–F fold lines. The measurement of 5 units below the horizontal plane isolates the exact position

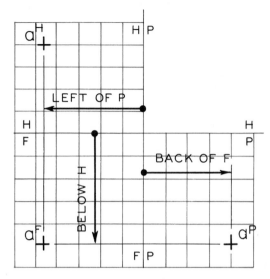

Fig. 3–8. Location of a point 5 units below the horizontal, 4 units back of the frontal, and 4.6 units left of the profile.

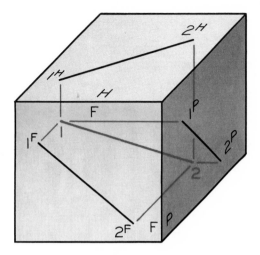

Fig. 3–9. A line in space.

of the frontal projection of point *A*. The right side view of point *A* will also lie on the projector 5 units below the horizontal plane. The third coordinate, 4 units back of the frontal plane, will complete the location of the top and side views of the point.

In the top, or horizontal view, the frontal and profile planes appear as edges. In the frontal view the horizontal and profile planes appear as edges, and in the profile view the frontal and horizontal planes appear as edges. This relationship permits two coordinates to be plotted in each view, since they are measured perpendicularly from planes that appear as edges. The edge view of the two other principal planes can be seen in each principal view.

3–5   LINES

A line is a straight path between two points in space. It can appear in three forms: (1) as a point, (2) as a line showing true length, or (3) as a foreshortened line. Line 1–2 appears foreshortened in each view in Fig. 3–9. The line of sight is always perpendicular to a true-length line or, in other words, a true-length line is

parallel to the plane on which it is projected. These relationships will be discussed further in the following examples.

Oblique Lines. An *oblique line* is a line that is neither perpendicular nor parallel to a principal projection plane, as shown in Fig. 3–9. When line 1–2 is projected onto the horizontal, frontal, and profile planes, it appears as represented in Fig. 3–10. The process of projecting a line is identical to that used in projecting a point, as discussed in Article 3–4. The two endpoints must be established and then connected to represent the line. An oblique or foreshortened line is the general case of a line. It may have any direction or length provided that it is not parallel to a principal plane in any view. Each end of a line is usually lettered for easy reference and to lessen the possibility of error in projection.

Principal Lines. If a line is parallel to a principal plane, it is referred to as a *principal line*. There are three principal lines, (1) horizontal, (2) frontal, and (3) profile, since there are three principal planes to which they can be parallel. The principal lines are true length in the view where the principal plane with which they are

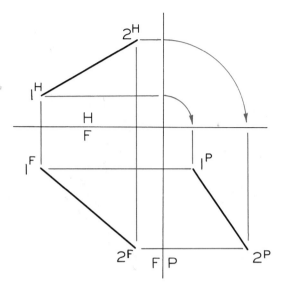

Fig. 3–10. Three views of a line.

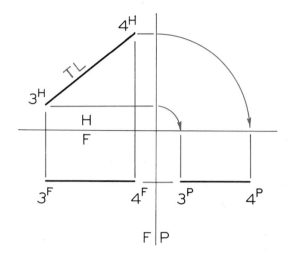

Fig. 3–12. Three views of a horizontal line.

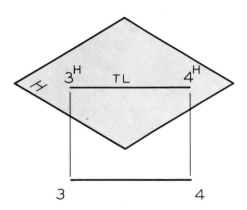

Fig. 3–11. A horizontal line.

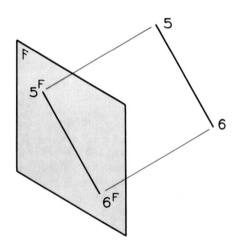

Fig. 3–13. A frontal line.

parallel appears true size. For example, horizontal lines are true length in the top view, which is the view that shows the true size of the horizontal plane.

3–6 HORIZONTAL LINES

A *horizontal line* is parallel to the horizontal plane, as illustrated in Fig. 3–11. A horizontal line may be shown in an infinite number of positions in the top view, provided that it is parallel to the horizontal plane in the frontal and profile projections, as shown in Fig. 3–12. The observer's line of sight is perpendicular to the horizontal plane when he is viewing the top view, which is the one that gives a true-shape view of the plane. Therefore, the horizontal line is shown true length in the top view.

Note that observation of the top view of any given line cannot reveal whether the line is

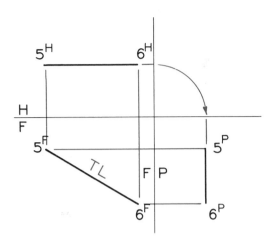

Fig. 3–14. Three views of a frontal line.

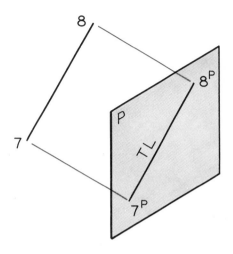

Fig. 3–15. A profile line.

horizontal. This can be established only from the front and side views. A line is horizontal if the representation of the line in these views is parallel to the H–F fold line. A line projecting as a point in either of these views is also horizontal. A line appearing as a point in the front view is a combination horizontal and profile line, while a point view of a line in the profile view indicates a combination horizontal and frontal line.

3–7 FRONTAL LINES

Recall that the front view of an object is projected onto a principal plane called the frontal plane. A line parallel to this plane is a principal line, and is called a *frontal line*. The frontal plane appears true shape in the front view, since the observer's line of sight is perpendicular to it (Fig. 3–13). His line of sight will also be perpendicular to any line parallel to the frontal plane. This line is projected as true length in the front view, as shown in Fig. 3–14.

A frontal line is projected parallel to the frontal plane in both the top and side views, where the frontal plane appears as an edge. It is possible to see in the top and side views that

line 5–6 is a frontal line, but in the front view it is not possible. A line that appeared as a point in the top view would be a combination frontal and profile line. A line projected as a point in the side view would be a combination horizontal and frontal line.

3–8 PROFILE LINES

The side view is projected onto the principal plane called the profile plane, which appears true shape in the side view. Line 7–8, which is parallel to the profile plane, is a principal line called a *profile line* (Fig. 3–15). Since the profile plane is shown true shape in the side view, a profile line will be projected true length in the side view.

The relationship of three views of a profile line is shown in Fig. 3–16. Line 7–8 is parallel to the profile plane in both of the views in which the profile plane appears as an edge, i.e., the top and front views. A line projecting as a point in the top view will be a combination profile and frontal line, while a line projecting as a point in the front view will be a combination profile and horizontal line.

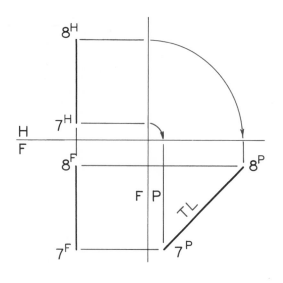

Fig. 3-16. Three views of a profile line.

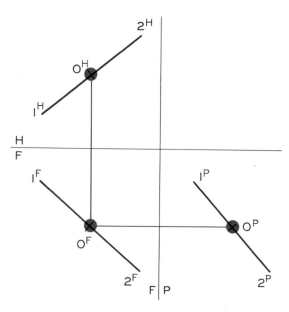

Fig. 3-17. Location of a point on a line.

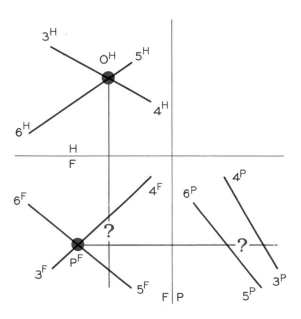

Fig. 3-18. Nonintersecting lines.

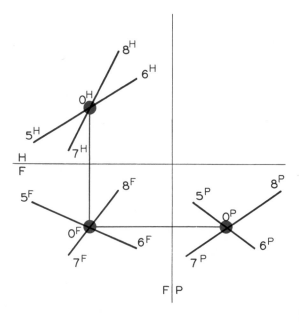

Fig. 3-19. Intersecting lines.

3-9 LOCATION OF A POINT ON A LINE

A line is composed of an infinite number of points. The solution of descriptive geometry problems requires that the locations of specific points on lines and surfaces in space be determined. Figure 3–17 gives the top, front, and side views of line 1–2. Since the endpoints of line 1–2 are located on projectors that are perpendicular to the fold lines, any point on the line can be found by applying the projection principles illustrated in the figure. For example, if point O is located on the line in the front view, the top view of the point may be found by projecting it perpendicular to the H–F fold line until O^H is found on the line in the top view. The side view is found by projecting the point perpendicular to the F–P fold line and then to the profile view of line 1–2.

Any point on the line can be found in the same manner. If the point is located at the midpoint of the line in any view, it will appear at the midpoint of the line in any other projection, although the line can vary in its projected length. Any other ratio of divisions of a line will remain constant in other views as well.

3-10 NONINTERSECTING LINES

Lines may cross in many views, but crossing lines are not necessarily intersecting lines. Lines 3–4 and 5–6 cross in the top and front views in Fig. 3–18, although when the side view is inspected, it is obvious that these lines do not intersect.

A point of intersection is a common point that lies on both lines, and must therefore project to both lines in all views as did point O in Fig. 3–17. Even if the side view were not given in Fig. 3–18, it would be possible to determine whether the lines intersected by projecting the crossing point, O^H, to the front view. Since the lines do not cross at a common point along this projection line in the front view, it is apparent that point O is not common to both lines at a single point, and thus there is no point of intersection.

On the other hand, Fig. 3–19 illustrates two lines, 5–6 and 7–8, that do intersect at a common point, point O, which is the intersection of the projections from all views, as was the case in Fig. 3–17. It is necessary to have at least two views before it is possible to determine whether two crossing lines intersect.

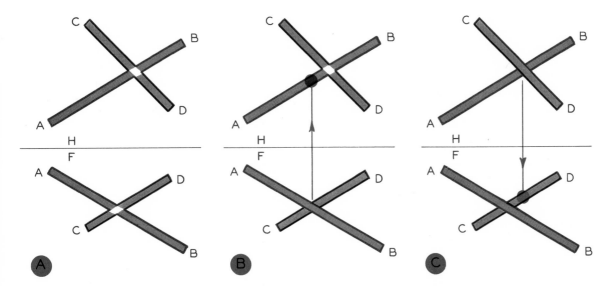

Fig. 3–20. Visibility of nonintersecting lines.

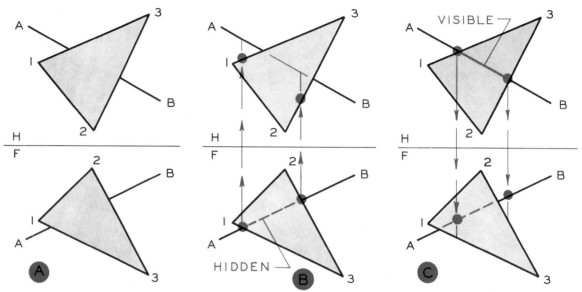

Fig. 3-21. Visibility of a line and a plane.

3-11 VISIBILITY OF CROSSING LINES

Two lines, *AB* and *CD*, are shown crossing in the top and front views of Fig. 3-20A. It is obvious that these lines do not intersect by application of principles outlined in Article 3-10. However, we want to determine which of the lines is visible in each view at the points of crossing.

The crossing point in the front view is projected to the top view in part B. This projector intersects line *AB* before line *CD*, indicating that line *CD* is farther back. This establishes line *AB* as being visible in the front view, since the horizontal view depicts true distances from the frontal plane and since the line that is closest to the front view would therefore be the one that is visible.

The visibility of the top view is determined by projecting the crossing point from the top view to the front view shown in part C of Fig. 3-20. This projector intersects line *CD* first, establishing line *CD* as being higher than or above line *AB* and therefore visible in the top view.

Visibility in a given view cannot be established by that view only. It is necessary to determine visibility by inspecting the preceding view, as outlined in this example.

3-12 VISIBILITY OF A LINE AND A PLANE

The principle of visibility of intersecting lines applies to an intersecting line and plane in much the same manner as outlined in Article 3-11. Part A of Fig. 3-21 shows that plane 1-2-3 and line *AB* cross in the top and front views.

Line *AB* crosses two lines of the plane, lines 1-3 and 2-3, in the front view of part B. To determine the visibility in the front view, we project these crossing points to the top view. In both cases, the projectors intersect the lines of the plane before they intersect line *AB*, which means that the plane is closer than the line in the front view. Therefore the portion of the line that crosses the plane in the front view is invisible and shown as a hidden line.

The visibility of the top view is found similarly by projecting the crossing points in the top view to the front view (part C). These projectors intersect line *AB* before lines 1-3 and 2-3. Consequently, line *AB* is higher than the plane in the top view and is drawn as being visible.

These methods can be used to find visibility in essentially all orthographic problems. Auxiliary view methods will be discussed in succeeding chapters.

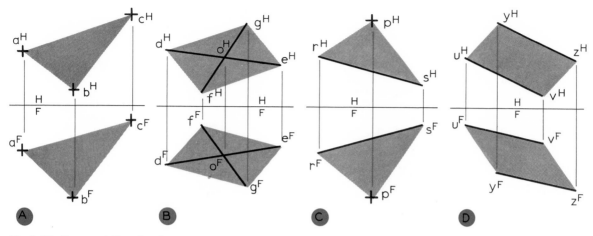

Fig. 3-22. Representation of a plane.

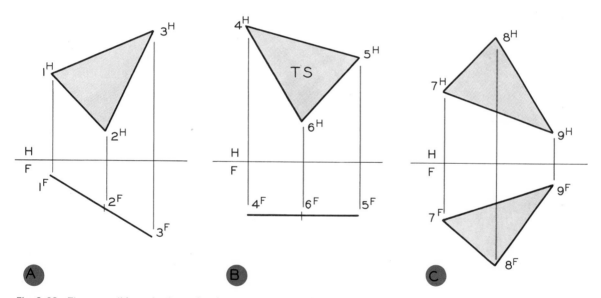

Fig. 3-23. Three possible projections of a plane.

3-13 PLANES

Whereas lines have only one dimension, length, planes have two dimensions that establish an area. Planes may be considered as infinite in certain problems. However, in most solutions segments of planes are used for convenience.

Four methods of representing planes are shown in Fig. 3-22. These are (A) three points not in a straight line, (B) two intersecting lines, (C) a point and a line, and (D) two parallel lines. The areas of the planes established by these methods need not be limited by the bounds of the points or lines used. The elements merely establish the necessary locations to orient the plane in space so it can be used in solving problems involving planes.

Planes may be projected in one of the following forms (Fig. 3-23): (A) as an edge, (B) as true

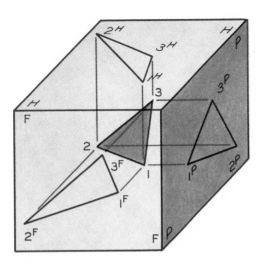

Fig. 3–24. A plane in space.

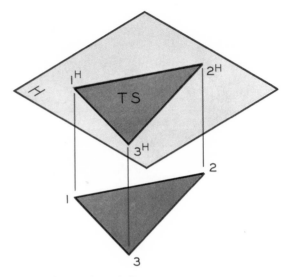

Fig. 3–26. A horizontal plane.

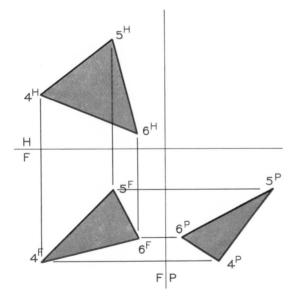

Fig. 3–25. Three views of a plane.

size, or (C) foreshortened. Planes parallel to one of the three principal projection planes—horizontal, frontal, and profile—are principal planes that will appear true size in a principal view. Each of these and the exception, the oblique plane, are discussed below.

The Oblique Plane. An oblique plane is a plane that is not parallel to a principal projection plane in any view, as shown in Fig. 3–24. Its projections may appear as lines or as foreshortened areas which are smaller than its true size. Figure 3–25 represents an oblique plane 4–5–6 in three views. This is the general case of a plane. Each of the vertex points is found in the same manner in each view as though it were an individual point.

The Horizontal Plane. A horizontal plane is parallel to the horizontal projection plane, as shown in Fig. 3–26. A horizontal plane is a principal plane and it appears true size in the top view. Three orthographic views of horizontal plane 7–8–9 are shown in Fig. 3–27. If the plane appears as an edge in both the front and side views or if it appears as an edge in either the front or side view and is parallel to the H–F fold line in the same view, it is a horizontal plane. Observation of the top view of a plane is not sufficient to determine whether it is a horizontal plane.

The Frontal Plane. A frontal plane is parallel to the frontal projection plane, as shown pictorially in Fig. 3–28. This principal plane appears true

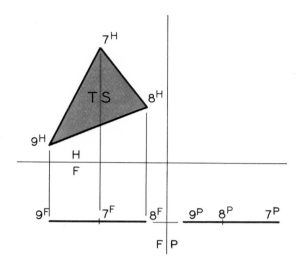

Fig. 3–27. Three views of a horizontal plane.

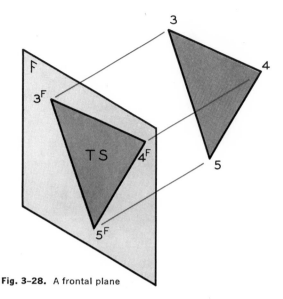

Fig. 3–28. A frontal plane

size in the front view and as an edge in the top
and side views. The edge views of plane 3–4–5
are shown parallel to the frontal plane in Fig.
3–29. There are an infinite number of shapes a
frontal plane may have in the front view, but the
top view and side views must be edges that are
parallel to the frontal plane.

The Profile Plane. The third principal plane is
the profile plane, which is parallel to the profile
projection plane (Fig. 3–30). Plane 6–7–8 is true
size in the profile view, or side view, as shown in
Fig. 3–31. Note that the plane appears as an
edge in the top and front views and that these
edges are parallel to the edge view of the profile
plane.

3–14   PROJECTION OF A LINE ON A PLANE

Plane 1–2–3–4 is given in Fig. 3–32A with line
AB drawn on the plane in the front view. We are
required to locate line *AB* on the plane in the top
view. Point *A* lies on line 1–4, while point *B* lies
on line 2–3; thus it is possible to find these
points in the top view by projecting them as
shown in part B. This is an application of the
principle covered in Article 3–9.

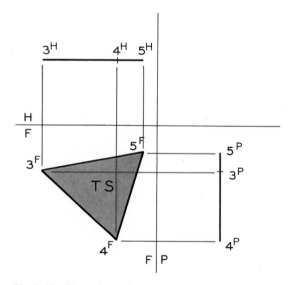

Fig. 3–29. Three views of a frontal plane.

The connection of points *A* and *B* will establish the line on plane 1–2–3–4 in the top view, as
shown in part C. This principle will have application in more advanced descriptive geometry
problems, which we shall discuss in succeeding
articles and chapters.

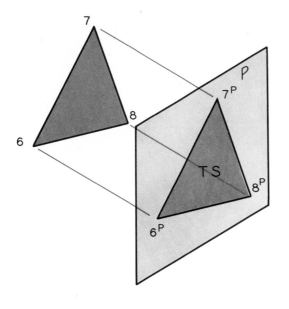

Fig. 3–30. A profile plane.

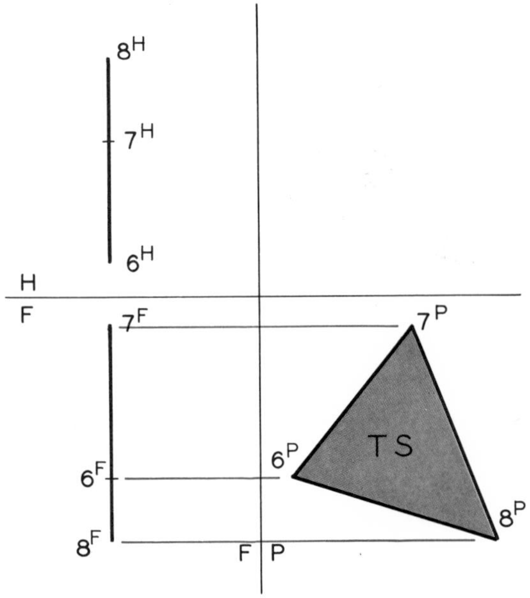

Fig. 3–31. Three views of a profile plane.

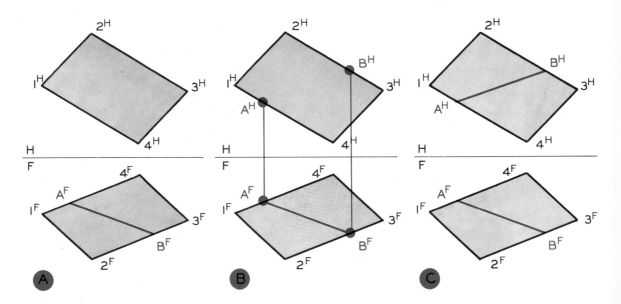

Fig. 3–32. Projection of a line on a plane.

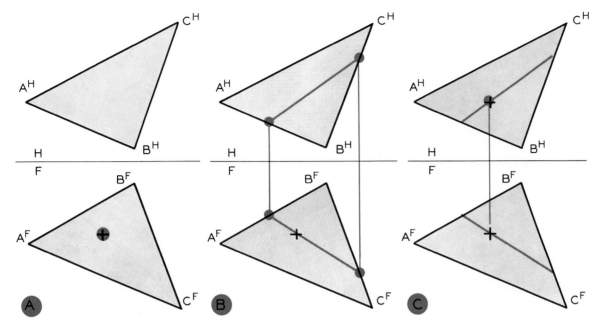

Fig. 3-33. Projection of a point on a plane.

3-15   LOCATION OF A POINT ON A PLANE

Many problems require that points be located on a plane in several views. Plane *ABC* (Fig. 3-33A) has a point indicated on its surface in the front view. We desire to locate the top view of this point as well. A line is drawn in any direction other than vertical through the point in the given view (part B). The points where this line intersects the edges of the plane in the front view are projected to these same respective lines in the top view (part B). The point can be located by projecting from the front view to this line in the top view (part C). Review Article 3-9 for a stronger understanding of this principle.

3-16   PRINCIPAL LINES ON A PLANE

Principal lines—horizontal, frontal, and profile—may be found in any view of a plane by application of the previously discussed principles. Principal lines are essential to the system of successive auxiliary views, which will be studied in later chapters.

Two horizontal lines are shown on plane 1-2-3 in Fig. 3-34. These were found by constructing lines on plane 1-2-3 that are parallel to the horizontal projection plane. The top views are found by projecting to the plane in the top view. These lines lie on the plane and are true length in the top view since they are horizontal.

Frontal lines which are parallel to the frontal projection plane are located in the top view of Fig. 3-35. The front view of the lines is found by projection. Frontal lines are true length in the front view.

Profile lines must be located in the front or top view and projected to the side view, as shown in Fig. 3-36. Profile lines are true length in the side views.

It should be observed that principal lines on any view of an oblique plane are parallel. For example, many profile lines could have been drawn in Fig. 3-36, but all would have been parallel and would have appeared true length in the side views.

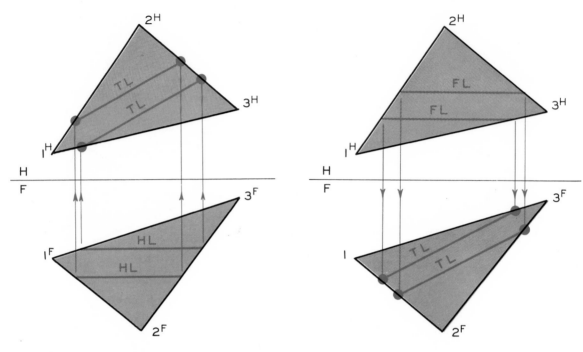

Fig. 3–34. Construction of horizontal lines on a plane.

Fig. 3–35. Construction of frontal lines on a plane.

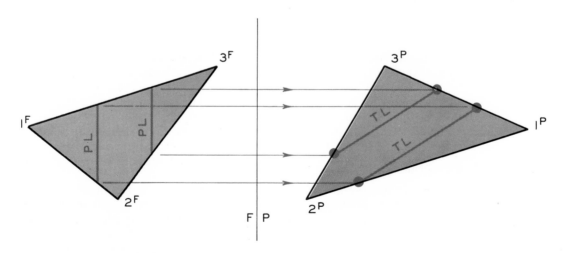

Fig. 3–36. Construction of profile lines on a plane.

3-17 PARALLELISM

In the solution of spatial problems it is often necessary to know whether lines or planes are parallel. This information can be determined by orthographic projection.

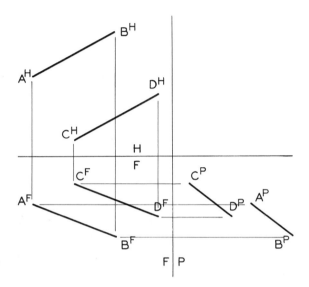

Fig. 3-37. Parallelism of lines.

Two lines that are parallel will be projected parallel in all views, except in the view where both lines appear as points. Lines *AB* and *CD* in Fig. 3-37 appear oblique in three views, but they are also parallel in each; therefore the lines are parallel in space.

When only one view of two lines is available, it cannot be assumed that the lines are parallel even though they are projected as parallel in this view. More than one view is necessary to determine whether two lines are parallel.

Figure 3-38 illustrates how this principle may be applied to a problem. Given in part A is line 3-4 and point *O*. We are required to construct a line equal in length and parallel to 3-4, with its midpoint at *O*. Since the midpoint of a line will be the midpoint of any projection of that line, the top view of the line is drawn through point *O* with its midpoint as shown in part B. The projection of this line is the same length as the projection of line 3-4. The front view of the line is drawn parallel to the front projection of line 3-4 in part C. The ends of the line are established by projecting from the top view. The frontal projections of the two lines are also equal in length, and the resulting line is parallel to the given line 3-4.

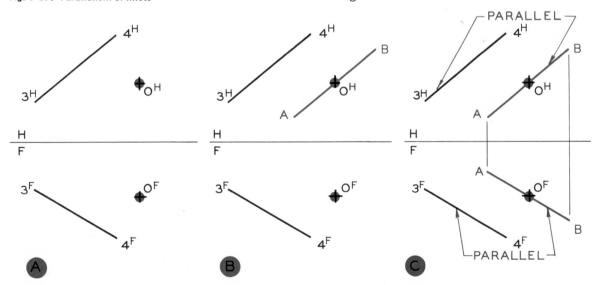

Fig. 3-38. Construction of a line parallel to a given line.

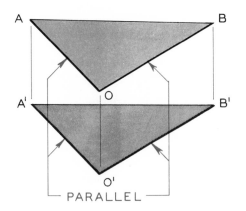

3–39

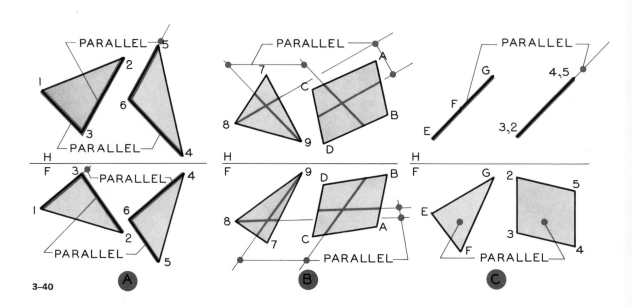

3–40

3-18 PARALLELISM OF PLANES

Two planes are parallel when intersecting lines in one plane are parallel to intersecting lines in the other, as shown pictorially in Fig. 3–39. Orthographic projections of parallel planes are shown in Fig. 3–40. Note that the same two sets of lines are parallel in the top view of part A as in the front view. These lines happen to be exterior lines of the planes concerned, but this does not have to be the case. The planes could be dissimilar in shape as shown in the example

in part B. Plane 7–8–9 and plane *ABCD* were found to be parallel by drawing parallel lines on each plane in one view and projecting them to the other. If these lines are parallel in this view also, then the planes are parallel. When two planes appear as parallel edges in one view, such as in part C, they are parallel in space.

The problem in Fig. 3–41A requires that a plane be constructed through point *O* parallel to plane 1–2–3. Line *AB* is drawn parallel to line 1–2 of the plane in the top and front views in part *B*. Line *CD* is then drawn through point *O*

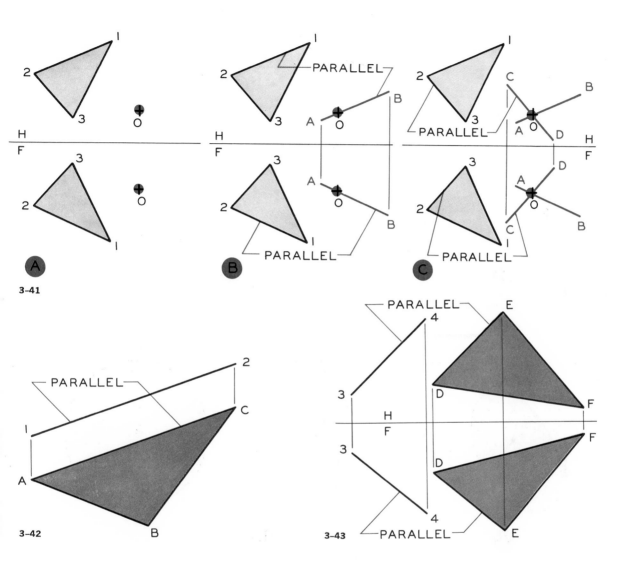

3-41

3-42

3-43

parallel to line 2-3 in both views in part C. Since these lines intersect at point O, they form a plane. This plane is parallel to plane 1-2-3, since two intersecting lines of one plane are parallel to two intersecting lines of the other.

3-19   PARALLELISM OF A LINE AND A PLANE

A line is parallel to a plane if it is parallel to any line in that plane. Line 1-2 is parallel to line AC in Fig. 3-42; therefore line 1-2 is parallel to plane ABC. Two orthographic views of a line and

a plane are shown in Fig. 3-43. Line 3-4 is parallel to line DE in the top view and in the front view, thus establishing these lines as parallel; therefore line 3-4 is parallel to plane DEF.

The problem given in Fig. 3-44A requires that a line drawn through point O be parallel to the plane formed by the two intersecting lines, 1-2 and 3-4. The line is constructed in part B through point O and parallel to line 1-2 in both views. This line is parallel to the plane, since it is parallel to a line in the plane. This line could have also been drawn parallel to line 3-4.

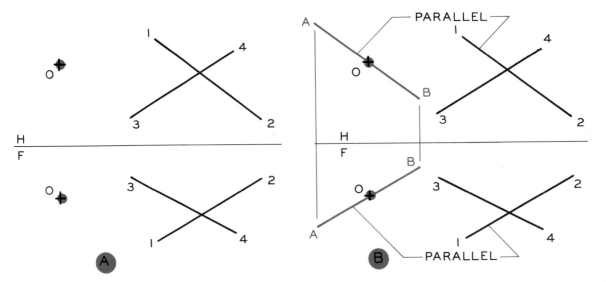

Fig. 3–44. Construction of a line through a point parallel to a given plane.

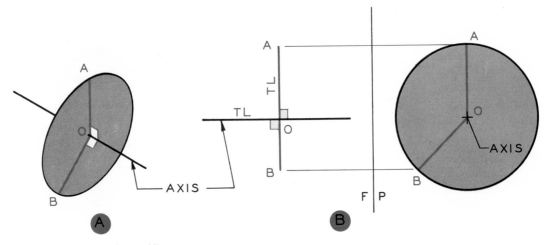

Fig. 3–45. Perpendicularity of lines.

3–20 PERPENDICULARITY OF LINES

The engineer will design many mechanisms that are composed of perpendiculars, whether they are lines or planes. It is therefore necessary that perpendicularity be understood sufficiently in order that it may be recognized or drawn when it occurs.

Figure 3–45 illustrates pictorially and orthographically the basic rules of perpendicularity.

Two perpendicular lines will be projected as perpendicular in any view where one or both are true length. As shown in part A, a line may be revolved around another line in an infinite number of positions and still be perpendicular to the other line, the axis.

In the orthographic view, part B, the lines *OA* and *OB* are projected such that they are perpendicular to the true-length axis. The axis and

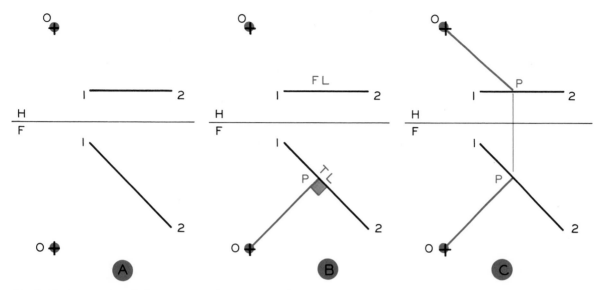

Fig. 3-46. Construction of a line perpendicular to a principal line.

line *OA* are both true length, but line *OB* is not true length. However, line *OB* is projected as perpendicular to the axis because the axis is true length, thereby satisfying the previously stated rule.

When two lines are perpendicular, but neither is true length, they will not project with a true 90° angle. The plane of the 90° angle will appear foreshortened and distorted.

3-21 A LINE PERPENDICULAR TO A PRINCIPAL LINE

Given in Fig. 3-46A are frontal line 1-2 and point *O*. Construct the top and front views of a line through point *O* that intersects line 1-2 and is perpendicular to it.

Line 1-2 is a principal line, a frontal line, and is consequently true length in the front view. By applying the rule of perpendicularity from Article 3-20, it is possible to construct line *OP* in the front view perpendicular to the true-length line (B). Since point *P* lies on the line, it may be found in the top view by projecting above its

front view to line 1-2, as shown in part C. These lines do not appear as perpendicular in the top view since neither are true length in this view.

3-22 A LINE PERPENDICULAR TO AN OBLIQUE LINE

The top and front views of an oblique line, 3-4 are given in Fig. 3-47A. We are required to construct a line through the midpoint of line 3-4 that would be perpendicular to it.

It is necessary that a true-length line be constructed before a perpendicular can be found. Thus in part B a horizontal line, *OP*, is drawn through the midpoint of the front view of line 3-4 to some convenient length. Line *OP* will be projected true length in the top view since it is horizontal. It may be drawn in any direction and still be true length; therefore, it is constructed perpendicular to line 3-4 through point *O*. The top view of point *P* is found by projecting from the front view. These two lines are perpendicular because they are perpendicular in the view where one of them is true length.

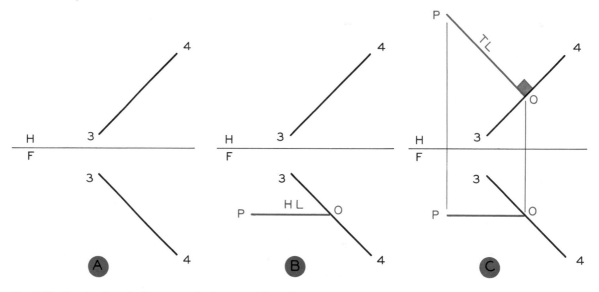

Fig. 3–47. Construction of a line perpendicular to an oblique line.

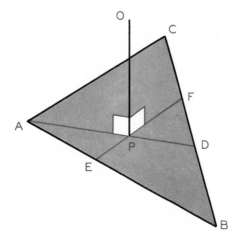

Fig. 3–48. A line perpendicular to a plane.

3–23   A LINE PERPENDICULAR TO A PLANE

It is possible to identify or to draw a line perpendicular to a plane in orthographic projection. *A line will be perpendicular to a plane if it is perpendicular to two intersecting lines on the plane.* This relationship is illustrated in Fig. 3–48. If a line is perpendicular to two intersecting lines in a plane, it will be perpendicular to all lines in the plane.

Plane *ABC* is given in Fig. 3–49A with point *O* located on the plane. We are required to construct a perpendicular to the plane through point *O*. It is possible to find a true-length line on any view of a plane by constructing a principal line, as covered previously. A true-length line is found in the front view by constructing a frontal line through point *O* in the top view and projecting it to the front view (part B). This line is true length and is a line on the plane, consequently, line *OP* can be drawn through point *O* perpendicular to the frontal line. If line *OP* is to be perpendicular to another line as well, we can draw a horizontal line on the plane in the front view (part C) and project it to the top view, where it appears true length. The top view of *OP* is constructed perpendicular to this line to establish the top view of line *OP*.

This line is perpendicular to the plane because it is perpendicular to two intersecting lines on the plane. This relationship is apparent where lines on the plane are shown true length.

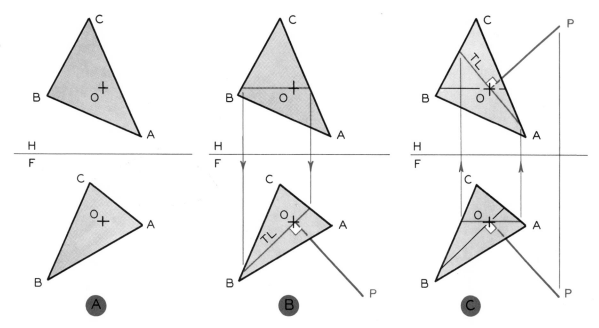

Fig. 3–49. Construction of a line perpendicular to a plane.

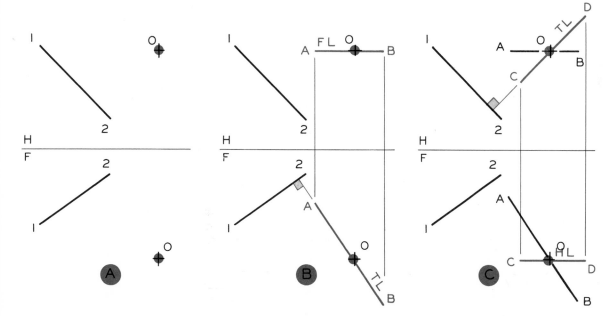

Fig. 3–50. Construction of a plane through a point perpendicular to an oblique line.

3–24 A PLANE PERPENDICULAR TO AN OBLIQUE LINE

Line 1–2 and point O are given in Fig. 3–50A. We are required to construct a plane through point O that will be perpendicular to line 1–2.

A plane may be established through point O by drawing two intersecting lines that intersect at point O. These lines will be true length if they are principal lines, which will permit perpendicularity to be established. Frontal line AB is drawn through point O in the top view and projected to the front view, where it is true length (part B). It is drawn perpendicular to line 1–2, which gives one line in the plane perpendicular to line 1–2.

A second line, CD, is drawn as a horizontal line (part C) in the front view and it is projected to the top view, where it will be true length and perpendicular to line 1–2. Line 1–2 is perpendicular to two intersecting lines in the plane, and we have now constructed a plane perpendicular to the given line.

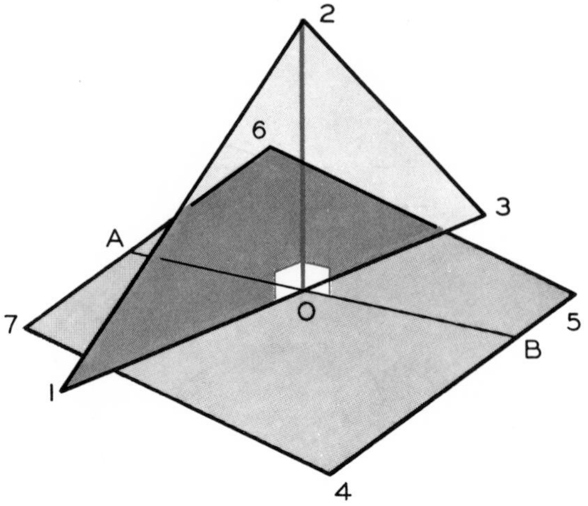

Fig. 3–51. Perpendicularity of planes.

3–25 PERPENDICULARITY OF PLANES

Planes may be perpendicular to other planes in many technological problems. The rule for determining perpendicularity of planes is a combination of the previously covered principles of perpendicularity.

A plane is perpendicular to another plane if a line in one plane is perpendicular to the other plane. This is illustrated in Fig. 3–51, where plane 1–2–3 is perpendicular to plane 4–5–6–7, because if line 2–O is perpendicular to two intersecting lines on a plane, then it is perpendicular to the plane. It can be seen from these principles that plane 1–2–3 is perpendicular to plane 4–5–6–7.

A plane and a line are given in Fig. 3–52A. We are required to construct a plane passing through line AB that is perpendicular to plane 1–2–3.

A plane can be passed through a line if the line lies in the plane that is constructed; therefore, an infinite number of planes can be established through line AB by intersecting it with another line. Two intersecting lines form a plane. If the line drawn to intersect line AB were drawn perpendicular to plane 1–2–3, the plane formed would be perpendicular to plane 1–2–3.

A true-length line is found in the front view of plane 1–2–3 in part B by constructing a frontal line in the top view and projecting it to the front view. Line CD is drawn through a convenient point on line AB perpendicular to the extension of the true-length line in the front view. A horizontal line is constructed in the front view of part C, and projected to the top view, where it is true length. The top-view projection of line CD is drawn perpendicular to this true-length line which goes through the top view of the point on line CD.

Line CD has been constructed perpendicular to two intersecting lines on the plane and is known to be perpendicular to the plane. Since the line CD intersects line AB, it forms a plane containing a line parallel to plane 1–2–3, which results in two perpendicular planes. These two

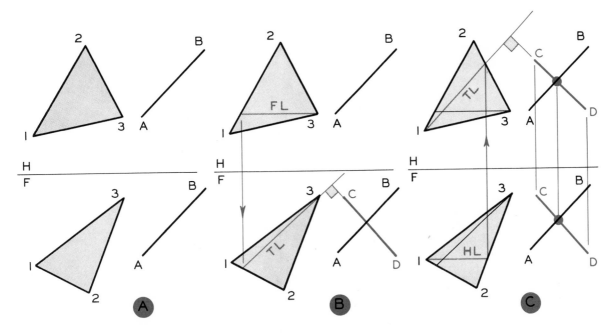

Fig. 3–52. Construction of a plane through a line perpendicular to a plane.

planes do not actually intersect as they are represented in this illustration; however, they are perpendicular and would intersect at a 90° angle if both were extended to their line of intersection.

3-26 SUMMARY

The principles of orthographic projection covered in this chapter are fundamentals that will be applied in the development of spatial problems involving descriptive geometry principles in succeeding chapters. A review of the basic elements—the point, line, and plane—and their relationship to each other in space is the basis of the solution of all graphical and descriptive geometry problems.

It is important that a solid understanding be gained of the principal projection planes in this chapter before continuing further. Principal lines and principal planes are related to the projection planes to which they are parallel. The principal planes are: (1) horizontal, (2) frontal, and (3) profile. Similarly, principal planes and principal lines are identified by these three terms. Principal lines are true length in the view where they are parallel to the projection plane being viewed; principal planes are true size in this view also.

Relationships such as parallelism and perpendicularity are common in essentially all engineering problems. The designer can prepare more accurate and efficient plans if he understands these projections.

The succeeding chapters will discuss the principles of projection as they relate to the auxiliary-view method of problem solution. The projection of auxiliary views is possible through a thorough understanding of the basic projection principles covered here. Frequent reference should be made to this chapter when necessary, to review projection principles that are used in other solutions.

PROBLEMS

The problems for this chapter can be constructed and solved on eight $8\frac{1}{2}'' \times 11''$ sheets as illustrated by the accompanying figures. Given that each grid represents $\frac{1}{4}''$, lay out and solve the problems on grid or plain paper. All reference planes and points should be labeled in all cases, using $\frac{1}{8}''$ letters and guidelines.

1. Use Fig. 3–53 for all parts of this problem. (A) Draw the missing view of point A. Locate point B from point A 3 units forward, 2 units to the right, and 2 units below. Show this in three views. (B) Find the missing view of point C. With respect to point C, locate in three views point D that is 4 units forward, 2 units to the right, and 3 units above. (C) Draw three views of line EF. Point F is 4 units in front, 5 units to the right, and 3 units below point E. (D) Draw three views of line GH. Point H is 4 units behind, 3 units below, and 5 units to the right of point G. (E) Line IJ is a horizontal line 3 units below the horizontal plane. Draw the line in all views and label its true-length view. (F) Line KL is a frontal line 4 units behind the frontal plane. Draw three views of the line and label its true-length view.

2. Use Fig. 3–54 for all parts of the problem. (A) Draw three views of line 1–2 with point 1 located 4 units to the left, 2 units below, and 3 units in front of point 2. (B) Draw three views of line 1–2 given that point 2 is located 4 units to the right, 2 units above, and 4 units in front of point 1. (C) Draw three views of frontal line 3–4 with point 4 located 3 units below point 3. Label its true-length view. (D) Draw three views of horizontal line 5–6 with point 6 located 4 units to the right and 3 units behind point 5. Label its true-length view. (E) Draw three views of horizontal line 7–8. Label its true-length view. (F) Draw three views of frontal line 1–2 and label its true-length view.

3. Use Fig. 3–55 for all parts of this problem. (A) Draw three views of profile line AB and label its true-length view. (B) Locate the midpoint of line CD in three views. (C) Divide line EF into three equal parts and show the divisions in

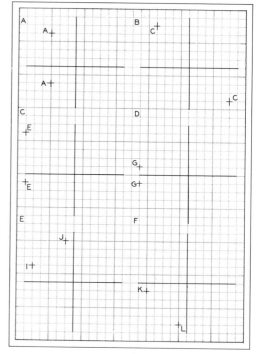

Fig. 3–53. Projections of a point.

three views. (D) Draw the side view of the two lines in part D. Determine whether they intersect. (E) Construct three views of the lines KL and IJ so that they will be intersecting lines. (F) Construct line PO in three views such that it will intersect line MN.

4. Use Fig. 3–56 for all parts of the problem. (A) Draw three views of profile line 1–2. Draw three views of a line 1'' long that intersects 1–2 at its midpoint and appears as a point in the profile view. (B) Draw three views of a line $\frac{1}{2}''$ long that intersects the given line at its midpoint and appears as a point in the front view. (C) Draw the side view of the given lines and determine whether they are intersecting lines. (D) Construct line OP that passes under the given line and does not intersect it. (E) Draw three views of the line and the plane and indicate visibility. (F) Draw three views of the line and the plane and indicate visibility.

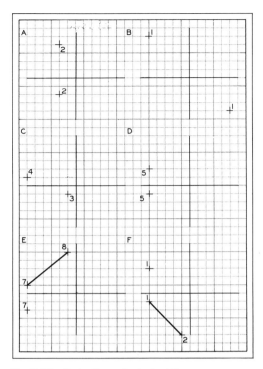

Fig. 3–54. Projections of principal lines.

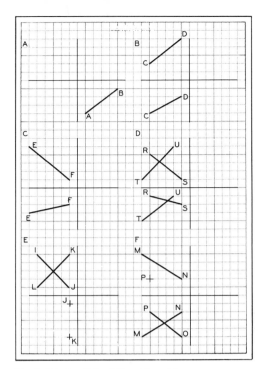

Fig. 3–55. Spatial relationships of lines.

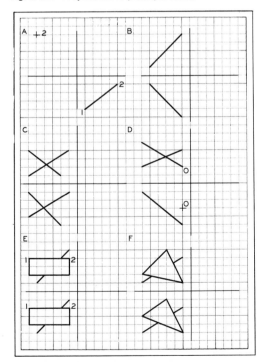

Fig. 3–56. Intersecting lines and visibility.

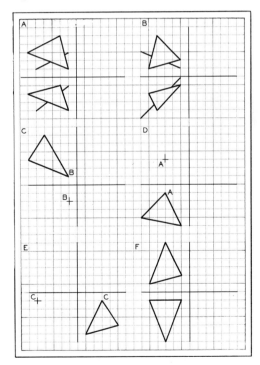

Fig. 3–57. Relationships of lines and planes.

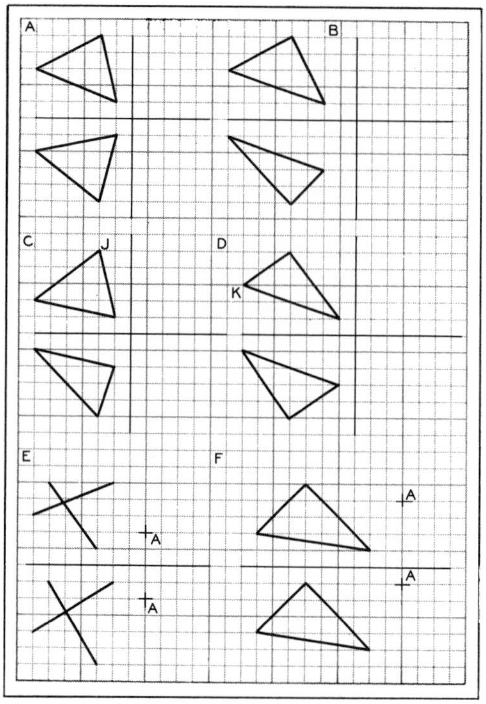

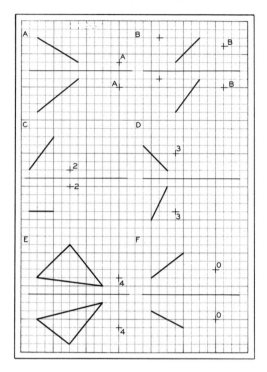

Fig. 3–58. Principal planes and spatial relationships.

Fig. 3–59. Perpendicularity problems.

5. Use Fig. 3–57 for all parts of this problem. (A) Draw three views of the line and the plane and indicate visibility. (B) Draw three views of the line and the plane and indicate visibility. (C) Construct three views of the horizontal plane and label its true-size view. (D) Construct three views of the frontal plane and label its true-size view. (E) Construct three views of the profile plane and label its true-size view. (F) Draw three equally spaced frontal lines on the plane in three views. Draw the side view.

6. Use Fig. 3–58 for all parts of this problem. (A) Draw two equally spaced horizontal lines on the plane and show them in three views. (B) Draw three equally spaced profile lines on the plane and show them in three views. (C) Construct line *JP* which lies on a plane that slopes upward to the left. Show the line and the plane in the side view also. (D) Construct line *KR* in a

plane that slopes downward and backward. Show the line and the plane in the side view also. (E) Construct a line through point *A* that is parallel to the plane. (F) Construct a line through point *A* that is parallel to the plane.

7. Use Fig. 3–59 for all parts of this problem. (A) Construct a line through point *A* that is parallel to the line and equal in length. (B) Construct a line through point *B* that is parallel to the plane formed by the line and point. (C) Construct a line from point 2 that is perpendicular to the line at its midpoint. (D) Construct a line from point 3 in the front view that will be perpendicular to the front view of the line. Show this line in three views. Is it perpendicular to the line? (E) Construct a line from point 4 that will be perpendicular to the plane. (F) Construct a plane through point *O* that will be perpendicular to the line.

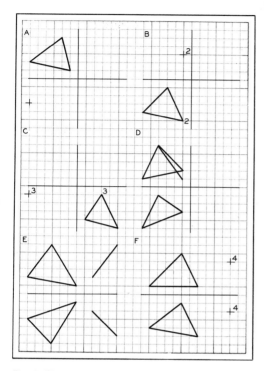

Fig. 3-60. Perpendicularity problems.

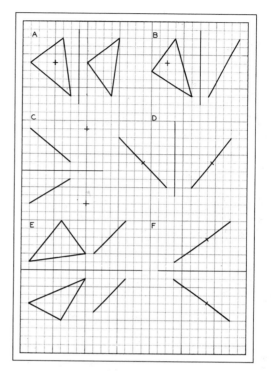

Fig. 3-61. Combination problems.

8. Use Fig. 3-60 for all parts of this problem. (A) Draw three views of the horizontal plane. Construct a line $\frac{1}{2}''$ long perpendicular to it and show the plane and the line in three views. (B) Draw three views of a line $\frac{1}{2}''$ long that is perpendicular to and intersecting the frontal plane on its back side. Show the line and the plane in three views. (C) Construct three views of a line $\frac{1}{2}''$ long that is perpendicular to and intersecting the profile plane on its right side. Show the line and the plane in three views. (D) Construct three views of the plane and line with the line lying on the plane as shown in part D of the figure. (E) Construct a plane through the line that is perpendicular to the plane given in part E of the figure. (F) Construct a plane through point 4 that is perpendicular to the plane given in part F of the figure.

9. Use Fig. 3-61 for all parts of this problem. (A) Construct a plane that passes through the point on the plane and is perpendicular to the plane. (B) Construct a plane that passes through the point on the plane and is perpendicular to the plane. (C) Construct a plane through the point that is perpendicular to the line. (D) Construct a line from the point on a line that is perpendicular to the line on the upward side. (E) Construct a plane through the line that is perpendicular to the plane. (F) Construct a plane that passes through the point on the line and is perpendicular to the line.

IDENTIFICATION

PRELIMINARY IDEAS

REFINEMENT

ANALYSIS

DECISION

IMPLEMENTATION

4

PRIMARY AUXILIARY VIEWS

4–1 INTRODUCTION

Chapter 3 reviewed principles of orthographic projection as applied to the principal views of points, lines, and planes in space. Although orthographic projection in principal views offers solutions to many spatial problems, auxiliary projections are necessary to analyze many designs for critical information that would be difficult to obtain by other means. Distances, lengths, angles, sizes, and areas must be determined during the refinement of preliminary designs to permit analysis in the next phase of the design process.

An example of a simple design problem appears in Fig. 4–1, which shows an exhaust pipe designed for installation in an automobile. It was necessary to determine the bend angles of the pipe and its length while providing the necessary clearance with other interior components. Design of the support brackets required that angular measurements, distances, and similar information be found by descriptive geometry methods prior to the preparation of the finished specifications. It should be easy to visualize problems of a greater complexity that would require considerably more refinement of dimensional properties of this type, but on more advanced levels.

Primary auxiliary views are necessary to determine spatial information pertaining to a design that cannot be found in the principal views. A *primary auxiliary view* is a view projected onto a projection plane that is perpendicular to only one of the principal planes. (If a projection plane is perpendicular to two principal planes,

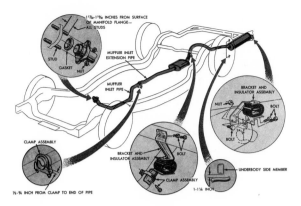

Fig. 4–1. The exhaust system of this automobile is an example of a spatial problem requiring the application of primary auxiliary views for solution. (Courtesy of Ford Motor Company.)

Fig. 4–2. The structural frame of the Mariner spacecraft illustrates many spatial relationships that must be determined during its design. (Courtesy of the National Aeronautics and Space Administration.)

it is a principal plane rather than an auxiliary view.) A primary auxiliary view is projected from one of the principal views—the top, front, or side views.

The Mariner spacecraft shown in Fig. 4–2 illustrates a number of applications of primary auxiliary views and secondary auxiliary views, which will be covered in the chapter that follows. The dimensions of each structural member must be found prior to the analysis of the frame for strength. Similarly, the dimensions of the members must be known to compute the weight of the vehicle, which is a critical aspect of space travel. The angles between the members must be obtained in order that the connecting joints may be designed. Knowledge of the angles between planes is necessary for fabrication of this system and for the determination of the true size of the planes formed by structural members. Graphical methods and descriptive geometry form the practical approach to solving realistic technological problems of the types shown in Figs. 4–1 and 4–2. Every effort should be made by the student to develop an understanding of these principles, since such understanding will enable him to recognize problems that can be solved graphically when this method is superior to mathematical methods.

Fig. 4–3. The inclined display panel of the Videx receiver is an example of a plane that must be found true size by a primary auxiliary view. (Courtesy of ITT Industrial Laboratories.)

4–2 TRUE SIZE OF INCLINED SURFACES

A plane that appears as an oblique edge in a principal view may be found true size in a primary auxiliary view. Such a plane will appear foreshortened in adjacent principal views from which the oblique edge view is projected. The inclined plane of the Videx unit in Fig. 4–3 will appear as an edge in one principal view and foreshortened in the other two. Since the plane does appear as an edge in one of the principal views, the true size of the plane can be found by a primary auxiliary view.

Primary auxiliary views are projected from any of the three principal views—the horizontal, frontal, or profile. A view projected from a horizontal view will require a horizontal reference plane, one projected from a front view will require a frontal reference plane, and one projected from a side view will require a profile reference plane. The procedure will be covered in the following explanation.

True Size of an Inclined Surface—Frontal Reference Plane. A plane that appears as an edge in front view (Fig. 4–4) can be found true size in a primary auxiliary view projected from the front view. Reference plane F–1 is drawn parallel to the edge view of the inclined plane in the front view at any convenient location. It is drawn to conform to the pictorial in part A of the figure, in this case, to relate with the orthographic views in part B. Note that primary auxiliary plane F–1 is perpendicular to the frontal plane and that the line of sight is perpendicular to the auxiliary plane and parallel to the frontal plane. When an observer views the object in the direction indicated by the line of sight, he will see the frontal projection plane as an edge, and consequently, he will see measurements perpendicular to the frontal plane true length. These dimensions are those of the depth, represented here by *D*, which is perpendicular to the edge view of the frontal plane in the top and side views (part B).

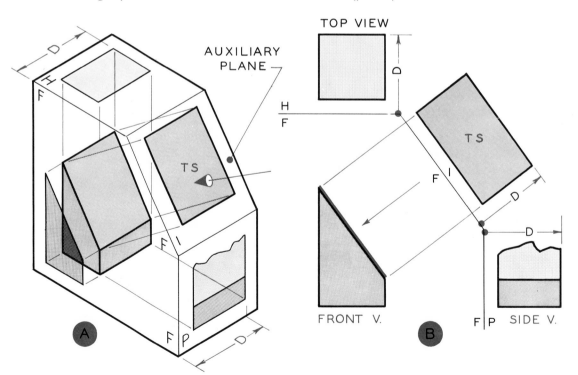

Fig. 4–4. True size of an inclined surface—frontal reference plane.

The inclined plane is projected from the front view perpendicular to the F–1 plane. Depth D is measured in the top or side views and transferred to the auxiliary view with dividers. Each of the four corners of the surface is found in this manner and then all four corners are connected with one another to give the true size of the inclined plane.

True Size of an Inclined Surface—Horizontal Reference Plane. The inclined plane in Fig. 4–5A is inclined to the frontal and profile planes and is perpendicular to the horizontal plane. It will appear true size when projected onto an auxiliary plane which is parallel to the inclined plane and perpendicular to the horizontal plane.

Reference plane H–1 is drawn parallel to the edge view of the inclined plane in part B of the figure. When the line of sight is perpendicular to an auxiliary plane projected from the horizontal (top) view, the horizontal plane will ap-pear as an edge, and the height dimension H will appear true length. Each corner of the inclined plane is projected perpendicularly to the H–1 plane and located by transferring the H distance from the front view to the auxiliary view with dividers. The four corner points are connected to give the true-size view of the inclined plane.

Since a plane can be represented by two intersecting lines, the true length of a curved pipe segment (Fig. 4–6), as well as its radius of curvature, can be found by application of a primary auxiliary view projected from the horizontal view. The plane of this curved section of pipe will appear as an edge in the top view. A primary auxiliary plane can be constructed parallel to the edge view of the plane of the curved pipe and perpendicular to the horizontal projection plane. The resulting auxiliary view locates the endpoints of the pipe, from which the curve can be designed to fulfill the requirements of this connection.

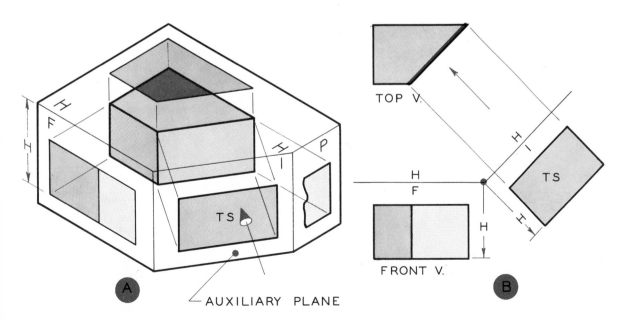

Fig. 4–5. True size of an inclined surface—horizontal reference plane.

Fig. 4–6. The lengths of the curved pipe segments can be found by auxiliary views during its design. The pipes here are part of a pneumatic conveying system at Phillips Chemical Company. (Courtesy of General American Transportation Corporation.)

Fig. 4–8. The bed of this Model 45 Haulpak truck was designed through the use of auxiliary views to determine sizes of oblique planes. (Courtesy of LeTourneau-Westinghouse Company.)

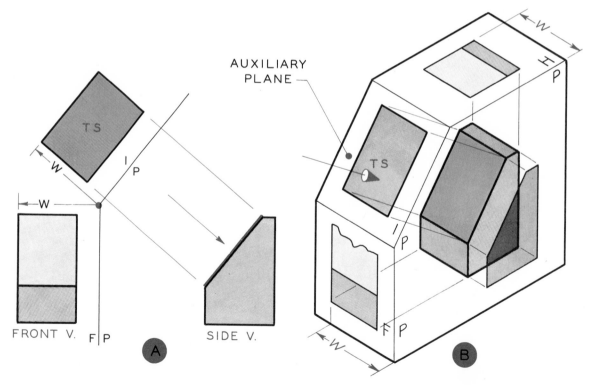

Fig. 4–7. True size of an inclined surface—profile reference plane.

True Size of an Inclined Surface—Profile Reference Plane. The inclined plane in Fig. 4–7 appears as an edge in the side view, which means it is inclined to the horizontal and frontal planes and perpendicular to the profile plane. Auxiliary plane P–1 is drawn parallel to the edge view of the inclined surface in the side view at some convenient location. An observer whose line of sight is perpendicular to the auxiliary plane will see the profile plane as an edge. Consequently, dimensions of width W will appear true length in the auxiliary view. The observer also sees the profile plane as an edge when he views the front view, so the width W dimensions are true length in this view. Therefore each measurement of W can be transferred from the front view to the auxiliary view to establish the corners of the inclined surface. The corners are connected to give the true-size view of the inclined surface.

The truck bed shown in Fig. 4–8 is composed of oblique planes that can be found true size by auxiliary views. Any two adjacent orthographic views of these planes can be used to find each plane true size by following the previously covered principles. It is necessary only for the planes to appear as edges in a principal view.

4–3 PRIMARY AUXILIARY VIEW OF A POINT

Point 3 is shown pictorially in Fig. 4–9A, where it is projected onto the horizontal, frontal, and auxiliary planes. Note that the auxiliary plane is perpendicular to the horizontal plane; consequently, the observer will see the horizontal plane as an edge when his line of sight is perpendicular to the auxiliary plane. Distances that are perpendicular to the horizontal plane will appear true length when the horizontal plane appears as an edge. Therefore point 3 can be located in the auxiliary view by measuring its distance, H, from the horizontal plane in the front view and transferring this distance to the auxiliary plane, where the horizontal plane appears as an edge also.

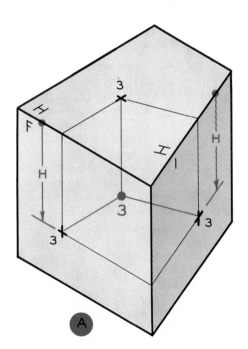

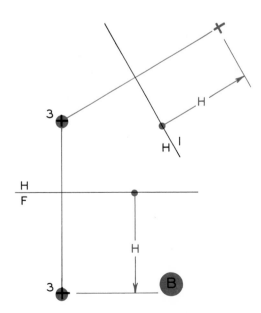

Fig. 4–9. Primary auxiliary view of a point shown pictorially and orthographically.

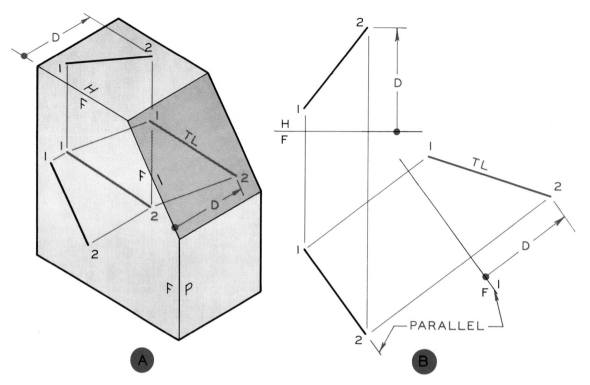

Fig. 4–10. Primary auxiliary view of a line.

The orthographic construction of the primary auxiliary view is illustrated in part B of the figure. It should be observed that there are an infinite number of positions for the auxiliary plane projected from the top view, but in every case point 3 would lie at the distance H from the horizontal plane. Similarly, an auxiliary view could have been projected from the front view through the use of an auxiliary plane that was perpendicular to the frontal plane, as introduced in Article 4–2. An auxiliary view of a point in space, such as that in this example, is of little value to the refinement or analysis of a preliminary design; however, it is a basic principle of projection that must be applied in all auxiliary view construction.

4–4 PRIMARY AUXILIARY VIEW OF A LINE

The projections of line 1–2 are shown pictorially in Fig. 4–10A. The line is projected onto the horizontal, frontal, and auxiliary planes with the

primary auxiliary plane constructed parallel to the frontal projection of line 1–2. When the observer's line of sight is perpendicular to the auxiliary plane, the frontal plane will appear as an edge, and all dimensions perpendicular to the frontal plane will be projected true length. Depth dimension D is perpendicular to the frontal plane and is therefore used as the measurement to construct the auxiliary view of line 1–2. Point 2 is the same distance from the frontal plane in the auxiliary view as it is in the horizontal projection (top view).

The orthographic construction of the primary auxiliary view is shown in part B of the figure. The auxiliary plane is drawn parallel to the front view of line 1–2 so that the observer's line of sight will be perpendicular to the line when it is perpendicular to the auxiliary plane. A line is projected true length in the view where the observer's line of sight is perpendicular to the line —in this case, the auxiliary view. We can measure the line's true length in this view.

FIGURE 4–11. TRUE LENGTH OF A LINE

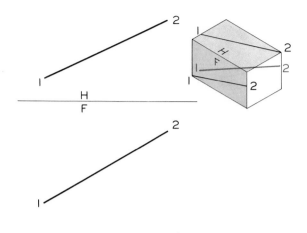

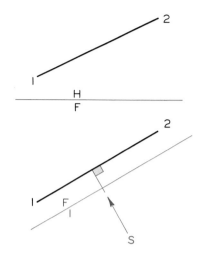

Given: The top and front views of line 1–2.
Required: Find the true length view of line 1–2 by the aux-iliary-view method.
Reference: Article 4–4.

Step 1: A line will appear true length when viewed in a perpendicular direction. Therefore we shall establish a line of sight perpendicular to the front view of 1–2 and draw reference plane F–1 parallel to line 1–2 and perpendicular to the line of sight. Label the reference plane F–1 since it is perpendicular to the frontal plane.

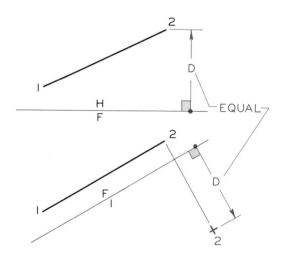

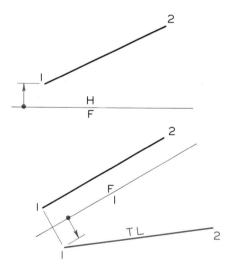

Step 2: We shall use the frontal plane as a reference plane for measurements since the auxiliary view is projected from the front view. Point 2 is distance *D* from the frontal plane in the top view. Measure this distance, which is perpendicular to the F–1 plane, in the auxiliary view along the projector from the front view of point 2.

Step 3: Locate point 1 in the auxiliary view in the same manner as we did point 2. Connect points 1 and 2 to establish the true-length view of line 1–2. We could also find the true length of line 1–2 by projecting from the top view and using an H–1 reference plane.

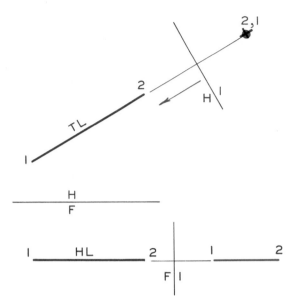

Fig. 4–12. A primary auxiliary view which is projected parallel to a true-length line gives a point view of the line.

Fig. 4–13. The diagonal structural members of the Saturn 1–B launch vehicle could have been designed by using primary auxiliary views to determine their true lengths. (Courtesy of National Aeronautics and Space Administration.)

Figure 4–11 separates the sequential steps required to find the true length of an oblique line. It is beneficial to letter all reference planes using the notation suggested in the example illustrations. The reference line drawn between the principal plane and the primary auxiliary plane is a line representing the line of intersection between the primary and auxiliary planes, as shown in Fig. 4–10. A primary view projected from a front view has a reference plane labeled F–1, from the horizontal view, H–1, and from the profile view, P–1. The true length of a line can be found by projecting from any of these views.

The point view of a line can be found in a primary auxiliary view when the line is true length in a principal view. Line 1–2 in Fig. 4–12 is horizontal in the front view, which makes the top view true length. When auxiliary plane H–1 is drawn perpendicular to the direction of the top view of line 1–2, the resulting auxiliary view will project as a point view of line 1–2. In order that the point view may be obtained, a line must

appear true length in the view from which the auxiliary view is projected. Note that the auxiliary view, which is projected from the frontal projection of line 1–2, does not result in a point view of the line, but instead gives a foreshortened view. This particular projection is actually a right-side view.

The true length of the diagonal structural members of the Saturn 1–B launch vehicle (Fig. 4–13) can be found by primary auxiliary views with a high degree of accuracy. These structural members would not appear true length in principal views. Numerous other examples of oblique lines requiring auxiliary view solution can be seen in the structural framework in the background of this illustration.

4–5 TRUE LENGTH BY ANALYTICAL GEOMETRY

The analytical approach to determining the true length of a line is illustrated in Fig. 4–14, where line 3–4 appears true length in the front view.

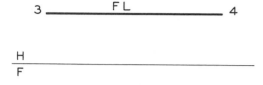

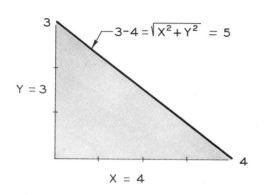

Fig. 4–14. The true length of a frontal line can be found analytically by the Pythagorean theorem.

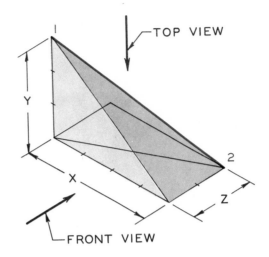

Fig. 4–15. The X-, Y-, and Z-coordinates used for finding the true length of an oblique line.

The line can be measured graphically for its true length or else its true length can be found by application of the Pythagorean theorem. The Pythagorean theorem states that the hypotenuse of a right triangle is equal to the square root of the sum of the squares of the other two sides. Line 3–4 is found to be 5 units long by application of this principle when the horizontal distance between the ends of the line is 4 units and the vertical distance is 3 units.

An oblique line that does not project true length in the principal views requires the manipulation of three coordinates—X, Y, and Z. Such a line is shown pictorially in Fig. 4–15. Note that the X- and Y-coordinates are projected true length in the front view while the Z-coordinate is true length in the top view. Two views are needed to determine the true length of an oblique line by analytical methods, just as two views were needed to find a graphical solution.

The steps for determining the true length of line 1–2 using the analytical method are illustrated in Fig. 4–16.

Part A. Right triangles are constructed with line 1–2 as the hypotenuse in the top and front views. The coordinates, or legs of the right triangles, are drawn parallel and perpendicular to the H–F reference plane.

Part B. The true length of the frontal projection of line 1–2 is found by application of the Pythagorean theorem as though the line were true length in the front view. The frontal projection of line 1–2 is found to be 5 units in length by substituting the units of 3 and 4 as the X- and Y-coordinates. The resulting length can be visualized by referring to the pictorial of the line in Fig. 4–15.

Part C. The true length of the line can be found by combining the true length of the frontal projection with the true length of the Z-coordinate in the top view. The total equation of line 1–2 becomes

$$1\text{–}2 = \sqrt{X^2 + Y^2 + Z^2} = \sqrt{29}.$$

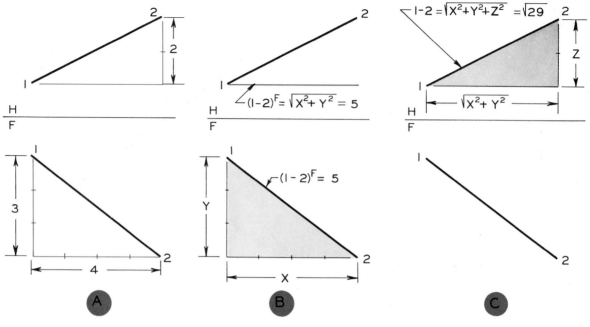

Fig. 4–16. The analytical method of finding the true length of an oblique line.

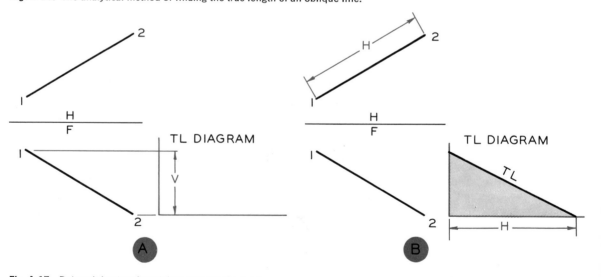

Fig. 4–17. Determining true length by a true-length diagram.

It can be seen by comparison that the analytical methods for determination of the true length of a line are very similar to the primary auxiliary method, where the projection of a line is used as the basis for an additional view in which the missing coordinate appears true length. For example, an auxiliary view projected from the front view of line 1–2 would result in a combination of coordinates where both the frontal projection of line 1–2 and the Z-coordinate appear true length, thus giving the true length of line 1–2. Both systems of spatial analysis should be used in combination to promote accuracy and to provide a means for a more thorough analysis.

4–6 TRUE LENGTH BY A TRUE-LENGTH DIAGRAM

The true length of line 1–2, or any oblique line, can be found by a true-length diagram such as that illustrated in Fig. 4–17. This is not an auxiliary view method, but a knowledge of primary auxiliary views is necessary to understand this method.

Part A. The top and front views of line 1–2 are given. The vertical distance between the ends of the front view is projected to form one leg of a right triangle that will be the true-length diagram. This diagram can be constructed equally well from either view.

Part B. The projected length of line 1–2 in the top view is transferred to the true-length diagram to represent the horizontal leg of the triangle. The hypotenuse of this right triangle is the true length of the line.

The true-length diagram method does not give a direction for the line, but merely its true length. In general, a true-length diagram can be projected from any two adjacent views, with one measurement being the distance measured between the two endpoints in a direction perpendicular to the reference plane between the two views. The other measurement is the projected length of the line in the other adjacent view.

4–7 ANGLE BETWEEN A LINE AND PRINCIPAL PLANES

When a primary auxiliary view is drawn, an edge view of a principal plane will appear in the resulting auxiliary view. When the auxiliary view is projected from the front view, the frontal plane will appear as an edge; when it is projected from the horizontal view, the horizontal plane will appear as an edge; and when it is projected from the profile view, the profile plane will appear as an edge. The true angle between a principal plane and a line can be found in the

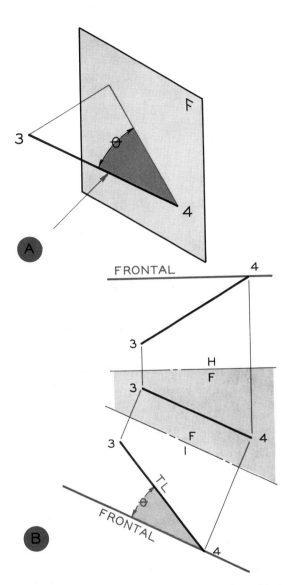

Fig. 4–18. Determining the angle made by a line with the frontal plane.

view where the principal plane in question appears as an edge and the line is true length.

Angle with the Frontal Plane. Figure 4–18 illustrates a technique for determining the angle between line 3–4 and the frontal plane. The line of sight in part A is parallel to the frontal plane and perpendicular to line 3–4 and is the view required to obtain the true angle, θ, between the line and the frontal plane. The orthographic construction of the auxiliary view is shown in part B, where the auxiliary view is projected from the front view. Note that the reference plane is located through point 4 in the top view, rather than between the two views as a folding line, as is usually the case. A reference plane can be located in any position in the top view, including through the line itself, provided that it is a frontal reference plane. Due to space

limitations on drawing layouts, the plane is usually drawn near the existing top view to conserve space in the auxiliary view. Point 3 in the top view is in front of the frontal reference plane and is located in front of the frontal plane in the auxiliary view as well.

Angle with the Horizontal Plane. Figure 4–19A pictorially illustrates the angle between the horizontal plane and line 1–2. In a projection from the top view of line 1–2, the horizontal

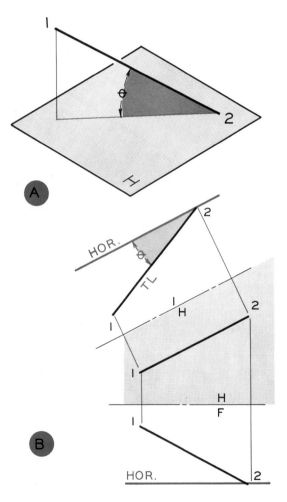

Fig. 4–19. Determining the angle made by a line with the horizontal plane.

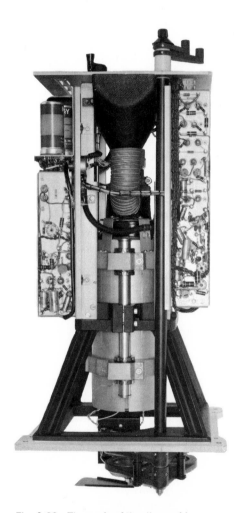

Fig. 4–20. The angle of the diagonal base supports with the horizontal base of the image orthicon camera could have been determined by an auxiliary view. (Courtesy of ITT Industrial Laboratories.)

plane will appear as an edge in the auxiliary view and the line will appear true length, as shown in part B of the figure. The true angle, θ, cannot be measured in the front view, where the horizontal plane appears as an edge, because line 1–2 is not true length in this view.

The structural mount used to attach the image orthicon camera (Fig. 4–20) to a telescope is an example of the need to determine the angle between a line and a principal plane. In this case, the line represents the diagonal base supports, while the horizontal plane is the plane of the base. This angle must be known to fabricate the design.

Angle with the Profile Plane. Figure 4–21A pictorially illustrates the angle between the profile plane and line 5–6. This angle can be determined by projecting from the profile view (part B). The profile plane appears true size in the profile view, and will therefore appear as an edge in the auxiliary view that is perpendicular to it, as in this example. The true size of the angle is found in the primary auxiliary view, where line 5–6 is true length and the profile plane appears as an edge.

4-8 SLOPE OF A LINE

Many engineering problems require that the slope of a line be determined or specified. Slope is the angle a line makes with the horizontal plane. It may be specified in angular degrees or as a percent grade. Figure 4–22A illustrates the slope of line 3–4 with the horizontal datum plane. The slope cannot be found in the top or front views, since the line is not true length in either. The slope of line 3–4 can be determined by finding the true length of the line in a view where the horizontal plane will appear as an edge. These requirements are fulfilled when a primary auxiliary view is projected from the top view, as shown in part B of the figure.

The grade of a line is the ratio of the rise to the run, with the rise being the vertical distance between each end of the line and the run being the horizontal distance between the ends in the top view. Both rise and run appear true length

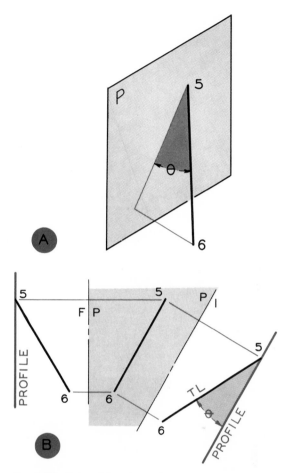

Fig. 4–21. Determining the angle made by a line with the profile plane.

in the auxiliary view that is projected from the top view. The grade of the line is 50 percent in this example. The grade of a line can be found only in a view where the horizontal plane appears as an edge and the line appears true length; consequently, the auxiliary view must be projected from the top view rather than from the frontal or profile views.

Sometimes slope is verbally referred to as being positive (+) or negative (−). Positive slope usually denotes that a line or a plane slopes upward from a reference point, and negative indicates that it slopes downward.

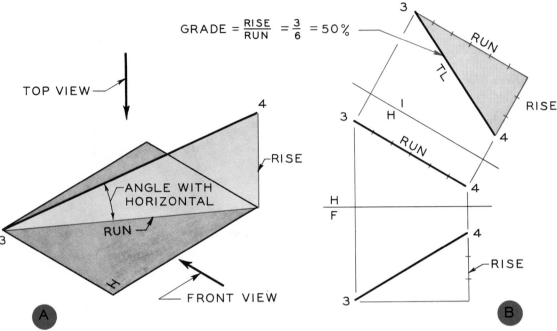

$$\text{GRADE} = \frac{\text{RISE}}{\text{RUN}} = \frac{3}{6} = 50\%$$

Fig. 4–22. The slope and percent grade of a line.

Fig. 4–23. The slope a pipe line is to follow at various intervals must be established during its design. (Courtesy of Trunkline Gas Transmission Company.)

All gravity-flow drainage systems must be analyzed to determine the slopes and percent grades within the system. In the pipeline in Fig. 4–23, for example, the slope was calculated from field data to determine the length and operational effectiveness of the pipeline.

4–9 EDGE VIEW OF A PLANE

The edge view of a plane can be found in any primary auxiliary view by applying previously covered principles. A plane will appear as an edge in any view where any line on the plane appears as a point.

This construction is illustrated in Fig. 4–24 by a sequence of steps. A true-length line can be constructed on any plane by drawing the line parallel to one of the principal planes and projecting it to the adjacent view, as shown in step 1, where a horizontal line is drawn. Since line 1–O is true length in the top view, its point view may be found as shown in Fig. 4–12. The remainder of the plane will appear as an edge

FIGURE 4–24. EDGE VIEW OF A PLANE

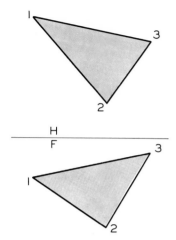

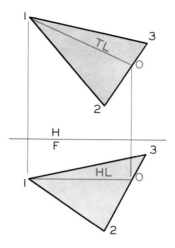

Given: The top and front views of plane 1–2–3.
Required: Find the edge view of plane 1–2–3.
References: Articles 4–4 and 4–9.

Step 1: Draw horizontal line 1–0 in the front view of plane 1–2–3, and project point 0 to line 2–3 in the top view. Line 1–0 is true length in the top view, since the horizontal plane appears true size in the top view and line 1–0 is parallel to the horizontal. *Note:* Any horizontal line other than line 1–0 could have been drawn in the front view.

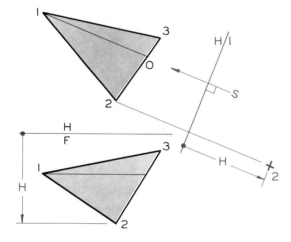

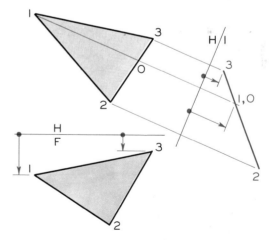

Step 2: A plane will project as an edge in the view where a line on the plane projects as a point. Line 1–0 will appear as a point if the line of sight is established parallel to the true-length view of 1–0. Draw the H–1 reference plane perpendicular to 1–0. Locate point 2 by projecting parallel to the line of sight and transferring the H-distance from the front to the auxiliary view.

Step 3: Determine points 1 and 3 in the same manner by projecting them parallel to the true-length line 1–0 (which is perpendicular to the H–1 reference plane). Find the location of each point from the H–1 plane by transferring the H-distance from the H–F plane in the front view to the auxiliary view, as in Step 2.

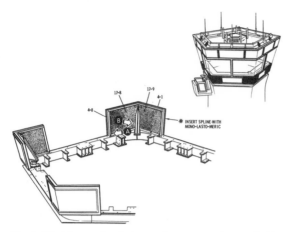

Fig. 4–25. The angles between the corner planes of this control tower had to be determined in order to design a connecting bracket. (Courtesy of the Federal Aviation Agency.)

Fig. 4–27. The angle between the planes of the basic structure of this Comsat satellite were determined prior to the design of a system for fabricating the joints. (Courtesy of TRW Systems.)

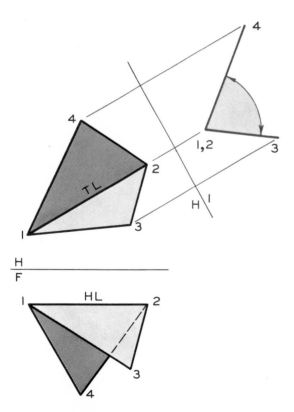

Fig. 4–26. The determination of the angle between two planes.

in this view. This is a basic projection that affords the designer a method for solving advanced problems such as those covered in following chapters.

4-10 ANGLE BETWEEN TWO PLANES

It is often necessary for the angle between two planes, which is called a dihedral angle, to be found in order for a design to be refined. Perhaps a connecting bracket must be designed to assemble planes in a desired position based on the angle between them, as in Fig. 4–25, where the angular planes of a control tower must be joined with an acceptable bracket. In another case, the planes might represent strata of ore under the ground.

The angle between two planes can be measured in the view where their line of intersection appears as a point.

The angle between planes 1–2–3 and 1–2–4 in Fig. 4–26 can be found in a primary auxiliary view, since the line of intersection, 1–2, is true length in the top view. Auxiliary plane H–1 is drawn so that it is perpendicular to the direction of the top view of 1–2. A view is projected to the auxiliary plane where the point view of line 1–2

FIGURE 4–28. PIERCING POINT OF A LINE ON A PLANE—PROJECTION METHOD

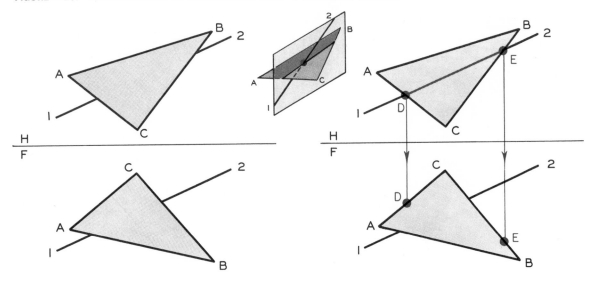

Given: The top and front views of plane *ABC* and line 1–2.
Required: Determine the piercing point of line 1–2 on the plane and the visibility of both views by the projection method.
References: Articles 3–12 and 4–11.

Step 1: Assume that a vertical cutting plane is passed through the top view of line 1–2. The plane intersects *AC* and *BC* at points *D* and *E*. Project points *D* and *E* to the front view.

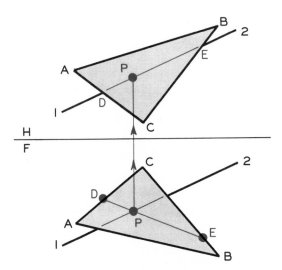

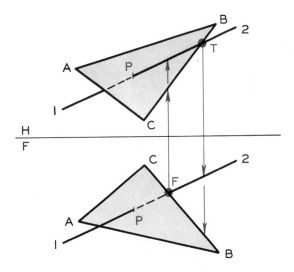

Step 2: Line *DE* represents the trace of the line of intersection between the imaginary vertical cutting plane and plane *ABC*. Any line that lies in the cutting plane and intersects plane *ABC* will intersect along line *DE*. Line 1–2 lies in the plane, therefore it intersects *ABC* at point *P* in the front view. Project point *P* to the top view.

Step 3: The visibility of line 1–2 in the front view is determined by analyzing point *F* where *P*–2 and *BC* cross. By projecting this point to the top view, we see that *BC* is in front of *P*–2; therefore *BC* is visible in the front view. The top-view visibility is determined by analyzing point *T* in the same manner; we find that *P*–2 is higher than *BC* in the front view and is therefore visible in the top view.

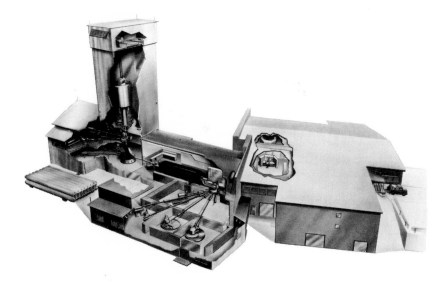

Fig. 4–29. The piercing points of the appendages of the tandem accelerator facility could have been determined by projection methods. (Courtesy Los Alamos Scientific Laboratory.)

is found. The edge views of both planes are found in this view since line 1–2 is a line common to both planes. The dihedral angle is measured in this view.

The satellite pictured in Fig. 4–27 illustrates intersecting planes for which the determination of the dihedral angles was required. These angles affect the inner structural members and the methods of connecting the planes.

4–11   PIERCING POINT WITH A LINE ON A PLANE BY PROJECTION

The location of a point where a line intersects a plane is necessary to the design of many engineering projects. The line may represent a structural member that must be attached to an oblique plane, or a cable that must have clearance through a plane of an enclosure.

Figure 4–28 gives the sequential steps necessary for the determination of the piercing point of a line passing through a plane by the application of projection principles similar to those covered in Chapter 3. The visibility of the line can be found by the application of the principles covered in Article 3–12. If a line intersects a plane it will be visible on one side of the piercing point and hidden on the other side.

The appendages of the tandem accelerator facility are shown piercing the protective walls in Fig. 4–29. These piercing points can be found graphically by the procedure given in Fig. 4–28.

4–12   PIERCING POINT OF A LINE WITH A PLANE BY AUXILIARY VIEW

An alternative method for finding the piercing point of a line intersecting a plane is the auxiliary view method illustrated in Fig. 4–30. The edge view of the plane is found by projecting from either view into the primary auxiliary view. The piercing point is found to be the point where the line and edge view of the plane intersect. Piercing point P is found in the principal views by projecting from the auxiliary view back to line AB in the top view and then to the front view. The front view of point P will also lie on line AB. However, in many cases it is helpful to check the location for greater accuracy by transferring the distance, H, from the auxiliary view to the front view. This is especially necessary when the front view of the piercing line approaches being a vertical line. Visibility is easily determined in the view from which the primary auxiliary was projected. The portion of the line on the upper side of the plane in the primary

FIGURE 4-30. PIERCING POINT OF A LINE THROUGH A PLANE—AUXILIARY METHOD

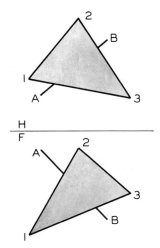

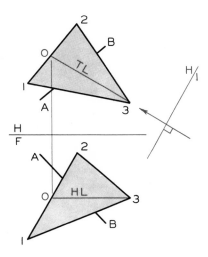

Given: The top and front views of plane 1-2-3 and line AB.
Required: Find the piercing point of line AB on plane 1-2-3 and the visibility in both views by the auxiliary-view method.
Reference: Article 4-12.

Step 1: Draw horizontal line, O-3 in the front view and project it to the top view. Line O-3 projects true length in the top view. Establish the line of sight for the primary auxiliary view parallel to O-3 in the top view. Reference plane H-1 is drawn perpendicular to the line of sight and O-3.

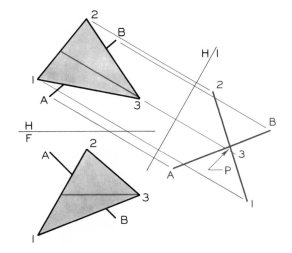

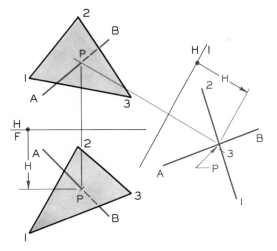

Step 2: Find the edge view of plane 1-2-3 by finding the point view of line O-3. Project line AB also. Point P in the auxiliary view is the piercing point of line AB on plane 1-2-3.

Step 3: Point P is projected to the top and front views in sequence. The front view of P can be checked by transferring distance H from the auxiliary view to the front view. Point A is closer to the H-1 plane in the auxiliary view, therefore, line AP is higher than the plane and visible in the top view. Visibility in the front view is found by the method used in Fig. 4-28.

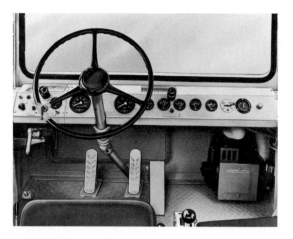

Fig. 4–31. The piercing point between the steering column and the firewall could be designed using descriptive geometry principles.   (Courtesy of LeTourneau-Westinghouse Company.)

Fig. 4–33. The solar panels of this satellite are designed to remain perpendicular to the sun's rays to take full advantage of its solar energy.   (Courtesy of Ryan Aeronautics, Incorporated.)

auxiliary is visible in the principal view—line *AP* in this case.

The piercing point between the steering column and the inclined firewall of the truck shown in Fig. 4–31 can be found by applying this principle of descriptive geometry.   The accurate location of this point is necessary to the function of the steering linkage.

4–13 A LINE PERPENDICULAR TO A PLANE

Economy of design dictates that materials be reduced to a minimum.   If a structural member were to be attached to an oblique plane, it would be more economical if the member were designed to be perpendicular to the plane, thus giving the shortest distance and requiring the minimum of materials.

Figure 4–32 is an example requiring that the shortest distance from a point to a plane be found.   The edge view of the plane is found by an auxiliary view.   The shortest distance (perpendicular distance) will be shown true length in this view when drawn from point *O* perpendicular to the edge view of the plane.   The piercing point is projected to the top view to intersect with a line drawn from point *O* parallel to the H–1 reference plane.   Line *O–P* must be parallel to the H–1 plane in the top view, since it is true length in the auxiliary view.   Line *O–P* is also perpendicular to the true-length lines in the top view, since perpendicular lines will project as perpendicular when one or both of two perpendiculars are true length, as covered in Article 3–20.   Line *O–P* is perpendicular to all lines in the plane; consequently, it is perpendicular to the true-length lines in the top view. The front view of the piercing point and its visibility is found in the manner outlined in Article 4–12.

A problem involving this principle is shown in Fig. 4–33.   The solar panels are attached to the satellite in such a manner that they can rotate to take full advantage of the available solar energy.   The orientation of the solar panels with respect to the perpendicular rays of the sun is an application of the principles covered in Fig. 4–32.

FIGURE 4-32. LINE PERPENDICULAR TO A PLANE

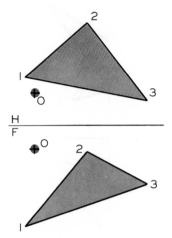

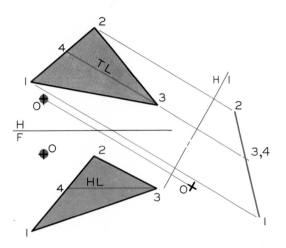

Given: Plane 1-2-3 and point O in two views.
Required: Find the shortest distance from point O to the plane 1-2-3 and show it in all views.
References: Articles 3-20 and 4-13.

Step 1: Draw horizontal line 3-4 in the front view of the plane 1-2-3. This line will be projected true length in the top view. Plane 1-2-3 will be projected as an edge in the auxiliary view where 3-4 appears as a point. Project point O to this view also.

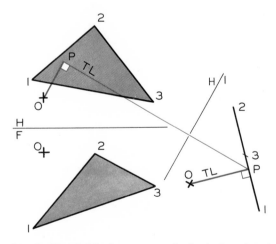

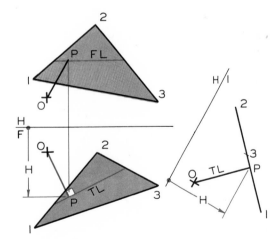

Step 2: Line O-P is drawn perpendicular to the edge view of plane 1-2-3, since the shortest distance is perpendicular to the plane. Because line O-P is true length in the auxiliary view, the top view of the line must be parallel to the F-1 reference plane. It is also perpendicular to the direction of a true-length line in the top view.

Step 3: The front view of line O-P is found by projecting point P to the front and locating it H distance from the H-F reference plane by transferring the H distance from the auxiliary view. Line O-P is visible in all views. Line O-P is also perpendicular to a true-length frontal line in the front view.

FIGURE 4–34.   INTERSECTION OF PLANES BY PROJECTION

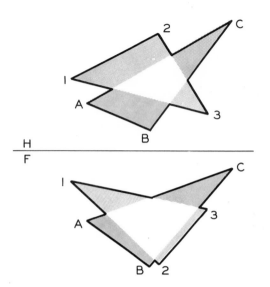

Given: The top and front views of planes 1–2–3 and *ABC*.
Required: Find the line of intersection between the planes and determine visibility in both views by projection.
References: Articles 4–11 and 4–14.

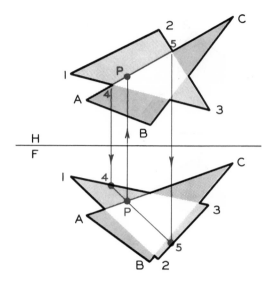

Step 1: Pass a vertical cutting plane through line *AC* in the top view to establish points 4 and 5. Project points 4 and 5 to lines 1–3 and 2–3 in the front view. Line *AC* pierces plane 1–2–3 where it crosses 4–5. Project point *P* to *AC* in the top view.

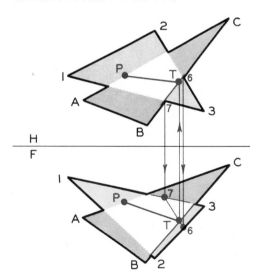

Step 2: Pass a vertical cutting plane through line *BC* in the top view to establish points 6 and 7. Project line 6–7 to the front view. Point *T* is the piercing point of line *BC* in plane 1–2–3. Line *PT* is the line of intersection between the planes. The piercing points of *AC* and *BC* are found as though they were independent lines rather than lines of a plane.

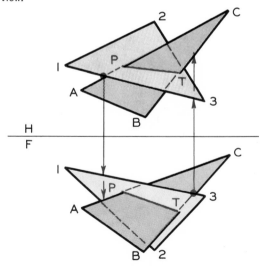

Step 3: Analyze the intersection of *AP* and 1–3 in the top view for visibility by projecting to the front view, where 1–3 is found to be higher and, consequently, visible in the top view. Line *PC* is also visible in the top view; therefore, *PCT* is visible. Frontal visibility is found by the analysis of the intersection of *CT* and 1–3, where 1–3 is in front and visible.

4-14 INTERSECTION BETWEEN PLANES BY PROJECTION

The line of intersection between two intersecting planes can be found by applying the principles covered in Article 4–11. The line of intersection is found by locating by projection on one plane the piercing points of two lines in the other plane. This procedure is shown by steps in Fig. 4–34. It can be determined by observation that lines 1–2, 2–3, and *AB* do not pierce either of the planes, since they fall outside of the planes in the given views. Therefore, lines *AB* and *BC* are selected to be lines which have a probability of intersecting plane 1–2–3. Line *AC* is analyzed as though it were a single line rather than a line on a plane. A vertical cutting plane is passed through the line in the top view, as in Fig. 4–28. The piercing point *P* is found and projected to both views, and line *BC* is analyzed in the same manner for piercing point *T*. *Note:* It is necessary to work with one plane, instead of finding the piercing point of one line of a plane and then skipping to a line on the other plane. The solution should be approached in a systematic fashion.

If the piercing points of two lines on a plane are found, then all lines in the plane that pierce the other plane must intersect along a line connecting the two piercing points. Points *P* and *T* are connected to form the line of intersection. The visibility is determined by analyzing the points where the lines of each cross. Visibility analysis is covered in Article 3–12.

4-15 INTERSECTION BETWEEN PLANES— AUXILIARY VIEW METHOD

An alternative method of finding the line of intersection between two intersecting planes is the auxiliary view method, illustrated in Fig. 4–35. An edge view of either of the planes is found in step 1 by a primary auxiliary view, with the other plane appearing foreshortened. Piercing points *L* and *M* are projected from the auxiliary view to their respective lines, 5–6 and 4–6, in the top view of step 2. The visibility of plane 4–5–6 in the top view is apparent in step 3 by

inspection of the auxiliary view, where sight line S_1 has an unobstructed view of the 4–5–*L*–*M* portion of the plane. Plane 4–5–*L*–*M* is visible in the front view, since sight line S_2 has an unobstructed view of the top view of this portion of the plane.

4-16 COMPASS BEARINGS OF A LINE

In civil engineering and geological applications, lines are often drawn from verbal information and field notes. Lines may also represent paths of motion in navigation, where verbal instructions are given by voice from a remote source. A commonly accepted method of locating a line verbally is by using the points of a compass.

Figure 4–36 gives the compass bearings of four lines. Note that the bearings begin with the north or south direction in all cases. The bearing of a line 30° to the west of north is given as North 30° West or N 30° W. A line making 60° with the south point of a compass is given as South 60° East or S 60° E. Since a compass can be read only when held horizontally, the bearings of a line can be determined in the horizontal (top) view only. A bearing is a horizontal direction.

Figure 4–37 is an example of an azimuth, which is measured from the north point of a compass in a clockwise direction. Azimuth readings are used to avoid the confusion that might be caused by reference to the four points of a compass. An azimuth of 120° is the direction making 120° with north. This is the same bearing as S 60° E shown in Fig. 4–36. The azimuth of 210° is equivalent to S 30° W. Figure 4–38 is an example of a constantly changing compass bearing in the case of an orbiting spacecraft.

Although bearings and azimuths are horizontal directions, these terms are often used to specify the construction of a drainage system or the design of a piping system whose pipes are inclined with the horizontal plane. In these cases, the bearings usually refer to the direction of the line with respect to the lower end. Figure 4–39 illustrates that lines 0–2, 0–1, and 0–3 each have a bearing of N 45° E, since the lines

FIGURE 4–35. INTERSECTION OF TWO PLANES BY AUXILIARY VIEW

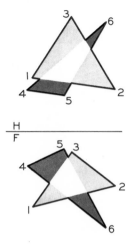

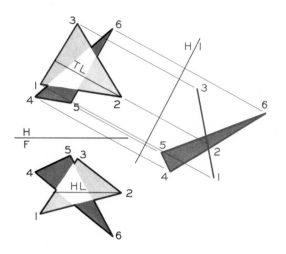

Given: The top and front views of planes 1–2–3 and 4–5–6.
Required: Find the line of intersection between the planes and determine the visibility in both views by the auxiliary view method.
References: Articles 3–12, 4–12, and 4–15.

Step 1: Draw a horizontal line in plane 1–2–3 and project it to the top view where the line is true length. Find the edge view of plane 1–2–3 by finding the point view of the true-length line. Project plane 4–5–6 to the auxiliary view also.

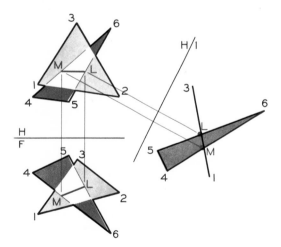

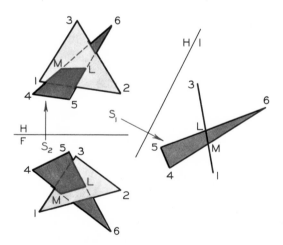

Step 2: Points L and M in the auxiliary view are the points of intersection of lines 5–6 and 4–6. These points are projected to the top and front views to give the line of intersection, *LM*.

Step 3: Visibility in the top view is found by viewing the auxiliary view in the direction of S_1, where plane 4–5–L–M is seen to be above plane 1–2–3 and is visible in the top view. Frontal visibility is found by viewing the top view in the direction of S_2, where 4–5 is in front of 1–3 and is therefore visible in the front view.

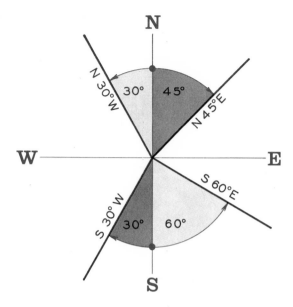

Fig. 4–36. Compass bearings of four lines.

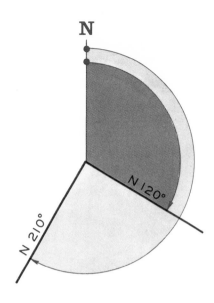

Fig. 4–37. Azimuth bearings of lines.

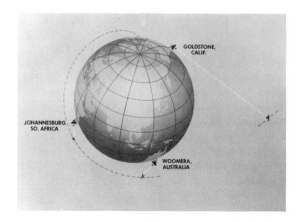

Fig. 4–38. During its launching orbit, a spacecraft has a constantly changing bearing. (Courtesy of the Jet Propulsion Laboratory of the California Institute of Technology and the National Aeronautics and Space Administration.)

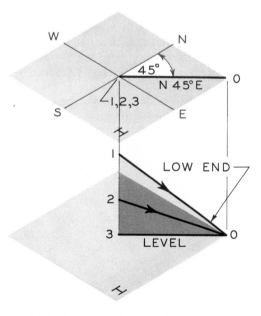

Fig. 4–39. The compass bearing of a line is in the direction of its low end.

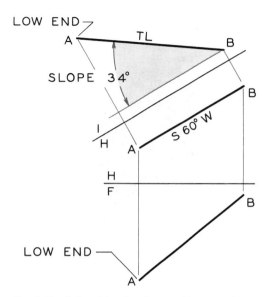

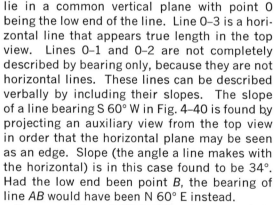

Fig. 4–40. Determining the slope and bearing of line by an auxiliary view.

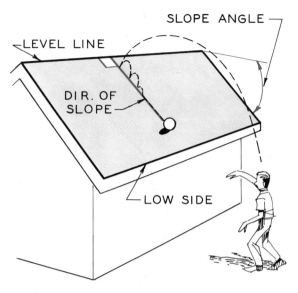

Fig. 4–41. The slope and direction of a slope of a plane.

lie in a common vertical plane with point 0 being the low end of the line. Line 0–3 is a horizontal line that appears true length in the top view. Lines 0–1 and 0–2 are not completely described by bearing only, because they are not horizontal lines. These lines can be described verbally by including their slopes. The slope of a line bearing S 60° W in Fig. 4–40 is found by projecting an auxiliary view from the top view in order that the horizontal plane may be seen as an edge. Slope (the angle a line makes with the horizontal) is in this case found to be 34°. Had the low end been point *B*, the bearing of line *AB* would have been N 60° E instead.

To accurately establish a line in space, it is sufficient to locate a single point in the top and front views and list the bearing and slope specifications of the line through the point. This method is often used in written specifications of construction contracts.

4–17 SLOPE OF A PLANE

Planes can be established in space by verbal specification of the *slope* and the *direction of slope* of the plane, as defined below.

Slope. The slope of a plane is the angle it makes with the horizontal plane.

Direction of slope. The direction of slope is the compass bearing of a line which is perpendicular to a true-length line in the top view of a plane taken toward its low side. This is the direction in which a ball would roll on the plane.

These terms are illustrated pictorially in Fig. 4–41. Note that the true angle of the slope is seen when it is viewed parallel to the ridge of the roof (the line of intersection). Since the ridge line is horizontal, a ball will roll perpendicular to it thereby establishing the direction of slope, which is given as a compass bearing.

Figure 4–42 gives the steps involved in determining the slope and direction of slope of the oblique plane 1–2–3 given in part A.

Part B. A horizontal line is drawn in the front view of plane 1–2–3 and projected to the top view where it is a true-length level line. The direction of slope is the compass bearing of a line perpendicular to the level line in the top view. The arrow head is placed on the low side toward line 1–3 to indicate the downward direction of slope.

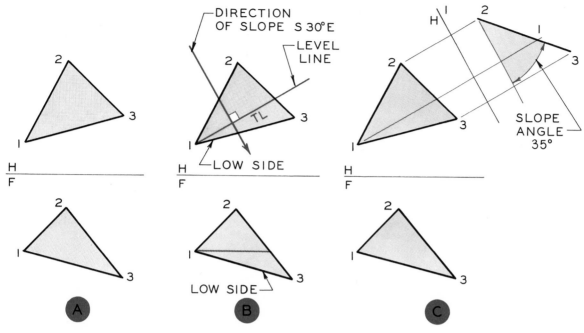

Fig. 4–42. The determination of slope and direction of slope of a plane.

Part C. The slope angle is found by measuring the angle between the edge view of the plane and the horizontal reference plane in the primary auxiliary view. Following verbal specifications, we can locate plane 1–2–3 in space as a plane passing through point 1 with a slope of 35° and a slope direction of S 30° E. This information is not sufficient to determine the limits of the plane, but merely establishes an infinite plane of which plane 1–2–3 is a part. The slope of the dam in Fig. 4–43 is an example of a plane that can be established verbally in written specifications by the engineer.

4–18 STRIKE AND DIP OF A PLANE

Strike and *dip* are terms used in geological engineering and mining to refer to strata of ore under the surface of the earth. It is important in these applications to locate the orientation of the strata by verbal terms that are somewhat similar to *slope* and *direction of slope*.

Fig. 4–43. The slopes of inclined surfaces of a dam are constructed from written specifications. (Courtesy of Kaiser Engineers.)

FIGURE 4–44. STRIKE AND DIP OF A PLANE

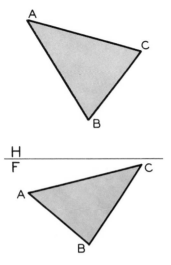

Given: The top and front views of plane *ABC*.
Required: The strike and dip of plane *ABC*.
Reference: Article 4–18.

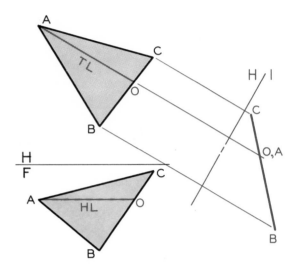

Step 1: Draw a horizontal line, *AO*, in the front view of plane *ABC*. This line will project true length in the top view. Project plane *ABC* as an edge in the auxiliary view where *AO* appears as a point. Project only from the top view in order to find the edge view of the horizontal plane.

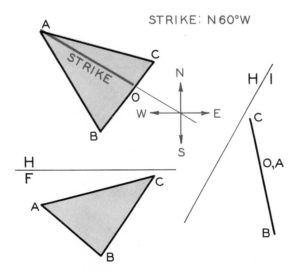

Step 2: The strike of a plane is the compass direction of a horizontal line in the plane. Line *AO* is the strike of *ABC* since it is a horizontal line. Its compass direction is measured in the top view as either N 60° W or S 60° E. The line has no slope, therefore either compass direction is correct.

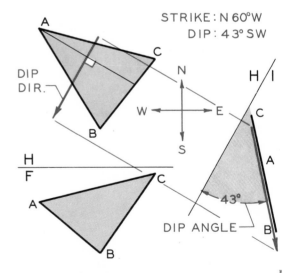

Step 3: The dip of a plane is its angle with the horizontal plane plus its general compass direction. This angle can be measured in the auxiliary view. The dip direction is perpendicular to the strike line in the top view. The dip of *ABC* is 43° SW. The strike and dip establishes the plane.

Fig. 4–45. Descriptive geometry principles have many applications to mining problems. (Courtesy of Joy Manufacturing Corporation.)

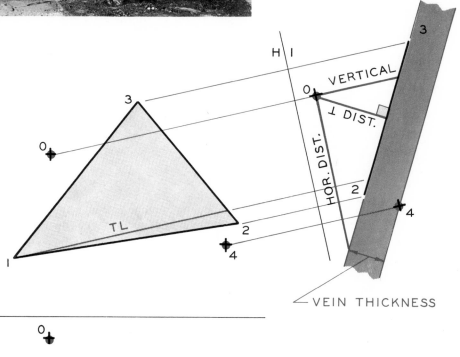

Fig. 4–46. Distances from a point to a vein of ore.

Strike. Strike is the compass direction of a level line in the top view of a plane. All level lines in a plane are parallel and have the same compass bearing.

Dip. Dip is the angle the edge view of a plane makes with the horizontal plane plus its general compass direction, such as NW or SW. The dip angle is found in the primary auxiliary view that is projected from the top view, and its general direction is measured in the top view. Dip direction is measured perpendicular to a level line in a plane in the top view toward the low inside.

Figure 4–44 illustrates the steps of finding the strike and dip of a given plane *ABC.*

4–19   DISTANCES FROM A POINT TO AN ORE VEIN

In the mining operation shown in Fig. 4–45 coal is being removed from its vein. Descriptive geometry principles can be used to find the

Fig. 4–47. The position of a stratum of oil-bearing sand with respect to the ocean floor would influence the location of offshore exploration. (Courtesy of Humble Oil and Refining Company.)

most economical distances from a point on the surface of the earth to a productive vein of ore.

Three points are located on the top plane of a stratum of ore which lies under the surface of the earth (Fig. 4–46). Point *O* is a point on the surface from which tunnels will be drilled to the vein of ore for mining purposes. Point 4 is a point on the lower plane of the stratum of the vein. We are required to determine the lengths of the following tunnels: (1) the shortest distance to the ore, (2) the vertical distance to the ore, and (3) the shortest horizontal distance to the ore. The edge view of the ore vein is found by projecting from the top view. The lower plane is drawn parallel to the upper plane through point 4. The vertical distance is perpendicular to horizontal plane H–1, and the horizontal tunnel is parallel to the H–1 plane. The shortest tunnel is perpendicular to the plane. The vein thickness can be approximated by measurement in the auxiliary view. The strike and dip of the plane can be found by referring to the principles covered in Article 4–18.

4–20 INTERSECTION BETWEEN TWO PLANES— CUTTING PLANE METHOD

The intersection between strata or planes is important to the exploration for minerals, which are usually contained in strata that approximate planes. For example, if a stratum of oil-bearing sand were located beneath the surface, it would be significant to approximate the general location of the intersection of the stratum with the ocean floor if it were continuous to a point of intersection. This information would influence the location of offshore explorations such as that shown in Fig. 4–47.

Planes 1–2–3 and 4–5–6 are segments of infinite planes in Fig. 4–48. We are required to find the line of intersection between them. Cutting planes are passed through either view at any angle and projected to the adjacent view. The two points where the lines formed by the cutting plane intersect in the top view establish the direction of the line of intersection. The compass direction of this line can be used to describe its orientation in space. The front view of the line of intersection is found by projecting the points from the top view to their respective planes in the front view.

4–21 INTERSECTION BETWEEN MINERAL VEINS— AUXILIARY METHOD

The locations of two mineral veins are given in a combination of verbal information and graphical representation in Fig. 4–49. We are required to locate the line of intersection, assuming that the two planes are continuous to a line of intersection.

The strike and dip of planes *A* and *B* are given in each view. Since the strike lines are true-length level lines in the top view, the edge view of the planes can be found in the view where the strike appears as a point. The plane can be drawn by the application of the dip angles given in specifications. Horizontal datum planes, H–F and H'–F', are used to find lines on each plane that will intersect when projected from the auxiliary views to the top views. Points *A* and *B* are connected to determine the line of

FIGURE 4–48.   INTERSECTION OF TWO INFINITE PLANES BY THE CUTTING-PLANE METHOD

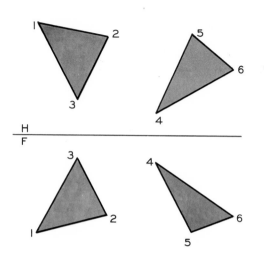

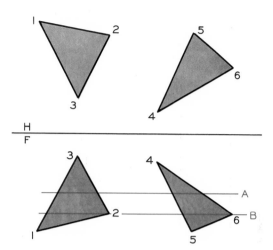

Given: The top and front views of two planes, 1–2–3 and 4–5–6.

Required: Find the line of intersection between these planes by projection given that they are infinite in size.

Reference: Article 4–20.

Step 1: Construct two cutting planes, A and B, in the front view. They are drawn parallel and horizontal in this case for convenience only. They could have been constructed in any direction and nonparallel.

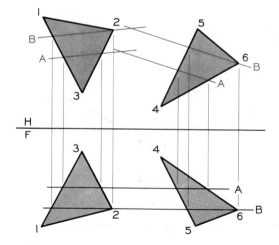

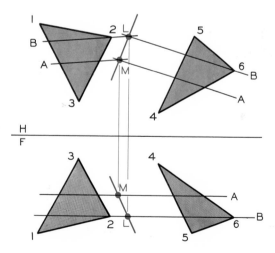

Step 2: The lines of intersection between the cutting planes and the given planes are projected to the top view. These lines are extended to cross their respective projections. Care should be taken to assure that the lines determined by the B cutting plane intersect and that those determined by the A cutting plane intersect.

Step 3: Points L and M in the top view are the points where lines in a common horizontal plane intersect to form a line of intersection. Point L is projected to the front view of plane B and point M to front view of plane A. The line of intersection is LM.

FIGURE 4–49. INTERSECTION BETWEEN ORE VEINS BY AUXILIARY VIEW

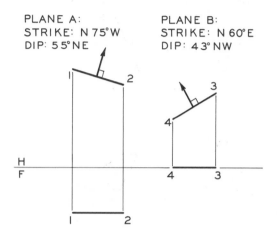

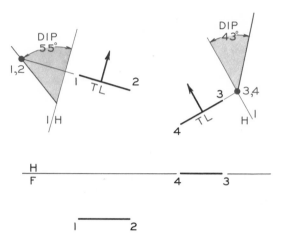

Given: The strike and dip of two ore veins, plane *A* and plane *B*.
Required: Find the line of intersection between the ore veins, assuming that each is continuous.
Reference: Article 4–21.

Step 1: Lines 1–2 and 3–4 are strike lines and are true length in the horizontal view. The point view of each strike line is found by an auxiliary view, using a common reference plane. The edge view of the ore veins can be found by constructing the dip angles with the H–1 plane through the point views. The low side is the side of the dip arrow.

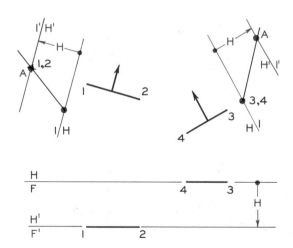

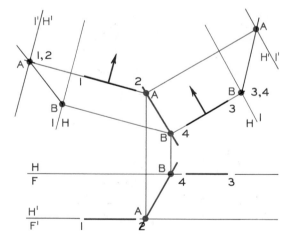

Step 2: A supplementary horizontal plane, H′–F′, is constructed at a convenient location in the front view. This plane is shown in both auxiliary views located *H* distance from the H–1 reference plane. The H′–1′ plane cuts through each ore vein edge in the auxiliary views.

Step 3: Points *A*, which were established on each auxiliary view by the H′–1′ plane, are projected to the top view, and they intersect at point *A*. Points *B* on *H*–1 plane are projected to their intersection in the top view at point *B*. Points *A* and *B* are projected to their respective planes in the front view. Line *AB* is the line of intersection between the two planes.

Fig. 4–50. Core samples are helpful in determining information about the orientation of a mineral vein under the ground. (Courtesy of Humble Oil and Refining Company.)

Fig. 4–51. A contour map and profiles.

4–50

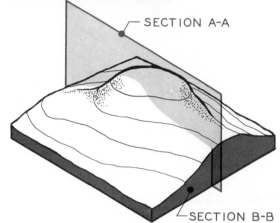

intersection between the two planes in the top view. These points are projected to the front view, where line *AB* is found.

Core samples taken from well sites are helpful in establishing information about the orientation of a mineral vein under the ground (Fig. 4–50). This information is used in the evaluation of the prospects for additional exploration in the immediate area.

4–22 CONTOUR MAPS AND PROFILES

Since the surface of the earth is rarely uniform or level, some system is required that will be acceptable for representing irregularities graphically in a drawing. A contour map is a widely accepted method employed by engineers to represent irregular shapes and surfaces of the earth. A pictorial view and a conventional map view of a contour map are shown in Fig. 4–51. The following definitions should be understood prior to further discussion:

Contour lines. Contour lines are lines that represent constant elevations from a common horizontal datum plane, such as sea level. Contour lines can be thought of as the intersection of horizontal planes with the surface of the earth. These horizontal planes are usually equally spaced in a vertical direction. The interval of spacing in Fig. 4–51 is 10′.

Contour maps. A contour map represents the irregularities on the surface of the earth with a network of contour lines, as shown in Fig. 4–51. Contour lines do not cross each other on a contour map. The closer the contour lines are to each other in the contour map, the steeper the terrain.

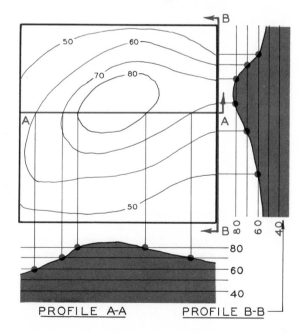

4–51

Fig. 4–52. Contours apply to irregular-shaped products as well as the earth's surface. (Courtesy of General Electric Corporation.)

Fig. 4–53. Geologists study the surface of the earth by viewing separate photographs which give a three-dimensional view of the terrain. (Courtesy of Humble Oil and Refining Company.)

Contoured surfaces. Contoured lines are also used to describe irregular shapes other than the surface of the earth. Examples are airfoils, irregular-shaped castings, automobile bodies, and household appliances. The steam iron shown in Fig. 4–52 was depicted by a contoured layout to represent its shape prior to manufacture. When applied to manufactured objects, this technique is called *lofting.* Contours are shown in three principal views to fully describe an irregular shape such as a ship's hull.

Profile. A profile is a vertical section through the surface of the earth which describes the contour of the earth's surface at any desired location. Two profiles are shown in Fig. 4–51. When applied to topography, a vertical section is called a profile regardless of the direction in which the view is projected. Contour lines appear as the edge views of equally spaced horizontal planes in the profiles. The true representation of a profile is drawn such that the vertical scale is equal to the scale of the contour map; however, this scale may be increased to emphasize changes in elevation that would not otherwise be apparent.

Geologists study irregularities on the surface of the earth through a three-dimensional viewer or stereoscope (Fig. 4–53). Each of the two photographs viewed through the stereoscope must be made with a separate camera lens which is calibrated to match the lens of the viewer. This three-dimensional analysis, which is called photogrammetry, can be used to study the contour of the surface and to determine contour lines.

An understanding of these definitions and their applications enables the designer to solve a variety of problems dealing with structures on the surface of the earth and the irregular shapes of some manufactured products.

4–23   CUT AND FILL OF A LEVEL ROADWAY

A level roadway routed through irregular terrain, such as the one pictured in Fig. 4–54, must cut through existing embankments in many locations. Also, volumes of fill must be provided to support the road at low points. It is more economical in most cases if the amount of fill is about equal to the cut volume in order that the earth removed by the cut can be transferred to

Fig. 4–54. This mountain road was constructed by cutting and filling volumes of the irregular hillside. (Courtesy of the Colorado Department of Highways.)

the low area and used as fill. This problem lends itself to graphical solution by application of primary auxiliary views.

The steps for solution of a cut-and-fill problem are given in Fig. 4–55. A contour map, the route of the level roadway to be constructed, and the angles of cut and fill are given. The contour lines located in the front view of step 1 are spaced 10′ apart, using the same scale that was used on the contour map. The profile of the contour lines shows the same lines as those given in the top view in the 20′ to 100′ elevation range. The roadway will project as an edge in the front view on the 60′ elevation line, the given level of the road.

The angle of cut is drawn on the upper side of the roadway, toward the higher elevations, by measuring the angle of cut with the horizontal plane on each side of the road. The fill angle is on the low side, or toward the contour lines of the smaller elevations. The top views of these planes are found in steps 2 and 3 by projecting points that lie on the cut-and-fill planes at each elevation line in the front view to their respective contour lines in the top view. These points are connected in sequence between each suc-

cessive pair of contour lines. The resulting line represents the line of intersection between the cut-and-fill planes and the surface of the earth.

The volume of earth involved in each area can be approximated by passing a series of vertical cutting planes through the top view to determine several profiles where the cut-and-fill planes will project as edges in the front view. The areas of cut and fill can be averaged in these views and multiplied by the linear distance in the top view to give the volume of cut and fill. This principle is illustrated in Article 4–24, where a sloping roadway is analyzed.

The cut-and-fill areas found in the map view should be crosshatched or shaded by some method to indicate the solution. The shading or cross-hatching used to represent the cut should be different from that used to indicate the fill area, and each symbol should be identified on the drawing. Crosshatching or shading used on an engineering drawing should be neatly presented to be as attractive as possible and to make the drawing more readable. Use sufficient notes and labels to fully explain the construction and the solution so that the drawing can be interpreted at a later date.

FIGURE 4–55. CUT AND FILL OF A LEVEL ROADWAY

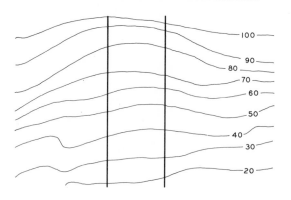

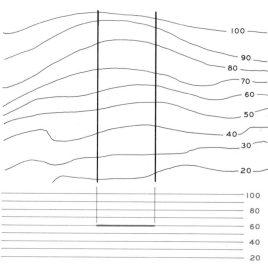

Given: A contour map with a level roadway given at an elevation of 60′.

Required: Find the top view given that the roadway is to have a 45° fill angle and a 30° cut angle.

Reference: Article 4–23.

Step 1: Draw a series of elevation planes in the front view at the same scale as the contour map. The elevations should have the same range as the contours—20′ to 100′. Locate the edge view of the level roadway on the 60′ elevation line in the front view.

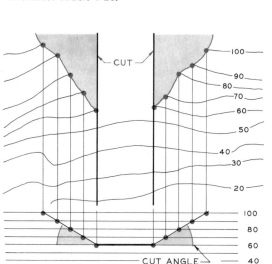

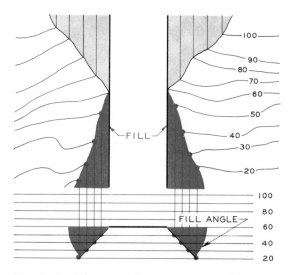

Step 2: Draw the cut angle of 30° with the horizontal on each side of the road in the upper portion of the front view. Project the points where the cut planes intersect the elevation lines to their respective contour lines in the top view. (*Example:* The points on the 100′ elevations in the front view are projected to the 100′ contour lines in the top view.) Connect these successive points to determine the cut area.

Step 3: The fill angles of 45° are drawn on each side of the roadway in the lower portion of the front view. The points on the plane of the fill are projected to the top view in the same manner that was used for the cut planes. The fill area is indicated by connecting the points. Note that the contour lines have been changed in the cut-and-fill areas to indicate the new contour of the land following construction.

4-24 CUT AND FILL OF A ROADWAY ON A GRADE

A highway cannot always be level; in many cases it will be constructed on a grade through irregular terrain. The problem given in Fig. 4–56 is an example of a road which required cut and fill during its construction on a grade. The following steps explain how the completed contour map view can be found and how an estimate can be made of the earth that must be cut and filled.

Step 1. A profile section, G–G, is taken through the center of the highway in order to show the true length and grade of the highway and its relationship to the terrain. The highway is constructed through a given point at the grade specified in this view. It can be seen in profile G–G that a portion of the highway is beneath the terrain, therefore requiring that a cut be made to route the road at the specified grade. Fill is necessary where the level of the highway is above the earth's surface.

Step 2. The top view of the cut and fill areas can be approximated by constructing a series of vertical sections through the map view (top view of the terrain). These cutting planes, A–A, B–B, C–C, D–D, and E–E, are drawn perpendicular to the center line of the highway. The sections cut by these planes appear as profiles in the front view.

Step 3. Each of the sections formed by the cutting planes is drawn as a profile in the front view by constructing horizontal elevation planes in these views to correspond to the contour lines in the map view. The contour planes appear as horizontal elevation planes in these sections, and the angles of cut and fill appear as edges at the location of the cutting plane.

Step 4. Each of the profiles corresponding to the cutting planes is found by projecting to the profile section the intersection of the cutting plane with each contour line in the top view. For example, Section B–B is drawn by projecting points on the 80′, 90′, and 100′ elevation contours to the profile to find the surface of the earth. The elevation of the highway at this

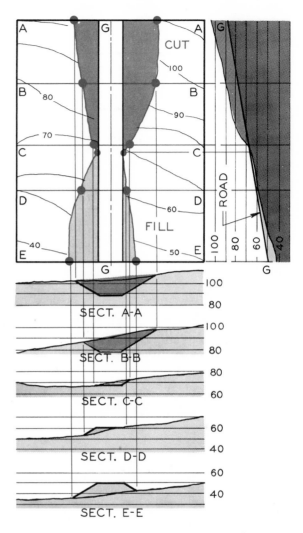

Fig. 4–56. Determining the cut and fill of a roadway on a grade.

section can be found in the profile by transferring the highway elevation found in profile G–G to profile B–B. The angles of cut and fill are constructed in each profile section by measuring their angle with the horizontal plane.

Step 5. The top view of the area of cut and fill is found by projecting the extreme points where the cut planes pierce the surface of the earth in each profile to the top view of the cutting

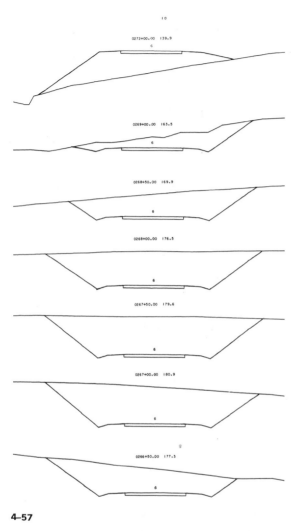

4–57

Fig. 4–57. The cut and fill areas of this roadway were plotted by a computer. (Courtesy of EAI.)

Fig. 4–58. Field data are transcribed into the language of a computer prior to plotting. (Courtesy of IBM.)

plane used to form the profile. When these points are connected, they establish the limits of the cut and fill, as labeled in the map view.

The spacing of the cutting planes in the top view must be determined by the designer's judgment, and is based on the characteristics of the terrain. The closer the sections are to each other, the more accurate the succeeding constructions and estimations of the volume of cut and fill will be. Note that the volume of fill can be determined by averaging the fill areas in profiles C–C, D–D, E–E, and multiplying this average cross section by the length of the road in the top view from section C–C to section E–E.

An example solution to this type of problem as plotted by a computer is shown in Fig. 4–57. A series of cross sections are plotted to indicate cut and fill from field data that were fed into a system similar to the one shown in Fig. 4–58. A basic knowledge of the graphical process must be understood to permit the drawings to be interpreted or programmed.

4–25 GRAPHICAL DESIGN OF A DAM

A dam is located on the contour map shown in Fig. 4–59. The angle on each side of the dam and its radius of curvature from center point C are given. The top of the dam is to be level to provide a roadway on the surface. The top view of the dam is to be drawn, and the level of the water is to be indicated in this view.

Step 1. The top view of the dam is constructed by drawing concentric arcs with point C as the center, using the given radii of curvature.

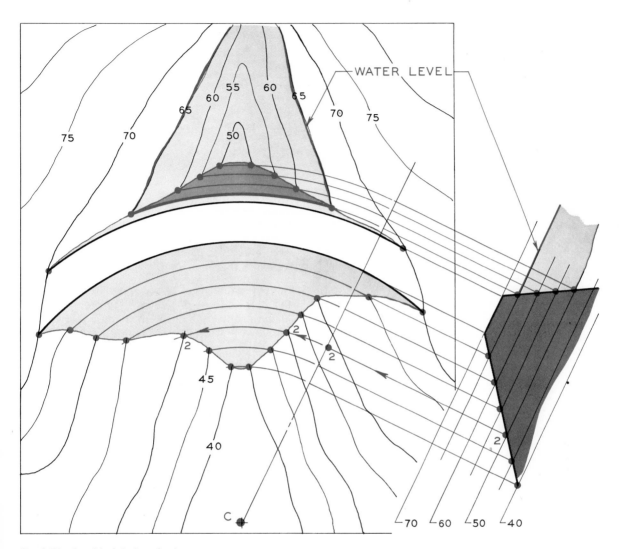

Fig. 4–59. Graphical design of a dam.

Step 2. A radial line is drawn at a convenient direction to serve as the top view of a vertical section that will be used to find a section through the dam, as shown. The crest of the dam is established at the specified level of 70', and the elevation planes shown in this view are equally spaced parallel planes drawn at the same scale as the contour map. The slope of the dam is established on each side to conform to given specifications.

Step 3. Points are located where each elevation plane intersects the slopes of the dam in the auxiliary profile view. These points are projected to the radial line drawn through point C in the top view. For example, Point 2 lies on the 50' elevation plane in the auxiliary profile. It is projected to the radial line in the top view where it is revolved using line C–2 as a radius until it intersects the 50' contour line in the top view at two points. These points represent the

4-60

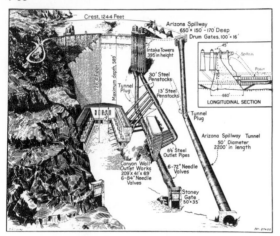

4-61

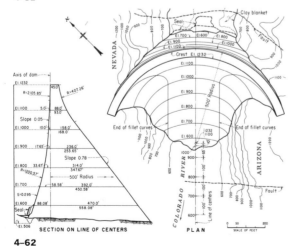

4-62

Fig. 4-60. An aerial view of Hoover Dam and Lake Mead, which were built during the period 1931 to 1935. (Courtesy of the Bureau of Reclamation, Department of Interior.)

Fig. 4-61. A schematic of the spillway system of Hoover Dam illustrates many spatial problems that could be solved graphically. (Courtesy of the Bureau of Reclamation, Department of Interior.)

Fig. 4-62. The top view and a sectional view of Hoover Dam. (Courtesy of the Bureau of Reclamation, Department of Interior.)

points on the surface of the earth where the downhill slope of the dam intersects the surface of the earth. The remaining points are projected in this manner.

Step 4. If the level of the water impounded by the dam is to be 5' beneath the crest, or at an elevation of 65', the area of the water can be found in the top view by using the 65' contour line as the limits of the water.

The volume of the water can be approximated as follows: Construct a series of vertical sections through the water in the top view and determine the average area for all the sections. Multiply this average cross section by the length of the water from the dam to its farthest-back point. This method is very similar to the method suggested in the preceding article for estimating volumes of cut and fill.

An application of these principles can easily be related to the Hoover Dam (Fig. 4-60), which was built for water control and power generation during the period from 1931 to 1935. Lake Mead, which is formed by this dam, originally had a capacity of 32,471,000 acre feet, the entire two-year flow of the Colorado River, making it the largest reservoir in the world. The dimensions of the dam are shown in Fig. 4-61 in a pictorial schematic of the generating system and spillways. The location and design of these systems involved many applications of graphics and descriptive geometry.

The top view of the dam and a view of a section taken through the center of the dam are shown in Fig. 4-62, which is closely related to the example given in Fig. 4–59. The top view of the dam is built in the shape of an arch to take advantage of the compressive strength of concrete. The section shows that the dam is progressively thicker as the depth of the water increases. This thickness is necessary to withstand the increased pressure at lower depths.

The Colorado River is shown in Fig. 4–63 as it begins backing up behind Hoover Dam in 1935, under control for the first time in the river's history. The water is shown approaching the upstream cofferdam which was used to divert the river around the damsite through four tunnels. The 726′ high structure required a total of 3,250,000 cu yd of concrete during its construction. Hoover Dam remains as one of engineering's wonders of the world, and Lake Mead is the world's largest man-made reservoir.

Fig. 4–63. The Colorado River begins backing up to form Lake Mead in 1935. (Courtesy of the Bureau of Reclamation, Department of Interior.)

4-26 OUTCROP OF AN ORE VEIN

Strata of ore or rock formations usually approximate planes of a somewhat uniform thickness. This assumption is employed in analyzing known data concerning the orientation of ore veins that are underground and are consequently difficult to study. A vein of ore may be inclined to the surface to the earth and may actually outcrop on its surface in some cases. Outcrops on the surface of the earth can permit open surface mining operations at the minimum of expense (Fig. 4–64). If the vein does not intersect the surface of the earth, its theoretical location of outcrop will serve as a site for further exploration.

Figure 4–65 is an example of a problem in which an inclined ore vein is analyzed graphically to determine its area of outcrop, assuming that the plane is continuous to the surface of the earth. The locations of sample drillings, A, B, and C, are shown in the contour map and their elevations are plotted on the surface of the upper plane of the ore vein in the front view. Point D is a point on the lower plane of the stratum. The edge view of plane ABC is found by auxiliary view, where the elevation planes are used as datum planes in step 1. The lower plane of the vein is drawn parallel to the upper

Fig. 4–64. Open mines are located on sites where ore veins outcrop to the surface of the earth. (Courtesy of LeTourneau-Westinghouse Company.)

FIGURE 4–65. ORE VEIN OUTCROP

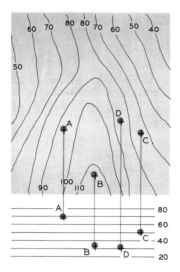

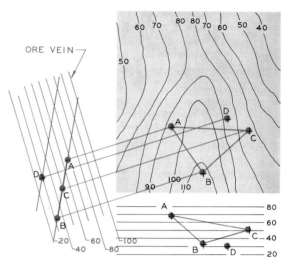

Given: Two views of points *ABC* on the upper plane of a stratum of ore and point *D* on the lower plane. The top view is a contour map and the front view is a series of elevation planes.

Required: Find the area where the vein outcrops on the surface, assuming that the vein is continuous.

Reference: Article 4–26.

Step 1: Connect points *ABC* to form a plane in each view. Find the edge view of plane *ABC* by projecting from the top view. Locate point *D* in the auxiliary view. Construct the lower surface of the vein parallel to the upper plane in the auxiliary view with the same position as in the front view.

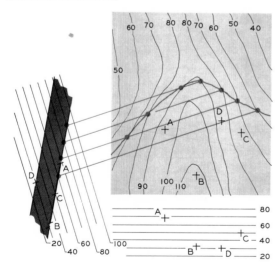

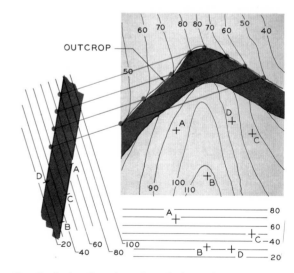

Step 2: Project the points where the upper plane of the vein crosses the elevation lines in the auxiliary view to their respective contours in the top view. For example, the point on the upper plane crossing the 90′ elevation line is projected to the 90′ contour line in the top view. Connect all points between contours in the top view.

Step 3: Project the points where the lower plane crosses the elevation lines to the top view in the same manner as the upper plane. Connect these points with a line. The area between the two lines in the top view is the area where the stratum would outcrop on the surface if the plane were continuous.

vein through point D to indicate the thickness of the vein. Points on the upper plane where the edge view intersects the elevation planes are projected to their respective contour lines in the contour map, as shown in step 2. These points are connected from contour line to contour line, resulting in the line of intersection between the upper plane of the vein and the surface of the earth. The lower plane is also projected to the top view in the same manner in step 3 to find its line of outcrop. The space between these lines is crosshatched to indicate the area where the plane would outcrop through the surface of the earth provided that the ore vein were continuous in this direction.

4-27 SUMMARY

The primary auxiliary view, which is projected from one of the principal views, has many applications similar to those covered in this chapter. Practically all engineering problems consist of a series of points, lines, and planes that represent most components of a design or project. Only a portion of the many applications of these principles have been covered in this chapter.

An understanding of the construction of auxiliary views of points, lines, and planes will enable the designer to solve many practical problems graphically when analytical solutions are impractical. Other applications of primary auxiliary views will become apparent when the principles are thoroughly understood.

Major emphasis has been placed on the theoretical concepts and principles throughout this chapter, as is the case in most chapters of this volume. However, the appearance of all drawings should be carefully considered for clarity; the drawings should clearly communicate ideas and specifications. A drawing presented with the minimum of notes and explanation may be very costly if insufficient information is given. The designer himself may be unable to interpret his own drawings after a few days unless he records each step of his solution as clearly as possible. The solution of a problem by the correct graphical procedures is insufficient unless the results, measurements, angles, and other findings are presented in an understandable form. The student can realize the importance of this if he attempts to interpret a problem unfamiliar to him that has been solved by a classmate.

PROBLEMS

The problems for this chapter can be constructed and solved on $8\frac{1}{2}'' \times 11''$ sheets, with instruments as illustrated by the accompanying figures. Each grid represents $\frac{1}{4}''$. Reference planes and points should be labeled in all cases using $\frac{1}{8}''$ letters with guidelines.

1. (A through D) In Fig. 4–66 find the true-size views of the inclined planes. Label all points and construction.

2. (A) In Fig. 4–67A find auxiliary views of point 2 as indicated by the lines of sight. Label all construction. (B) In part B of the figure find auxiliary views of the lines 1–2 as indicated by the lines of sight.

3. (A) In Fig. 4–68A find the true length of the line by projecting auxiliary views from the top and front views. Find the true length of the line by true-length diagrams projected from the top and front views. (B) In part B of the figure find auxiliary views of the lines as indicated by the lines of sight.

4. Use Fig. 4–69 for all parts of this problem. (A) Find the angle the line makes with the horizontal plane. (B) Find the angle the line makes with the frontal reference plane. (C) Find the angle between the line and the profile reference plane. (D) Find the slope of the line in the given top and front views.

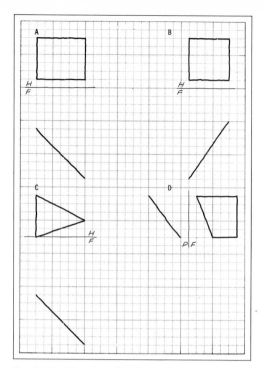

Fig. 4-66. Edge view of inclined planes.

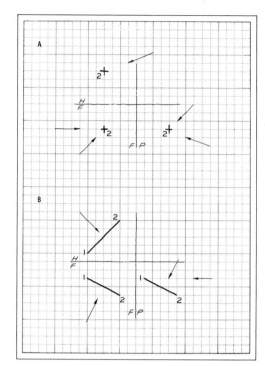

Fig. 4-67. Primary auxiliary views of a point and line.

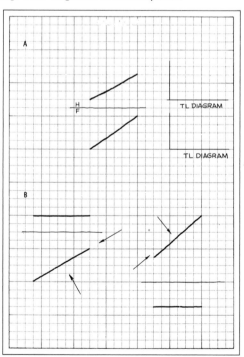

Fig. 4-68. True length of a line by auxiliary view and by true-length diagram.

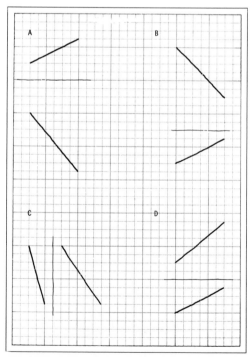

Fig. 4-69. Angle made by a line with principal planes.

5. (A and B) In Fig. 4–70 find the edge views of the two planes.

6. Use Fig. 4–71 for all parts of this problem. (A) Find the angle between the two intersecting planes. (B) Find the piercing point and determine the visibility of the plane and line by projection methods. (C) Find the piercing point and determine the visibility of the plane and line by the auxiliary view method.

7. (A) In Fig. 4–72A construct a line $\frac{1}{2}''$ long on the upper side of the plane through point O on the plane. (B) In part B of the figure construct a line from point C that will be perpendicular to the plane. Indicate the piercing point and visibility.

Fig. 4–70. Edge view of planes.

Fig. 4–71. Angle between planes and intersection of a line and plane.

Fig. 4–72. Line perpendicular to a plane.

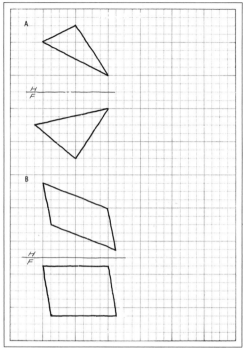

4–70

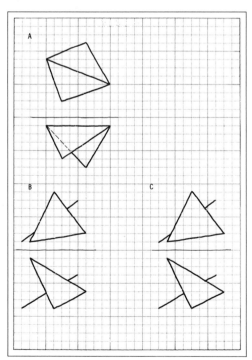

4–71

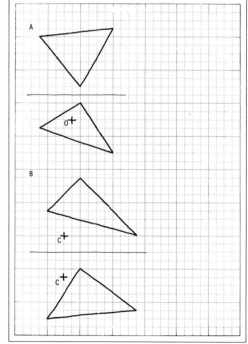

4–72

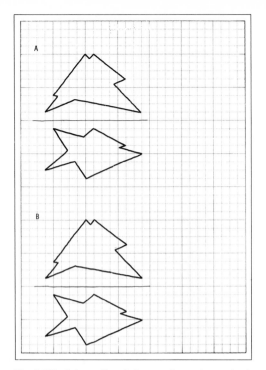

Fig. 4–73. Intersection between planes by projection and auxiliary views.

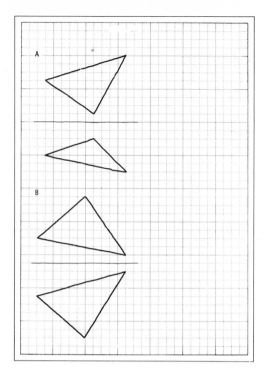

Fig. 4–74. Slope, strike, and dip of a plane.

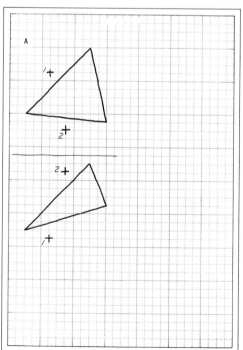

Fig. 4–75. Distance to an ore vein.

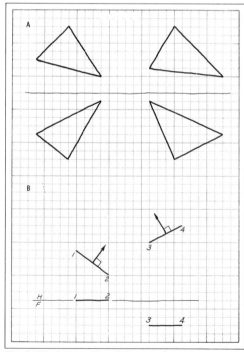

Fig. 4–76. Intersections between planes.

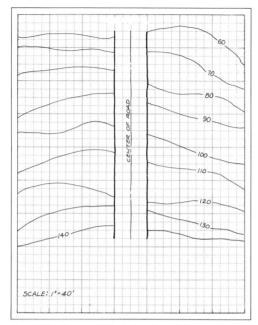

Fig. 4–77. Cut and fill of a level roadway.

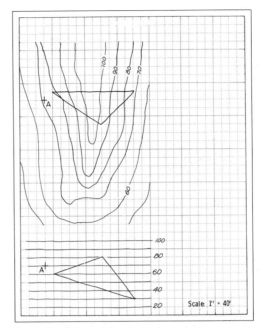

Fig. 4–78. Outcrop of an ore vein.

8. (A) In Fig. 4–73A determine the line of intersection and the visibility between the two planes by projection. (B) In part B of the figure find the line of intersection and the visibility of the two planes by the auxiliary-view method.

9. Use Fig. 4–74 for all parts of this problem. (A and B) Find the slope and direction of slope of each of the planes. Indicate all measurements. (C and D) Find the strike and dip of each of the planes in parts A and B on a separate sheet of paper.

10. The plane represents the location of points on the upper plane of a stratum of ore under the ground. Point 2 is a point on top of the surface; point 1 is a point on the bottom plane of the stratum of ore. Find the shortest distance, the shortest horizontal distance, and the shortest vertical distance from point 2. What is the thickness of the stratum? Use Fig. 4–75.

11. In Fig. 4–76A find the line of intersection between the two planes by cutting planes, assuming that the two are continuous planes.

In part B of the figure two strike lines of an ore vein are given—1–2 and 3–4. The plane with strike 1–2 dips 30° northeast, and the plane with strike 3–4 dips 45° northwest. Find the line of intersection between the two views in both views.

12. (A) In Fig. 4–77 the level road has an elevation of 100′. Find the cut and fill in the top view given that the cut angle is 30° with the horizontal and the fill angle is 35° with the horizontal. Label all construction. (B) Assume that the roadway is sloping at a 10-percent grade with its low end toward the bottom of the sheet. Determine the cut and fill areas for this situation, using the same angles as in the previous problem. Use a separate sheet. Estimate the amount of earth to be cut and filled.

13. In Fig. 4–78 the plane represents two views of the top plane of a stratum of ore under the ground. Point A is in the bottom plane of the stratum of ore. Find the area of outcrop where the stratum pierces through the surface of the earth in the top view. Scale: $1'' = 40'$.

IDENTIFICATION

PRELIMINARY IDEAS

REFINEMENT

ANALYSIS

DECISION

IMPLEMENTATION

5

SUCCESSIVE AUXILIARY VIEWS

5-1 INTRODUCTION

Many industrial problems cannot be solved by primary auxiliary views, but instead they require that secondary auxiliary projections be made before the desired information can be obtained. The designer is concerned with much the same type of design information as that covered in Chapter 4, namely, physical dimensions and shapes. For example, a basic requirement of a design involving intersecting planes of irregular shapes is the true shape and size of the planes (Fig. 5-1). A design cannot be detailed with the complete specifications necessary for construction unless all details of fabrication have been determined; these details include true shapes of planes, angles between planes, distances from points to lines, and angles between lines and planes. An example of a typical project that required the solution of many descriptive geometry problems is a structural frame for a 65-ton truck (Fig. 5-2). Prior to its fabrication, drawings and specifications were prepared to describe completely each component of this system through the application of graphic principles. It should be rather obvious from observation of the problems covered in this chapter that many of the solutions that are obtained graphically would be quite complicated if attempted from an analytical approach or through the application of mathematical principles. The best method for solving complicated spatial problems is a mixture of graphical and analytical procedures which combines the advantages of each. The graphical analysis required to solve a spatial problem aids in the application of analytical methods.

Fig. 5–1. The many facets of the U.S. pavilion dome at Expo 67 provide an example of the interrelationships between lines, points, and planes that require spatial analysis. (Courtesy of Rohm and Haas Company.)

Fig. 5–2. This frame for a 65-ton Haulpak truck illustrates the many design problems that require the application of descriptive geometry. (Courtesy of LeTourneau-Westinghouse Company.)

Primary auxiliary views are supplementary views projected from primary orthographic views—the horizontal, frontal, or profile views. A *secondary* auxiliary view is a view projected from a primary auxiliary view. The reference plane between the principal plane and the auxiliary view is labeled F–1, H–1 or P–1, but the reference plane between a primary auxiliary view and a secondary auxiliary view is labeled 1–2, regardless of the primary view from which it is projected (Fig. 5–3). A *successive auxiliary view* is a view projected from a *secondary* auxiliary view or from another successive auxiliary view. In other words, an infinite sequence of auxiliary views can be produced by continuing to project successively from auxiliary view to auxiliary view.

Auxiliary views have the same relationship between their adjacent views as the principal views have with each other. A secondary auxiliary plane is perpendicular to the primary auxiliary plane, and the plane of a successive auxiliary view projected from a secondary auxiliary view is perpendicular to the secondary auxiliary plane. It should be remembered that all sequential auxiliary planes are perpendicular to the preceding plane from which the projection was made.

5–2 SECONDARY AUXILIARY VIEW OF A SOLID

It is easier to understand spatial relationships of abstract lines and planes in space if a familiar three-dimensional solid is used to introduce the principles of projection. A simple rectangular prism is therefore used to introduce secondary auxiliary-view construction in Fig. 5–3.

A line of sight is arbitrarily chosen in the top and front views. Since we are required to view the prism in the direction of the line of sight, we must construct a view in which the line of sight will appear as a point. In step 1, a primary auxiliary view is drawn to find the true length of the line of sight; the object is also projected to this view. The secondary auxiliary plane, 1–2, is located perpendicular to the true-length line of sight in step 2. The two edge views of the prism are projected to the secondary auxiliary view as independent planes to simplify the formation of the solid and the determination of visibility.

It can be seen in step 3 that plane 1–2–3–4 is a visible plane in the secondary auxiliary view; that is, the line of sight from the secondary auxiliary view gives an unobstructed view of the plane in the primary auxiliary view. Since plane 1–2–3–4 is visible in the secondary auxiliary view, all lines crossing the plane must be behind

FIGURE 5-3.   SECONDARY AUXILIARY VIEW OF A SOLID

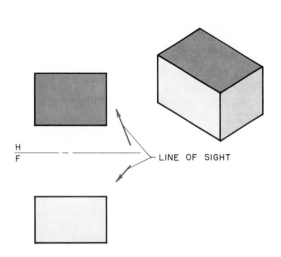

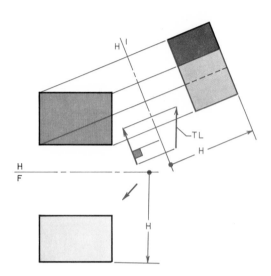

Given: The top and front views of a solid and a line of sight.
Required: Find the view of the solid indicated by the line of sight.
References: Articles 4-4 and 5-2.

Step 1: Project a primary auxiliary view from one of the given views so that it is perpendicular to the line of sight. The primary auxiliary will give the true length of the line of sight since it is viewed perpendicularly. Project the solid to this view in the same manner. Transfer dimension H from the front view to establish points in the primary auxiliary view.

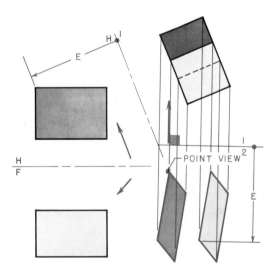

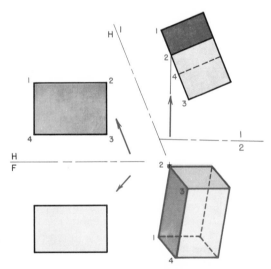

Step 2: Since the line of sight is true length in the primary auxiliary, a point view of the line can be found in a secondary projection plane, which is drawn perpendicular to the line. This will give the required view of the object. Project the upper and lower planes to the secondary auxiliary by transferring all dimensions from the H-1 plane in the manner of measurement E.

Step 3: Complete the object by connecting the respective corners with the missing lines. Plane 1-2-3-4 will appear visible in the secondary auxiliary view since the line of sight gives an unobstructed view of the plane in the primary auxiliary view. Any line crossing this plane must be behind it and therefore is hidden, as shown above. The outlines of a solid are always visible.

FIGURE 5-4. POINT VIEW OF A LINE

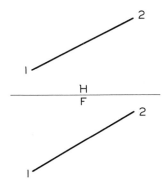

Given: The top and front views of oblique line 1-2.
Required: Find the point view of the line by a secondary auxiliary view.
References: Articles 4-4 and 5-3.

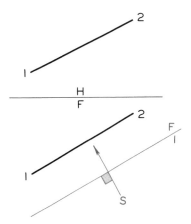

Step 1: Project an auxiliary view from one of the principal views. In this case, the reference plane is established parallel to the front view of line 1-2. The projectors will be parallel to the given line of sight, which is perpendicular to the F-1 plane. The primary auxiliary view could have also been projected from the horizontal view.

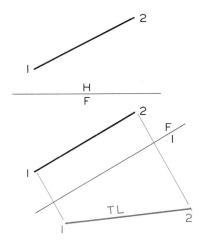

Step 2: Find the primary auxiliary view by projecting as specified in step 1. Line 1-2 is true length in this view, since the line is parallel to the reference plane in the preceding view. This construction is illustrated in Fig. 4-11.

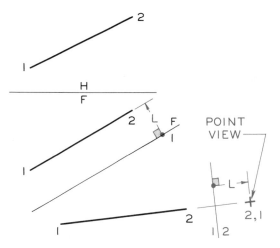

Step 3: Draw a secondary plane, 1-2, perpendicular to the true-length view of line 1-2. Transfer measurement L, which is taken from the F-1 plane to the front view of the line, to the secondary auxiliary view to find the point view. Measurement L will appear true length in these positions, since it is perpendicular to the primary auxiliary plane, which appears as an edge in the front and secondary auxiliary views.

it and consequently are hidden. All outlines of a solid are visible. The respective points of each of the two similar planes are connected in the secondary auxiliary view with solid and dashed lines to indicate visibility.

5-3 POINT VIEW OF A LINE

The principle involved in the determination of the point view of a line is a basic one that must be utilized to solve many problems in spatial geometry. The preceding problem has provided an introduction to this principle in relationship to a familiar solid object. Figure 5-4 reviews the steps involved in finding the point view of line 1-2 in its isolated form. The true length of the line must be found before its point view can be found in a secondary auxiliary view. The secondary auxiliary plane is constructed perpendicular to the true-length view of line 1-2 in step 3 and projectors are drawn parallel to line 1-2. The secondary auxiliary plane is perpendicular to the primary auxiliary plane, as is the frontal plane; consequently, a dimension perpendicular to the primary auxiliary plane will project true length in the front and secondary auxiliary views, as shown in step 3.

When two adjacent views are given, the point view of a line can be found by projecting a secondary auxiliary view from either view. For example, we could have found the true length of line 1-2 in Fig. 5-4 by projecting it from the top view, and then developing a secondary auxiliary view from this projected view. Similarly, the primary auxiliary could have been projected from the profile view.

5-4 ANGLE BETWEEN TWO PLANES

Nearly all designs involve the intersection of planes at many unusual angles that must be specified in detail by the designer before fabrication. These angles must be known so that a means for connecting the two planes may be devised, or perhaps so that a form may be designed for casting the design in concrete, metal, or even glass. The nuclear detection

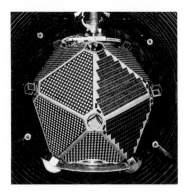

Fig. 5-5. A nuclear detection satellite is composed of planes and angles that can be determined with successive auxiliary views. (Courtesy of TRW Space Technology Laboratories.)

satellite shown in Fig. 5-5 is an example of an assembly for which angles need to be determined. The dihedral angles between the planes of the exterior surface are very critical. These angles must be formed within a high degree of tolerance to permit a highly accurate joint, which is a necessity for the successful function of the satellite in outer space.

Two planes, 1-2-3 and 1-2-4, are joined by an oblique line of intersection, 1-2, in Fig. 5-6. Since this line of intersection does not appear true length in either view, we must develop a secondary auxiliary view to solve the problem. The true angle between two planes can be measured in the view in which the line of intersection appears as a point and both planes project as edges. The true length of the line of intersection is found in step 1, and the line is found as a point in step 2 by applying the procedures outlined in Fig. 5-4. The true angle is measured in step 3, where the plane of the angle, which is perpendicular to the line of intersection, appears true size. This sequence of auxiliary views could have also been projected from the front view.

5-5 TRUE SIZE OF A PLANE

Most products and engineering designs contain many oblique surfaces and planes whose true size must be found in order that appropriate

FIGURE 5-6.   ANGLE BETWEEN TWO OBLIQUE PLANES

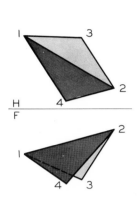

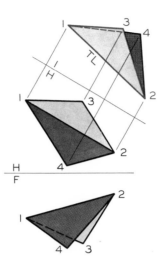

Given: The top and front views of two intersecting planes
Required: The angle between the two planes.
References: Articles 4-10 and 5-4.

Step 1: The angle between two planes can be seen in a view where the line of intersection appears as a point. Project a primary auxiliary view perpendicularly from a principal view of the line of intersection. In this case, a view is projected from the top view. Line 1-2 will appear true length in the primary auxiliary view.

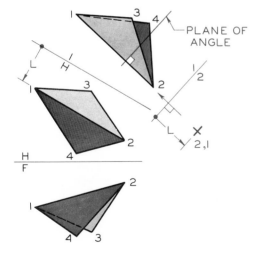

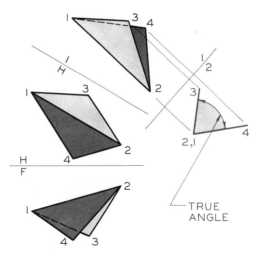

Step 2: The point view of the line of intersection 1-2 is found in the secondary auxiliary view. Locate this view by transferring measurement *L* from the edge view of the primary projection plane as indicated. The plane of the angle appears as an edge perpendicular to the true-length view of the line of intersection in the primary auxiliary.

Step 3: The edge views of the planes are completed in the secondary auxiliary view by locating points 3 and 4 in the same manner as in step 2. The angle between the planes can be measured in this view since the line of intersection appears as a point and the planes appear as edges.

FIGURE 5-7.   TRUE SIZE OF A PLANE

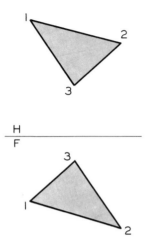

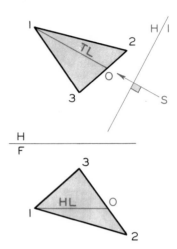

Given: The top and front views of a plane.
Required: Find the true size of the plane.
References: Articles 4-4 and 5-5.

Step 1: Draw horizontal line 1-0 in the front view of plane 1-2-3 and project it to the top view, where the line appears true length. Project a primary auxiliary view from the top view parallel to the direction of line 1-0. The H-1 reference plane is perpendicular to 1-0 and the line of sight.

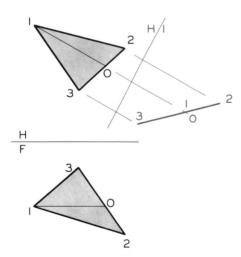

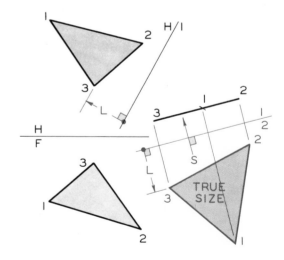

Step 2: The point view of line 1-0 is found in the primary auxiliary view. Project points 2 and 3 to this view where the plane will appear as an edge.

Step 3: A secondary auxiliary view plane 1-2 is drawn parallel to the edge view of plane 1-2-3. The line of sight is drawn perpendicular to the 1-2 plane. The true-size view of the plane is found by locating each point with measurements taken perpendicularly from the edge view of the primary auxiliary plane, as indicated.

working drawings may be prepared for the construction of the finished design. The nuclear detection satellite in Fig. 5–5 illustrates an assembly in which there is a need for finding the true size and shape of each of the oblique surface planes. These surfaces are precisely assembled to close tolerances. The determination of the true size of a plane is a fundamental procedure that is applied to many subsequent spatial problems.

The true size of plane 1–2–3 is found in sequential steps in Fig. 5–7. The edge view of the plane is found in step 1 by a primary auxiliary view. The secondary auxiliary projection plane, 1–2, is constructed parallel to the edge view of plane 1–2–3. The true size of the plane is found in the secondary auxiliary view by projecting perpendicular to the 1–2 plane and transferring the measurements from the H–1 plane in the top view to the secondary auxiliary view, as shown in step 3.

It should be noted at this point that the representation of a plane, as defined in descriptive geometry, can take a variety of forms, including two intersecting lines, two parallel lines, three points, or a line and a point. This allows many applications of the principle for finding the true size of a plane. For instance, Fig. 5–8 illustrates the fuel system for a gas turbine engine; the

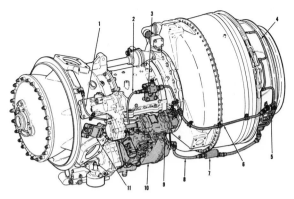

Fig. 5–8. The determination of the bends in a fuel line is an application of the principle of finding the angle between two lines. (Courtesy of Avco Lycoming.)

tubing for the system must be bent to fit the contours of the engine properly. The determination of the lengths of tubing and the angular bends is an application of the principle for finding the true size of a plane. A problem similar to this is shown in Fig. 5–9, where the top and front views of points on the center line of a fuel line are given. The true angle, 1–2–3, can be found in the view where plane 1–2–3 appears true size. The primary auxiliary view is found by projecting in a direction parallel to line 1–2 in

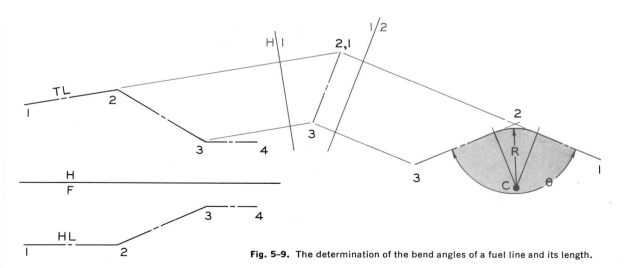

Fig. 5–9. The determination of the bend angles of a fuel line and its length.

Fig. 5–10. The base of the Unisphere ®, symbol of the New York World's Fair, is shown under construction. This is an application of the principle of finding the angle between two lines. (Courtesy of U.S. Steel Corporation.)

Fig. 5–11. A detailed pictorial of the XV-5A aircraft illustrates many applications of ellipse construction. (Courtesy of Ryan Aeronautical Company.)

Fig. 5–12. The elliptical paths of satellites are shown in the partially completed Unisphere ®. (Courtesy of U.S. Steel Corporation.)

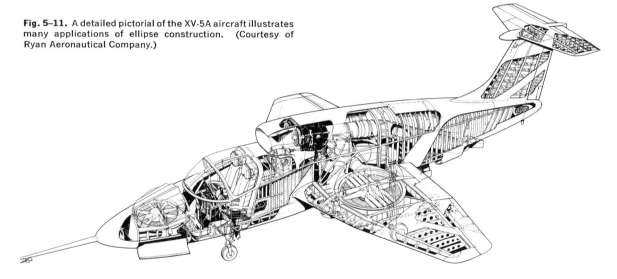

the top view, which is true length, to find the edge view of the plane. A secondary auxiliary view projected perpendicular to the edge view gives the plane true size, where both lines are true length and the angle between them is true size. A given bend radius can be used to construct the curvature arc at point 2 with point C as the center. The straight lengths can be scaled directly, while the arc distance can be found mathematically by application of the formula for finding the circumference of a circle. The solution to this problem would be quite complex if it had to be solved entirely by mathematical methods.

Another application of the angle between two lines is illustrated in Fig. 5–10, which shows a connecting joint designed to support the structural members of the 1965 New York World's Fair Unisphere ®. It was necessary to construct a view in which the angle between the chordal member and the support element appeared true size. It was also necessary to find the angles between the intersecting planes at this point of support so that the details could be prepared for fabrication and erection. A structural project of this type is designed to be erected on the site with a minimum of modification of the structural forms.

5-6 ELLIPTICAL VIEWS OF A CIRCLE

Circular and cylindrical shapes are commonly used in most designs. Many uses of these are illustrated in Fig. 5–11, the pictorial of the aircraft, where the circular features appear as ellipses rather than circles. The orbital paths of satellites will project as ellipses in most views, whether in actual space or as depicted symbolically in Fig. 5–12, which shows the Unisphere ® in the final stages of its construction. Circles appear true size and shape when the observer's line of sight is perpendicular to the plane of the circle. However, there are many instances when the line of sight is oblique to the plane of the circle; in the resulting foreshortened views the circles will appear as ellipses. The representation of circular features requires an understanding of the principles of ellipse construction.

The following definitions are given to explain terminology associated with ellipses. Refer to Fig. 5–13.

Ellipse. A view of a circle in which the line of sight is oblique to the plane of the circle.

Major Diameter. The greatest possible diameter that can be measured across an ellipse. By definition, a diameter passes through the center of the ellipse. The major diameter is always true length in any view of a circle.

Minor Diameter. The shortest possible diameter that can be measured across an ellipse. This diameter is perpendicular to the major diameter at its midpoint in all views.

Ellipse Angle. The angle between the line of sight and the edge view of the plane of the circle, usually found in a primary auxiliary view.

Cylindrical Axis. In a right circular cylinder, an imaginary line connecting the centers of all right sections and perpendicular to them.

Ellipse Template. A template composed of a series of various sizes of ellipses, used for drawing the ellipses when the major and minor diameters are known. Ellipse guides are graduated in 5° intervals (ellipse angles) in most cases. A set of ellipse guides is illustrated in Fig. 5–14.

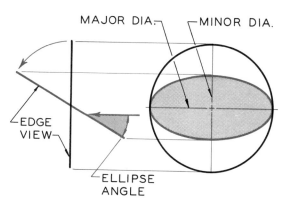

Fig. 5–13. The relationship of an ellipse to a circle.

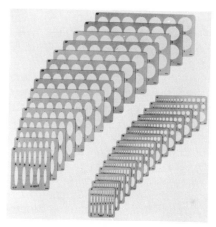

Fig. 5–14. Typical ellipse templates used for ellipse representation. (Courtesy of The A. Lietz Co.)

Fig. 5–15. It can be seen by inspection of tire molds that circles appear as ellipses when viewed obliquely. (Courtesy of ALCOA.)

An example of an elliptical view of a circular shape can be seen in Fig. 5–15, where the line of sight is oblique to the circular plane of the tire mold. Note that the major diameter is true length in any view and the minor diameter is perpendicular to it, as indicated, whether the object is viewed in actuality or depicted in a drawing.

Suppose that we are required to construct a circle passing through points 1, 2, and 3 as shown in all views in Fig. 5–16. The true size of plane 1–2–3 must be found in order to construct the circle in true shape. The circle is found in step 1 by locating the center, where the three perpendicular bisectors of each line of the plane intersect, and by selecting a radius that will pass through each point. In step 2, the major and minor diameters are drawn in the secondary auxiliary view parallel and perpendicular to the 1–2 reference plane. Both will be true length in this view since the plane is true size. Next, the diameters of the circle are projected to the edge view in the primary auxiliary view, where the major diameter coincides with the edge view and the minor diameter is equal to zero. Then the diameters are projected to the top view, where major diameter *CD* is parallel to a true-length line on the plane, since the major diameter is always true length. The major-diameter length is found by transferring the measurements from the secondary auxiliary view, as shown in step 2. The minor diameter is drawn perpendicular to the major diameter through point *O*. Its length is found by projecting points *A* and *B* from the edge view. These diameters will be used to position the ellipse template that will be used to draw the ellipse in the top view. The ellipse template angle is found in the primary auxiliary view by measuring the angle between the line of sight and the edge view of the plane. The ellipse size is selected from the ellipse template such that it will be as nearly equal to the major diameter as possible. The ellipse can be drawn by aligning the cross markings on the template with the major and minor diameters.

The construction of the ellipse in the front view is found in much the same manner as in step 2; however, the true-size view is unnecessary since the center of the circle has been found in step 1. Point *O* is projected to the front view of plane 1–2–3. The edge view of the plane is found by projecting from the front view, where the ellipse guide angle can be found as shown in step 3. Note that the edge view of the plane is extended on each side of point *O* in order for the diameter to appear true length in this view. The major diameter is drawn true length in the front view through point *O* parallel to a true-length line in the plane. The minor diameter is perpendicular to the major diameter and its length is found by projecting its extreme points from the edge view of the circle. The ellipse template can be used to construct the completed elliptical view as well as to find the top view.

There are several methods of constructing ellipses graphically without the use of an ellipse template; however, these methods are tedious and require considerable time. The ellipse template affords the designer the most practical method of constructing ellipses. Today's technology demands that time be used as economically as possible, thereby emphasizing methods that will expedite all phases of the engineering process.

Right circular cylinders are closely related to ellipses in that they are composed of a series of circles that may project as ellipses in conventional views. The construction of cylinders that appear foreshortened requires that the procedures outlined in Fig. 5–16 be followed, with the addition of one step. This additional step is the construction of the axis of the cylinder. The right sectional ends of a cylinder will be perpendicular to the axis of a cylinder, as shown in Fig. 5–17B. It is rather obvious even to the untrained eye that the ends of the cylinder in part A of the figure are not perpendicular to the cylindrical axis. When a line is perpendicular to a plane, it is perpendicular to all of the lines in that plane intersecting at the piercing point. Such a line will project as perpendicular to any true-length line in a perpendicular plane; consequently, the axis of a right cylinder will always be perpendicular to the major diameter

FIGURE 5-16.   ELLIPTICAL VIEWS OF A CIRCLE

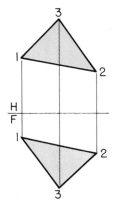

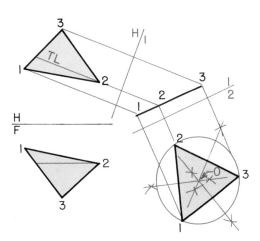

Given: The top and front views of plane 1-2-3.
Required: Construct a circle that will pass through each vertex of the plane. Show the circle in all views.
References: Articles 5-5 and 5-6.

Step 1: Determine the true size of plane 1-2-3 in the manner illustrated in Article 5-5. Draw a circle through the vertexes in the true-size view. The center of the circle, *O*, is found at the intersection of the perpendicular bisectors of each of the triangle's sides.

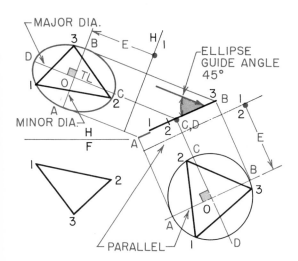

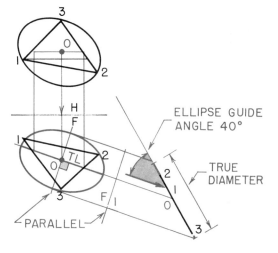

Step 2: Draw the diameters, *AB* and *CD*, parallel and perpendicular to the 1-2 plane, respectively, in the secondary auxiliary view. Project these lines to the primary auxiliary and top views, where they will represent the major and minor diameters of an ellipse. Select the ellipse template for drawing the top view by measuring the angle between the line of sight and the edge view of the plane.

Step 3: Determine the particular ellipse template for drawing the ellipse in the front view by locating the edge view of the plane in an auxiliary view which is projected from the front view. The ellipse angle is measured in the auxiliary view as shown. Note that the major diameter is true length and that it is parallel to a true-length line on the plane in the front view. The minor diameter is perpendicular to it.

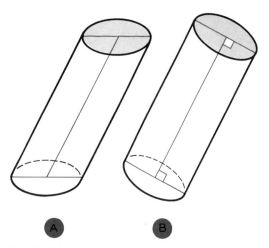

Fig. 5–17. Relationship of a cylinder's axis to its right section.

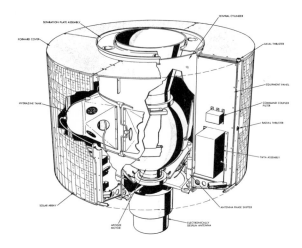

Fig. 5–18. The satellite is an example of the representation of a cylindrical shape in an oblique view. (Courtesy of TRW Space Technology Laboratories.)

of the elliptical right section in a foreshortened view. This is illustrated in Fig. 5–17B. An example of the application of this principle is shown in Fig. 5–18, a pictorial of a cylindrical satellite. Note that there are elliptical holes projected onto oblique planes in the internal portion of the device; the drawing of these required the application of the previously covered principles.

5–7 SHORTEST DISTANCE FROM A POINT TO A LINE

The shortest distance from a given point to a line must be known in order to make the most economical use of material, whether it is pipe, structural members, or power conductors. The steps required to find this shortest distance are given in Fig. 5–19.

The true length of the line is found in step 1 and its point view is found in step 2. The perpendicular distance from the point to the line can be seen true length in the view in which the line appears as a point. This line is projected to the primary auxiliary view, where it will be perpendicular to the line that is true length. Since line 3–0 is true length in the secondary

auxiliary view, it must be parallel to the 1–2 reference plane in the preceding view, as shown in step 3. Line 3–0 is projected back to the other views in sequence.

The shortest distance from a point to a line can also be found by an alternative method covered in Article 5–5. The true size of plane 1–2–3 can be found where the perpendicular distance can be drawn perpendicular to line 1–2 and measured true length in the same view.

It can be seen in Fig. 5–20 that in industry the determining of the shortest distances from points to lines is a frequent necessity to conserve expensive materials and labor.

5–8 SHORTEST DISTANCE BETWEEN SKEWED LINES—LINE METHOD

The determination of the shortest clearance between two lines is applicable to a number of industrial situations encountered by the engineer and technician. The high-voltage power lines shown in Fig. 5–21 must have a minimum clearance, which is specified by regulations. The design of the support towers will be affected by this specified clearance, as will the safety factors related to the clearance.

FIGURE 5–19. SHORTEST DISTANCE FROM A POINT TO A LINE

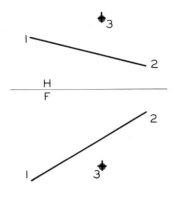

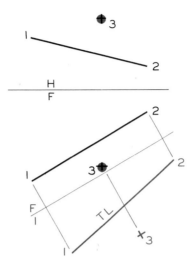

Given: The top and front views of line 1–2 and point 3.
Required: Find the shortest distance from point 3 to line 1–2 and show it in all views.
References: Articles 5–3 and 5–7.

Step 1: Find the true length of line 1–2 by projecting a primary auxiliary view from the front view. Draw the reference plane, F–1, parallel to the front view of line 1–2 and make all projections perpendicular to the F–1 plane. Project point 3 to this view also.

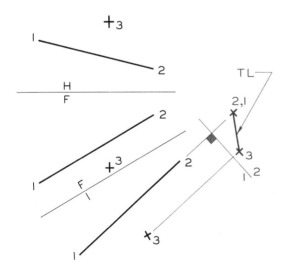

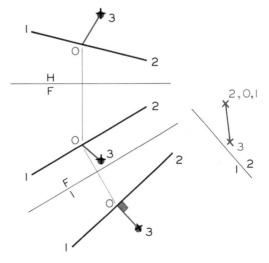

Step 2: Draw a secondary reference plane, 1–2, perpendicular to line 1–2, in order to find the point view of line 1–2. The perpendicular distance from point 3 to line 1–2 can be seen true length in this view.

Step 3: Since line 3–0 is true length in the secondary auxiliary view, it must be parallel to the 1–2 plane in the primary auxiliary view and perpendicular to line 1–2. When one or both perpendicular lines are true length, they will project as perpendicular. Determine the front and top views of line 3–0 by projecting from the primary auxiliary view in sequence.

Fig. 5–20. This top structure of a blast furnace involves applications of finding a shortest distance from a point to a line. (Courtesy of Jones & Laughlin Steel Corporation.)

Fig. 5–21. The shortest distance between two crossing high-voltage power lines can be found by descriptive geometry theory. (Courtesy of the Tennessee Valley Authority.)

Two methods—the line method and the plane method—are used to find the shortest distance between two lines. The line method is presented in Fig. 5–22 in sequential steps. Since the shortest distance between two lines will be a line perpendicular to both, the line will appear true length in the secondary auxiliary view, where line 3-4 projects as a point. To establish point *P*, line *OP* is projected to the primary auxiliary view, where it is drawn perpendicular to line 3–4, which is true length in this view. Points *O* and *P* are projected to the front and top views to represent the shortest distance between the two lines.

5–9 SHORTEST DISTANCE BETWEEN SKEWED LINES—PLANE METHOD

The problem covered in Article 5–8 can be solved by the application of the plane method, as illustrated in Fig. 5–23. We shall use the projection principles discussed in Chapter 3 to construct in the top and front views a plane that is parallel to line 1–2. A line is constructed

through a point (point 4 in this case) parallel to line 1–2 in both views. Two intersecting lines, 4–0 and 3–4, form a plane. A number of planes could be constructed in this manner, but all would lie on a common infinite plane. When an edge view of the plane is found in a primary auxiliary view, the two lines will be projected as parallel, as shown in step 1. The plane has served its purpose when the auxiliary view is found and can be ignored in the remaining steps of the solution.

The shortest distance between the two lines will be projected as perpendicular to each of the lines in the primary auxiliary view, where the lines are parallel (step 2). Although a number of lines can be drawn apparently perpendicular to the lines, only one will be truly perpendicular —the one that appears true length in the primary auxiliary view. This line will appear as a point in the secondary auxiliary view, which is projected perpendicularly from the primary auxiliary view, as shown in step 3. Both lines, 1–2 and 3–4, appear true length in this view; consequently, the shortest distance between them is

FIGURE 5-22. SHORTEST DISTANCE BETWEEN SKEWED LINES—LINE METHOD

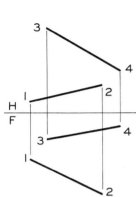

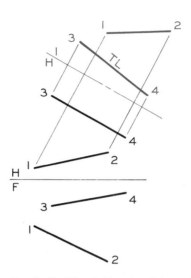

Given: The front and top views of lines 1–2 and 3–4.
Required: Find the shortest distance between the two lines by the line method and show it in all views.
References: Articles 5–3 and 5–8.

Step 1: Find line 3–4 true length in a primary auxiliary view projected from the horizontal view. Project line 1–2 to this view also. The primary auxiliary view could have been projected from the front view equally well.

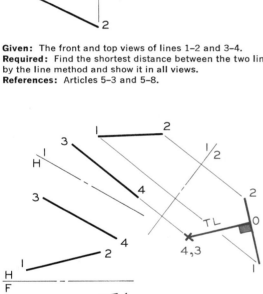

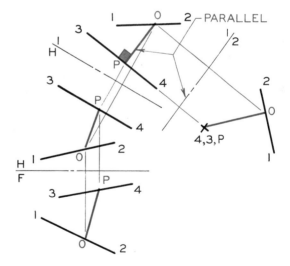

Step 2: Draw a secondary auxiliary view to find line 3–4 as a point. The shortest distance between the two lines is a line perpendicular to both. This line will appear true length in the secondary auxiliary view, where it is drawn perpendicular to line 1–2.

Step 3: Locate O in the primary auxiliary view by projection. Locate point P on line 3–4 by constructing line O–P through point O perpendicular to line 3–4. These points are projected back to the top and front views to represent the line. Note that line O–P is parallel to the 1–2 reference plane in the primary auxiliary view since it is true length in the secondary view.

FIGURE 5–23. SHORTEST DISTANCE BETWEEN SKEWED LINES—PLANE METHOD

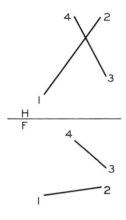

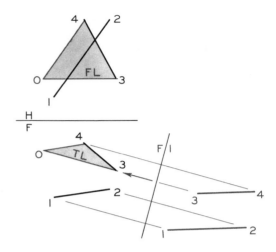

Given: The top and front views of line 1–2 and 3–4.
Required: Find the shortest distance between the two lines by the plane method. Show this distance in all views.
References: Articles 3–19 and 5–9.

Step 1: Construct a plane through line 3–4 that is parallel to line 1–2. Line 4–0 is drawn parallel to line 1–2 in both views. Since plane 3–4–0 contains a line parallel to line 1–2, the plane is parallel to the line. Both lines project parallel in an auxiliary view where plane 3–4–0 projects as an edge.

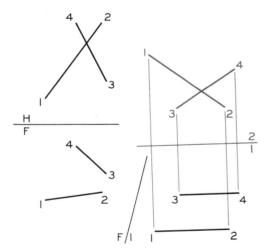

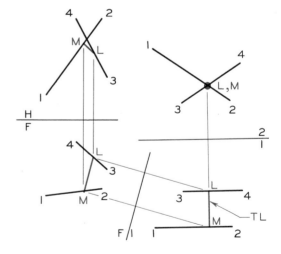

Step 2: The shortest distance will appear true length in the primary auxiliary view, where it will be perpendicular to both lines. Draw a secondary auxiliary view by projecting perpendicularly from the lines in the primary auxiliary view. Lines 1–2 and 3–4 cross in this view.

Step 3: The crossing point of lines 1–2 and 3–4 establishes the point view of the perpendicular distance, *LM*, between the lines. This distance is projected to the primary auxiliary view, where it is true length. The line is found in the front and top views by projecting points *L* and *M* to their respective lines in these views.

at the point of crossing, where line *LM* projects as a point. The true-length view of line *LM* is found in the primary auxiliary view. The line is projected to the two principal views to complete the requirements of the problem.

This method of solving for the shortest distance between two lines is the general case that can be used in the solution of problems covered in Articles 5-10 and 5-11. Complicated traffic systems, such as that shown in Fig. 5-24, must be analyzed to determine the clearances between the center lines of the crossing highways. Also, the vertical clearances are critical to the design of the overpasses. Vertical distances between skewed lines appear true length in the front view directly beneath the point where the two lines cross in the top view.

5-10   SHORTEST LEVEL DISTANCE BETWEEN TWO SKEWED LINES

The shortest level, or horizontal, distance between two lines is found by using the plane method in the initial steps, as illustrated in Article 5-9. A plane is constructed through one of the lines to be parallel to the other given line in step 1, Fig. 5-25. An edge view of the plane is projected from the *top view* in order that the horizontal reference plane may appear as an edge in the primary auxiliary view, where the level distance can be drawn parallel to the horizontal plane. This problem *cannot* be solved by projecting from the front view, because in that case the frontal plane, rather than the horizontal plane, will appear as an edge. The direction of the shortest level line will appear true length in step 2 and parallel to the H–1 reference plane. Only the *shortest* level line will appear true length in this view. A secondary auxiliary view is required to locate its position. The point view of line *LM* is found in the secondary auxiliary view and is projected to the primary auxiliary view, where it appears true length. As a check on the accuracy of the construction, line *LM* should appear level in the front view.

An application of this problem is the connection of two roadways with a level tunnel (Fig.

Fig. 5-24. The interchange of Harbor and Santa Monica Freeways in downtown Los Angeles illustrates a variety of skewed line applications. (Courtesy of the California Division of Highways.)

Fig. 5-26. Construction of a three-mile tunnel to be used for a rapid transit system in the Berkeley Hills area of San Francisco. (Courtesy of Kaiser Engineers.)

5-26). This principle is also used to connect mining shafts with tunnels which must remain level, but which also must be as short as possible for reasons of economy.

FIGURE 5–25. SHORTEST LEVEL DISTANCE BETWEEN SKEWED LINES

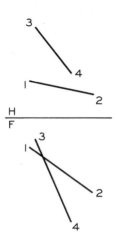

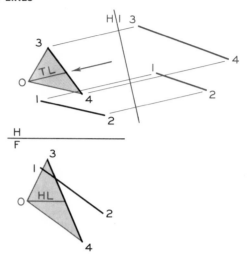

Given: The top and front views of lines 1–2 and 3–4.
Required: Find the shortest level distance between the lines and project it to all views.
References: Articles 3–19, 5–9 and 5–10.

Step 1: Construct plane 3–4–0 parallel to line 1–2 by drawing line 4–0 parallel to line 1–2 in the top and front views. Plane 3–4–0 is found as an edge in the primary auxiliary view where the lines are projected as parallel. *Note:* The primary auxiliary *must* be projected from the *top view* to find the horizontal plane as an edge.

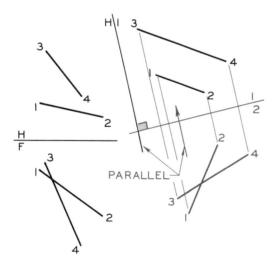

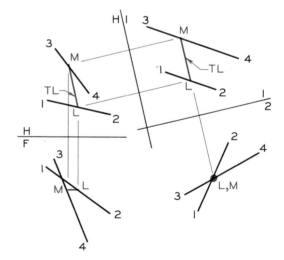

Step 2: An infinite number of horizontal (level) lines can be drawn parallel to H–1, between the lines in the primary auxiliary view, but only the shortest level line will project true length in the primary auxiliary view. Draw the secondary auxiliary plane, 1–2, perpendicular to the H–1 plane, where lines 1–2 and 3–4 are projected.

Step 3: The point where lines 1–2 and 3–4 cross in the secondary auxiliary view establishes the point view of line *LM* that will appear true length in the primary auxiliary view. Project line *LM* to the top view and front views. Line *LM* is parallel to the H-plane in the front view, which verifies that it is a level line.

FIGURE 5-27. GRADE DISTANCE BETWEEN SKEWED LINES

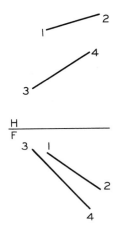

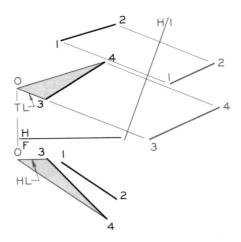

Given: The top and front views of lines 1–2 and 3–4.
Required: Find the shortest line having a 50 percent grade between the two lines.
References: Articles 3–19 and 5–11.

Step 1: Draw 3–4–O parallel to line 1–2 by drawing line 4–O parallel to line 1–2 in both views. The edge view of the plane is found where both lines project as parallel. *Note:* The primary auxiliary *must* be projected from the *top* view in order that the horizontal plane may appear as an edge in the primary auxiliary view.

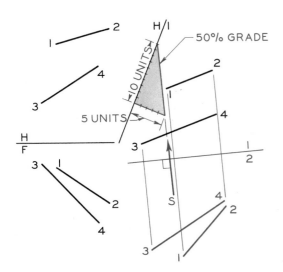

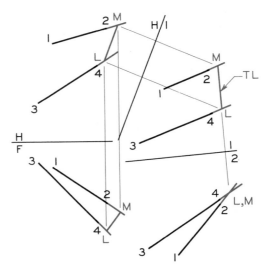

Step 2: Construct a 50-percent grade line with respect to the edge view of the H–1 plane in the primary auxiliary view. Draw this line in the direction nearest to that which a line perpendicular to the two lines would assume. Project a secondary auxiliary parallel to the direction of the grade line. The shortest grade distance will appear true length in the primary auxiliary view.

Step 3: Extend the lines in the secondary view to establish their point of intersection, where the point view of *LM* is located. *LM* will appear true length at a 50% grade in the primary auxiliary. Line *LM* is projected back to the top and front views. Lines 1–2 and 3–4 must be extended in each view.

5–11 SHORTEST GRADE DISTANCE BETWEEN SKEWED LINES

The plane method introduced in Article 5–9 must be employed in solving for the shortest grade line between two skewed lines. It can be seen from this series of problems that the plane method is a general approach to solving all skewed-line problems, whereas the line method is applicable only to the perpendicular distance between two skewed lines.

The lines are projected as parallel in the primary auxiliary view by finding the edge view of a plane constructed parallel to one of the lines through the other, as shown in step 1 of Fig. 5–27. This primary auxiliary view must be projected from the *top view* in order for the horizontal plane to appear as an edge, from which the percent grade of a line can be drawn. Recall that grade is the ratio of the vertical rise to the horizontal run of a line, expressed as a percentage. These components can be used to establish the specified grade in the primary auxiliary view, as shown in step 2. The grade could be drawn in two directions with respect to the H–1 reference plane. However, the shortest grade between two lines will be the line drawn in

the direction that is most nearly perpendicular to the lines. This direction can be determined by visual inspection in the primary auxiliary view. The secondary auxiliary plane, 1–2, is drawn perpendicular to the grade line that has been constructed, and the view is projected parallel to the direction of the grade line. The lines in this example do not cross in the secondary auxiliary view. Since lines 1–2 and 3–4 are only segments of longer, continuous lines, they can be extended to their point of intersection, as shown in step 3. This locates the point view of the shortest line that can be drawn at a 50-percent grade. This line, *LM*, can be projected back to the horizontal and frontal views, as illustrated.

Figure 5–28 illustrates a multitude of pipes that had to be designed to conform to grade specifications in order for the system to function under design conditions. Figure 5–29 shows a complex traffic interchange where highways connect with intermediate arteries on a grade. Drainage problems and sewer systems must also be critically analyzed with respect to grade distances between drainage channels and culverts.

Fig. 5–28. Clearances between interrelated pipes must be evaluated to reduce cost of materials and installation. (Courtesy of Standard Oil Corporation of New Jersey.)

Fig. 5–29. Highways often present skewed line problems requiring graphical solutions. (Courtesy of the California Division of Highways.)

FIGURE 5–30. A LINE THROUGH A POINT WITH A GIVEN ANGLE TO A LINE

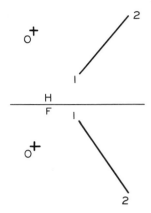

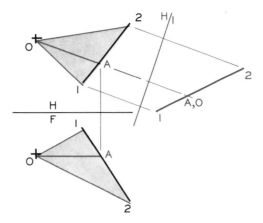

Given: The top and front views of line 1–2 and point O.
Required: Construct a line from point O that will make an angle of 45° with line 1–2.
References: Articles 5–5 and 5–12.

Step 1: Connect point O to each end of the line to form plane 1–2–O in both views. Draw a horizontal line in the front view of the plane and project it to the top view, where it is true length. Determine the edge view of the plane by finding the point view of line OA.

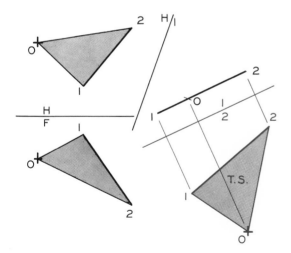

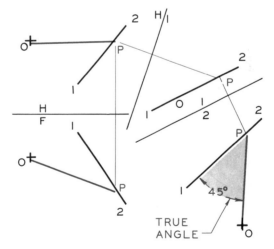

Step 2: Determine the true size of plane 1–2–O by perpendicularly projecting an auxiliary view from the edge view of the plane in the primary auxiliary view. The plane need not be drawn in the secondary auxiliary view since it will not be used further.

Step 3: Line OP can be constructed at the specified angle of 45° with line 1–2 in the secondary auxiliary view, since point O and line 1–2 lie in the same plane. Project point P back to the primary auxiliary, top, and front views, and connect it with point O. This problem could have also been solved by projecting from the front view.

5-12 A LINE THROUGH A POINT AT A GIVEN ANGLE TO A LINE

Seldom is it necessary to design all of the components of a single system. In fact, to reduce expense and delay it is customary to utilize as many standard, commercially available parts as possible. Standard connectors are available for joining pipes, structural beams, and other engineering forms encountered in industrial projects. Of course, the standard connectors have been designed for only the most commonly used angles, since it would be economically impossible to provide connectors that varied from 0° to 90° at 1° intervals. Consequently, it is important to know how to design connections corresponding to a given common angle.

The example problem in Fig. 5-30 illustrates the procedure for constructing a line from a given point to another line such that a standard 45° angle will be formed between the lines. This procedure could be utilized practically to design a connection that would allow a standard connector to be used. Point *O* is connected with points 1 and 2 to form plane 1-2-0, which is found as an edge in step 1 and as true size in step 2. Since this plane is true size, any line connecting point *O* with line 1-2 will be true length in the secondary auxiliary view. Consequently, line *O-P* is drawn from point *O* to intersect line 1-2 at 45°, the standard angle, in

step 3. Line *O-P* is projected back to the given views in sequence.

Designing for standard connectors is common practice in the complex chemical and petroleum industry, as illustrated in Fig. 5-31. The details of construction of a refinery or processing plant are so complicated that often three-dimensional models are used to assist in the solution of the design problems (Fig. 5-32).

5-13 ANGLE BETWEEN A LINE AND A PLANE—PLANE METHOD

Although standard connectors and hardware components should be considered for connecting structural members to a plane, there will be cases where a particular nonstandard angle is unavoidable, so the designer must be able to determine the angle between a line and a plane to design the special connector. This principle has many applications; for instance, in space vehicles the angle of the observer's line of sight to the plane of the instrument panel must fall within the operational limitations previously determined. In addition to a line of sight, a line may also represent a center line of a pipe, a structural member, a power line, or many other components.

These problems are solved by establishing a segment of the plane in question and the line in two views, as given in Fig. 5-33. The plane is

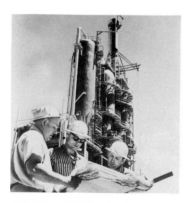

Fig. 5-31. The design of a processing plant such as this involves problems which lend themselves to solution by successive auxiliary views. (Courtesy of Standard Oil Corporation of New Jersey.)

Fig. 5-32. In complicated systems, clearances and optimum distances are often checked by analysis of three-dimensional models. (Courtesy of Esso Research of New Jersey.)

FIGURE 5-33. ANGLE BETWEEN A LINE AND A PLANE—PLANE METHOD

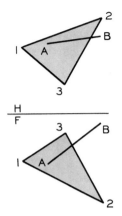

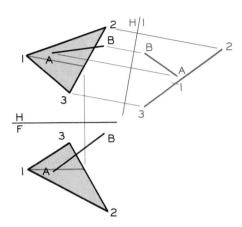

Given: The top and front views of plane 1–2–3 and line *AB*.
Required: Find the angle between the line and plane and determine its visibility in all views.
References: Articles 5–5 and 5–13.

Step 1: Determine the edge view of plane 1–2–3 by projecting from either the front or top view. Find the edge view by projecting from the top view in this example; project line *AB* also. The angle cannot be measured in this view since the line is not true length.

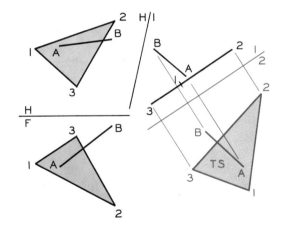

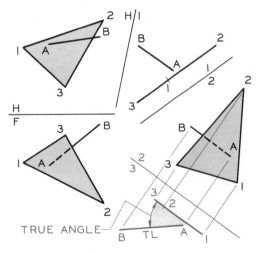

Step 2: Determine the true size of plane 1–2–3 in a secondary auxiliary view projected perpendicularly from the edge view of the plane. Line *AB* is not true length in this view. Draw line *AB* lightly since visibility must be determined.

Step 3: A view projected in any direction from a true-size view of a plane will result in an edge view of the plane. Since line *AB* must be true length at the same time, project a third auxiliary view perpendicularly from line *AB*. The line appears true length and the plane appears as an edge, thus satisfying the conditions for measuring the angle between them. Visibility is shown in all views.

found as an edge in the primary auxiliary view in step 1, and true size in step 2. Since the plane is true shape in this view, any auxiliary view projected from it will result in an edge view of the plane. The third auxiliary view plane, 2–3, is drawn parallel to line *AB* in step 3 in order to find the true length of line *AB* and an edge view of the plane. The true angle between a line and a plane can be measured in the view where the plane appears as an edge and the line appears true length. This condition exists in step 3; therefore, the true angle can be measured in the third auxiliary view.

An application of this principle can be seen in Fig. 5–34 in the Hydra 5 sea-test vehicle. A series of tripods have been constructed at intervals along the body of the vehicle. Finding the angle which one leg of each tripod forms with the other two is the same as finding the angle between a line and a plane, since two intersecting lines form a plane. This information was necessary to design the tripods. Similarly, the angles between the guy rods and the plane of the cylindrical collar at the left end were required for design of the bracing connectors.

Fig. 5-34. The Hydra 5 sea-test vehicle required application of the principle for finding the angle between a line and plane by successive auxiliary views. (Courtesy of Pacific Missile Range, Naval Missile Center.)

5-14 ANGLE BETWEEN A LINE AND A PLANE— LINE METHOD

An alternative method for finding the angle between a line and a plane is the line method illustrated in Fig. 5–35. The true length of line *AB* is found in step 1 and the point view of the line is found in step 2. Any view of a line projected from its point view will show the true length of the line. A line is constructed on the plane in the primary auxiliary view that is parallel to the 1–2 reference plane. This line is projected to the plane in the secondary auxiliary view, where it appears true length on plane 1–2–3. Since line *AB* appears as a point in the secondary auxiliary view, any view projected from it will result in a true-length view of the line. Therefore the edge view of the plane can be found in the third auxiliary view by projecting a point view of the true-length line on the plane (step 3). The line appears true length and the plane appears as an edge, making possible the measurement in the final view. The point of intersection is located in each view and the visibility is determined.

5-15 SUMMARY

Successive auxiliary views can be used to great advantage to refine preliminary designs and to determine information that is needed for design finalization and analysis. Many of the solutions illustrated would be virtually impossible without using the principles of descriptive geometry and graphical methods. The engineer and technician should have command of these methods in order to recognize problems that lend themselves to graphical solutions but which would be difficult to solve by other methods.

It should be remembered that auxiliary views are merely orthographic projections that have the same relationship to each other as do principal views. Fundamentals of orthographic projection can be reviewed in Chapter 3. A thorough understanding of these basic principles is a prerequisite to the solution of problems by successive auxiliary views, since each construction step must be analyzed for spatial relationships before the next view is projected.

FIGURE 5-35. ANGLE BETWEEN A LINE AND A PLANE—LINE METHOD

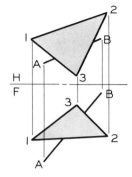

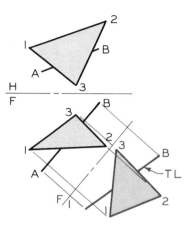

Given: The top and front views of plane 1–2–3 and line *AB*.
Required: Find the angle between line *AB* and plane 1–2–3 by the line method.
References: Articles 5–13 and 5–14.

Step 1: Determine the true length of line *AB* in a primary auxiliary view by projecting from either principal view. Plane 1–2–3 is projected also; however, it does not appear true size in this view except in a special case.

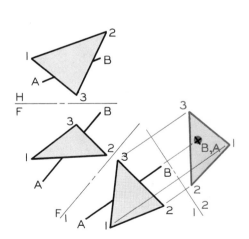

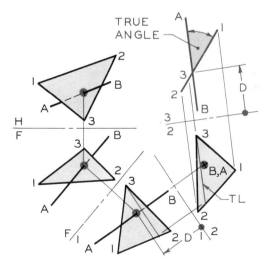

Step 2: Construct the point view of line *AB* in the secondary auxiliary view. Plane 1–2–3 does not appear true size in this view unless the line is perpendicular to the plane. The point view of the line in this view is also the piercing point on the plane.

Step 3: Construct a true-length line on plane 1–2–3 in the secondary auxiliary view, from which the edge view of the plane can be found in the third auxiliary view. Line *AB* will be true length in this view, since it appeared as a point in the secondary auxiliary view. Measure the angle in the third auxiliary view and determine the piercing point and visibility in the previous views.

PROBLEMS

Lay out the following problems on graph paper with a $\frac{1}{4}''$ grid. The method of locating the starting points on each problem is illustrated in Fig. 5-36. These problems can be drawn on blank paper with a scale if preferred. Refer to Article 1-12.

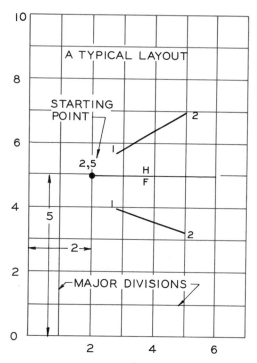

Figure 5-36

Point View of a Line

1 and 2. Find the point views of the lines in Fig. 5-37.

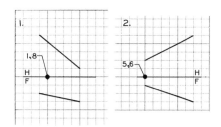

Figure 5-37

Angle between Two Planes

3 and 4. Find the angle between the intersecting planes shown in Fig. 5-38.

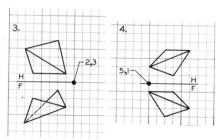

Figure 5-38

True Size of a Plane

5. Find the true size of the plane in Fig. 5-39.

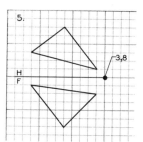

Figure 5-39

6. Find the bend angle at point 2 in Fig. 5-40. Find the length of pipe from point 1 to point 3, including the arc distance, given that the radius of bend is 3' with the center line of the pipe. Scale: $\frac{1}{4}'' = 1'\text{-}0''$.

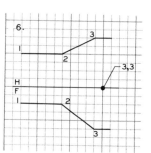

Figure 5-40

Elliptical View of a Circle

7. Points 1, 2, and 3 in Fig. 5–41 are points on the earth which are located vertically beneath a great-circle path of an orbiting satellite. Plot the path of the satellite in all views.

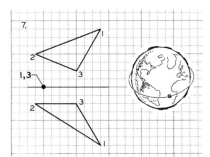

Figure 5–41

8. Line 1–2 in Fig. 5–42 represents the center line of a right cylinder in which each circular end is perpendicular to the axis. Show the cylinder in all views with a 1″ diameter.

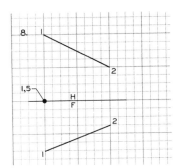

Figure 5–42

Shortest Distance from a Point to a Line

9. A pipe is to be connected with a standard 90° tee to the pipe represented by line 3–4 in Fig. 5–43. Find the shortest distance from point *O* to line 3–4, where the tee will be inserted.

10. Find the shortest distance from point *P* to line 5–6 in Fig. 5–43. Show it in all views.

Skewed Lines

11. The two skewed lines in Fig. 5–44 represent nearly straight segments of two high-voltage

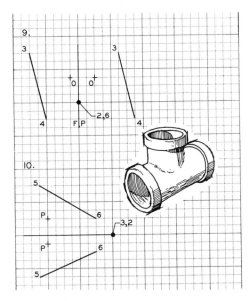

Figure 5–43

power lines that cross on irregular terrain. Determine the clearance between the lines by the line method. Scale: $\frac{1}{8}'' = 1'\text{-}0''$.

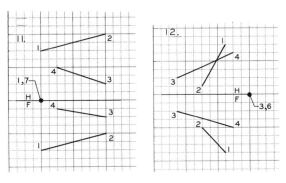

Figure 5–44   **Figure 5–45**

12. On one page, find the shortest distance between the skewed lines in Fig. 5–45 by the plane method.

13. On a separate page, solve problem 12 by the line method.

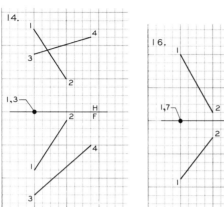

Figure 5–46

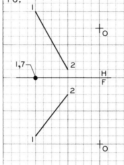

Figure 5–47

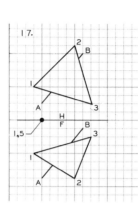

Figure 5–48

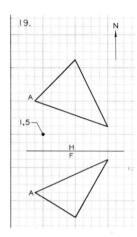

Figure 5–49

14. Find the shortest horizontal distance between the two skewed lines in Fig. 5–46 and show it in all views.

15. Find the shortest 50 percent grade distance between the lines given in problem 14 on a separate sheet.

Angle from a Point to a Line

16. In Fig. 5–47, find the shortest distance from point O to line 1–2 that will intersect at 60°, thus allowing standard connecting hardware to be used. Lay out and solve this problem on a separate sheet.

Angle between a Line and a Plane

17. Find the angle between the plane and the line in Fig. 5–48 by the plane method and show visibility in all views.

18. On a separate sheet, find the angle between the plane and the line given in problem 17, using the line method. Show visibility.

Combination Problem

19. In Fig. 5–49, a line that is 2.3″ long is to be constructed through point A that will have a bearing of N 66° E and slope upward from point A with a 20° slope. Draw this line in all views. Find the angle between this line and the plane.

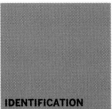

IDENTIFICATION

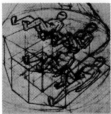

PRELIMINARY IDEAS

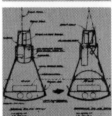

REFINEMENT

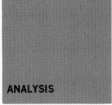

ANALYSIS

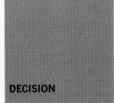

DECISION

IMPLEMENTATION

6
REVOLUTION

6–1 INTRODUCTION

The F-111, the world's first variable-geometry aircraft, is shown in Fig. 6–1 in a sequence of photographs which illustrate the full range of positions of its wings during flight. The wings are shown revolved from a 16° spread at takeoff to a fully swept 72.5° they assume for supersonic speed.

This plane will be able to do everything the military services want—take off from or land on a relatively rough, unimproved forward-area airfield or a naval carrier deck; cruise long distances or "loiter" for extended periods; dash to the attack at more than twice the speed of sound; fly supersonically at high altitudes or fly "hugging the deck"; have transoceanic range; be able, with aerial refueling, to be ferried anywhere in the world within one day.

The development of an aircraft of this type involved many hours of testing, planning, and design. The wing system of the plane is an example of an application of revolution to the design of an aircraft that permits variable positions during flight.

Revolution is another method of solving problems that could also, in most cases, be solved by auxiliary views. It is sometimes more advantageous to use the revolution method than the auxiliary view method, which was covered in Chapters 4 and 5. An understanding of revolution will reinforce an understanding of auxiliary view principles, which is necessary for the solution of spatial problems. Many engineering designs utilize rotating or revolving mechanisms that must be analyzed for critical information by means of the principles of revolution.

Fig. 6–1. The F-111, the world's first variable-geometry aircraft designed as an operational plane, involves principles of revolution in the design of its wings. (Courtesy of General Dynamics Corporation.)

The basic relationship between the projection method and revolution is shown in Fig. 6–2, where the observer, located at point 1, is viewing line *AB* from the front. Note that line *AB* is drawn as though it were an element of a cone, with line *AO* as the axis of the cone. The observer at point 1 will not see the true length of the line since his line of sight is not perpendicular to plane *ABO* in which line *AB* lies. The observer can change his position by moving to point 2, and, looking perpendicularly at plane *ABO*, he then sees line *AB* at its true length. This illustrates the auxiliary view method, as covered in Chapter 4. The observer moves his position to obtain the desired view, while the object being viewed remains stationary.

The true-length view of the line could be found by the observer located at position 1 in Fig. 6–2 if the line were revolved while he remained stationary. To demonstrate this principle, we revolve line *OC* in Fig. 6–3 into plane *AOC'*, which is perpendicular to the observer's line of sight. An observer whose line of sight is perpendicular to the axis of a cone will always see a triangular section of the cone in true size and shape. In this case, the observer is standing at the conventional front view position and he is viewing an

oblique line that does not appear true length in the front view. Then point *C* is revolved in the horizontal plane of the base into the true-size frontal plane, *AOC'*. The observer has not moved, but the line has been revolved into a plane perpendicular to his line of sight. In the auxiliary view method the observer changes positions, whereas in the revolution method the line is revolved to a new position while the observer remains stationary.

6–2 TRUE LENGTH OF A LINE IN THE FRONT VIEW BY REVOLUTION

The Saturn S-IVB, shown in Fig. 6–4, has a conical configuration composed of intersecting structural members. The lengths of these and the angles they make with the circular planes at each end can be determined by applying revolution principles as well as by applying auxiliary views. The procedure for this is developed in the following explanation.

The observer is positioned in the conventional front-view location where he is viewing oblique line *AB* in Fig. 6–5. His line of sight is not perpendicular to plane *ABO*, in which line *AB* lies; consequently, the true length of line *AB*

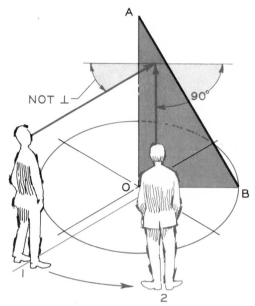

Fig. 6-2. The observer in the conventional front-view position will not see the true length of line *AB*, whereas the line will appear true length when viewed from position 2.

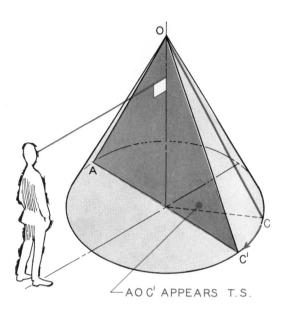

Fig. 6-3. The observer located in the front-view position can see the true length of line *OC* if it is revolved to position *OC'* as though it were an element of a cone.

Fig. 6-4. The true length of the structural members of Saturn S-IVB could be found by revolution during the refinement process. (Courtesy of National Aeronautics and Space Administration.)

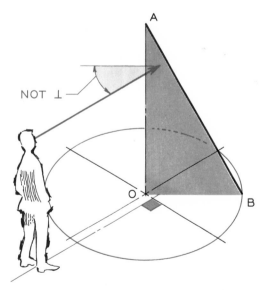

Fig. 6-5. The observer does not see the true length of line *AB* in the front view, because his line of sight is not perpendicular to plane *AOB*.

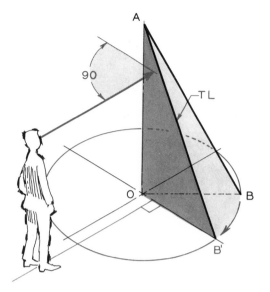

Fig. 6–6. The observer will see line *AB* true length in the front view when it has been revolved in the horizontal plane until the line becomes frontal line *AB'*.

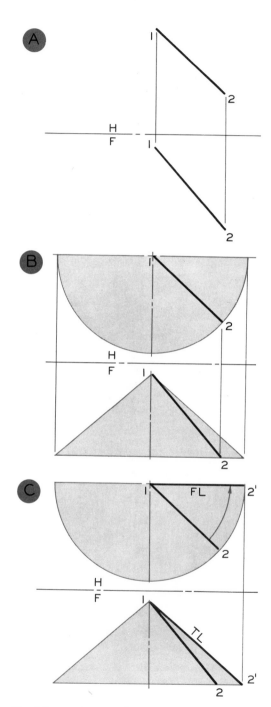

Fig. 6–7. Determining the true length of a line in the front view by revolution.

will not be seen in the front view. Therefore we revolve line *AB* as an element of a cone (Fig. 6–6), with point *B* traveling in a horizontal plane and point *A* remaining stationary at the apex of the imaginary cone. Line *AB* will now appear true length, since it is revolved into the frontal plane, which is perpendicular to the observer's line of sight. We have rotated the line to show its true length in the front view by revolving it parallel to the horizontal plane, which appears as an edge in the front view.

The true length of a similar line, 1–2, is found in the front view by revolving it parallel to the horizontal plane in Fig. 6–7. Part A shows the top and front views of an oblique line, 1–2. Point 1 is used as the apex of a cone, and the half view of the top view of the cone is drawn in part B, using line 1–2 as a radius. The front view of the cone is projected from the top view. The top view of line 1–2 is revolved into the frontal plane of the cone and its projection found in the front view in part C. Since line 1–2 has been revolved into the frontal plane, its true length is found in the front view where it is an

Fig. 6–8. The spindle speed lever on the lathe was designed through the use of principles of revolution and with consideration of human factors. (Courtesy of Jones and Lamson Corporation.)

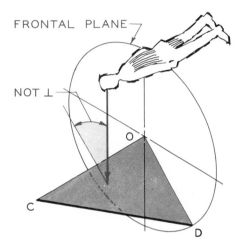

Fig. 6–9. The observer does not see the true length of line CD from the top view.

extreme element of the cone. Point 2 traveled in the horizontal plane, so the vertical height between points 1 and 2 was not changed. Consequently, the front view of point 2′ is found by projecting horizontally from the front view of point 2 to the projector from the top view of point 2′.

6–3   TRUE LENGTH OF A LINE IN THE HORIZONTAL VIEW BY REVOLUTION

The handle for operating the speed control on the lathe shown in Fig. 6–8 allows the operator to apply the principle of revolution of a line about an axis. The handle has been positioned to take into account the human factors involved in the operation of the lathe and the position of the operator.

When an observer views a line in the top view, the line will appear true length if it lies in a horizontal plane. In Fig. 6–9, line CD is not seen at true length in the top view, since the line is not horizontal, thus causing the observer's line of sight to be oblique to the line. Line CD is revolved in a direction parallel to the frontal plane, the plane that appears as an edge in the top view, until the observer's line of sight is perpendicular to plane OCD′ as shown in Fig. 6–10.

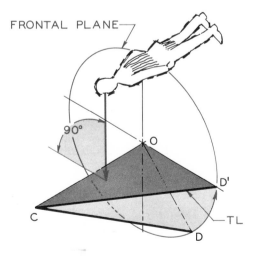

Fig. 6–10. The observer will see the true length of line CD when it has been revolved in a frontal plane to become horizontal line CD′.

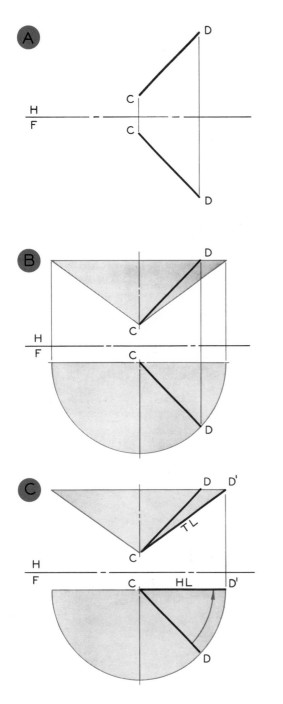

Fig. 6–12. The crucible used to pour 700-pound ingots of aluminum was designed to revolve about an axis to the position required for efficient flow of metal. (Courtesy of ALCOA.)

Fig. 6–11. Determining the true length of a line in the horizontal view by revolution.

The orthographic views of line *CD* are shown in part A of Fig. 6–11. The front view of line *CD* is used as a radius to draw the front view of the cone that is obtained when point *D* is revolved parallel to a frontal plane (part B). The triangular view of the cone is constructed in the top view by projection, as shown in part B. Line *CD* is revolved in the front view to position *CD'*, where it is horizontal (part C). It becomes the extreme, outside element of the cone in the top view, where it appears true length. Note that points *D* and *D'* are in the same frontal plane in the top view. Point *D'* is found by projecting parallel to the H–F reference plane until it intersects the projector from the front view.

Figure 6–12 shows a crucible that revolves about an axis, pouring aluminum to form ingots. As viewed in the photograph, the center line of the spout will revolve about its axis parallel to the frontal projection plane. The design of this crucible and its operating system was analyzed through the use of the principles of revolution to establish its limits of operation.

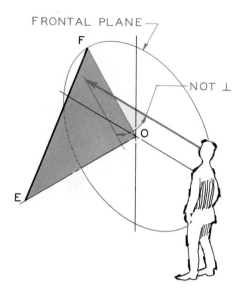

Fig. 6–13. The observer will not see the true length of line *EF* in the profile view, since his line of sight is not perpendicular to plane *EFO*.

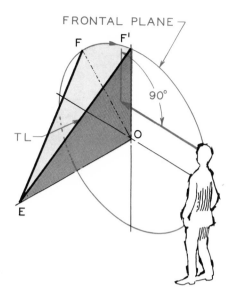

Fig. 6–14. The observer will see the true length of line *EF* when it has been revolved until it is in position *EF'*, parallel to the profile plane.

6–4   TRUE LENGTH OF A LINE IN THE PROFILE VIEW BY REVOLUTION

The observer viewing line *EF* from the conventional right-side view position will see the line foreshortened, since his line of sight is not perpendicular to plane *EFO*, as shown in Fig. 6–13. When line *EF* is revolved about the edge view of the frontal plane (Fig. 6–14) until it is parallel to the profile plane, the observer will see the true length of the line from his conventional profile-view vantage point.

The orthographic projections and revolutions of line *EF* are shown in Fig. 6–15. In order for the line to be true length in the side view shown in part A, it is revolved in the front view as though it were an element of a cone (part B). The circular view of the cone is projected to the side view, where its triangular shape is seen. In part C, point *F* is revolved to *F'* in the front view and projected to the side view, where the line represents the extreme element of the cone and is true length, since it is a profile line in this position.

It should be noted that the true length of any line can be found by revolution in either view when two adjacent views are given. The true length of line *EF* could have been found in the front view of Fig. 6–15 by revolving the line into a position that was parallel to the frontal plane instead of the profile plane. The examples previously covered revolve each line about one of its given ends, because this is a simple way of introducing the principles of revolution. However, the line could be revolved about any point on its length equally as well.

The portable well work-over equipment and the pump shown in Fig. 6–16 illustrate revolutions about an axis. The design of each was analyzed by revolution principles to refine and develop operational functions.

6–5   ANGLES BETWEEN A LINE AND PRINCIPAL PLANES BY REVOLUTION

The process of pouring hot metal into the tilted basic oxygen furnace in Fig. 6–17 illustrates the revolution of a line to make a specified angle

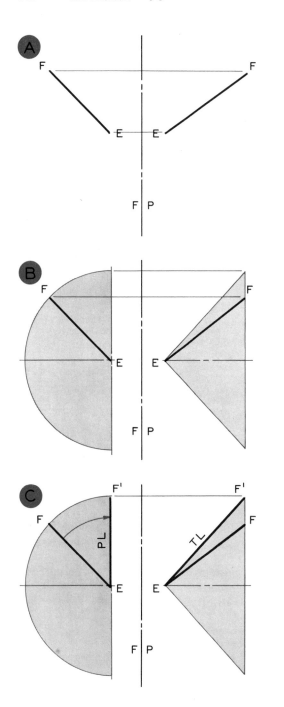

Fig. 6–16. The portable well work-over equipment and the pump are examples of mechanisms that were designed to revolve about an axis into a variety of positions. (Courtesy of Humble Oil and Refining Company.)

Fig. 6–17. Two smelting components were designed to revolve into a position that will permit hot metal to be charged into a basic oxygen furnace. (Courtesy of Jones and Laughlin Steel Corporation.)

Fig. 6–15. Determining the true length of a line in the profile view by revolution.

with a principal plane. The furnace is tilted to a required angle with this imaginary plane in order to best receive the charge of hot metal.

It should be remembered that the angle between a line and a plane will appear true size in the view where the plane is an edge and the line is true length. In all principal views, two principal planes appear as edges. Consequently, when a line appears true length in a principal

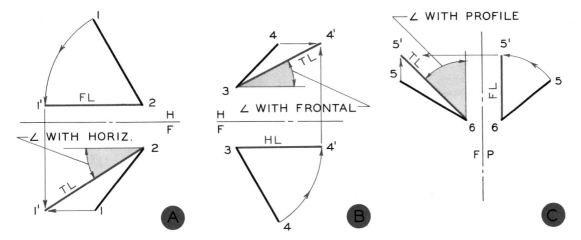

Fig. 6–18. Determining angles between lines and principal planes.

Fig. 6–19. The 45-ton Haulpak truck was designed to permit the bed to revolve about an axis, as required for functional operation. (Courtesy of LeTourneau-Westinghouse Corporation.)

view, the angle between the line and at least one principal plane can be measured.

A line may be revolved to find its true length in any principal view, as illustrated in Fig. 6–18. Since the horizontal plane appears as an edge in the front view, the true angle between the horizontal plane and an oblique line, 1–2, can be found by constructing the true length of the line in the front view by revolution, as shown in

part A. The frontal plane projects as an edge in the top view (part B). The angle between line 3–4 and the frontal plane can be found in the top view by revolving point 4 to a horizontal position in the front view and then projecting to find the true length of 3–4 in the top view, as shown in part B.

The angle between line 5–6 and the profile plane can be found in the front view, where the profile plane is a vertical edge (part C). Line 5–6 is revolved in the side view until it becomes a frontal line and is projected to the front view. The true length of the line is found in the front view by projecting point 5 parallel to the edge view of the profile plane until it intersects with the projector from point 5′ in the profile view. The angle line 5′–6 makes with the profile plane can be measured in the front view.

6–6   TRUE SIZE OF A PLANE BY REVOLUTION

A plane can be revolved about an axis until it becomes true size in much the same manner as a truck bed is revolved about an axis (Fig. 6–19). This principle of revolving a plane is closely related to the revolution of a line when the plane being revolved appears as an edge.

FIGURE 6–20. TRUE SIZE OF A PLANE BY REVOLUTION

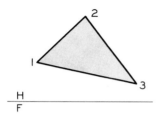

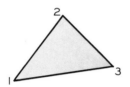

Given: The top and front views of plane 1–2–3.
Required: Find the true size of the plane by revolution.
References: Articles 4–9 and 6–6.

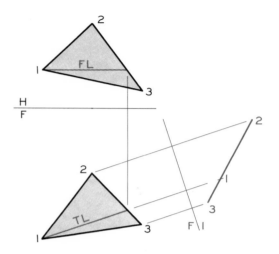

Step 1: Construct a true-length line in the front view of plane 1–2–3. Since the plane will appear as an edge in a view where the true-length line projects as a point, project a primary auxiliary view of the plane from the front view. The edge view could have been projected from the top view as well.

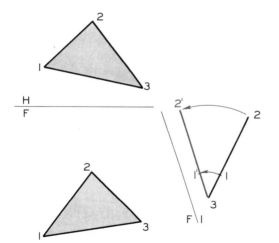

Step 2: Revolve the edge view of the plane about an axis through point 3 until the plane is parallel to the F–1 plane. The plane, 1'–2'–3, will be a true-size projection when projected to the front view since it has revolved into a plane which is parallel to the frontal projection plane.

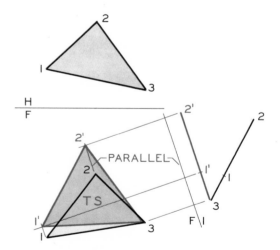

Step 3: Project points 1' and 2' from their revolved positions to the front view. Locate points 1' and 2' in the front view by extending projectors from the original points 1 and 2 parallel to the F–1 plane, because the plane was revolved to a position parallel to the auxiliary plane in Step 2.

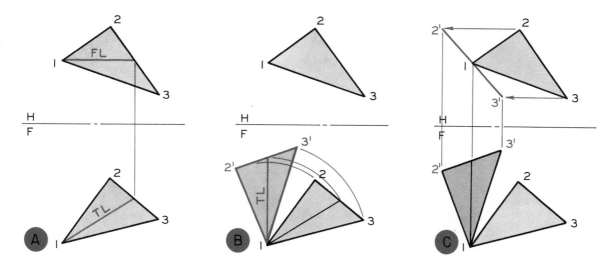

Fig. 6–21. Determine the edge view of a plane by revolution.

The steps required to find the true size of a plane by revolution are presented in Fig. 6–20 through a combination of auxiliary-view and revolution methods. The plane is found as an edge in the primary auxiliary view by locating the point view of a line on the plane (step 1). Because the edge view is oblique to the F–1 plane in this projection, it has to be revolved in the primary auxiliary view until it is parallel to the F–1 plane in step 2. Any point could have been selected for the axis of revolution. Since the plane was revolved parallel to the auxiliary plane, the true size of the plane is obtained by projecting the original points in the front view parallel to the F–1 plane to intersect the projectors from 1' and 2'. These form the true-size plane 1'–2'–3 in the front view. The true size of the plane could have also been found by projecting the edge view from the top view and revolving the plane in this auxiliary view.

6–7 EDGE VIEW OF A PLANE BY REVOLUTION

The edge view of a plane can also be found by revolution without using auxiliary views as was done in Fig. 6–20. The revolution method is

illustrated in Fig. 6–21. In this case, plane 1-2-3 is given in the top and front views in part A, where a frontal line is drawn on the plane in the top view and projected to the front view. This line appears true length in the front view. The plane is revolved until the true-length line becomes vertical in the front view (part B). The true-length line will project as a point in the top view. The edge view of the plane is found in part C by projecting original points, 2 and 3, in the top view parallel to the H–F reference plane to intersect the projectors from the revolved points, 2' and 3', in the front view. This can be done because the plane was revolved parallel to the frontal plane.

A second revolution, sometimes called a *double revolution,* can be made to revolve the edge view of the plane in the top view until it is parallel to the edge view of the frontal plane. Since frontal planes are true size in the front view, we can obtain the true size of the plane through a procedure similar to that covered in the sequential steps of Fig. 6–20. This last step is not illustrated, since it should be an apparent extension of previously covered principles.

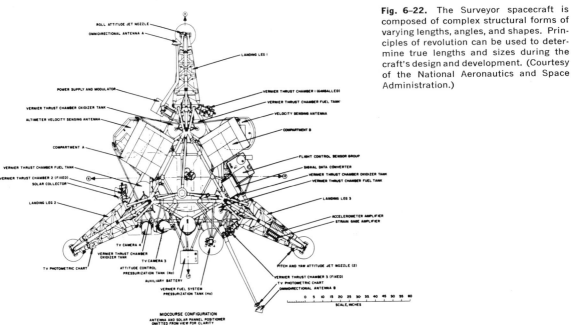

Fig. 6–22. The Surveyor spacecraft is composed of complex structural forms of varying lengths, angles, and shapes. Principles of revolution can be used to determine true lengths and sizes during the craft's design and development. (Courtesy of the National Aeronautics and Space Administration.)

The Surveyor spacecraft shown in Fig. 6–22 involves many complex relationships between lines and planes that had to be studied in great detail so that the structure could be refined prior to its analysis and construction. In some cases, the true lengths of the lines were found with less difficulty by revolution than by using auxiliary views. Determining the true sizes of the planes was also necessary for the completion of design specifications. The methods covered in the articles that follow would also prove useful in designing a spatial structure of this type.

6–8 ANGLE BETWEEN TWO PLANES BY REVOLUTION

The line of intersection of the two intersecting planes given in Fig. 6–23A is true length in the top view. The plane of the angle between the two planes will appear as an edge, in this view, since it is perpendicular to the true-length line of intersection. Points 1, 2, and 3 in the plane of the angle are projected to the front view where

the plane of the angle appears foreshortened (part 2). The true size of this plane can be found in the front view by revolving the edge view of the plane in the top view until it becomes a frontal plane (part 3). Points 1′, 2′, and 3 are then projected from the top view to the front view and located in the same horizontal planes as the original points in the foreshortened view. Angle 1′–2′–3 appears true size in the front view.

Often the line of intersection between two intersecting lines will not project as true length in a principal view. Such is the case in Fig. 6–24, which shows an engine mount frame of a helicopter. The angle between these planes must be determined to design the joints and to analyze the clearances within the frame.

In the top and front views of two intersecting planes in part A of Fig. 6–25, the line of intersection does not appear true length in either view. The true length of the line of intersection is found in a primary auxiliary view which is projected perpendicularly from the line of intersection in the top view. The plane of the angle between the two planes projects as an edge that

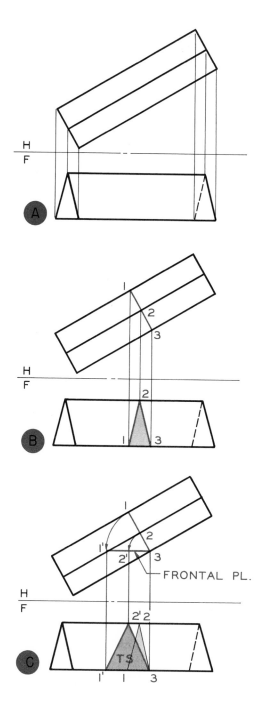

Fig. 6–23. Determining the angle between two planes by revolution.

Fig. 6–24. The angular measurements between the two planes of the helicopter engine mount can be determined by revolution principles. (Courtesy of Bell Helicopter Corporation.)

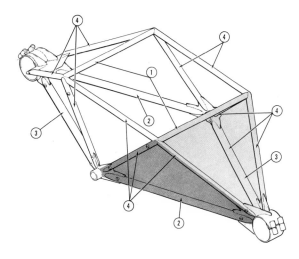

is perpendicular to the true-length view of the line of intersection (part B). Plane 1–2–3 is projected as a foreshortened plane in the top view. The edge view of plane 1–2–3 is therefore revolved about the axis, 3–1, in the primary auxiliary view until it is parallel to the H–1 plane (part C). It is then projected back to the top view. Angle 1–2'–3 appears true size in the top view when point 2' has been located by projecting from point 2 parallel to the H–1 plane.

6–9 REVOLUTION OF A POINT ABOUT AN OBLIQUE AXIS

Handwheels and hand cranks are mechanical means of adjusting all types of machines from common household appliances to mass-production equipment such as the machine shown in Fig. 6–26. Note that the hand cranks are positioned to be accessible to the operator while having sufficient clearance with the other components of the machine. Principles of revolution were applied to these hand adjustments in the early stages of their design. The same principles

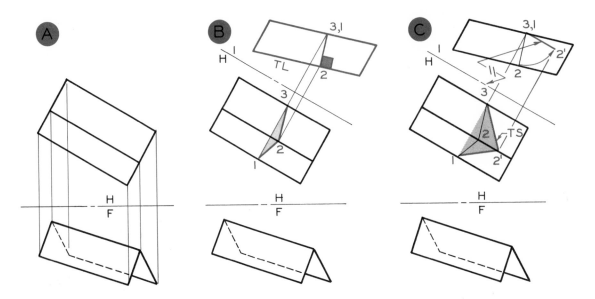

Fig. 6–25. Determining the angle between two oblique planes by revolution.

Fig. 6–26. The hand cranks on the mass-production machine were designed to permit adequate clearance when they are revolved about their axes. (Courtesy of Ex-Cell-O Corporation.)

can be applied to the location of a power line with respect to another by revolving a point on one wire about the axis of the other to determine the required minimum clearance.

The revolution of a point about a line is illustrated in Fig. 6–27. The top and front views of axis 1–2 and point *O*, the point to be revolved, are given. We are to revolve point *O* into its highest position to determine its location in the given views and its relationship to adjacent components. The circular path of revolution of point *O* about line 1–2 can be seen in the view where line 1–2 appears as a point (step 1). The highest position of point *O* is found in step 2 by constructing line 1–3 in an upward direction in the two given views. This directional line is then projected back to the secondary auxiliary view where the highest point is located on the circular path. Point *O'*, the highest point on the path, is found in each view by projecting to the primary auxiliary view, the front view, and the top view (step 3). The measurements from the reference planes are used to establish accurately these views of the point. Note that the circular path of the point projects as an edge which is perpendicular to axis 1–2 in the primary auxiliary view.

FIGURE 6–27.   REVOLUTION OF A POINT ABOUT AN AXIS

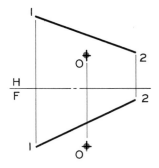

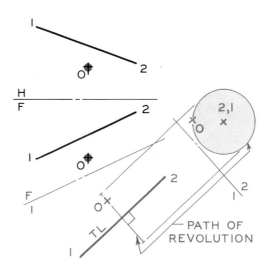

Given: The top and front views of axis 1–2 and point O.
Required: Revolve point O about the axis, locate its highest position, and show it in all views.
References: Articles 3–3, 5–3, 5–6, and 6–9.

Step 1: Locate the true length of axis 1–2 in a primary auxiliary view, and construct its point view in the secondary auxiliary view. Project point O to these views also. Using as a radius the distance from the point view of axis 1–2 to point O, construct the circular path of revolution in the secondary auxiliary view. The path of revolution appears as an edge in primary auxiliary view.

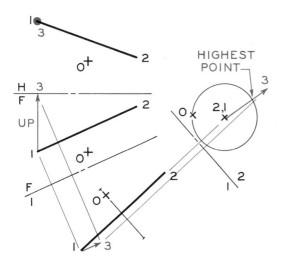

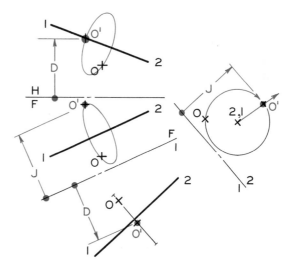

Step 2: Determine the highest point by constructing line 1–3 upward in the front view and projecting it as a point in the top view. This line is then projected back through the primary auxiliary view to the secondary auxiliary view. The point where this directional arrow crosses the circular path locates the highest point of the path of point O.

Step 3: Point O' is projected from its circular view back through the successive views. Note that the highest point, O', lies on line 1–2 in the top view, which verifies that it is in its highest position. This problem could have been solved by projecting from the top view as well. The circular path appears elliptical in the front and top views.

Projection principles in Chapter 3 covering the directions of forward, backward, up and down, and left and right should be reviewed if necessary, since those principles are used in locating the positions of a point that is revolved about a given axis.

The elliptical paths of point O can be constructed in principal views by application of the principles covered in Article 5–6. The ellipse guide angle for the front view is the angle formed by the line of sight from the front view and the edge view of the circular path of revolution. The ellipse angle for the top view must be found by an auxiliary view projected from the top view in which the axis appears true length and the circular path appears as a perpendicular edge. The angle formed by the line of sight from the top view and the edge view of this circular path establishes the ellipse angle that will be used in selecting the proper ellipse template for drawing the ellipse in the top view.

The point could have been located in any specified position, such as its highest, lowest, or most forward position, by constructing a line

of the required direction in the principal views and projecting it into all views. The point would be located in the circular view indicated by the position of the directional line constructed in the principal views.

6–10 REVOLUTION OF A LINE ABOUT AN AXIS

A line can be revolved about another line, as shown in Fig. 6–28, if the line to be used as an axis is found as a point. The point view of line 1–2 is obtained in part A of the figure in the primary auxiliary view, since the top view of line 1–2 is true length. A circle is drawn tangent to line 3–4 with its center at the axis, 1–2. Each end of line 3–4 is revolved the specified number of degrees and drawn in its new position as shown in part A. The top view of line 3'–4' is found by projecting parallel to the H–1 plane from the original points of 3 and 4 in the top view, as shown in part B. These projectors will intersect the projectors from the primary auxiliary view. The front view is obtained by projecting from the top view and transferring

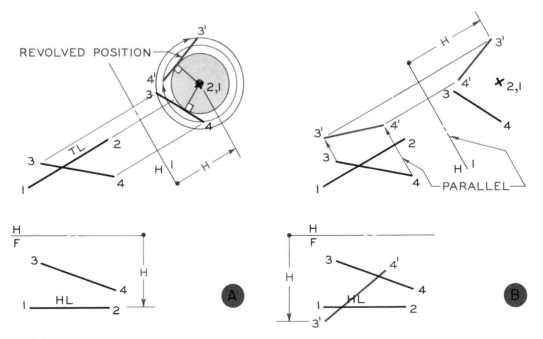

Fig. 6–28. Determining the revolution of a line about an axis.

6–29

Fig. 6–29. This 60-ft diameter antenna is used for precision tracking of communication satellites. Its shell is formed by the revolution of a parabola about its axis of symmetry. (Courtesy of Ryan Aeronautical Company.)

Fig. 6–30. The Ranger spacecraft is revolved about three axes to position its cameras for photographing the moon. (Courtesy of National Aeronautics and Space Administration.)

Fig. 6–31. This photograph, taken through a telescope in September 1919, is a view of the expected landing area of Ranger. (Courtesy of the Jet Propulsion Laboratory, California Institute of Technology.)

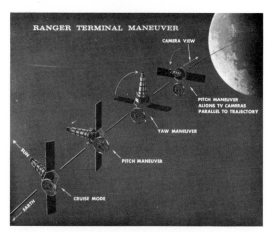

6–30

6–31

the height dimensions from the primary auxiliary view, as shown in part A.

A closely related application of this principle is the revolution of a plane about an axis to form a geometric shell or solid. An example of a shell is the tracking antenna in Fig. 6–29. This parabolic shell is formed by the theoretical revolution of a parabola about its axis of symmetry.

The orientation of a spacecraft by command signals from the earth is an application of the theory of revolution; the craft is revolved about an axis to a specified position. In Fig. 6–30, the Ranger spacecraft is revolved to position its cameras to obtain medium resolution pictures of the moon's surface and to determine the presence of radioactive elements. The photograph of the landing area of the Ranger, shown in Fig. 6–31, was taken through a telescope in September 1919. Thanks to successful flights by Ranger and other spacecraft, we now have much clearer photos of the moon's surface. The path of Ranger was controlled by commands that revolved it about its three axes with maneuvers of pitch, yaw, and roll. Note that the antenna in Fig. 6–30 is designed to maintain a constant position for reception of command signals from earth even though the spacecraft revolves in space.

The contributions to spacecraft technology by the Ranger project were instrumental in the development of the Mariner 2 spacecraft shown in Fig. 6–32. Mariner 2 was man's first successful voyager through space; its mission was

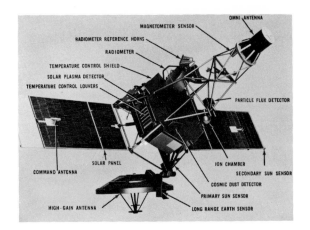

Fig. 6–32. Mariner 2 was man's first successful voyager through space that scanned Venus. (Courtesy of National Aeronautics and Space Administration.)

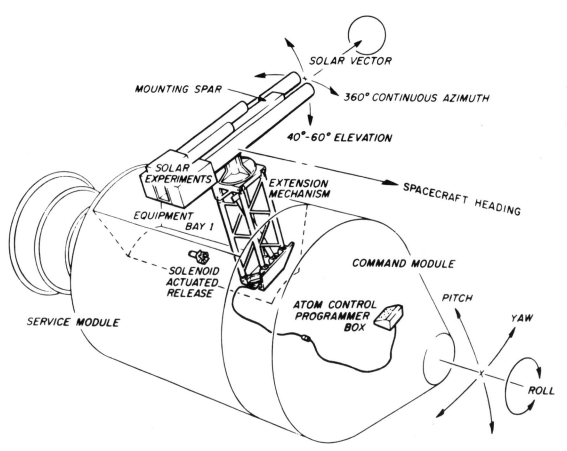

Fig. 6–33. The Apollo command service module was designed to permit the automatic revolution of a telescope to keep it directed toward the sun as the vehicle travels through space. (Courtesy of National Aeronautics and Space Administration.)

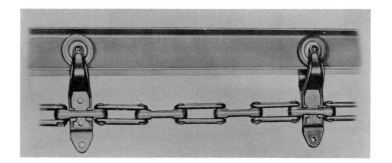

Fig. 6–34. The overhead track of this conveyor system must be designed in such a manner that the track web is positioned in a vertical plane at all times. (Courtesy of Mechanical Handling Systems, Inc.)

to scan Venus and gather information on the temperature and composition of its cloud cover.

An artist's drawing of the atom system in the Apollo command service module is shown in Fig. 6–33. The maneuvers of pitch, roll, and yaw are illustrated with respect to the path of the spacecraft. Pitch is the up-and-down revolution with respect to the spacecraft heading, while yaw is the left-or-right rotation, and roll is the revolution of the spacecraft along the path of its heading. The commands given to a module will be for revolutions about these three axes, whether the commands come from the earth by radio waves or from the astronauts aboard. The telescopes are mounted on a spar that will extend outside the service module on a two-axis gimbal that can automatically correct for the yaw or the pitch of the spacecraft. This system will be used for observing the sun through telescopes.

It is our understanding of the revolution of geometric shapes in space that enables us to control the revolutions of a spacecraft in flight. These principles are very similar to the revolution of a point about a line, as discussed in Article 6–9, and the revolution of a line about an axis, as covered in this article.

6–11 REVOLUTION OF A RIGHT PRISM ABOUT AN AXIS

The handling of materials in mass-production plants is a complex engineering problem that requires considerable skill and engineering experience. Many plants employ automatic

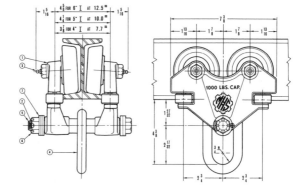

Fig. 6–35. A detail view of a trolley that will utilize a track like that shown in Fig. 6–34. (Courtesy of Mechanical Handling Systems, Inc.)

tow lines located overhead or under the floor to transport parts and materials through the manufacturing process. An example of a portion of an overhead system is shown in Fig. 6–34. The track is an I-beam and the trolleys are designed to roll on its lower flange, as shown in Fig. 6–35. The tracks are designed to be suspended from the structural beams of the plant's interior structure. It is obvious that the trolley system will work effectively only when the track's right section is positioned so that the interior web of the beam is positioned in a vertical plane and the lower flange is positioned horizontally. If the web were not vertical, the trolley would bind and not roll properly. Consequently, it is necessary to design a method for suspending the track in

FIGURE 6–36. REVOLUTION OF A RIGHT PRISM ABOUT ITS AXIS

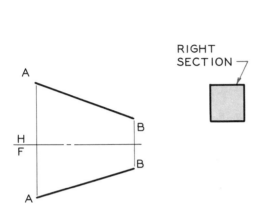

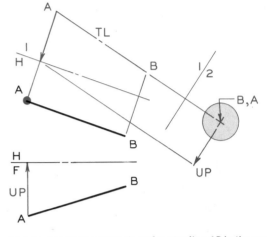

Given: The top and front views of line *AB*, the center line of a prism.
Required: Revolve the given right section about the axis to establish the prism with two surfaces in the vertical plane. Show the prism in all views.
References: Articles 3–3, 5–3, 6–9, and 6–11.

Step 1: Locate the point view of center line *AB* in the secondary auxiliary view by drawing a circle about the axis with a diameter equal to one side of the square right section. Draw a vertical arrow in the front and top views and project it to the secondary auxiliary view to indicate the direction of vertical in this view.

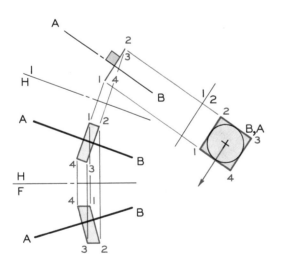

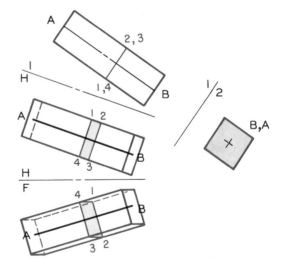

Step 2: Draw the right section, 1–2–3–4, in the secondary auxiliary with two sides parallel to the vertical directional arrow. Project this section back to the successive views by transferring measurements with dividers. The edge view of the section could have been located in any position along center line *AB* in the primary auxiliary view, so long as it was perpendicular to the center line.

Step 3: Draw the lateral edges of the prism through the corners of the right section so that they are parallel to the center line in all views. Terminate the ends of the prism in the primary auxiliary where they appear as edges that are perpendicular to the center line. Project the corner points of the ends to the top and front views to establish the ends in these views.

Fig. 6–37. Each of the chutes for transporting iron ore in this installation was designed so that two edges of its right section are vertical and the other two are horizontal. These designs were developed by applying the principle of revolving a prism about its axis. (Courtesy of Kaiser Steel Corporation.)

such a way that the web is positioned in a vertical plane.

A problem of this type is illustrated in Fig. 6–36, in which a prism with a square right section is revolved about its axis until two of its planes are vertical. This prism could represent the I-beam mentioned above; for simplicity, the details of each flange are not drawn. The center line is found as a point in a secondary auxiliary view in step 1. The direction of vertical is found in this view by projecting a vertical directional arrow in the front view to the secondary auxiliary view. In step 2, the square right section is positioned about the point view of the center line so that two sides are parallel to the directional arrow. The sides of the prism are found by drawing the lateral sides parallel to the center line through the corner points of the right section in all views. The length of the prism is drawn from specifications in the primary auxiliary view; the ends will be perpendicular to the center line (step 3). They are found in the top and front views by projection.

These principles apply to structural members, hallways, and conveyor belts which, to function properly, must be designed so that their surfaces are positioned with respect to certain planes. A chute connecting two planes through which material will be conveyed must have two sides of its right section in the vertical plane and the other two sides in the horizontal plane (Fig. 6–37). The revolution of a prismatic shape about its axis to a desired position is a necessary step in the design of the connections at all chute supports and the openings at the ends of the chutes where they join other structures.

6-12 ANGLE BETWEEN A LINE AND A PLANE BY REVOLUTION

A third way of finding the angle between a line and a plane is by revolution, as shown in Fig. 6–38. This problem was solved by auxiliary view methods in Articles 5–13 and 5–14.

The true size of the plane is found in a secondary auxiliary view in step 1 of Fig. 6–38. The

FIGURE 6–38. ANGLE BETWEEN A LINE AND A PLANE BY REVOLUTION

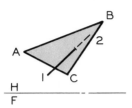
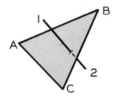

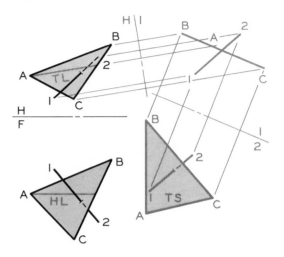

Given: The top and front views of plane *ABC* and line 1–2.
Required: Find the angle between the line and plane by revolution.
References: Articles 5–13, 5–14, and 6–12.

Step 1: Construct plane *ABC* as an edge in a primary auxiliary view, which can be projected from either view. Determine the true size of the plane in secondary auxiliary view, and project line 1–2 to each view.

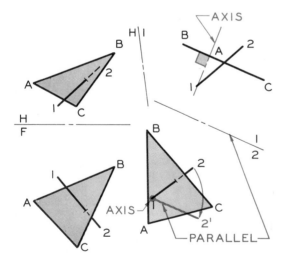

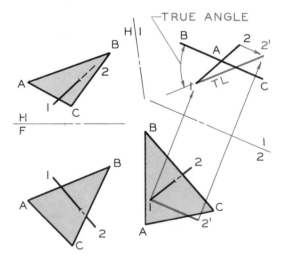

Step 2: Revolve the secondary auxiliary view of the line until it is parallel to the 1–2 reference plane. The axis of revolution appears as a point through point 1 in the secondary auxiliary view. The axis appears true length and is perpendicular to the 1–2 plane and plane *ABC* in the primary auxiliary.

Step 3: Point 2′ is projected to the primary auxiliary where the true length of line 1–2′ is found by projecting the primary auxiliary view of point 2 parallel to the 1–2 plane as shown. Since the plane appears as an edge and the line appears true length in this view, the true angle between the line and the plane can be measured.

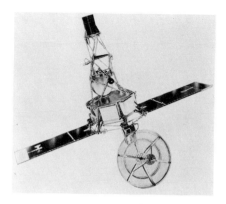

Fig. 6–39. Angles between the structural members and planes of the spacecraft can be determined by revolution. (Courtesy of the National Aeronautics and Space Administration.)

Fig. 6–40. The cradle of these image orthicon cameras was designed to permit revolution to any position for tracking space vehicles and astronomical bodies. (Courtesy of ITT Industrial Laboratories.)

line is revolved in the secondary auxiliary view until it is parallel to the 1–2 reference plane (step 2). Line 1–2' will project true length in the primary auxiliary view because it was parallel to the edge view of the primary auxiliary plane. Point 2' is found by projecting point 2 parallel to the 1–2 plane in the primary auxiliary view, as shown in step 3. Since the line appears true length and the plane appears as an edge, the true angle between the line and plane can be measured in this view.

The spacecraft shown in Fig. 6–39 is an example of planes formed by intersecting lines that connect with other lines. These angles must be determined during the refinement stages of developing the final design. Revolution principles can be used to good advantage in many cases for finding these angles once the preliminary configuration has been drawn.

6–13 A LINE AT SPECIFIED ANGLES WITH TWO PRINCIPAL PLANES

The facet-eye camera shown in Fig. 6–40 can be revolved about three axes, giving it full mobility and flexibility for viewing any point in the sky. These television cameras are used for tracking satellites and bodies in space, and they receive excellent contrast even under poor

visibility conditions. The design of the camera's cradle involves applications of revolution about several axes. These cameras can be positioned to make a required angle with the two adjacent principal planes. For instance, the direction of the cameras could be positioned to make an angle of 44° with the horizontal and 35° with the frontal plane. This example is illustrated in Fig. 6–41.

In step 1 of Fig. 6–41, cone A is drawn to contain all the lines making an angle of 35° with the frontal plane. These lines are the elements on the surface of the cone. Cone A will be triangular in the top view and circular in the front view. Cone B is drawn in step 2 to contain elements which make an angle of 44° with the horizontal plane. The elements are drawn equal in length to element E of the previously drawn cone A. The two cones will intersect with common elements, since the elements of each cone are equal in length. Two lines, 0–1 and 0–2, satisfy the requirements of the problem. If the requirements had specified that the line slope to the right or left, then only one of the lines would have satisfied the requirements.

These principles can also be applied to determining the intersections between piping systems that must be joined with standard connectors which are cast in standard angles.

FIGURE 6-41. A LINE AT SPECIFIED ANGLES TO TWO PRINCIPAL PLANES

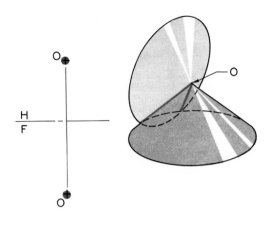

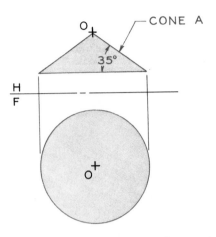

CONE A

35°

Given: The top and front views of point O.
Required: Construct a line through point O that will make angles of 35° with the frontal plane and 44° with the horizontal plane, sloping forward and downward.
Reference: Article 6-13.

Step 1: Draw a triangular view of a cone in the top view such that the extreme elements make an angle of 35° with the edge view of the frontal plane. Construct the circular view of the cone in the front view, using O as the apex. All elements of this cone make an angle of 35° with the frontal plane.

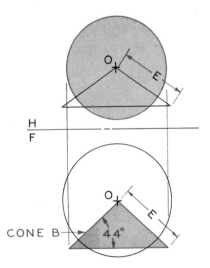

CONE B   44°

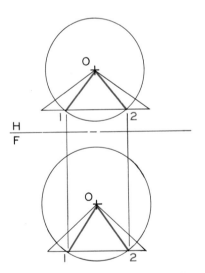

Step 2: Draw a triangular view of a cone in the front view such that the elements make an angle of 44° with the edge view of the horizontal plane. Draw the elements of this cone equal in length to element E of cone A. All elements of cone B make an angle of 44° with the horizontal plane.

Step 3: Since the elements of cones A and B are equal in length, there will be two common elements that lie on the surface of each cone, elements 0-1 and 0-2. Locate points 1 and 2 at the point where the bases of the cone intersect in both views. Either of these lines will satisfy the problem requirements.

6-14 SUMMARY

Principles of revolution are closely related to principles of auxiliary-view projections. In revolution, the observer maintains his position to view principal views in the conventional direction while the object is revolved into the desired position to give the required view. The auxiliary view method of projection moves the observer's position about the stationary object so that the object is viewed from auxiliary positions.

In many instances, the principles of revolution can be used to supplement those of auxiliary views, allowing the designer to find the true sizes and shapes of geometric figures with greater ease than would be possible with auxiliary views alone. Spatial problems should always be analyzed to determine the most appropriate method of solution available. Once the preliminary designs have been scaled and drawn in preliminary form, the configurations can be refined through the application of revolution principles and auxiliary views. Angles, true lengths, true sizes, and other physical properties must be found to permit further analysis of the final design, as will be discussed in the succeeding chapters.

PROBLEMS

The problems for this chapter should be constructed and solved on $8\frac{1}{2}'' \times 11''$ sheets, as illustrated by the accompanying figures, in accordance with the practices outlined in Article 1-12. Each grid represents $\frac{1}{4}''$. All reference planes and points should be labeled using $\frac{1}{8}''$ letters with guidelines.

1. Use Fig. 6–42 for all parts of this problem. (A) Find the true length of the line in the front view by revolution. Indicate the angle this line makes with the horizontal plane. (B) Find the true length of the line in the front view by revolution. Indicate the angle this line makes with the horizontal plane. (C) Find the true length of the line in the horizontal view by revolution. Indicate the angle this line makes with the frontal plane. (D) Find the true length of the line in the horizontal view by revolution. Indicate the angle this line makes with the frontal plane.

2. Use Fig. 6–43 for all parts of this problem. (A) Find the true length of the line in the profile view by revolution. Indicate the angle this line makes with the frontal plane. (B) Find the true length of the line in the profile view by revolution. Indicate the angle this line makes with the frontal plane. (C) Find the true size of the plane by a primary auxiliary view and a single revolution.

3. (A) In Fig. 6–44A find the edge view of the plane by revolution. (B) Find the true size of the plane by double revolution in part B of the figure.

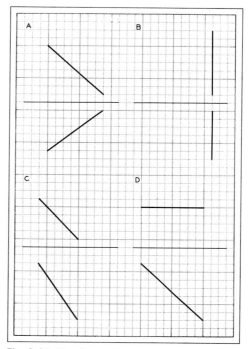

Fig. 6–42. Revolution of lines.

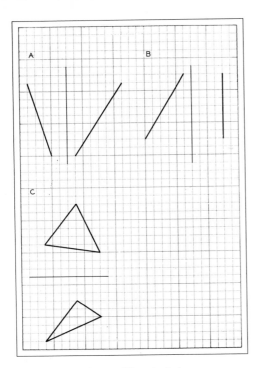

Fig. 6–43. Revolution of lines and planes.

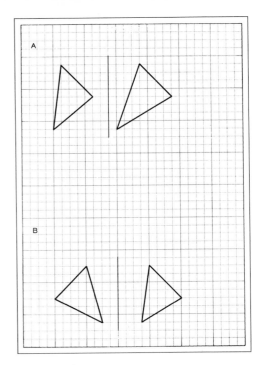

Fig. 6–44. Revolution of a plane.

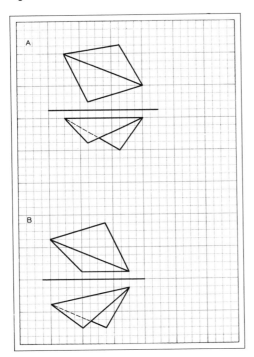

Fig. 6–45. Determining the angle between planes by revolution.

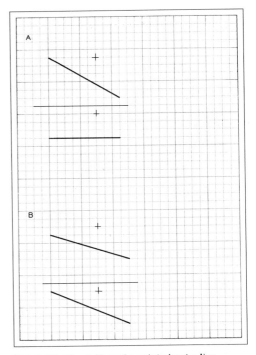

Fig. 6–46. Revolution of a point about a line.

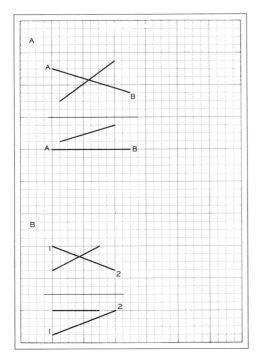

Fig. 6–47. Revolution of a line about an axis.

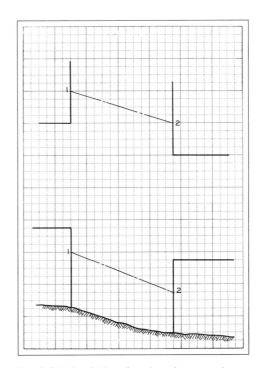

Fig. 6–48. Revolution of a prism about an axis.

4. (A) In Fig. 6–45A find the angle between the two intersecting planes by revolution. (B) Find the angle between the intersecting planes in part B of the figure by revolution.

5. (A) In Fig. 6–46A revolve the point about the line and locate its highest and lowest positions. (B) Revolve the point about the oblique line in part B of the figure. Locate its highest and most forward positions. Indicate it in all views.

6. (A) In Fig. 6–47A revolve the line about the axis *AB* 90° in a clockwise direction. Show the revolution in all views. (B) Revolve the line about axis 1–2 90° in a counterclockwise direction in part B of the figure. Show the revolution in all views.

7. Line 1–2 in Fig. 6–48 is the center line of a conveyer chute, such as that shown in Fig. 6–49, which has a 10-ft-square cross section.

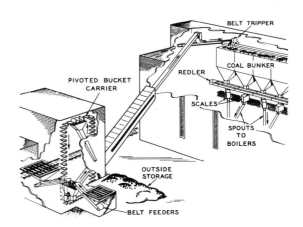

Fig. 6–49. An example of a coal chute between two buildings which is similar to that represented by Fig. 6–48. (Courtesy of Stephens-Adamson Manufacturing Company.)

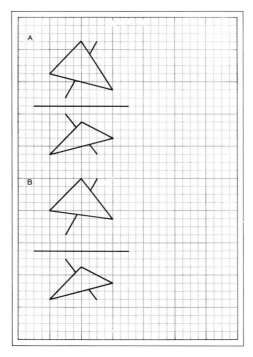

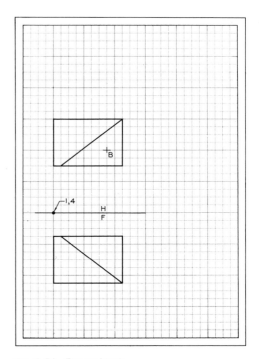

Fig. 6–50. Determining angle between a line and a plane by revolution and by auxiliary view.

Fig. 6–51. Fixture block.

Construct the necessary views to revolve the 10-ft square into a position where two sides of the right section will be vertical planes. Show the chute in all views. Scale: $1'' = 10'$.

8. In Fig. 6–50A find the angle between the line and plane by two auxiliary views and one revolution. Show all construction. (B) Find the angle between the line and plane in part B of the figure by the auxiliary-view method. Compare the solutions obtained in both parts.

9. Locate two views of a point $3\frac{1}{2}''$ apart on an $8\frac{1}{2}'' \times 11''$ sheet. Using a conical element of $2''$, find the direction of a line that slopes for-

ward and makes an angle of 30° with the frontal plane and slopes downward and makes an angle of 50° with the horizontal plane. Show all construction.

10. A fixture block (Fig. 6–51) must have a hole drilled perpendicular to the inclined surface with its center at point B, which lies on the plane. Using principles of revolution, determine the angles of revolution necessary to position the block under a vertically mounted drill for drilling. This information will be needed to design a jig for holding the block during this operation. Show the new positions of the block after revolution in all views.

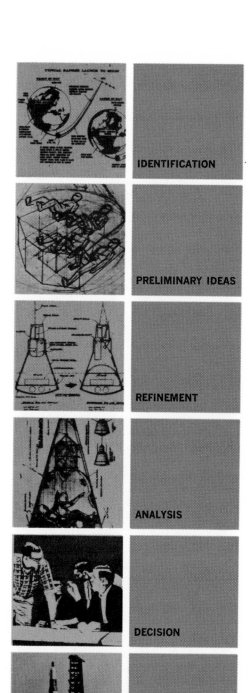

IDENTIFICATION

PRELIMINARY IDEAS

REFINEMENT

ANALYSIS

DECISION

IMPLEMENTATION

7

INTERSECTIONS

7-1 INTRODUCTION

Practically every product or engineering project designed is composed of planes, lines, or solids that intersect, often at unusual angles. The simple attachment of a rear-view mirror on the exterior body of an automobile is an intersection problem that must be solved prior to production. Massive concrete structures often involve the intersection of geometric forms with each other. The engineer must understand the principles of intersections in order to present his designs and to supervise the construction of the concrete forms into which the concrete will be poured.

The design of the dashboard of an automobile requires the solution of many intersection problems (Fig. 7-1). The forms that intersect vary from lines to contoured shapes. All intersections must be developed graphically in the early stages of the design refinement, since the intersections will influence the final configuration and appearance of the instrument panel and the included accessories.

Many of the principles of intersection covered in this chapter are of a conventional nature and involve planes and regular geometric shapes. An understanding of the principles given will be sufficient for practically any problem encountered, since all intersection applications will involve variations of fundamental examples. As often as possible in our discussion, we shall include industrial examples to illustrate applications of the principles being covered.

It is advantageous to letter the significant points and lines that are used in the solution of intersection problems, as shown in the examples that follow. It is unnecessary to letter each and every point, but key points should be labeled to clarify construction and projection. Guidelines

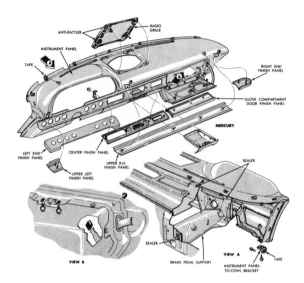

and constructions should be drawn very lightly to avoid the need for erasure upon completion of the problems.

7–2 INTERSECTION OF A PLANE AND A PRISM

One of the more common types of intersection is the intersection of a plane with a prism, as shown in Fig. 7–2.

Given: This is a special case in which the plane appears as an edge in the side view, thus per-

mitting the application of the piercing-point principles covered in Articles 4–11 and 4–12.

Step 1: The lateral corners of the prism intersect the edge view of the plane at points 1′, 2′, 3′, and 4′. These points are projected to their respective lines in the front view.

Step 2: The points 1′, 2′, 3′, and 4′ are connected to form the line of intersection in the front view. Visibility of the line of intersection on the prism can be determined in the front view by inspecting the top view. The surface

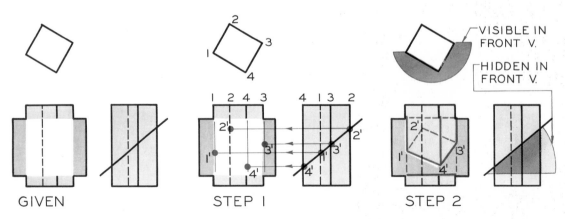

Fig. 7–2. Intersection of a plane and a prism.

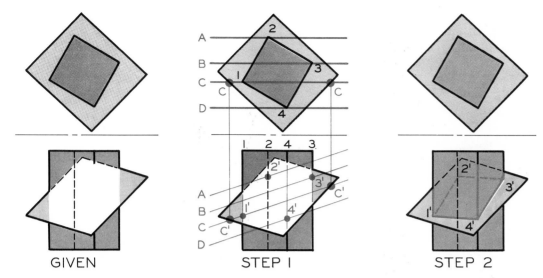

Fig. 7–3. Intersection of an oblique plane and a prism.

area shown in the top view will appear visible in the front view. The back surface will be hidden in the front view. Inspection of the right side view indicates that portions of the prism will be hidden by the plane in the front view. The lines on the prism shown lying within the hidden zone are invisible in the front view and are therefore represented by dashed lines.

A general case of intersection between a plane and a prism is shown in Fig. 7–3. The lateral corners of the prism project true length in the front view and the plane appears foreshortened in both views.

Given: The top and front views of an oblique plane and a prism. We are required to locate the line of intersection between the two figures.

Step 1: Four vertical cutting planes are passed through the four corner points of the vertical prism in the horizontal view. These planes are constructed through to the lateral corners of the prism, and can be drawn in any direction in the top view. The projections of cutting planes *A, B, C,* and *D* are located on the front view of the plane. *Example:* Since line 4 lies in vertical cutting plane *D,* the line must intersect the plane at point 4′, where the front view of cutting plane *D* crosses line 4. All piercing points of the

lateral edges are located in the front view in this manner.

Step 2: The line of intersection between any two planes is a straight line; therefore, the piercing points 1′, 2′, 3′ and 4′ are connected to form the line of intersection. Visibility is found in the front view by inspection of the top view and is indicated by solid and dashed lines as shown in Fig. 7–3.

The general case of the intersection between an oblique plane and an oblique prism is shown in Fig. 7–4. Since both the plane and the prism are oblique in the given views, neither the plane nor any of the planes of the prism appears as an edge. This problem can be solved in the same manner as the example in Fig. 7–2, if a view can be found where the plane projects as an edge. This view can be found in a primary auxiliary view by taking the point view of a line on the plane by projection from either view. The lateral edges of the prism do not appear true length in the auxiliary view, but this does not complicate the problem. In the figure, points 1, 2, and 3 are located in the auxiliary view where the corner edges of the prism intersect the plane. These points are projected to the top and front views as shown. Visibility is deter-

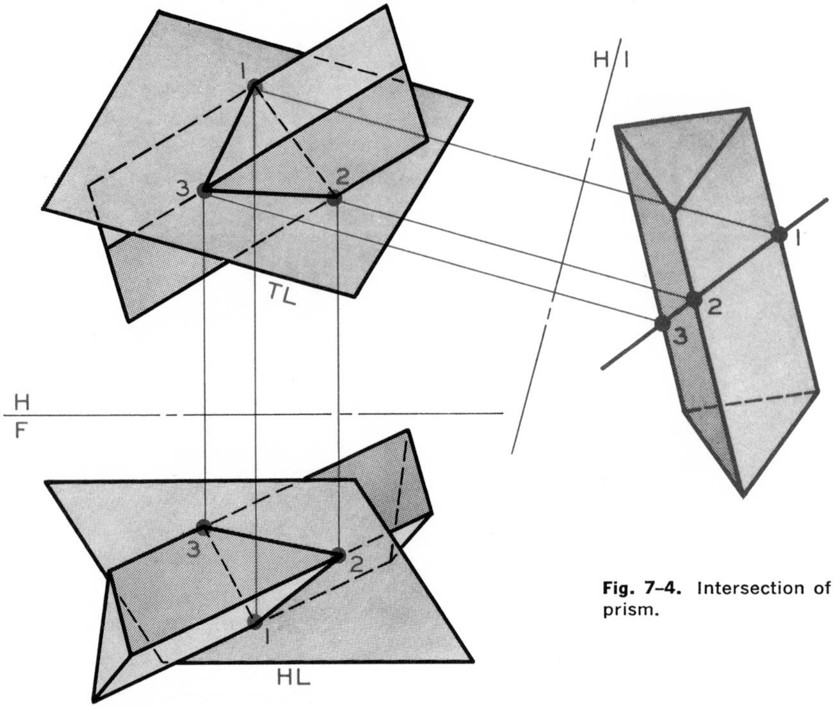

Fig. 7–4. Intersection of an oblique plane and an oblique prism.

Fig. 7–5. Many examples of intersections can be seen in this truck body.   (Courtesy of LeTourneau-Westinghouse Company.)

mined in both views by inspection. Principles of visibility can be reviewed in Article 3–12.

The truck body and bed shown in Fig. 7–5 illustrate a number of applications of intersections of planes and prisms. These intersections were determined prior to the development of the sheet-metal shapes which were used to form the body of the truck and to add strength to its design.

7–3 INTERSECTION BETWEEN PRISMS

The intersection between two prisms can be found by applying the principles that were used to find the intersection between a single plane and a prism in the preceding article. Prisms are composed of planes; consequently, it is possible to work with each plane individually until all lines of intersection are found. An example is solved by steps in Fig. 7–6.

FIGURE 7–6. INTERSECTION BETWEEN TWO PRISMS

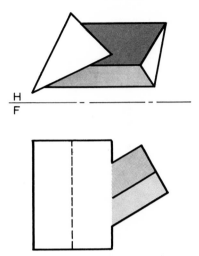

Given: The top and front views of two prisms.
Required: The line of intersection between the two prisms in both views with visibility indicated.
References: Articles 7–2 and 7–3.

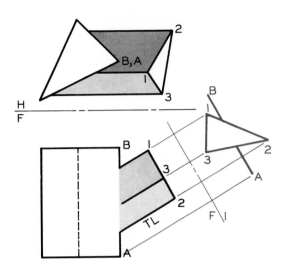

Step 1: Construct the end view of the inclined prism by projecting an auxiliary view from the front view. Show only line *AB*, the corner line of the vertical prism, in the auxiliary view because this is the only critical line. Letter the points.

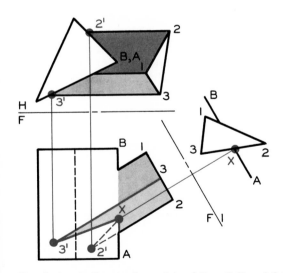

Step 2: Locate the piercing points of lines 2–2' and 3–3' in the top view and project them to the front view to the extension of the corner lines. It is rather obvious that a line connecting points 2' and 3' will not be a straight line, but will bend around the corner line *AB*. The point where this line intersects the corner is found to be point *X* in the primary auxiliary. Project it back to the front view.

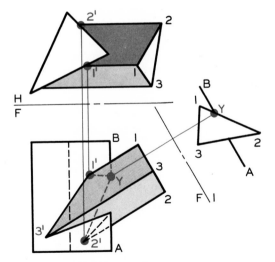

Step 3: It can be seen in the primary auxiliary view that line 1'–2' bends around corner line *AB* at point *Y*. Draw line 1'–*Y*–2' in the front view. This line is found to be invisible in the front view by inspection of the primary auxiliary view. Draw line 1'–3' as a visible straight line; it does not bend around a corner.

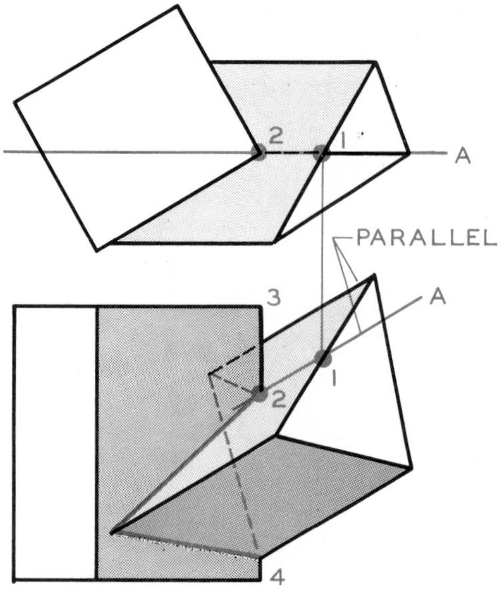

Fig. 7-7. Intersection between prisms by projection.

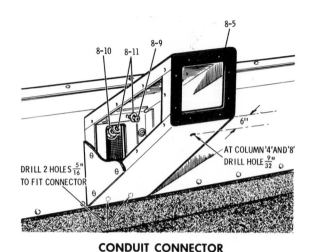

CONDUIT CONNECTOR

Fig. 7-8. This conduit connector was designed through the use of the principles of intersection of a plane and a prism. (Courtesy of Federal Aviation Agency.)

The top and front views of two intersecting prisms are given, and we are required to find their lines of intersection. The surfaces of one prism appear as edges in the top view, which makes it possible to see where the corner edges of the other prism intersect. It is necessary to draw an auxiliary view (step 1) in order to find the relationship between line *AB* and the end view of the prism, since two of the lines of intersection must bend around this corner line. The points of intersection, 3' and 2', are found in the top view in step 2, and then are projected to the front view. Point *X*, the point where line 2'–3' bends around line *AB*, is found in the auxiliary view and projected to the front view. Line 2'–*X*–3' is completed in the front view and visibility is indicated. The remaining lines of intersection are found, as explained in step 3, by repeating this procedure.

An alternative method of finding the line of intersection between two prisms is illustrated in Fig. 7-7. Vertical cutting plane *A* is passed through the point view of corner line 3-4 in the top view, and points 1 and 2 are established on

the second prism. Since the cutting plane is parallel to the corner edges of the upper surface of the oblique prism, line 1–2 will be drawn parallel to these sides in the front view, where it is found to intersect line 3–4 at point 2. Point 2 is the point where the line of intersection bends around corner line 3–4. The other piercing points are found in the manner described in Fig. 7-6.

The conduit connector shown in Fig. 7-8 is an example of the intersection of planes and prisms. This connector is designed to intersect an oblique wall at an angle.

7-4 INTERSECTION OF A PLANE AND A CYLINDER

The catalytic cracking unit shown in Fig. 7-9 illustrates many intersections of cylindrical shapes with geometric forms. Cylinders are fundamental shapes that are used extensively in processing plants of this type and have many engineering applications in all other industries as well.

Fig. 7–9. Many intersections of cylinders and planes can be seen in this refinery. (Courtesy of Humble Oil and Refining Company.)

A special case of a plane intersecting a cylinder is shown in Fig. 7–10. The plane appears as an edge in the side view.

Given: The principal views of a plane and a cylinder. We are required to find the line of intersection between these intersecting forms.

Step 1: The line of intersection is located in the front view by finding the piercing points with the plane of a number of lines lying on the surface of the cylinder. Four example points, 1, 2, 3, and 4, are found in the front view by projection from the top and side views. Other piercing points should be located in this same manner so that the line of intersection can be found accurately.

Step 2: Visibility is determined as indicated in the figure, to complete the solution of the problem.

A number of planes intersecting cylinders are shown in Fig. 7–11. This is a model of a refinery that has been constructed to analyze the

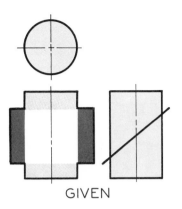

GIVEN

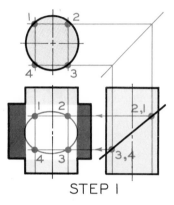

STEP I

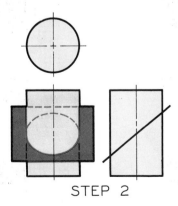

STEP 2

Fig. 7–10. Determining the line of intersection of a plane and a cylinder.

Fig. 7–11. Models are sometimes used to refine a design of a complicated installation. Cylindrical shapes are prominent in this design. (Courtesy of Standard Oil Company of New Jersey.)

relationships of the components and to serve as a guide during construction.

A similar problem is solved in Fig. 7–12, in which the plane is oblique in the principal views.

Given: The top and front views of a cylinder which is intersected by an oblique plane. We are required to find the line of intersection between the two geometric forms.

Step 1: Vertical cutting planes are passed through the top view of the cylinder to establish lines on its surface and lines on the plane. *Example:* Points 1 and 2 are found to lie on plane C and on the surface of the cylinder in the top view. These points are projected to the front view, where they lie on the line of intersection of cutting plane C and the oblique plane. Additional points are found in the same manner until the total line of intersection is found.

Step 2: The piercing points found in step 1 are connected to form an elliptical line of intersection. The visibility is determined as indicated in the figure, to complete the problem solution.

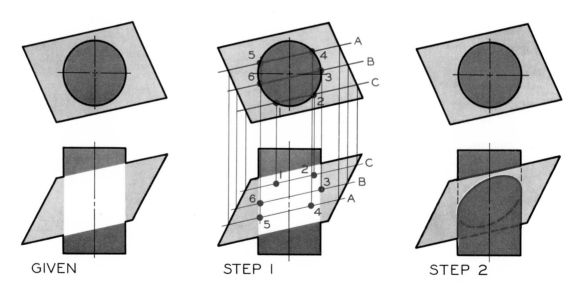

GIVEN   STEP I   STEP 2

Fig. 7–12. Determining the line of intersection between an oblique plane and a cylinder.

Fig. 7–13. Determining the line of intersection between an oblique plane and an oblique cylinder.

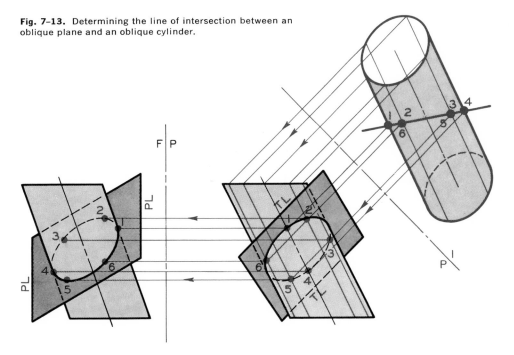

The general case for the intersection between an oblique plane and an oblique cylinder is shown in Fig. 7–13, in which the cylinder does not appear true length, and the plane does not appear as an edge. The line of intersection between these forms is determined by finding an edge view of the plane in a primary auxiliary view, where the projection of the cylinder is foreshortened. Cutting planes are used to establish lines on the surface of the cylinder in the primary auxiliary view. These lines are found to intersect the edge view of the plane at points 1, 2, 3, 4, 5, and 6. The lines on the surface of the cylinder are projected from the auxiliary view to the profile view. Each of the points of intersection found in the auxiliary view is projected to its respective line in the profile view. These points are connected to establish the elliptical line of intersection. Visibility is shown. The line of intersection is found in the front view by transferring measurements of points from the primary auxiliary view to the front view using dividers.

Aircraft designs require the solution of many intersection problems because of the many intersecting geometric forms. Examples of intersections can be seen in the F-105 shown in Fig. 7–14. In addition to the intersections made by the tail assembly and the wings with the fuselage, the cockpit represents the principle of a cone intersecting an approximate cylinder.

Fig. 7–14. The F-105 fighter-bomber is composed of many intersections between a variety of geometric shapes. (Courtesy of Republic Aviation Corporation.)

FIGURE 7–15.   INTERSECTION BETWEEN A CYLINDER AND A PRISM

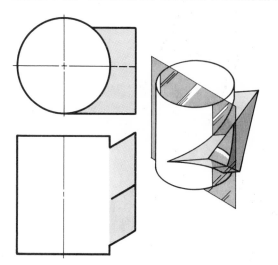

Given: The top and front views of an intersecting cylinder and prism.
Required: Find the line of intersection between the cylinder and prism.
Reference: Article 7–5.

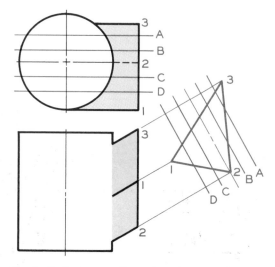

Step 1: Project an auxiliary view of the triangular prism from the front view to show three of its surfaces as edges. Pass frontal cutting planes through the top view of the cylinder and project them to the auxiliary view. The spacing between the planes is equal in both views.

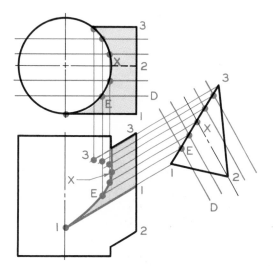

Step 2: Locate points along the line of intersection of the cylinder and plane 1–3 in the top view and project them to the front view. The intersection of these projectors with those coming from the auxiliary view establishes points on the line of intersection in the front view. *Example:* Point *E* on cutting plane *D* is found in the top and primary auxiliary views and projected to the front view where the projectors intersect. Point *X* on the center line is the point where visibility changes from visible to hidden in the front view.

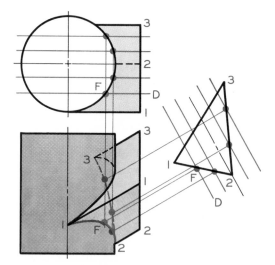

Step 3: Determine the remaining points of intersection by using the same cutting planes. Point *F* is shown in the top and primary auxiliary views and is projected to the front view on line of intersection 1–2. Connect the points and determine visibility. Judgment should be used in spacing the cutting planes so that they will produce the most accurate representation of the line of intersection.

7–5 INTERSECTION BETWEEN A CYLINDER AND A PRISM

A series of cutting planes are used in Fig. 7–15 to establish lines that lie on the surfaces of the cylinder and the prism. Since these lines lie in a common cutting plane, they will intersect where they cross in the views of projection. A primary auxiliary view is necessary to locate the lines on the surface of the prism in the front view (step 1). Rather than attempting to find the lines of intersection of two or more planes simultaneously, we shall analyze each plane independently. The line of intersection is projected from the edge view of plane 1–3 in the auxiliary view to the front view in step 2. A plane intersects a curved surface with a curved line. Note that the change in visibility of a line passing around a cylinder in the front is found to be point X in the top view. Step 3 is a continuation of this system of locating points until the final line of intersection is found with the visibility shown.

A practical example of intersections such as we have been discussing can be seen in an electric coffee pot. The lines of intersection made by the spout and handle with the cylindrical body of the container can be determined by constructing a series of horizontal cutting planes and projecting points of intersections to the other views. Determining these lines of intersection is a preliminary step in designing the components for accurate assembly.

7–6 INTERSECTION BETWEEN TWO CYLINDERS

The intersection between the two cylinders shown in Fig. 7–16 is found with the cutting-plane method. Frontal cutting planes are drawn in the top view to establish points common to each cylinder. For example, the locations of points 1 and 2 in the front view are determined by the intersections of the projectors coming from the top and primary auxiliary views where plane D intersects the cylinders. These points are on the line of intersection in the front view. The trace of the cutting plane D is shown in the front view to illustrate the path of the cutting plane. Additional points are found and con-

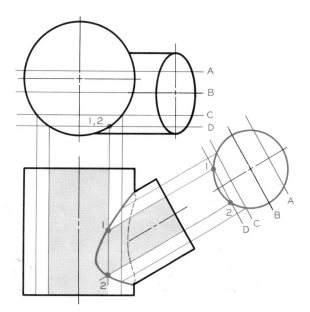

Fig. 7–16. Determining the intersection between cylinders.

Fig. 7–17. Many intersections between cylinders can be seen in this gas processing plant. (Courtesy of Humble Oil and Refining Company.)

nected to find the complete line of intersection. Visibility is indicated in the front view.

Many intersections between cylinders are shown in Fig. 7–17, in which a thermometer at an Oklahoma gas-processing plant is being checked. Intersections of this type must be found to permit the shapes to be formed for proper joining on the site.

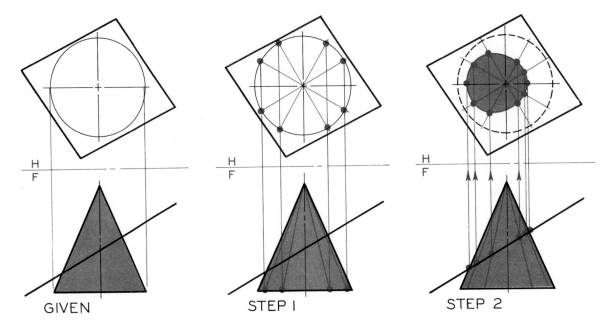

Fig. 7–18. Determining the line of intersection between a plane and a cone.

7-7 INTERSECTION BETWEEN A PLANE AND A CONE

A cone is a geometric shape which is used in many engineering designs in combination with other forms. The determination of the intersection of a plane with a cone is shown in Fig. 7–18.

Given: The top and front views of a cone and a plane, with the plane appearing as an edge in the front view. We are required to find the line of intersection between the plane and cone.

Step 1: A series of elements is drawn in the top view on the surface of the cone. These elements are projected from the top view of the base to the front view of the base, and their projected points are connected with the apex in both views.

Step 2: The top view of the line of intersection is found by connecting in sequential order the piercing points of the elements of the cone, which are projected from the front view. The front view of the line of intersection coincides with the edge view of the plane.

A cone and an oblique plane are given in Fig. 7–19, in which the line of intersection is determined with a series of cutting planes.

Given: The top and front views of a plane and cone. We are required to find the line of intersection between the two.

Step 1: A series of horizontal cutting planes is passed through the cone perpendicular to its axis, to cut circular sections in the top view of the cone and lines on the plane. Points 1 and 2 have been constructed to illustrate the method of locating points on the line of intersection. Cutting plane *A* cuts circle *A* in the top view and line *DE* on the plane. Since each of these lies in the same plane, points 1 and 2 are points of intersection of this interval of circle *A* and line *DE* in the top view.

Step 2: Additional points are found by projecting from planes *B* and *C*. These points are connected sequentially to form the lines of intersection in the top and front views as shown. Visibility is indicated.

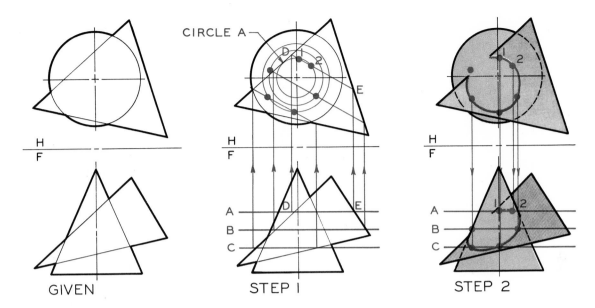

Fig. 7–19. Determining the line of intersection between an oblique plane and a cone.

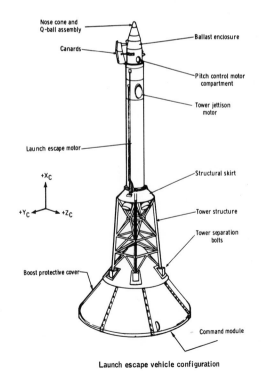

Fig. 7–20. Intersections with a conical shape were solved in designing the launch escape vehicle. (Courtesy of the National Aeronautics and Space Administration.)

Launch escape vehicle configuration

The cutting-plane method could have been used to solve the example shown in Fig. 7–18 as an alternative method.   Most descriptive geometry problems have more than one method of solution.

Figure 7–20 illustrates the utilization of conical shapes in the configuration of a launch escape vehicle.   Points of intersection, as well as lines of intersection, were determined in the final refinement of this spacecraft.

7-8 INTERSECTION BETWEEN A CONE AND A PRISM

A primary auxiliary view is drawn in Fig. 7–21 to show the lateral planes of the prism as edges so that the line of intersection between the prism and cone may be found. Cutting planes that radiate from the apex of the cone in the

FIGURE 7–21. INTERSECTION BETWEEN A CONE AND A PRISM

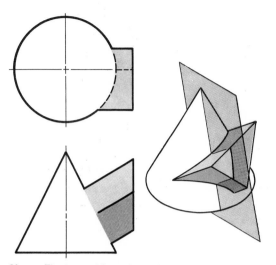

Given: The top and front views of a cone intersecting with a prism.

Required: Find the line of intersection between the cone and prism and determine visibility.

Reference: Article 7–8.

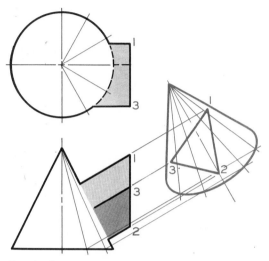

Step 1: Construct a primary auxiliary view to obtain the edge views of the lateral surfaces of the prism. In the auxiliary view pass cutting planes through the cone which radiate from the apex to establish elements on the cone. Project the elements to the principal views.

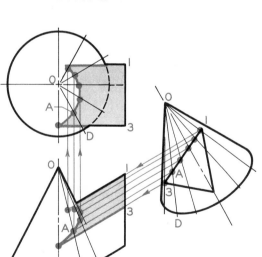

Step 2: Locate the piercing points of the cone's elements with the edge view of plane 1–3 in the primary view and project them to front and top views. *Example:* Point A lies on element OD in the primary auxiliary, so it is projected to the front and top view of element OD. Locate other points along the line of intersection in this manner.

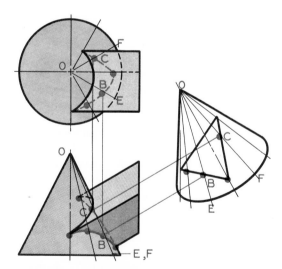

Step 3: Locate the piercing points where the conical elements intersect the edge views of the other planes of the prism in the primary auxiliary. *Example:* Point B is found on OE in the primary auxiliary and is projected to the front and top views of OE. Show visibility in each view after the location of a sufficient number of points.

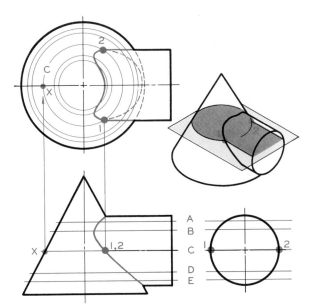

Fig. 7–22. Intersection between a cone and a cylinder.

Fig. 7–23. This electrically operated distributor illustrates intersections between a cone and a series of cylinders. (Courtesy of GATX.)

primary auxiliary view are used to establish lines lying on the surface of the cone and the surface of the prism, as shown in step 1. Inspection of the auxiliary view in step 2 shows that point *A* lies on cutting plane *OD*. Point *A* is projected to the front and top views of element *OD*, which was established on the surface of the cone by the cutting plane.

Other piercing points are found by repeating this system on the other two planes of the prism in step 3. All projections originate in the auxiliary view, where the cutting planes and the planes of the prism appear as edges.

The horizontal cutting-plane method for finding the line of intersection between a cylinder and a cone is shown in Fig. 7–22. This is not a feasible method if the axis of the intersecting cylinder is not horizontal and the axis of the cone not vertical, since the sections cut by the cutting planes would be irregular in shape and would require the tedious plotting of many points.

An unusual example of cylinders intersecting a cone can be seen in Fig. 7–23. The lines of intersection between the cones of this distributor housing were determined through the use of the auxiliary view method, as illustrated in Fig. 7–21.

7–9 CONIC SECTIONS

Conic sections—the parabola, hyperbola, ellipse, and circle—are, in effect, intersections of a plane with a cone. These are basic mathematical figures that can be found graphically as well as mathematically. The graphical method of finding the line of intersection between the imaginary plane and the cone is illustrated in the following examples.

Parabola. The parabola is the line of intersection formed by a cutting plane that passes through the cone, making the same angle with the cone's base as with its elements, as illustrated in Fig. 7–24A. This figure can be described mathematically as a plane curve, each point of which is equidistant from a directrix (a straight line) and its focal point.

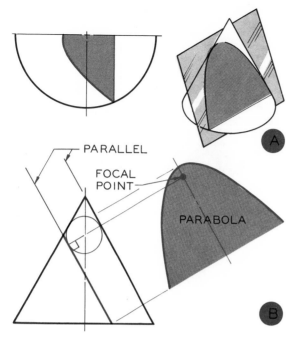

Fig. 7–24. Constructing a parabolic section of a cone.

Fig. 7–25. This tracking antenna is an application of a parabolic shell. (Courtesy of Ryan Aeronautics.)

The edge view of the cutting plane is drawn in the front view of the cone in part B of the figure, and it is projected to the top view by using a series of horizontal cutting planes, as introduced in Fig. 7–19. Having the top view of the line of intersection, it is now possible to find the true-size view of the parabola by a primary auxiliary view that is projected perpendicularly from the edge view of the cutting plane. The circle drawn at the apex of the cone represents a sphere that is drawn tangent to the cone and to the edge view of the parabola. The point of tangency of the sphere with the edge view of the parabola locates the focal point of the parabola. All lines entering the open end of the parabola parallel to its axis of symmetry will be reflected to a common point called the focal point. This shape is used for light reflectors, in which the bulb is located at the focal point, resulting in emission of parallel beams of light from the parabola. It is also used in the design of huge tracking antennas which send radio signals millions of miles into space and receive signals from satellites in space (Fig. 7–25).

The equation of a parabola can be written in the following form:

$$y = ax^2 + bx + c, \qquad \text{when} \quad a \neq 0.$$

When the parabola's equation is known, it can be plotted on grid paper by substituting values for x and y.

Hyperbola. The hyperbola is the line of intersection that is formed by a cutting plane which is passed through a cone in a manner such that it intersects the cone's base at an angle of 90° or less and makes an angle greater than the angle made by the elements with the base. Figure 7–26A illustrates a hyperbola constructed by the intersection of a cutting plane with two cones.

The edge view of the cutting plane is drawn in the front view of part B of the figure. The line of intersection of this cutting plane is found in the top view by using horizontal cutting planes, as shown in Fig. 7–19. An auxiliary view, a right side view in this case, is used to find the true size of the hyperbola. A circle is constructed at the apex of the cone to be tangent to the hyperbola and to the sides of the cone in the front view. The point where the circle is tangent to the plane is the focal point.

A hyperbola is defined as the path of a point which moves in a direction such that the difference of its distances from the two focal points is constant. Its mathematical equation is written in the following form:

$$\frac{x^2}{a^2} - \frac{y^2}{b^2} = 1, \quad \text{where} \quad a, b \neq 0.$$

Ellipse. The line of intersection of a plane that cuts across the axis of a cone at an angle other than 90° above the base is an ellipse (Fig. 7–27). An ellipse is the path of a point which is moving in such a way that the sum of the distances from two focal points is a constant.

The edge view of the cutting plane is passed through the cone in part B of the figure, and the top view of the line of intersection is found by projecting points which are established by the projections of horizontal cutting planes to the top view. The auxiliary view results in a true-size view of the plane of the ellipse. The focal points are located by drawing two circular arcs in the front view which represent spheres that are tangent to the cone and to the plane of the ellipse. The points where the spheres are tangent to the ellipse are the focal points. These are projected to the auxiliary view.

An ellipse is also formed by passing an oblique plane through the axis of a cylinder at an angle other than 90°. This principle is employed in experimental designs of ditches at the sides of highways which are to lessen the impact of cars leaving the highway at an angle at high speeds (Fig. 7–28). Mathematics and the laws of motion can be applied to determine the effect on acceleration and deceleration caused by the curvature of the bottom of the ditch. The actual path of the car can be plotted graphically in an auxiliary view, which would show the true size of the plane of the elliptical path.

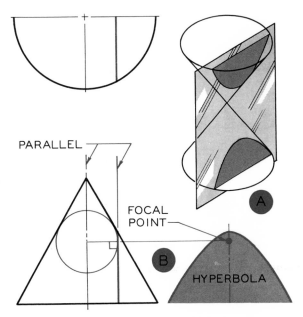

Fig. 7–26. Constructing a hyperbolic section of a cone.

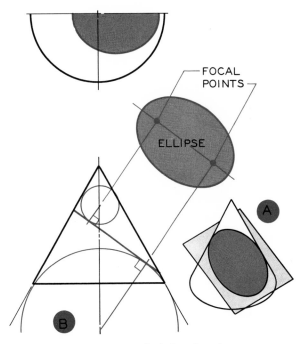

Fig. 7–27. Constructing an elliptical section of a cone.

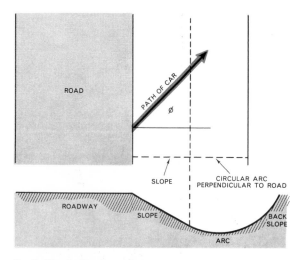

Fig. 7–28. A side ditch which has a circular cross section causes a wayward car to assume an elliptical path. This ditch configuration is effective in safely decelerating the vehicle. (Courtesy General Motors Corporation.)

The equation of the ellipse can be written in the following form:

$$\frac{x^2}{a^2} + \frac{y^2}{b^2} = 1, \quad \text{where} \quad a, b \neq 0.$$

When the equation is written in this form, a and b are equal to the major and minor diameters of the ellipse, respectively.

Circle. The line of intersection of a plane that is passed through a cone perpendicular to its axis is a circle (Fig. 7–29A). The circle is the path of a point which is moving in a direction such that its distance from the center is a constant. Its equation is written in the following form:

$$\frac{x^2}{r^2} + \frac{y^2}{r^2} = 1, \quad \text{where} \quad r \neq 0.$$

In this form, r is equal to the radius of the circle. The circular intersection formed by the cutting plane is shown in Fig. 7–29B.

7–10 INTERSECTION BETWEEN A PYRAMID AND A PRISM

The intersection between a prism and pyramid can be found by a method similar to that used in Fig. 7–21. An auxiliary view is constructed to show the lateral planes of the prism as edges in step 1 of Fig. 7–30. Cutting planes are drawn to radiate from apex 0 through the corner edges of the prism in the auxiliary view (step 2). Lines 0A and 0B are found in the principal views by projection. The lateral edges of the prism are projected to these lines in steps 2 and 3 to find piercing points, which are connected to determine the line of intersection. A pictorial located adjacent to step 1 illustrates the cutting-plane principle used in solving this intersection problem.

The intersection between a horizontal prism and a pyramid is determined in Fig. 7–31 through the use of the horizontal cutting-plane method. An auxiliary view is projected from the top view to find the edge views of the lateral surfaces of the prism. Horizontal cutting planes are passed through the front and auxiliary

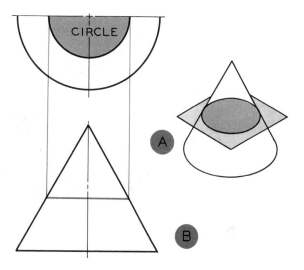

Fig. 7–29. Constructing a circular section of a cone.

FIGURE 7-30. INTERSECTION BETWEEN A PRISM AND A PYRAMID

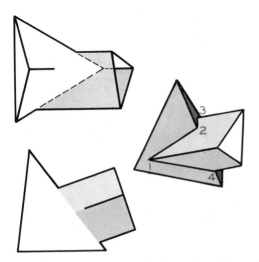

Given: Top and front views of a prism intersecting a pyramid.
Required: Find the line of intersection between the two geometric shapes.
Reference: Article 7-10.

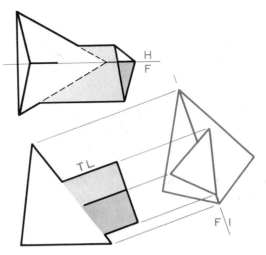

Step 1: Find the edge view of the surfaces of the prism by projecting an auxiliary view from the front view. Project the pyramid into this view also. Only the visible surfaces need be shown in this view.

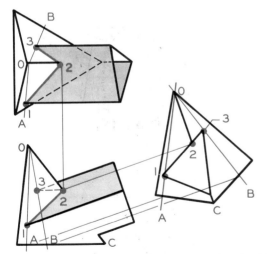

Step 2: Pass planes *A* and *B* through apex 0 and points 1 and 3 in the auxiliary view. Project the intersections of the planes *OA* and *OB* on the surfaces of the pyramid to the front and top views. Project points 1 and 3 to *OA* and *OB* in the principal views. Point 2 lies on line *OC*. Connect points 1, 2, and 3 to give the intersection of the upper plane of the prism with the pyramid.

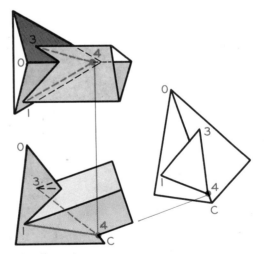

Step 3: Point 4 lies on line *OC* in the auxiliary view. Project this point to the principal views. Connect point 4 to points 3 and 1 to complete the intersections. Visibility is indicated. Note that these geometric shapes are assumed to be hollow as though constructed of sheet metal.

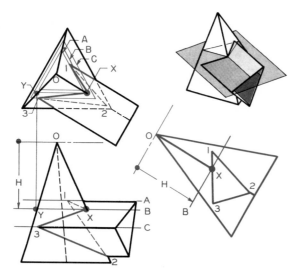

Fig. 7-31. Determining the line of intersection between a pyramid and a prism by horizontal cutting planes.

Fig. 7-32. Examples of intersections of a variety of geometric shapes can be seen in this compressor station installation. (Courtesy of Trunkline Gas Company.)

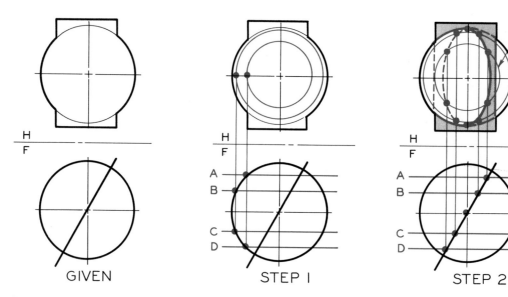

Fig. 7-33. Determining the intersection between a plane and a sphere.

views, where they appear as edges that are parallel to the horizontal. These planes will cut triangular sections in the top view which have sides that are parallel to the base of the pyramid. Note that these planes are drawn to pass through the given corner edges of the prism. Each corner edge is extended in the top view to the point of intersection with the section of the pyramid formed by the cutting plane passed through that particular line. Plane *B* is used to locate point *X* in the auxiliary view, which is where the line of intersection 1–*X*–3 bends at line 0-2. Visibility is determined in each view.

The intersection could have been found by using radial cutting planes, as in Fig. 7–30. As can be seen in these examples, the use of a systematic lettering procedure to plot each important point is helpful in intersection problems.

Figure 7–32 shows the interior of a compressor station where natural gas is compressed for transmission through pipelines over long distances. Many intersection problems are apparent in this complex facility. Complicated layouts of this type are presented in combinations of drawings and models to improve visualization and communication of spatial relationships.

7-11 INTERSECTION OF A SPHERE AND PLANE

The sphere is a shape that has many engineering applications, from petroleum storage tanks to the plotting of the paths of satellites traveling in space. An example of the determination of the intersection between a plane and a sphere is shown in Fig. 7–33.

Given: The top and front views of a sphere and an intersecting plane. We are required to find the line of intersection between the two.

Step 1: The intersecting plane appears as an edge in the front view. Horizontal cutting planes are passed through the sphere in the front view to establish circular sections in the top view.

Step 2: Points are projected from the cutting-plane intersections with the sphere in the front view to their respective circular sections in the

top view. The resulting line of intersection will be an ellipse in the top view, but a circle when the line of sight is perpendicular to the intersecting plane.

The ellipse could have been drawn with an ellipse template which was selected by measuring the angle between the edge view of the plane in the front view and the projections coming from the top view. The major diameter of the ellipse would be equal to the true diameter of the sphere, since the plane passes through the center of the sphere.

In the partially constructed Unisphere® shown in Fig. 7–34, the structural members represent intersections between imaginary cutting planes and the surface of the sphere. All the circles passing through the poles are equal in size, while those passing perpendicularly to the axis of the sphere vary in size. Straight members are used to approximate the spherical shape in which it appeared in its finished form (Fig. 7–35). The paths of the satellites, depicted by metal rings, can be projected to the surface to the globe to form circular paths that would appear as ellipses in the view shown.

Fig. 7-34. Structural members of this spherical shape represent the intersection between imaginary cutting planes and the sphere. (Courtesy of U. S. Steel Corporation.)

Fig. 7–35. The orbital paths depicted by metal rings which encircle the sphere can be projected to the surface of the sphere to locate support brackets. (Courtesy of U. S. Steel Corporation.)

Fig. 7–37. Tracking stations are used to project the path of a satellite to the spherical surface of the earth. (Courtesy of the Coast and Geodetic Survey.)

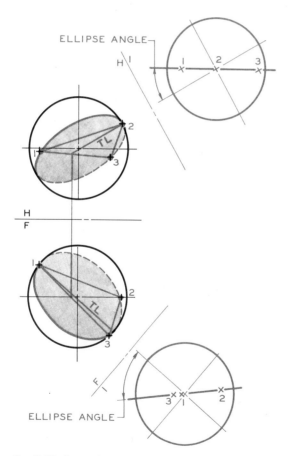

Fig. 7–36. Determining the location of an orbital path on a sphere.

The sphere in Fig. 7–36 has three points, 1, 2, and 3, located on its surface. A circle is to be drawn through these points so that it will lie on the surface of the sphere. This problem is solved by drawing the plane of the circle, plane 1–2–3, in the top and front views. The plane is found as an edge in the primary auxiliary view when projected from the top and front views as shown. The circle on the sphere cut by plane 1–2–3 will appear as an ellipse in the top and front views. The ellipse-guide angle for each view is found by measuring the angle made by the projectors with the edge view of the plane in the primary auxiliary view. The major diameters of the ellipse are drawn parallel to the true-length lines on plane 1–2–3 in the top and front views.

Satellites circling the earth are tracked by determining the lines of intersection made by the planes of their flight with the surface of the earth. Tracking stations (Fig. 7–37) receive signals from the satellite that give its location in space at a particular instant. Additional locations in space establish its plane of travel and, consequently, its projected path on the earth's surface. The intersection of the plane of a satellite's orbit with the surface of the earth is shown in Fig. 7–38. The path on the earth is found by projecting the orbital path toward the center of the earth to locate points *M* and *P*.

7-12 INTERSECTION BETWEEN A SPHERE AND A PRISM

A prism which intersects a sphere is shown in Fig. 7–39. Cutting planes are passed through the sphere in the top and side views so that they are parallel to the frontal plane; they appear as circles in the front view. In the side view, the intersections made by the cutting planes with the edges of the prism are projected to the front view, where they are found to intersect with their respective circles, i.e., those formed by the same cutting plane. *Example:* points 1 and 2 are found to lie on cutting plane *A* in the side view. These are projected to the front view to circle *A*, which was established by cutting plane *A*. Point *X* in the side view locates the point where the visibility of the intersection in the front view changes. Point *Y* in the side view is the point where the visibility of the intersection changes in the top view. Note that both these points lie on center lines of the sphere in the side view.

7-13 INTERSECTION BETWEEN TWO OBLIQUE CYLINDERS

To determine the line of intersection of two cylinders, as shown in Fig. 7–40, a plane must be drawn in space such that it is parallel to both cylinders. This will be the case if the plane contains lines that are parallel to the axes of each cylinder, as shown in step 1. It is necessary that the planes be passed through the top views of the intersecting cylinders as cutting planes; consequently, a line is constructed in the plane that is parallel to the edge view of the base planes of the cylinder in the front view. This line is projected to the top view, where its direction will represent the line of intersection of the cutting planes on the circular bases of the cylinders in the top view. A series of planes is passed through the bases, as shown in step 1, where the elements are formed on the surface of the cylinders parallel to their axes, as shown in step 2. Elements that lie in common cutting planes establish points on the line of intersection when they cross in the top view. A systematic lettering procedure will assist in plotting the points as they are found. The points are con-

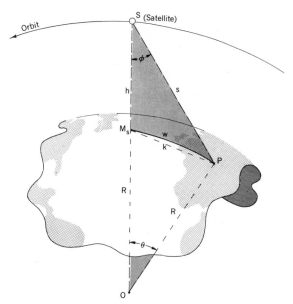

Fig. 7–38. The projection of a satellite's path to the surface of the earth. (Courtesy of the Coast and Geodetic Survey.)

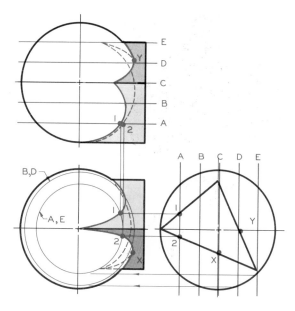

Fig. 7–39. Determining the intersection between a sphere and prism.

FIGURE 7–40. INTERSECTION BETWEEN OBLIQUE CYLINDERS

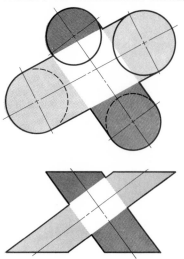

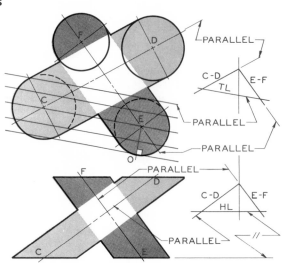

Given: The top and front views of two intersecting cylinders.
Required: Determine the line of intersection between the two cylinders in both views.
Reference: Article 7–13.

Step 1: Construct a triangular plane so that it will contain lines which are parallel to both axes of the cylinders. Draw a horizontal line in the front view of the triangular plane so that it lies in the base plane of the cylinders. Project this line to the triangular plane in the top view, where its direction is used as the direction for the cutting planes that will be drawn in the top view to pass parallel to the axes of the cylinders.

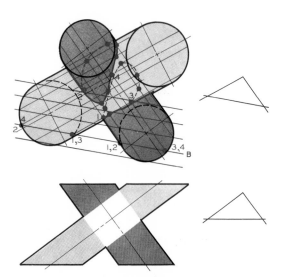

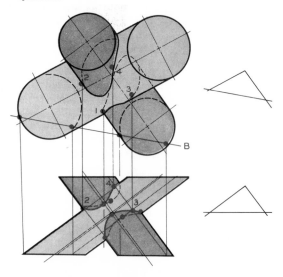

Step 2: Where the cutting planes intersect the bases of cylinders in the top view, elements are formed on the cylinders and they are parallel to the axes of each cylinder. Note that four elements are cut by each cutting plane. Where these common elements intersect, a point on the line of intersection is found. These points should be labeled, as are the four example points shown.

Step 3: Project the elements on the cylinders from the top view to the front view. The points found to lie on specific elements in the top view are projected to their respective elements in the front view. Several points have been projected as examples. Visibility in this view is determined by analysis of the top view.

Fig. 7–41. The intersection between these cylindrical shapes is an example of the principle covered in Article 7–13. (Courtesy of Ryan Aeronautical Company.)

nected in sequence to obtain the continuous lines of intersection shown in step 2 in the top view.

The elements on each cylinder are projected to the front view, where they will be parallel to the axes of both cylinders. The points on the lines of intersection lying on the cutting planes are projected to the front view and connected to form the desired lines of intersection. The visibility of each is determined by examining each pair of intersecting elements. If both elements are visible, their points of intersection will be visible. If only one element is visible, the point of intersection is hidden.

The ducts which intersect at unusual angles in Fig. 7–41 require the same type of analysis as that covered in Fig. 7–40. The lines of intersection were used to design the joints of the intersecting ducts.

7–14 INTERSECTING CONES

We are required to determine the line of intersection between the two cones shown in Fig. 7–42. A series of cutting planes is needed to

cut elements on each cone, which can be used to find piercing points on the lines of intersection. A plane drawn to contain a line that passes through both apexes of the cone and a line passing through both bases of the cones will cut elements in each cone. Such a plane is established in step 1. Five cutting planes are drawn in step 2, where line *OA* is a common side and the base lines radiate from point *O*. Elements established by the cutting planes are projected to their points of intersection. Note that cutting plane 3 is used to plot points *E*, *F*, *G*, and *H*. All points are connected in sequence to form the lines of intersection of the two cones in the top view.

The elements formed by the cutting planes are projected to the front view so that the front views of the points that have been projected from the top views may be located. Points *J* and *K* are projected to the front view as an example. Visibility is determined in each view by analyzing the elements that were used to plot the points. Both elements must be visible in a view before the point at their intersection can be visible.

7–15 SUMMARY

It can be seen from the examples given in this chapter that principles of intersection have many applications to engineering, technology, and science. Use of the principles of intersections involves most of the previously covered techniques of descriptive geometry and orthographic projection. Piercing points and visibility analysis can be reviewed in Chapter 3 to assist in a better understanding of intersections. Auxiliary views—primary and secondary—are used to find intersections of geometric shapes, as was covered in Chapters 4 and 5.

The fundamental principles covered in this chapter are basic to practically any problem that involves intersections. An attempt should always be made to identify an intersection in terms of its geometric elements. Perhaps several shapes are joined in combination to form the configuration of a design. The intersections will be easier to find if the problem is

FIGURE 7–42. INTERSECTING CONES

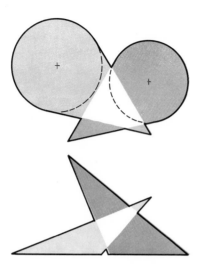

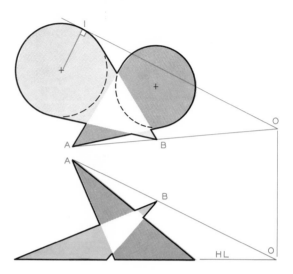

Given: The top and front views of two intersecting cones.
Required: Find the lines of intersection between the two cones in each view.
Reference: Article 7–14.

Step 1: Draw a line through apexes *A* and *B*, and extend it to point *O* on the plane of the bases of the two cones in the front view. Project line *ABO* to the top view, and draw line *O*–1 to intersect the two bases, as shown. This plane will cut elements on each cone, since the apexes lie on a common line. Note that line *OC* is tangent to cone *B*.

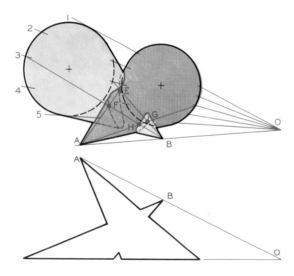

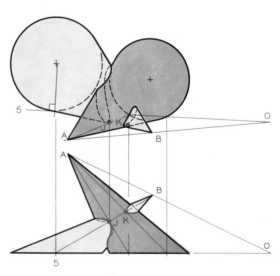

Step 2: Draw a series of planes with line *AO* common to each plane and to a second line in the horizontal plane of the cone bases. These cutting planes establish four elements on each cone, which are connected as illustrated where points *E, F, G,* and *H* are found at the intersection of common elements. Locate additional points and connect them to form the two lines of intersection.

Step 3: Project the elements used in the top view to the front view and project the points lying on them in the top view to the front views of these elements. Points *J* and *K* on plane *AO5* are projected to illustrate this technique of finding the line of intersection in the front view. Determine the visibility. Cutting plane *AO5* establishes only two points, since it is tangent to one of the cones.

treated as though it involved an intersection between two geometric elements, then two more, etc., in sequence, until the complete line is found.

The student must understand intersection principles before proceeding to Chapter 8, which deals with developing flat patterns that are used to fabricate products that are composed of geometric shapes. Many of these shapes will be intersected by other forms; consequently, the lines of intersection must be found before the patterns can be completed.

PROBLEMS

The problems for this chapter should be constructed from the given sketches with *instruments* on $8\frac{1}{2}'' \times 11''$ sheets, as illustrated in the accompanying figures. For laying out the problems on grid or plain paper, assume that each grid represents $\frac{1}{4}''$. All reference planes and figure points should be labeled, using $\frac{1}{8}''$ letters with guide lines. Solutions should be sufficiently noted and labeled to explain all construction. Refer to Article 1–12.

1. (A) In Fig. 7–43A find the intersection between the prism and the plane. (B) In part B of the figure find the intersection between the two prisms using the projection method. (C) In part C of the figure find the line of intersection by the projection method. Lay out the same problem on a separate sheet and solve it by the auxiliary-view method.

2. (A) In Fig. 7–44A find the intersection between the cylinder and the plane. (B) In part B of the figure find the intersection between the cylinder and the prism.

3. In Fig. 7–45A find the intersection between the two cylinders. In part B of the figure find the intersection between the two cylinders.

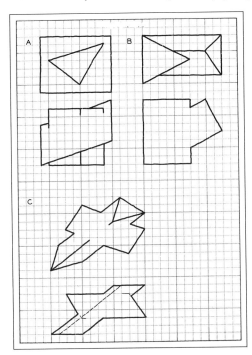

Fig. 7-43. Intersections of planes and prisms.

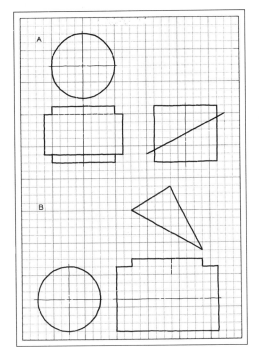

Fig. 7-44. Intersections of cylinders and planes.

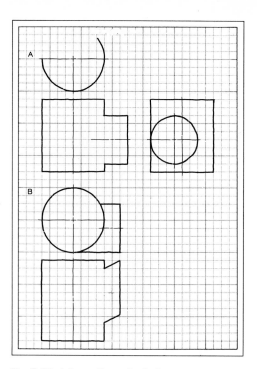

Fig. 7-45. Intersections of cylinders.

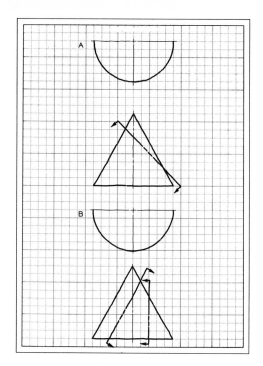

Fig. 7-46. Conic sections.

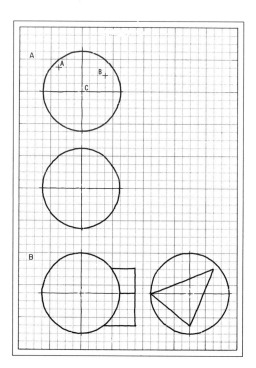

Fig. 7-47. Spherical intersections.

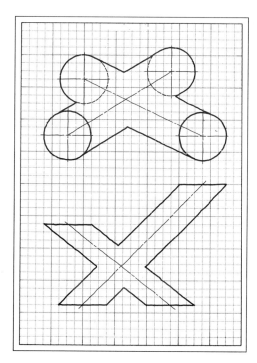

Fig. 7-48. Intersection between oblique cylinders.

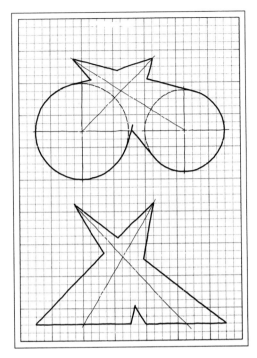

Fig. 7–49. Intersection between oblique cones.

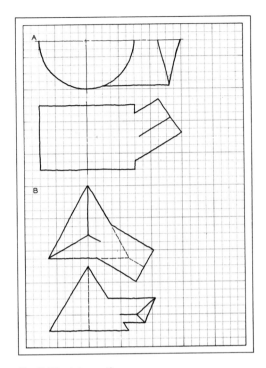

Fig. 7–50. Intersections.

4. (A) In Fig. 7–46A find the top view of the intersection formed by the cutting plane, and construct the auxiliary view of the section. What type of conic section is this? (B) In part B of the figure find the intersections formed by the cutting planes in the front view. Construct the sections indicated by the cutting planes. Identify the types of conic sections in each case.

5. (A) Two views of a sphere are given in Fig. 7–47A, in which points *A* and *B* are located on the upper surface and point *C* is located at the sphere's center. Find the line of intersection formed by a plane that passes through these

points and extends through the surface of the sphere. Show the line of intersection in all views. (B) In part B of the figure find the intersection between the prism and the sphere.

6. In Fig. 7–48 determine the line of intersection of the two oblique cylinders in both views.

7. Determine the lines of intersection of the two oblique cones in Fig. 7–49. Show these in both views and determine visibility.

8. Construct the lines of intersection in parts A and B of Fig. 7–50. Determine visibility and show in all views.

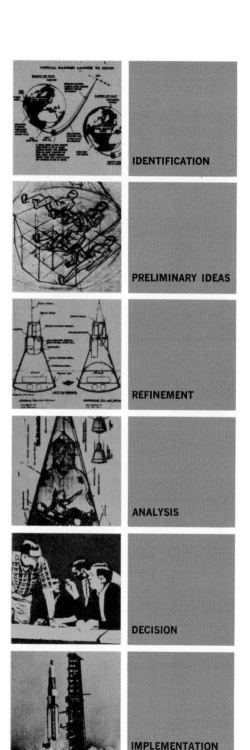

IDENTIFICATION

PRELIMINARY IDEAS

REFINEMENT

ANALYSIS

DECISION

IMPLEMENTATION

8
DEVELOPMENTS

8-1 INTRODUCTION

The Supersonic F–105 Thunderchief shown in Fig. 8–1 is an example of a highly complicated shape that has been formed with sections of flat sheet metal. This chapter is concerned with the geometric principles and techniques used in the fabrication of such a shape from flat materials.

Creating a flat pattern for a three-dimensional object involves a *development* ("unfolding") of the object. Developments are closely related to the intersections we studied in Chapter 7, since provision for the joining of component parts must be made in the flat pattern of an object.

We may make developments for all applications, from small, simple shapes made of thin sheet metal to sophisticated pieces of hardware such as space capsules, which must be fabricated within a high degree of accuracy. The model of the processing plant shown in Fig. 8–2 illustrates a wide variety of shapes that must be designed, developed, and specified by the designer. Whether the design is fabricated by bending flat metal or by casting a solid object, the designer must have a grasp of development principles. This chapter will cover the fundamentals of this area, and will relate these principles to industrial applications where possible.

8-2 DEVELOPMENT OF A PRISM

A cylinder or a prism (Fig. 8–3) can be laid out to result in either an inside or an outside pattern. An inside development is more frequently desired, because (1) most bending machines are designed to fold metal such that the markings are folded inward, and (2) markings and lines etched on the patterns will be hidden when the development is assembled into its finished

Fig. 8-1. The surface of this F-105 Thunderchief is an application of developed surfaces which were designed to conform to a specified shape. (Courtesy of Republic Aviation Corporation.)

Fig. 8-2. Many examples of intersections and developments can be seen in this model of a processing installation. (Courtesy of Bechtel Corporation.)

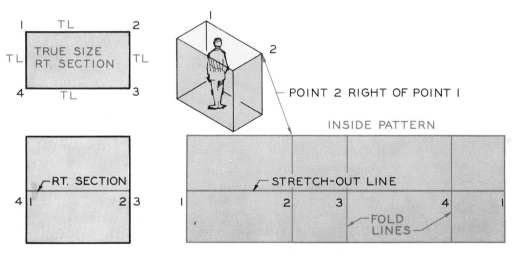

Fig. 8-3. The development of a rectangular prism to give an inside pattern.

form. Whether the pattern is an inside or an outside pattern will depend upon the material and the equipment being used. In any case, it is important that the pattern *always* be labeled as inside or outside when presented. The patterns in the following examples will be inside patterns, since these are the most common; however, the principles for finding inside patterns can be applied to outside patterns.

The following rules apply generally to cylinders and prisms. These should be reviewed as example problems are studied. The most important rule in developing patterns is that *all lines of a development must be true length*.

Rules for Developing Cylinders or Prisms

1. Find the view in which the right section appears as an edge.

2. Lay out the stretch-out line of the development parallel to the edge view of the right section.

3. Locate the distances between the lateral corner edges by measuring from the true-size views in the right section and transferring these measurements to the stretch-out line. Letter these points.

4. Construct the lateral fold lines perpendicular to the stretch-out line.

5. Establish the lengths of the fold lines by projecting from the view in which the right section appears as an edge.

6. Make sure that the line where the development will be spliced is the shortest line, so that the least amount of welding or joining effort will be required.

7. Connect all points in the proper sequence to give the complete pattern.

8. Verify that the point where the development ends is the same point as the beginning point on the right section.

9. Indicate by a note whether the development is an inside or an outside pattern.

These rules have been applied to the problem in Fig. 8–3. Note that the lateral fold lines of the prism are true length in the front view and that the right section appears as an edge in this view also. The stretch-out line is drawn parallel to the edge view of the right section, beginning with point 1. If an inside pattern is desired, it is necessary to select the point that lies to the right of point 1, since the development will be laid out in this direction. The observer assumes that he is inside the prism, as illustrated pictorially in Fig. 8–3, and that he is looking at the inside view of fold line 1. Note that the top view of the prism can be used for this analysis. Point 2 is seen to lie to the right of line 1 whereas line 4 is to the left; consequently, distance 1–2 is transferred from the top view to the stretch-out line, with point 2 to the right of point 1. Note that all lines on the surface of the right section are true length in the top view. Lines 2–3, 3–4, 4–1 are then laid out in sequence along the stretch-

out line. The length of each fold line is found by projecting its true length from the front view. The ends of the fold lines are connected to form the limits of the developed surface. Fold lines are drawn as thin lines on the development.

The body of the toaster shown in Fig. 8–4 is an example of the application of the principle of developments in the design of a household appliance. Construction is more economical when it consists of forming one continuous piece of material that is bent into shape than it is when the operation demands joining a series of sections together. The forms that are used for the pouring of concrete are applications of developments of a different type.

A prism with a beveled end can be developed in the same manner as was the example in Fig. 8–3, except that the lengths of the fold lines will have to be determined by projecting from the front view. In this case, the lines will be unequal in length, resulting in a pattern such as that shown in Fig. 8–5. The use of a lettering system will assist in identifying the points of projection, as shown in this example. Note that the right section is used for the direction of the stretch-out line and as a source of measurements for determining the space between fold lines.

The mammoth coal hauler in Fig. 8–6 was developed as a flat pattern and joined to form this finished shape. Regardless of the size of the problem, the principles of solution are identical. The material used in this example was sheet aluminum, which can support ten times its weight.

8–3 DEVELOPMENT OF OBLIQUE PRISMS

The standard views of an oblique prism may be presented in a preliminary sketch which must be analyzed for further refinement. For example, an inclined prism might not show the right section as an edge nor a surface area as true size in the standard views. If this is the case, an auxiliary view must be used to provide the additional information necessary to complete the development.

Fig. 8–4. The surface of this toaster is an application of the development of a rectangular shape. (Courtesy of General Electric Company.)

Fig. 8–6. The all-aluminum body of this coal hauler is an example of an industrial development application. (Courtesy of ALCOA.)

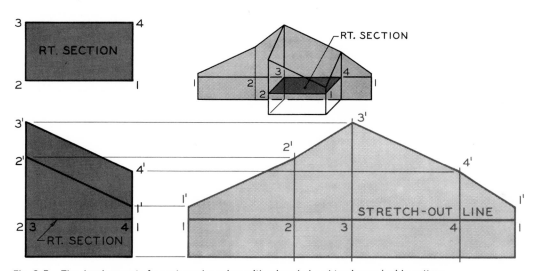

Fig. 8–5. The development of a rectangular prism with a beveled end to give an inside pattern.

A prism is shown inclined to the horizontal plane, but parallel to the frontal plane, in Fig. 8–7. The lateral corner edges of the prism appear true length in the front view, in which they are frontal lines. The right section can be drawn as an edge in the front view perpendicular to the fold lines. An auxiliary view of the edge view of the section will show the true size of the right section (step 1). The pattern is laid out in the conventional manner, which was covered in Article 8–2, and the stretch-out line is drawn parallel to the edge view of the right section in

the front view. The measurements between the fold lines are transferred from the true sizes of the right section to the development (step 2). The developments of the end pieces can be found by a secondary auxiliary view, which is projected perpendicular to the edge view of the end of the prism. These projections are drawn as part of the total pattern in the developed view.

A prism which does not project true length in either view, but which is oblique to the principal planes, can be developed as illustrated in

FIGURE 8–7. DEVELOPMENT OF AN OBLIQUE PRISM

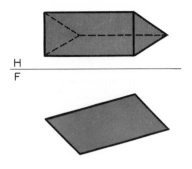

Given: The top and front views of an oblique prism.
Required: The inside pattern of the developed surface of the prism and the end sections.
Reference: Article 8–3.

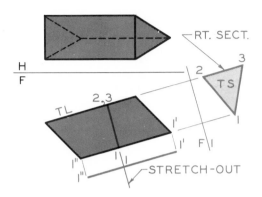

Step 1: The edge view of the right section will appear as perpendicular to the true-length axis of the prism in the front view. Determine the true-size view of the right section by constructing an auxiliary view. Draw the stretch-out line parallel to the edge view of the right section. Project bend line 1'–1'' as the first line of the development.

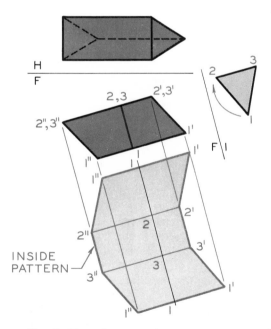

Step 2: Since the pattern is developed toward the right, beginning with line 1'–1'', the next point is found to be line 2'–2'' by referring to the auxiliary view. Transfer true-length lines 1–2, 2–3, and 3–1 from the right section to the stretch-out line to locate the elements. Determine the lengths of the bend lines by projection.

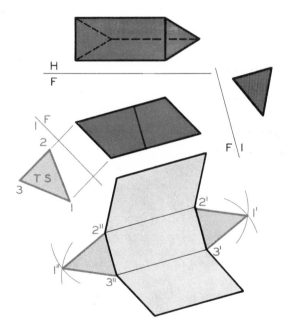

Step 3: Find the true-size views of the end pieces by projecting auxiliary views from the front view. Connect these surfaces to the development of the lateral sides to form the completed pattern. Fold lines are drawn with thin lines, while outside lines are drawn as regular object lines.

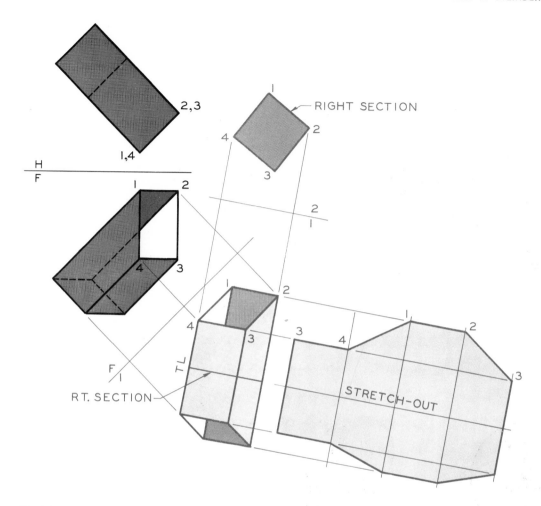

Fig. 8-8. The development of an inside pattern of an oblique prism.

Fig. 8-8. From the front view we find the true length of the lateral corners by projecting them to an auxiliary view in a direction perpendicular to that of the lateral corners in the front view. The right section will appear as an edge in the primary auxiliary view. The stretch-out line is drawn parallel to this edge view. The true size of the right section is found in an auxiliary projected perpendicularly from the edge view of the right section. The fold lines are located on the stretch-out line by measuring around the right section in the secondary auxiliary view.

The lengths of the fold lines are then projected to the development from the primary auxiliary view.

8-4 DEVELOPMENT OF CYLINDERS

Cylinders are basic shapes that are used extensively in practically all areas of technology. The large storage tanks shown in Fig. 8-9 are typical of the cylindrical developments that can be found in the petroleum industry. These tanks are efficient and economical vessels for

Fig. 8–9. Storage tanks are designed through the use of cylindrical developments. (Courtesy of Shell Oil Company.)

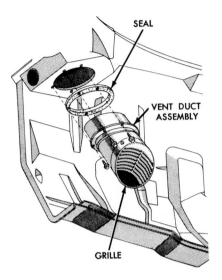

Fig. 8–11. This ventilator air duct was designed through the use of development principles. (Courtesy of the Ford Motor Company.)

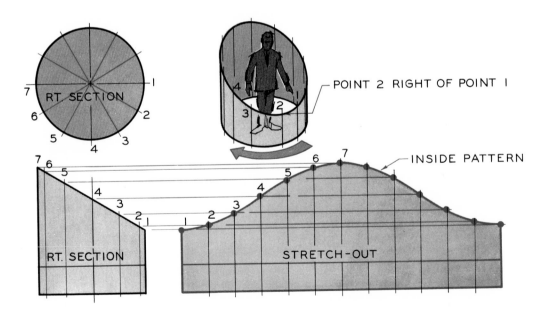

Fig. 8–10. The development of a cylinder.

storage of petroleum products. Note that these cylinders have no fold lines, since their surfaces are smooth and curving; however, they were developed by using a series of lines on their surface as though they were fold lines.

The example in Fig. 8–8 illustrates the manner in which an inside pattern of a cylinder is developed. The axis of the cylinder appears true length in the front view, which allows the right section to be seen as an edge, since it is perpendicular to the axis. The stretch-out line is drawn parallel to the edge view of the section, and point 1 is chosen as the beginning point, since it is on the shortest possible line on the surface. Since an inside pattern is desired, the observer must assume that he is standing inside the cylinder in the top view, as illustrated pictorially in Fig. 8–10. The pattern will be laid out to the right, so the observer is interested in determining which lines are to the right of point 1. The first point to the right of point 1 is point 2, which establishes the sequence of points to be followed in laying out the distances between the lines in the development along the stretch-out line. These distances are transferred from the true-size right section in the top view as chordal distances

to approximate the circumference around the cylinder. The closer the intervals between the lines on the right section, the closer the graphical solution will be to the theoretical circumference. If accuracy is a critical factor, the circumference can be determined mathematically, laid out true length along the stretch-out line, and divided into the number of divisions desired. The ends of the lines on the surface are projected from the top to the front view. The ends of these lines on the beveled end of the cylinder are projected to their respective lines in the developed view, where they are then connected with a smooth curve.

A practical application of this principle is shown in Fig. 8–11, in which an air-conditioning vent duct is shown as used on an automobile. This vent was developed through the use of the same principles as those covered in this article. The Hydra 5 test vehicle (Fig. 8–12) is composed of a number of cylindrical developments that required graphical solutions.

Gun ranges that are used to simulate meteoroid impact on spacecraft utilize cylindrical forms, as shown in Fig. 8–13. Other applications of cylindrical developments can be seen in the background of this laboratory.

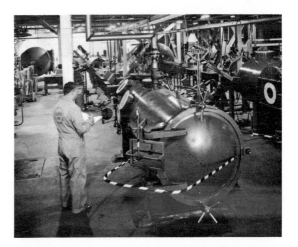

Fig. 8–12. Cylindrical developments were necessary in the design of the Hydra 5 launch vehicle. (Courtesy of the U. S. Navy.)

Fig. 8–13. Gun ranges, which are used to simulate meteoroid impact on aircraft, are examples of cylindrical developments. (Courtesy of Arnold Engineering Development Center.)

FIGURE 8–14. DEVELOPMENT OF AN OBLIQUE CYLINDER

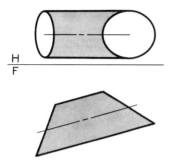

Given: The top and front views of an oblique cylinder.
Required: Find an inside development of the cylinder and its end pieces.
Reference: Article 8–5.

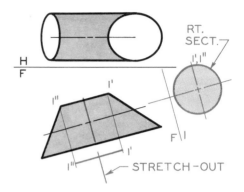

Step 1: The right section appears as an edge in the front view, in which it is perpendicular to the true-length axis. Construct an auxiliary view to determine the true size of the right section. Draw a stretch-out line parallel to the edge view of the right section. Locate element 1′–1″.

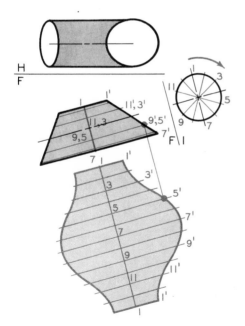

Step 2: Divide the true-size right section into equal points which represent the point views of elements on the cylinder's surface. Project these elements to the front view. Transfer measurements between the lines from the auxiliary view to the stretch-out line to locate the elements in the development. Determine the lengths of the elements by projection to complete the development.

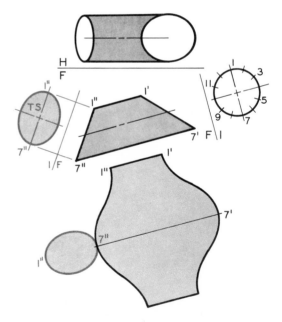

Step 3: The development of the end pieces will require auxiliary views that project these surfaces as ellipses, as shown for the left end. Attach this true-size ellipse to the pattern at a point on the pattern. Note that the line of departure for the pattern was made along line 1″–1′, the shortest element, for economy.

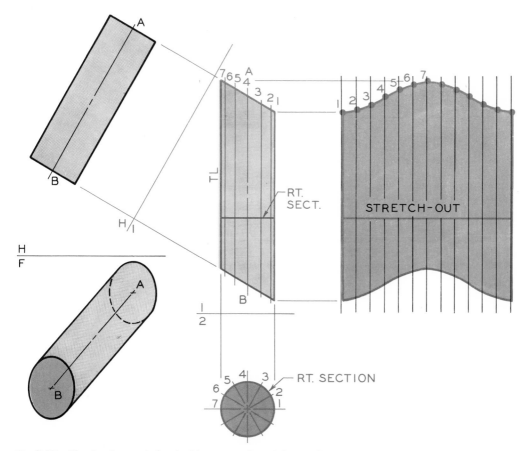

Fig. 8-15. The development of an inside pattern of an oblique cylinder.

8-5 DEVELOPMENT OF OBLIQUE CYLINDERS

The oblique cylinder in Fig. 8-14 appears true length in the front view, in which its right section projects as an edge that is perpendicular to its center line. The stretch-out line for the development is drawn parallel to the edge view of the right section (step 1). The true-size view of the right section is found in an auxiliary view. Lines lying on the surface of the cylinder are projected from the right section to the front view. These elements are spaced the same distance apart on the stretch-out line in the development view as they were in the right section in the auxiliary view. All element lengths are pro-

jected to the development from the front view, where they are true length. The ends of the elements are connected with a smooth curve (step 2). The true size of one elliptical end of the cylinder is found by auxiliary view, as shown in step 3. This shape is drawn attached to the development. The development of the opposite end can be found by auxiliary view in the same manner.

Figure 8-15 is an example of a cylinder that is oblique to the principal planes in both views. The edge view of the right section is found in an auxiliary view, where the elements on the surface of the cylinder project true length. The stretch-out line is drawn parallel to this

Fig. 8–16. Cylindrical developments are used to design electronic components. (Courtesy of ITT.)

Fig. 8–17. Wind tunnels are designed through the extensive application of cylindrical developments. (Courtesy of Arnold Engineering Development Center.)

edge view. The elements are separated on the stretch-out line by the distance between the point views of the elements in the secondary auxiliary view, where the right section appears true size. The lengths of the elements in the developments are found by projecting from the true-length view of the elements in the primary auxiliary view. These points are connected by a smooth curve. The elliptical development of the beveled end can be found by a secondary auxiliary view which is projected from the primary auxiliary view in a manner similar to that shown in step 3 of Fig. 8–14.

Applications of cylindrical developments vary in size from small to large. Cylindrical developments are necessary for the construction of electronic components such as those shown in Fig. 8–16. On the larger side, the 16′ wind tunnels shown in Fig. 8–17 are also examples of the application of development principles. Regardless of their size, however, all applications of cylindrical developments are solved in the same manner.

8–6 DEVELOPMENT OF PYRAMIDS

The development of a pyramid is given in Fig. 8–18 through a series of steps. Since all fold lines will have point 0 as a common point,

the stretch-out line will not be used on this type of problem; instead, a series of adjacent triangles will be drawn in the development.

Recall that *all lines* in a development must be true length. Lines 1–0 and 2–0 are revolved into the frontal plane in the top view so that their true length will be seen in the front view, as shown. All bend lines are equal in length, since the pyramid is a right pyramid; consequently, in the development line 1–0 is used as a radius for constructing an arc that will contain all corner points lying on the base of the pyramid. The lines of the base appear true length in the top view since the base is a horizontal plane. Distance 1–2 is measured in the top view and transferred to the development, where it is a chord on the arc from point 1 to point 2. Lines 2–3, 3–4, and 4–1 are found in the same manner. The bend lines are drawn with thin lines from the base to the apex, point 0.

A variation of this problem is given in Fig. 8–19, in which the pyramid has been truncated or cut at an angle to its axis. The development of the inside pattern is found in the same manner as covered previously; however, an additional step is required to establish the upper lines of the development. The development is first laid out as though it were a continuous pyramid from the apex 0, to the base. The true-

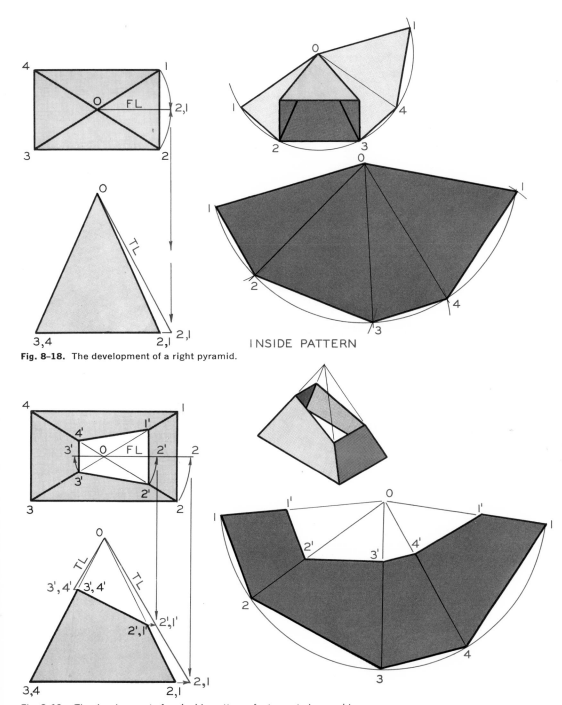

INSIDE PATTERN

Fig. 8-18. The development of a right pyramid.

Fig. 8-19. The development of an inside pattern of a truncated pyramid.

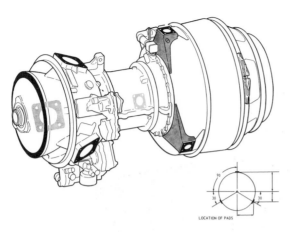

Fig. 8–20. Examples of pyramid shapes in the design of mounting pads for an engine. (Courtesy of Lycoming Division of the Avco Corporation.)

length lines from the apex to points 1′, 2′, 3′, and 4′ are found by revolution, as shown. These true-length distances are measured along their respective lines from point 0 to locate the upper limits of the development. These points are then connected to complete the inside development of the truncated pyramid.

The mounting pads in Fig. 8–20 are sections of pyramids that intersect an engine body. This is an example of a design problem involving both intersections and developments.

An oblique pyramid is developed in sequential steps in Fig. 8–21 to illustrate the procedure for constructing the development. The true lengths of all bend lines are determined in step 1 by revolving the lines into the frontal plane and projecting them to the front view. These lines are found to vary in length since the pyramid is not a right pyramid. The planes of each triangular surface of the pyramid are shown true size in the development by triangulation, in which the revolved lengths and the true-length base lines taken from the top view are used. The triangles are drawn adjacent to each other, with point 0 common to each (step 2). To determine the upper limits of the developed surface (step 3), we find the true-length distances from point 0 to points 1′, 2′, 3′, and 4′

FIGURE 8–21. DEVELOPMENT OF AN OBLIQUE PYRAMID

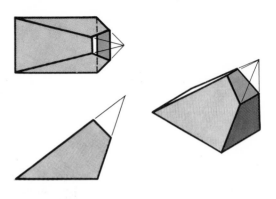

Given: The top and front views of an oblique, truncated pyramid.
Required: Find the inside development of the pyramid's surface.
Reference: Article 8–6.

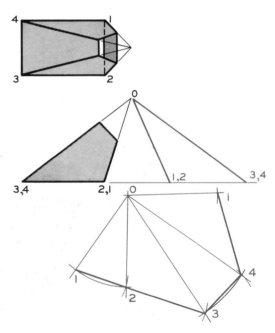

Step 2: The base lines appear true length in the top view. Using these true-length lines from the top view and the revolved lines in the front view, draw the development triangles. All triangles have one side and point 0 in common. This gives a development of the surface, excluding the truncated section.

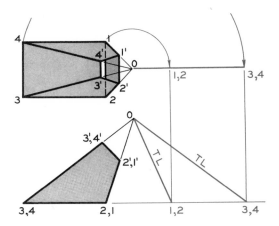

Fig. 8–22. The Apollo command module is an example of a conical development. (Courtesy of the National Aeronautics and Space Administration.)

Step 1: Revolve each of the bend lines in the top view until they are parallel to the frontal plane. Project these views to the front view where the true-length views of the revolved lines can be found. Let point 0 remain stationary but project points 1, 2, 3, and 4 horizontally in the front view to the projectors from the top view.

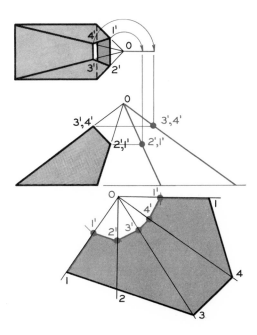

Step 3: The true lengths of the lines from point 0 to the points 1′, 2′, 3′, and 4′ are found by revolving these lines. These distances are laid off from point 0 along their respective lines to establish points along the upper edge of the developed pattern. The points are then sequentially connected by straight lines to complete the development.

by revolution and transfer these lengths to the respective bend lines in the developed view. The limits of the development are connected with straight lines, and fold lines are indicated with thin lines.

8–7 DEVELOPMENT OF CONES

The Apollo command module, shown in Fig. 8–22, is an example of a conical development. Many other examples of cones and other irregular shapes can be seen in the Charger and its missiles, shown in Fig. 8–23. Development principles are used to fabricate these irregular shapes from flat materials.

Cones are developed by a procedure similar to that used to develop pyramids. A series of triangles is constructed on the surface through the use of the elements of the cone and a chordal connection between points on the base of the cone. Figure 8–24 illustrates the division of the surface of the cone into triangular sections in the top and front views. The element 0–10 appears true length in the front view since it is a frontal line in the top view. All elements on a right cone are equal; therefore, line 0–10 will be used to construct the arc upon which the developed base will lie. The inside pattern of

Fig. 8–23. The body of this aircraft and the irregularly shaped missiles were fabricated through the application of development principles. (Courtesy of General Dynamics Corporation.)

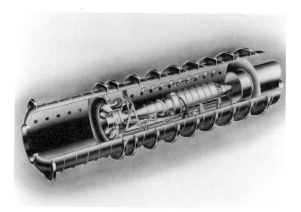

Fig. 8–25. Conical developments were used as an integral part of this wind tunnel design. (Courtesy of Arnold Engineering Development Center.)

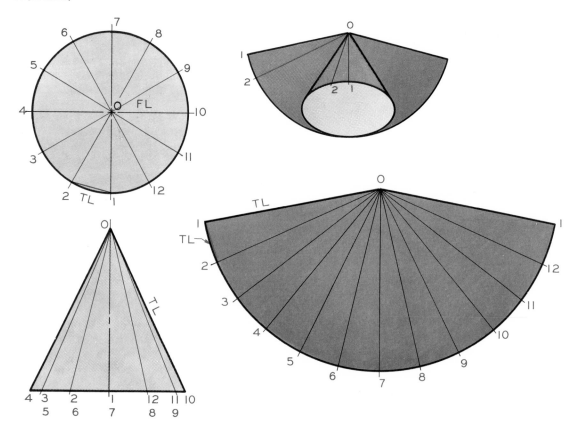

Fig. 8–24. The development of an inside pattern of a right cone.

the cone is drawn beginning with point 1 and moving toward the right. The point to the right of point 1 is point 2, which is found by inspection of the top view and the pictorial view of the cone. Point 2 is found in the top view and in the development by measuring the true-length chordal distance from point 1 along the arc. Successive triangles are found in this manner until point 1 is again reached at the extreme edge of the development. The base of the development is drawn as an arc rather than the series of chords along the arc that were connected by triangulation.

A more accurate approximation of the distance between the base points on the arc can be determined by finding the circumference of the base by mathematics and laying off this distance in equal increments along the arc formed by radius 0-1. The graphical approximation is sufficient in most cases.

Conical developments are used as an integral part of the wind tunnel design shown in Fig. 8-25. Cylindrical and spherical sections were also developed during the design of this facility.

A cone that has been truncated as shown in Fig. 8-26 can be developed by applying the principles illustrated in Fig. 8-24. It is advisable to construct the total development as though it were a complete cone that had not been modified. This portion of the development is identical to that shown in Fig. 8-24. A conical section has been removed from the upper

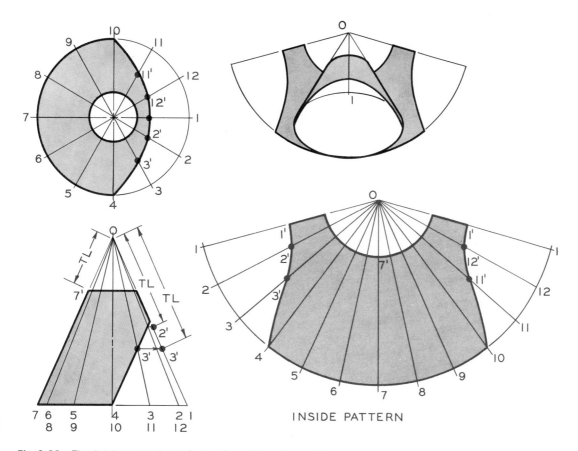

INSIDE PATTERN

Fig. 8-26.   The development of a conical surface with a side opening.

Fig. 8-27. Huge conical developments are used in the construction of a blast furnace. (Courtesy of Jones & Laughlin Steel Corporation.)

portion of the cone. This part of the pattern can be removed by constructing an arc in the development, using as the radius the true-length line 0–7', which is found in the front view. The true-length measurements from point 0 to the limits of the development, on the hyperbolic surface that is formed by the modification of the cone in the front view, are found by revolution. Lines 0–2' and 0–3' are projected horizontally to the extreme element, 0–1 in the front view, where they will appear true length. These distances are measured along their respective lines in the development to establish points through which the smooth curve will be drawn to outline the development.

Huge conical developments are necessary in the construction of a blast furnace (Fig. 8–27). Cylindrical developments are also frequently used in structures of this type. The developments must be carefully constructed to enable on-the-site assembly with considerable accuracy.

The development of an oblique cone is shown in Fig. 8–28. Elements on this cone are of varying lengths, but the resulting development will be symmetrical, since the top view is symmetrical. Elements in the given views are revolved into the frontal plane, as shown, so that their true lengths can be determined in the front view. The development is begun by constructing a series of triangles which are composed of elements and the chordal distances found on the base. The line of separation for the cone is chosen to be 0–1, since this is the shortest line on the cone's surface. The base is connected with a smooth curve. The true-length lines from apex 0 to the upper surface of the approximate cone are found by projecting from the front view to the true-length diagram. Points 1' and 7' are projected from the front view to their true-length lines in the true-length diagram found by revolution. Lines 0–1' and 0–7' are shown in the development, where they are used to locate points along the upper edges of the developed surfaces. These points are connected with a smooth line, but this line will not be an arc, since the geometric shape is not a true right cone and the edge view of the plane through points 7' and 1' in the front view is not perpendicular to the axis of the cone.

8-8 DEVELOPMENT OF WARPED SURFACES

The geometric shape shown in Fig. 8–29 is an approximate cone with a warped surface and is similar to the oblique cone shown in Fig. 8–28. The development of this surface will be merely an approximation, since a truly warped surface cannot be laid out on a flat surface. The surface is divided into a series of triangles in the top and front views by dividing the upper and lower views as shown. The true lengths of all lines are found in the true-length diagrams, which are drawn on each side of the front view, by project-

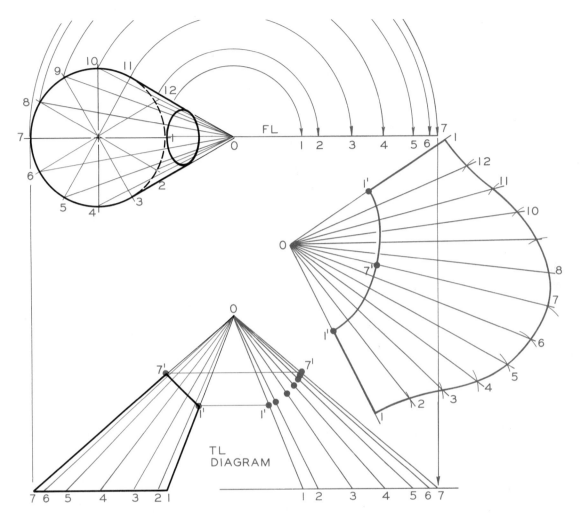

Fig. 8–28. The development of an oblique cone.

ing horizontally from the front view the vertical distances between the lines. To complete the true-length views of the lines, the horizontal distance between the ends of the lines is measured along the actual projection of the top view of the lines. A true-length line found in this manner is equivalent to a line that has been revolved, such as those illustrated in Fig. 8–28.

The chordal distance between the points on the base appears true-length in the top view

since the base is horizontal. The chordal distance between the points on the upper edge of the lateral surface will appear true-length in a view that shows a true-size plane of this end. The developed surface is found by triangulation using true-length lines from (1) the true-length diagram, (2) the horizontal base in the top view, and (3) the primary auxiliary view. Each point should be carefully lettered to facilitate construction in all views.

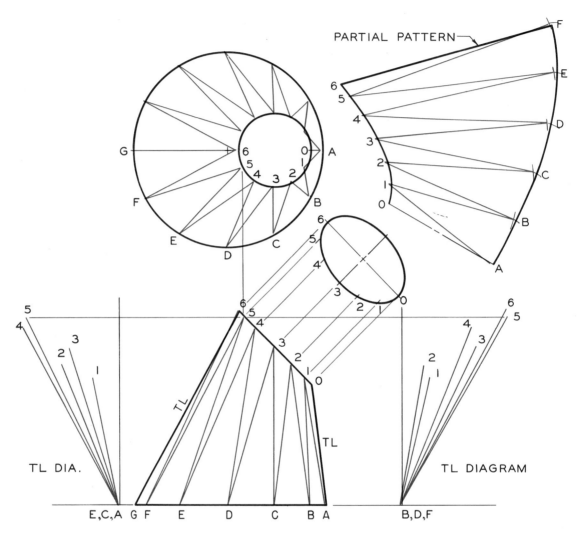

Fig. 8–29. The development of a partial inside pattern of a warped surface.

8–9 DEVELOPMENT OF TRANSITION PIECES

A transition piece is a figure that transforms its section at one end to a different shape at the other. This change is made gradually and uniformly. A duct with a rectangular cross section is connected to a cylinder with a transition piece in Fig. 8–30. Another example of a transition piece is the interior of the supersonic circuit of

the wind tunnel shown in Fig. 8–31. Note that the cross section of the tunnel is changed from a rectangle to a circle at this point with a transition piece. Many other examples of these shapes can be seen in concrete structures.

The problem in Fig. 8–32 is solved by steps. The circular view of the transition piece is divided into equal units from which radial lines are

Fig. 8–30. Transition-piece developments are used to join a circular shape with a rectangular section. (Courtesy of Western Precipitation Group, Joy Manufacturing Company.)

Fig. 8–31. An example of a transition application is the interior of this supersonic circuit of a wind tunnel. (Courtesy of Arnold Engineering Development Center.)

drawn to each corner of the base. The true lengths of these lines are found by revolution (step 1). The chordal lines between the points on the circular section appear true length and the lines on the rectangular base appear true length, since these planes are horizontal. The line of separation for the development is line 1–A, the shortest line.

A portion of the development is laid out by triangulation in step 2, utilizing the true lengths of the lines. The remaining planes of the surface are found in step 3 to complete half of the symmetrical development. The upper points are connected with a smooth curve and the points on the base are connected with straight lines. Thin fold lines are given to indicate the curving surface at the corners.

Transition pieces and other examples of intersections and developments can be seen in Fig. 8–33. All of these components were developed and constructed through the use of the principles of intersections and developments.

8–10 DEVELOPMENT OF SPHERES

Among the applications of spherical developments, an important one is the projection and preparation of maps used to chart the surface of the earth. No ideal development has been found that will permit the earth's surface to be projected without distortion on a two-dimensional surface. The globe therefore remains the most satisfactory surface on which to represent the areas of the earth. Nevertheless, the limitations of this surface are rather obvious: Spherical surfaces are unwieldy and bulky when drawn at sufficiently large scales to permit the analysis of a relatively small area, as represented on most charts. The advent of space travel has increased interest in charting spherical paths. Spherical developments are also used in the study of domes and geodesic structures, such as that shown in Fig. 8–34. The sphere is used as an efficient storage vessel, as illustrated in Fig. 8–35. Undersea diving capsules are designed as spheres to take advantage of the sphere's ability to withstand the excessive pressures to which a diving capsule is subjected in the depths of the ocean.

An understanding of spherical surfaces will permit the designer to lay out developments for constructing an approximately true sphere with flat materials. Two methods of development are presented below.

FIGURE 8–32. DEVELOPMENT OF A TRANSITION PIECE

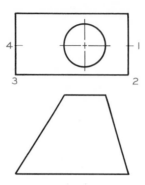

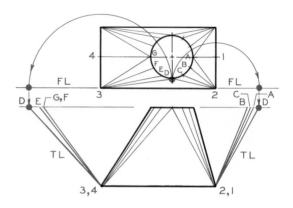

Given: The top and front views of a transition piece.
Required: Find an inside development of the surface from point 1 to point 4.
Reference: Article 8–9.

Step 1: Divide the circular edge of the surface into equal parts in the top view. Connect these points with bend lines to the corner points, 2 and 3. Find the true length of these lines by revolving them into a frontal plane and projecting them to the front view. These lines represent elements on the surface of an oblique cone.

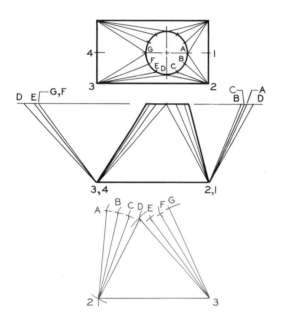

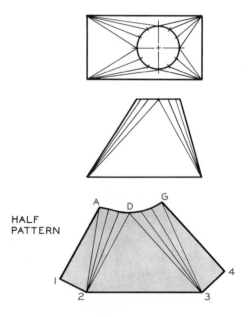

Step 2: Using the true-length lines found in the TL-diagram and the lines on the circular edge in the top-view, draw a series of triangles, which are joined together at common sides, to form the development. *Example:* arcs 2D and 2C are drawn from point 2. Point C is found by drawing arc DC from point D to find point C. DC is true length in the top view.

Step 3: Construct the remaining planes, A–1–2 and G–3–4, by triangulation to complete the inside, half pattern of the transition piece. Draw the fold lines as thin lines at the places where the surface is to be bent slightly. The line of departure for the pattern is chosen along A–1, the shortest possible line, for economy.

Fig. 8-33. Transition pieces and other examples of intersections and developments can be seen in this industrial installation. (Courtesy of Kirk and Blum Manufacturing Company.)

Fig. 8-34. An all-aluminum spherical shape is being assembled as a corn storage and conditioning unit. (Courtesy of ALCOA.)

Fig. 8-35. These spherical tanks, which were constructed through developments, make efficient storage tanks. (Courtesy of Shell Oil Company.)

8-11 SPHERICAL DEVELOPMENT—ZONE METHOD

The zone method is a conventional method of developing a sphere on a flat surface. A series of parallels, called latitudes in mapping, are drawn in the front view of Fig. 8-36. The parallels are spaced so that they establish equal arcs, D, on the surface of the sphere in the front view. Note that unit D was determined mathematically and set off on the sphere. This was done to establish uniformity in the development so that each of the developed zones would be equal in breadth. Cones are passed through the sphere's surface so that they form truncated cones in which one parallel serves as a base of a cone, and the other as the truncated top. The largest cone, which has an element equal to R_1, is found by extending line R_1 through the points where the equator and the next parallel intersect the sphere's surface in the front view, until R_1 intersects the extended center line of the sphere. Spherical elements R_2, R_3, and R_4 are found by repeating this process. The development is begun by laying out the largest zone, using R_1 as the radius of an arc which represents the base of an imaginary cone. The breadth of the zone

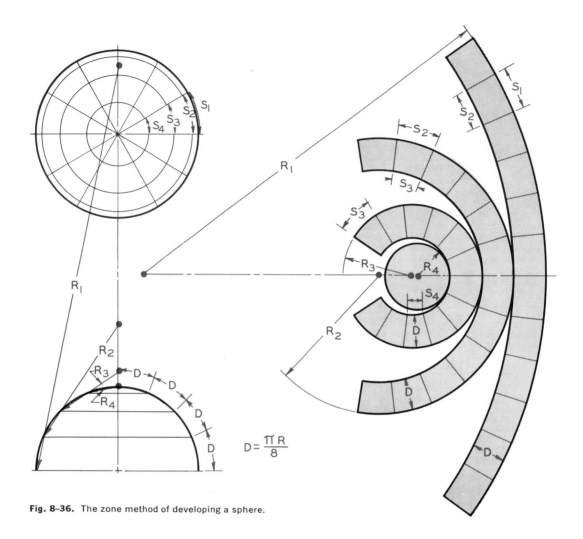

$$D = \frac{\pi R}{8}$$

Fig. 8–36. The zone method of developing a sphere.

is found by transferring distance D from the front view to the development and drawing the upper portion of the zone with a radius equal to R_1–D, using the same center. No regard is given to finding the arc lengths at this point. The next zone is drawn using the radius R_2 with its center located on a line through the center of arc R_1. The center of R_2 is positioned along this line such that the arc to be drawn will be tangent to the preceding arc, which was drawn with radius R_1–D. The upper arc of this second zone

is drawn with a radius R_2–D. The remaining zones are constructed successively in this manner. The last cone will appear as a circle with R_4 as its radius.

The lengths of the arcs can be established by dividing the top view with vertical cutting planes that radiate through the poles. These lines, which lie on the surface of the sphere, are called longitudes in cartography. Arc distances S_1, S_2, S_3, and S_4 are found on each parallel in the top view. These distances are measured off on the

Fig. 8-37. The giant dome of the United States Exhibit at Expo 67 is an example of a geodesic dome formed by straight structural members. (Courtesy of Rohm and Haas Company.)

Fig. 8-38. Individual panels of Plexiglas® are installed in the giant dome. (Courtesy of Rohm and Haas Company.)

constructed arcs in the development. In this case, there are twelve divisions, but smaller divisions would provide a more accurate measurement. A series of zones found in this manner can be joined to give an approximate sphere.

The giant dome of the United States Exhibit at the International Exhibition in Montreal is an example of a geodesic dome formed by straight structural members. This dome, shown in Fig. 8-37, is 250′ in diameter and 187′ high. Individual panels of Plexiglas® are shown being installed in Fig. 8-38. Most panels measured 10′ by 12′. This dome is another example of a unique application of the sphere. Domes of this type have been considered as possible enclosures for entire cities to control weather conditions and environment.

8-12 SPHERICAL DEVELOPMENT—GORE METHOD

Figure 8-39 is an alternative method of developing a flat pattern for a sphere. This method uses a series of spherical elements called gores. Equally spaced vertical cutting planes are passed through the poles in the top view. Parallels are located in the front view by dividing the surface into equal zones of dimension *D*. A front view of one of the gores is projected to the front view. A true-size view of one of the gores is developed by projecting from the top, which represents an approximation of the surface between two of the vertical cutting planes. Dimensions can be checked mathematically at all points. A partial pattern of the sphere is shown, in which the gores are drawn tangent to each other at the equator.

The Unisphere® was designed by determining chordal lengths of longitudes and latitudes on the surface of the sphere, as shown in Fig. 8-40. The chordal lengths made it possible to fabricate the structure with straight members. The land areas attached to the sphere were developed by a method similar to the gore method. Segments of these surfaces can be seen in Fig. 8-41, where they are being attached to the framework for later assembly on the site.

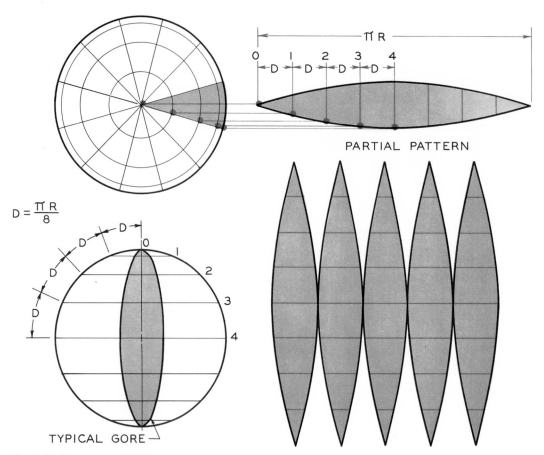

$$D = \frac{\pi R}{8}$$

PARTIAL PATTERN

TYPICAL GORE

Fig. 8–39. The gore method of developing a sphere.

Fig. 8–40. The Unisphere® was designed by determining chordal lengths of longitudes and latitudes on the surface of the sphere. This method is similar to the gore method of development. (Courtesy of U. S. Steel Corporation.)

Fig. 8–41. Surface areas are being attached to the structural frame of the Unisphere®. (Courtesy of U. S. Steel Corporation.)

FIGURE 8–42.   STRAP DEVELOPMENT

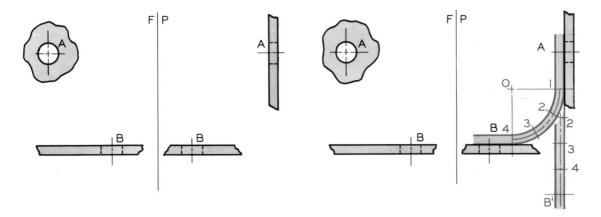

Given: The front and side views of two planes that are to be connected at points *A* and *B* with a metal strap.
Required: Find the true development of the strap and show it in both views.
Reference: Article 8–13.

Step 1: Construct the edge view of the strap in the side view using the specified radius of bend. Locate points 1, 2, 3, and 4 on the neutral axis at the bend. Revolve this portion of the strap into the vertical plane and measure the distances along this view of the neutral axis. Check the arc distances by mathematics. The hole is located at *B'* in this view.

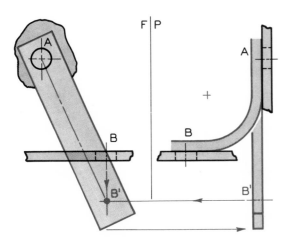

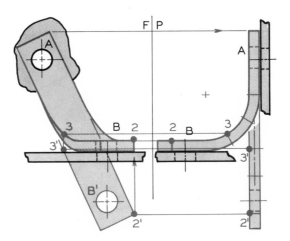

Step 2: Construct the front view of *B'* by revolving point *B* parallel to the profile plane until it intersects the projector from *B'* in the side view. Draw the center line of the true-size strap from *A* to *B'* in the front view. Add the outline of the strap around this center line and around the holes at each end, allowing enough material to provide sufficient strength.

Step 3: Determine the projection of the strap in the front view by projecting points from the given views. Points 3 and 2 are shown in the views to illustrate the system of projection used. The ends of the strap are drawn in each view to form true projections.

8–13 DEVELOPMENT OF A SUPPORT STRAP

Strap metal is universally used in mass-produced products such as brackets, connectors, and supports. It is more economical to form these shapes to the desired configuration by stamping and bending than by any other fabrication method. Almost all designs contain a variety of oblique surfaces and structures which must be connected by brackets that have been stamped. Figure 8–42 illustrates the steps necessary to the design of a developed view of a support bracket. The bracket is to connect two surfaces in different planes whose points of connection are oblique to each other. The strap is drawn in the view in which the planes appear as edges (step 1), using the specified radius of bend. The arc of the bend is divided into smaller arcs and developed as a straight strap without a bend in the side view. Point *B'* is found in this view to indicate the location of the hole. The hole in the front view, shown at *B*, is projected to its position on the developed strap, as shown in step 2. This per-

mits the true-size development of the strap to be drawn, and allowance to be made for the appropriate amount of metal on each side of the hole for strength. The projected front view of the strap in its bent position is constructed in step 3 to indicate its final configuration. An accurate design that reduces surplus material would result in considerable savings when mass-produced.

Observe that principles of revolution have been applied to this development, as well as the techniques of three-view projection. Most industrial problems tend toward a combination of graphical principles rather than the application of a single concept. Mathematics could also be used to verify the arc measurements in step 2. The designer should develop versatility in applying every tool at his disposal to the solving and checking of problems.

Figure 8–43 illustrates many examples of stamped metal components used in the body of an automobile. Each of these components was developed during the design process to obtain flat patterns from which the finished shapes could be fabricated.

8–14 SUMMARY

The examples and applications covered in this chapter should serve to illustrate the many uses of the principles of developments. Essentially all engineering and technological problems are concerned with a wide assortment of geometric shapes that must be constructed from flat materials. Developments are made possible through the application of basic graphical and descriptive geometry principles in conjunction with mathematics.

Principles of intersections are closely related to developments, since different shapes must be joined together in many instances. Any development problem will be easier to solve if it is first resolved into its basic geometric elements; this process will facilitate the application of the principles covered in this chapter. A lettering system should be utilized in laying out a pattern, to avoid confusion with the projections and constructions.

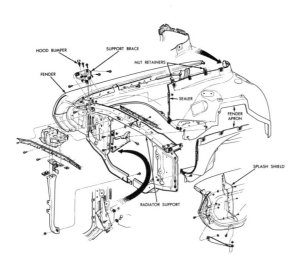

Fig. 8–43. Many examples of stamped metal developments can be seen in this exploded assembly drawing of a portion of an automobile body. (Courtesy of the Ford Motor Company.)

PROBLEMS

The problems for this chapter should be constructed with *instruments* from the given
sketches on $8\frac{1}{2}'' \times 11''$ sheets, as illustrated
in the accompanying figures. Each grid repre-
sents $\frac{1}{4}''$. All reference planes and figure points
should be labeled, using $\frac{1}{8}''$ letters with guidelines. Solutions should be sufficiently noted
and labeled to explain all construction.

1. (A through C) Using Fig. 8–44, lay out an
inside pattern for the prisms in parts A, B, and C
of the figure. Number representative points.

2. (A and B) Using Fig. 8–45, lay out an inside
pattern for each of the prisms in parts A and B
of the figure. Show all construction and number
the points.

3. (A through C) Lay out an inside half pattern
for each cylinder in parts A,B, and C of Fig. 8–46.

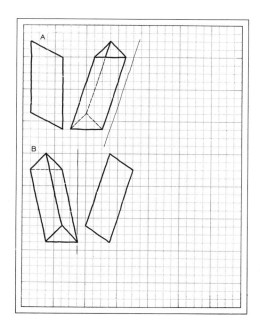

Fig. 8–45. Development of prisms.

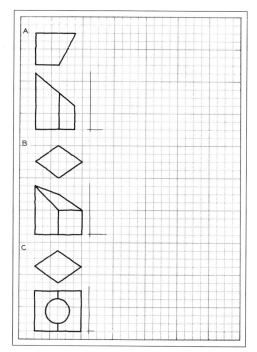

Fig. 8–44. Development of prisms.

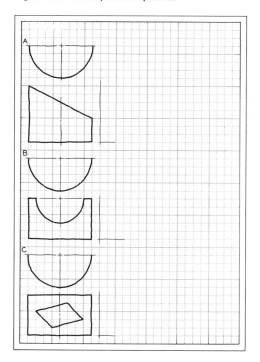

Fig. 8–46. Development of cylinders.

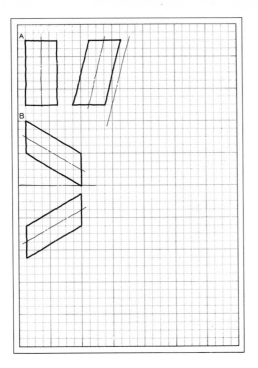

Fig. 8–47. Development of cylinders.

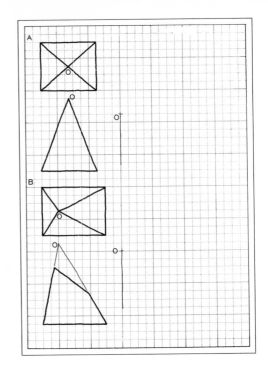

Fig. 8–48. Development of pyramids.

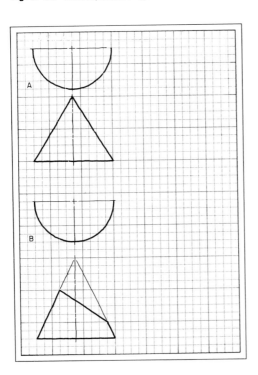

Fig. 8–49. Development of a cone.

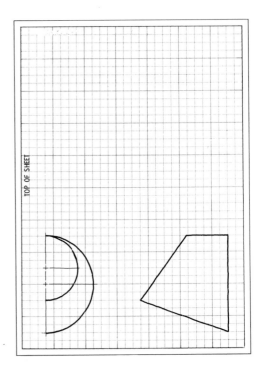

Fig. 8–50. Development of warped surface.

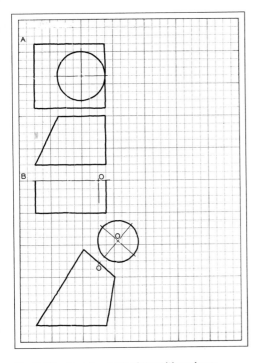

Fig. 8–51. Development of transition pieces.

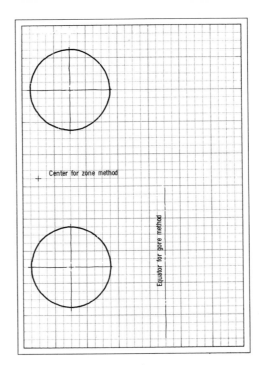

Fig. 8–52. Development of a sphere.

4. (A and B) Lay out an inside pattern for each cylinder in parts A and B of Fig. 8–47. Show all construction and number the points.

5. (A and B) Lay out an inside half pattern for each pyramid in parts A and B of Fig. 8–48.

6. (A and B) In Fig. 8–49 lay out inside half patterns for each of the cones in parts A and B.

7. Lay out an inside pattern for the warped surface in Fig. 8–50. Show a half development.

8. (A and B) Lay out inside half patterns for the transition pieces in parts A and B of Fig. 8–51.

9. (A) Lay out an inside developed pattern of the sphere in Fig. 8–52 using the gore method. (B) Using a separate sheet of paper, lay out an inside developed pattern of the sphere in Fig. 8–52 by the zone method.

10. Complete the front and side views of the $1\frac{1}{4}''$ strap which is shown in Fig. 8–53 bent into position at holes *A* and *B*. Give the complete development of the strap, including squared-off ends that extend $\frac{3}{4}''$ beyond the center line of the holes.

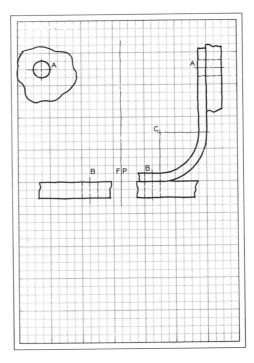

Fig. 8–53. Development of a strap.

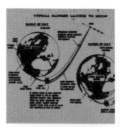

IDENTIFICATION

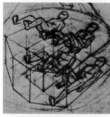

PRELIMINARY IDEAS

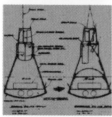
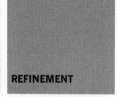

REFINEMENT

ANALYSIS

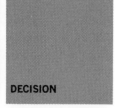

DECISION

IMPLEMENTATION

9
VECTOR ANALYSIS

9-1 INTRODUCTION

After a design of a structural system has been refined and drawn to scale, and angular and linear dimensions have been determined, it is necessary to analyze the system for strength and stresses. When the forces are known, members of an appropriate size may be selected to withstand the forces within the system. Principles of strength of materials can be applied to the graphical solutions in selecting the shapes and sizes of the structural members used in the final design.

In analyzing a system for strength it is necessary to consider the forces of tension and compression within the system. These forces are represented by vectors. Vectors may also be used to represent other quantities. For example, they can represent distance, velocity, and electrical properties.

Graphical methods are useful in the solution of vector problems, which are often very complicated to solve by conventional trigonometric and algebraic methods. This does not mean that only the graphical method should be used. The designer should strive to integrate all methods available to him in solving problems. Each method can serve as an effective check on the solutions determined by other methods.

9-2 BASIC DEFINITIONS

A knowledge of the terminology of graphical vectors is prerequisite to an understanding of the techniques of problem solving with vectors. The following definitions will be used throughout this chapter.

220

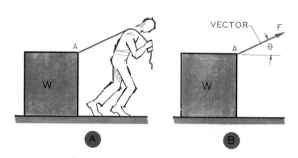

Fig. 9-1. The representation of a force by a vector.

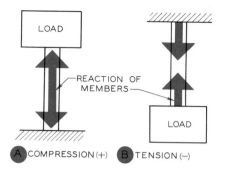

Fig. 9-2. A comparison of tension and compression in a member.

Force: A push or a pull that tends to produce motion. All forces have (1) magnitude, (2) direction, (3) a point of application, and (4) sense. A force is represented by the rope being pulled in Fig. 9-1A.

Vector: A graphical representation of a quantity of force which is drawn to scale to indicate magnitude, direction, sense, and point of application. The vector shown in Fig. 9-1B represents the force of the rope pulling the weight, *W*.

Magnitude: The amount of push or pull. In drawings, this is represented by the length of the vector line. Magnitude is usually measured in pounds of force.

Direction: The inclination of a force (with respect to a reference coordinate system).

Point of application: The point through which the force is applied on the object or member. This is point *A* in Fig. 9-1A.

Sense: Either of the two opposite ways in which a force may be directed, i.e., toward or away from the point of application. The sense is shown by an arrowhead attached to one end of the vector line. In Fig. 9-1A, the sense of the force is away from point A. It is shown in part B of the figure by the arrowhead at *F*.

Compression: The state created in a member by subjecting it to opposite pushing forces. A member tends to be shortened by compression

(Fig. 9-2A). Compression is represented by a plus sign (+).

Tension: The state created in a member by subjecting it to opposite pulling forces. A member tends to be stretched by tension, as shown in Fig. 9-2B. Tension is represented by a minus sign (−).

Force system: The combination of all forces acting on a given object. Figure 9-3 shows a force system.

Resultant: A single force that can replace all the forces of a force system and have the same effect as the combined forces.

Equilibrant: The opposite of a resultant; it is the single force that can be used to counterbalance all forces of a force system.

Components: Any individual forces which, if combined, would result in a given single force. For example, Forces *A* and *B* are components of resultant R_1 in step 1 of Fig. 9-3.

Space diagram: A diagram depicting the physical relationship between structural members. The force system in Fig. 9-3 is given as a space diagram.

Vector diagram: A diagram composed of vectors which are scaled to their appropriate lengths to represent the forces within a given system. The vector diagram is used to solve for unknowns that are required in the solution of the problem.

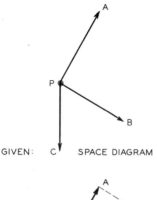

GIVEN: C   SPACE DIAGRAM

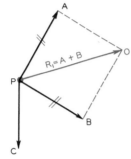

STEP I   C

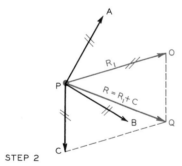

STEP 2

Fig. 9–3. The resultant of a coplanar, concurrent system as determined by the parallelogram method.

A vector diagram may be a polygon or a parallelogram.

Statics: The study of forces and force systems that are in equilibrium.

Additional definitions will be introduced throughout the chapter at appropriate times. The terms given above will be more extensively defined when applied to actual examples.

9–3 COPLANAR, CONCURRENT FORCE SYSTEMS

When several forces, represented by vectors, act through a common point of application, the system is said to be *concurrent.* Vectors *A, B,* and *C* act through a single point in Fig. 9–3; therefore this is a concurrent system. When only one view is necessary to show the true length of all vectors, as in Fig. 9–3, the system is *coplanar.*

Engineering designs are analyzed to determine the total effect of the forces applied in a system. Such an analysis requires that the known forces be resolved into a single force—the *resultant*—that will represent the composite effect of all forces on the point of application. The resultant is found graphically by two methods—(1) the parallelogram method and (2) the polygon method. In either case, the selection of a proper scale is important to the final solution. A larger drawing will result in a higher degree of accuracy.

9–4 RESULTANT OF A COPLANAR, CONCURRENT SYSTEM—PARALLELOGRAM METHOD

In the system of vectors shown in Fig. 9–3, all the vectors lie in the same plane and act through a common point. The vectors are scaled to a known magnitude.

Step 1. Two of the vectors, *A* and *B*, are resolved into one *resultant* that will replace the effects of the two vectors on the point of application. The two missing sides of a parallelogram are drawn from the ends of vectors *A* and *B*, to find point *O*. Note that *AO* is drawn through *A* parallel to *PB* and that *OB* is drawn parallel to *AP* through point *B*. The resultant is the diagonal of the parallelogram, *OP.* It is said to be the *vector sum* of vectors *A* and *B.* Its point of application is the same as that of the component vectors *A* and *B.*

Step 2. Since vectors *A* and *B* have been replaced by R_1, they can be disregarded in the next step of the solution. Again, resultant R_1 and vector *C* are resolved by completing a parallelogram, i.e., by drawing a line parallel to each vector. The diagonal of this parallelogram, *PQ*, is the resultant of the entire system and is the vector sum of R_1 and *C*. This resultant, *R*, can be analyzed as though it were the only force acting on the point; therefore the analysis of a particular point-of-force application is simplified by finding the resultant.

9–5 RESULTANT OF A COPLANAR, CONCURRENT SYSTEM—POLYGON METHOD

The system of forces shown in Fig. 9–3 is shown again in Fig. 9–4, but in this case the resultant is found by the polygon method. The forces are drawn to scale and in their true directions, with each force being drawn head-to-tail to form the polygon. In this example, the vectors are drawn in a counterclockwise sequence, beginning with vector *A*. Vector *B* is drawn with its tail at the arrowhead end of vector *A* and vector *C* is similarly attached to *B*. (Note that the polygon does not close; this means that the system is not in *equilibrium*. In other words, it would tend to be in motion, since the forces are not balanced in all directions.) The resultant *R* is drawn from the tail of vector *A* to the head of vector *C* to close the polygon. It can be seen by inspection that the resultant is equal in length, direction, and sense to the resultant found by the parallelogram method of the previous article.

9–6 RESULTANT OF A COPLANAR, CONCURRENT SYSTEM—ANALYTICAL METHOD

Vectors can be solved analytically by application of algebra and trigonometry. The graphical method is generally much faster, and presents less chance of error due to an arithmetical mistake. The designer should, however, be well-versed in all methods, since each will have ad-

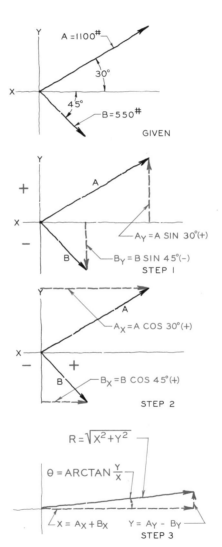

Fig. 9–5. The resultant of a coplanar, concurrent system as determined by the analytical method.

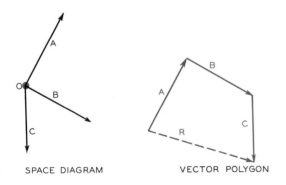

SPACE DIAGRAM   VECTOR POLYGON

Fig. 9–4. The resultant of a coplanar, concurrent system as determined by the polygon method.

vantages over the others in certain situations. The following example (Fig. 9–5) is given to afford a comparison between the graphical and analytical methods.

Given. Forces A and B of the magnitudes and directions shown in Fig. 9–5 are acting through a common point at the origin of the X- and Y-axes. Since the analytical approach will be used, it is unnecessary for the vectors and angles to be drawn accurately to scale. A freehand sketch is sufficient. However, it is advantageous if the sketch approximates the true measurements.

Step 1. The vertical components, which are parallel to the Y-axis, are drawn from the ends of both vectors to form right triangles. The lengths of these components are found through the use of the trigonometric functions of the angles the vectors make with the X-axis. The vertical component of vector A is found to be $A_y = A \sin 30°$ in a positive sense. The vertical component of B is $B_y = B \sin 45°$ in a negative sense. The positive sense of Y is conventionally considered to be upward from the X-axis, while the negative sense is thought of as being downward from the X-axis.

Step 2. The horizontal component of each vector is drawn parallel to the X-axis through the end of each vector. The lengths of these components are found to be the cosine functions of the given vectors, which form the hypotenuses of right triangles. The horizontal component of vector A is $A_x = A \cos 30°$ in a positive sense. The horizontal component of vector B is $B_x = B \cos 45°$ in a positive sense. The positive sense is considered to be to the right of the Y-axis and the negative sense is to the left of the Y-axis.

Step 3. The Y-components of each vector, A_y and B_y, can be added, since each lies in the same direction. The resulting value is $Y = A_y - B_y$, since the components have opposite senses. The horizontal component is $X = A_x + B_x$, since both components have equal directions and senses. A right triangle is sketched using the X- and Y-distances that were found trigonometrically. The vertical and horizontal components are laid off head-to-tail and the head of the hori-

zontal component is connected to the tail of the vertical to form a three-sided polygon of forces. The resultant is the hypotenuse of the triangle. The magnitude of the resultant is found by the Pythagorean theorem,

$$R = \sqrt{X^2 + Y^2}.$$

The direction of the resultant is

$$\text{angle } \theta = \arctan Y/X,$$

and it is measured from the horizontal X-axis. The sense is determined by the hypotenuse, and it runs from the tail of the horizontal component to the head of the vertical component. All measurements and magnitudes are found mathematically, so no graphical measurements are needed. The diagrams used to analyze the system of forces need not be drawn to scale when the problem is solved in this manner.

It can be seen in this example that a system of only two forces requires a considerable degree of mathematical manipulation to arrive at the resultant. Although these manipulations are relatively simple, there are many possibilities for making a mistake that would nullify the entire sequence of calculations. Errors are often difficult to detect when the solution is derived in this manner. A quickly drawn vector polygon can be used as a readily available method of checking analytical answers in the minimum of time. Graphical solutions can be made with the same degree of accuracy as slide-rule solutions, provided that the appropriate scale is chosen.

An *equilibrant* has the same magnitude, direction, and point of application as the *resultant* in any system of forces. The difference is the sense. Note that the resultant of the system of forces shown in Fig. 9–6 is solved for through the parallelogram method. The sense of the resultant is toward point C along the direction OC, the diagonal of the parallelogram. The equilibrant is drawn so that its arrowhead is at the opposite end, toward point O. The equilibrant E can be applied at point O to balance the forces A and B and thereby cause the system to be in a state of equilibrium. Note that this problem is the same as the one solved mathematically in Fig. 9–5.

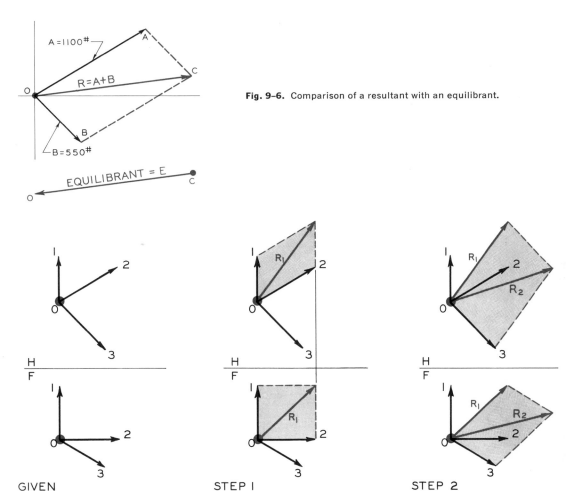

Fig. 9-6. Comparison of a resultant with an equilibrant.

Fig. 9-7. The resultant of noncoplanar, concurrent forces as determined by the parallelogram method.

9-7 RESULTANT OF NONCOPLANAR, CONCURRENT FORCES—PARALLELOGRAM METHOD

When vectors lie in more than one plane of projection, they are said to be *noncoplanar;* therefore more than one view is necessary to analyze their spatial relationships. The resultant of a system of noncoplanar forces can be found, regardless of their number, if their true projections are given in two adjacent orthographic views. The solution of an example of this type is shown through sequential steps of the parallelogram method in Fig. 9-7.

Given. The top and front views of a system of three vectors are given in Fig. 9-7, and we are required to find the resultant of the system.

Step 1. Vectors 1 and 2 are used to construct the top and front views of a parallelogram. The diagonal of the parallelogram, R_1, is found in both views. As a check, the front view of R_1 must be an orthographic projection of its top view; if it is not, there is an error in construction. Since R_1 is used to replace vectors 1 and 2, they may be omitted in further construction.

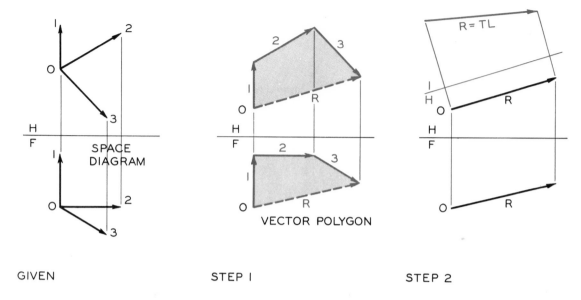

Fig. 9–8. The resultant of noncoplanar, concurrent forces as determined by the polygon method.

Step 2. Resultant R_1 and vector 3 are resolved to form resultant R_2 by the parallelogram method in both views. The top and front views of R_2 must project orthographically if there is no error in construction. Resultant R_2 can be used to replace vectors 1, 2, and 3. Since R_2 is an oblique line that is not true length in the top or front views, its magnitude cannot be measured. The true length can be found by auxiliary view, as shown in Fig. 9–8 or by revolution, as previously covered.

9–8 RESULTANT OF NONCOPLANAR, CONCURRENT FORCES—POLYGON METHOD

Given. The same system of forces that was given in Fig. 9–7 is given in Fig. 9–8. In this instance, we are required to solve for the resultant of the system by the polygon method.

Step 1. The given orthographic views of the vectors are transferred to a vector diagram, or vector polygon, in which each vector is laid head-to-tail in a clockwise direction, beginning with vector 1. The vectors are drawn in each view to

be orthographic projections at all times. Since the vector polygon did not close in the horizontal view or the front view, the system is not in equilibrium. The resultant R is constructed from the tail of vector 1 to the head of vector 3 in both views.

Step 2. Resultant R is an oblique line and so requires an auxiliary view to find its true length. The magnitude of the resultant can be measured in the true-length auxiliary view by using the same scale as was used to draw the original views. This method could have been used to find the resultant in Fig. 9–7.

9–9 RESULTANT OF NONCOPLANAR, CONCURRENT FORCES—ANALYTICAL METHOD

Given. The same system of forces that was given in Fig. 9–7 are given in Fig. 9–9. We are required to solve for the resultant of the system by the analytical method, using trigonometry and algebraic equations. The projected lengths of the vectors are known in both views, as indicated in Fig. 9–9.

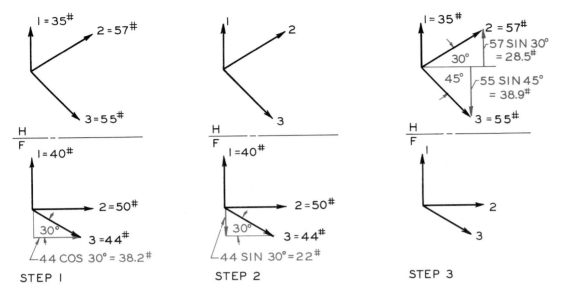

Fig. 9–9. The resultant of noncoplanar, concurrent forces as determined by the analytical method.

Step 1. The summation of the forces in the X-direction is found in the front view. Since this left and right direction can be seen in either the top view or front view, either view can be used for finding the X-component of the system. The summation in the X-direction is expressed in the following equation:

$$\sum F_x = (2) + (3) \cos 30°$$
$$= 50 + 44 \cos 30° = 88.2 \text{ lb } (+).$$

The X-component is found to be 88.2 lb in the positive direction, which is considered to be to the right. Vector 1 is vertical and consequently has no component in the X-direction.

Step 2. The summation of forces in the Y-direction is found in the front view. Positive direction is considered upward and negative downward. This summation is expressed in the following equation:

$$\sum F_y = (1) - (3) \sin 30°$$
$$= 40 - 44 \sin 30° = 18 \text{ lb } (+).$$

The vertical component of vector 3 is subtracted from vector 1, resulting in a summation

of 18 lb in the positive direction. Vector 2 is horizontal and has no vertical component.

Step 3. The summation of forces in the Z-direction is found in the top view. Positive direction is considered to be backward and negative, to be forward. This summation is expressed in the following equation:

$$\sum F_z = (1) + (2) \sin 30° - (3) \sin 45°$$
$$= 35 + 57 \sin 30° - 55 \sin 45°$$
$$= 24.6 \text{ lb } (+).$$

The Z-component is found to be 24.6 lb in a positive (backward) direction.

The resultant that can be used to replace vectors 1, 2, and 3 can be found from these three components. The true-length of a line can be determined from these three components by the following equation:

$$R = \sqrt{X^2 + Y^2 + Z^2}.$$

By substitution of the X-, Y-, and Z-components found in the three previous summations, the equation can be solved as follows:

$$R = \sqrt{88.2^2 + 18^2 + 24.6^2} = 93.3 \text{ lb.}$$

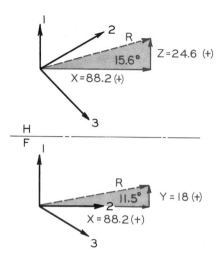

Fig. 9–10. The direction and sense of resultant R.

These two angles, found in the top and front views, establish the direction of the resultant vector, whose sense can be described as upward, to the right, and back. The force system and the various steps of solution need not be drawn to scale for analytical solution, since no attempt is made to measure lines or angles.

The advantages of the graphical solution of this problem should be apparent after this example is completed in its entirety. Errors are more likely in the analytical solution due to the number of components involved. The accuracy of both methods is essentially the same if a sufficiently large scale is selected for the graphical solution. Both methods should be used in combination for the most satisfactory solution.

Step 4. The resultant force of 93.3 lb is of no value unless its direction and sense are known. To find this information, we must refer to the two orthographic views of the force system, as shown in Fig. 9–10. The X- and Z-components, 88.2 lb and 24.6 lb, are drawn to form a right triangle in the top view. The hypotenuse of this triangle depicts the direction and sense of the resultant in the top view. Note that both the X-component and the Z-component have a positive sense. The angular direction of the top view of the resultant is found in the following equation:

$$\tan \theta = \frac{24.6}{88.2} = 0.279; \qquad \theta = 15.6°.$$

The angular direction of the resultant is found in the front view by constructing a triangle with the X- and Y-components, 88.2 lb and 18 lb. The hypotenuse of this right triangle is the direction of the resultant. Each of the components is drawn in a positive direction, and they act on the point of concurrency. The direction of the resultant in the front view is expressed in the following equation:

$$\tan \phi = \frac{18}{88.2} = 0.204; \qquad \phi = 11.5°.$$

9–10 STRUCTURES IN EQUILIBRIUM

In all the previous examples, the vectors were drawn from given or known magnitudes and directions. The same principles can be applied to structural system in which the magnitudes and senses are not given. All engineering structures are analyzed for their stresses as the first step in designing and selecting members to adequately support the loads for which the structure is designed. An example of coplanar structures in equilibrium can be seen in the loading cranes in Fig. 9–11, which are used for the handling of cargo on board ship. These can be considered as coplanar, concurrent force systems. The stresses in the members are dependent on the magnitude of the loading and the position of the members.

The coplanar, concurrent structure given in Fig. 9–12 is designed to support a load of $W = 1000$ lb. The maximum loading is used to determine the type and size of structural members used in the structural design.

Step 1. The only known force, $W = 1000$ lb, is laid off parallel to the given direction. Unknown forces A and B are drawn as vectors that are acting at a common point of application. The sense of these vectors can be determined so as to balance the system. Note that if either force A or B had been drawn with an opposite sense,

Fig. 9–11. The cargo cranes on the cruise ship "Santa Rosa" are examples of coplanar, concurrent force systems that are designed to remain in equilibrium. (Courtesy of Humble Oil and Refining Company.)

the system could not be in equilibrium. The magnitude of these vectors is not known, but their directions must lie along the lines of the structural members.

Step 2. Force *W* is drawn to a convenient scale as a vector. Forces *A* and *B* are laid off head-to-tail parallel to their given views to close the polygon formed by the three lines. The re-

sulting polygon can be scaled to give the magnitude of vectors *A* and *B* by applying the same scale as that used for drawing vector *W*. The structural lengths of the members do not affect the forces derived in the polygon. A column 3 ft long may support the same weight as a column 30 ft long. The length versus the cross section of a member will be considered when selecting a member, but the determination of force in the

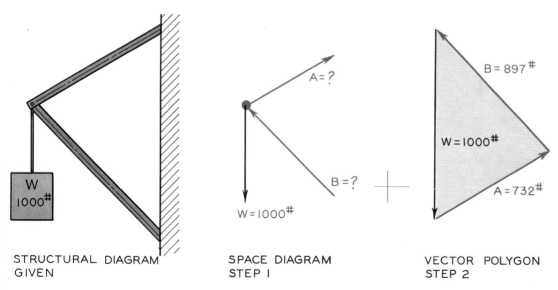

STRUCTURAL DIAGRAM
GIVEN

SPACE DIAGRAM
STEP I

VECTOR POLYGON
STEP 2

Fig. 9–12. The determination of stresses in a coplanar, concurrent structure in equilibrium.

member is found in the same manner in the vector polygon regardless of member length.

Tension is a force tending to stretch a member while compression is a force tending to shorten a member. Forces are considered to produce tension or compression in relation to a point of application. A rope is a member that is in tension when in use, while a car jack is a mechanism that is in compression when in use. When the sense of a vector is toward the point of application, an object is in compression; when its sense is away from the point, the object is in tension.

The members in Fig. 9–12 can be analyzed to determine whether they are in tension or compression by inspecting the diagram drawn in step 1. Vector A can be compared with the member it represents. The sense of this vector is away from the point of application; therefore the member is in tension. Vector B has its sense toward the point of application, indicating that the member is in compression. Compression and tension can also be determined by visually relating the vector polygon in step 2 to the given structural diagram.

9–11 FORCES IN EQUILIBRIUM—ANALYTICAL SOLUTION

The force system shown in Fig. 9–12 has been sketched in Fig. 9–13 for solution by the analytical method. The load W must be known along with the angular directions of members A and B. Forces A and B are unknown; however, they can be used in the equations where the X- and Y-forces will be summed. Since the system is in equilibrium, the summation of forces in any direction will equal zero, which indicates balance or equilibrium. The summation of forces in the Y-direction can be expressed in the following equation:

(1) $\sum F_y = A \sin 30° + B \sin 45° - 1000 = 0.$

The summation of forces in the X-direction can be expressed in the following equation:

(2) $\sum F_x = A \cos 30° - B \cos 45° = 0.$

We can solve Eq. (2) for A by rearranging the

equation to the following form:

(3) $A = \dfrac{B \cos 45°}{\cos 30°} = .816\ (B).$

When Eq. (3) is substituted into Eq. (1), the equation can be rewritten as:

(4)
$$\sum F_y = .816\ (B) \sin 30° + B \sin 45° - 1000$$
$$= 0 = 0.408\ B + 0.707\ B = 1000;$$

$$B = \frac{1000}{1.115} = 897\ \text{lb.}$$

The value of $B = 897$ lb is substituted into Eq. (2) so that we may solve for A in the following manner:

$$\sum F_x = A \cos 30° - 897 \cos 45° = 0,$$

$$A = \frac{897 \cos 45°}{\cos 30°} = 732\ \text{lb.}$$

In comparing the graphical and analytical methods, we should note that both methods are limited to two unknowns. Although we obtained

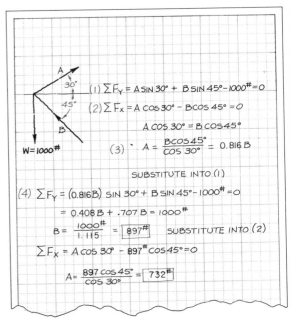

Fig. 9–13. Analytical determination of the forces in a concurrent, coplanar system in equilibrium.

the same answer by the analytical method as we did by the graphical method, there was a considerably greater chance of error in the analytical approach. The analytical method also required more time. The student should nevertheless complete all steps of the analytical solution, so that he will be familiar with this method as well as the graphical method.

9–12 TRUSS ANALYSIS

Structural trusses, such as those pictured in Fig. 9–14, can be analyzed graphically to determine (1) the stresses in each member and (2) whether the members are in compression or tension. The information needed for such an analysis includes the physical size of the truss, the location of the supports, the maximum loads to be supported, and the directions of the loads. Usually, wind loads, dead loads, live loads, and snow loads are analyzed separately to determine the maximum stress on any single member.

The supporting structure in Fig. 9–15, called a Fink truss, is analyzed to determine the stress in the structural members due to the loads that are concentrated at the points shown. For ease of analysis, loads are considered to be concentrated at points of concurrency even though the loads may actually be uniformly distributed along the upper surface. Since the truss is symmetrical and is loaded symmetrically, the resultants, R_1 and R_2, can be found by dividing the total load of 9000 lb (denoted in the Figure by #) by two, resulting in a reaction of 4500 lb at each end.

The structural analysis is begun by analyzing the extreme left joint independently, as shown in step 1 of Fig. 9–15. There are two unknowns, A–1 and E–1. Note the method of lettering the structural members. In this system, called *Bow's notation*, a letter or a number is placed in the spaces between the system of vectors. For example, the truss in step 1 has numbers placed in the interior panels and letters placed outside, between the exterior forces. A force is denoted by the letters appearing on either side of it. Their order is chosen by either a clockwise or counterclockwise system. The first letter is used

Fig. 9–14. These roof trusses can be analyzed for their stresses by application of graphical principles. (Courtesy of General Dynamics Corporation.)

to denote the tail while the second letter represents the head of the vector. Resultant R_1 is referred to as EA and R_2 as DE. This method of notation gives the vectors a more distinct relationship with each other and facilitates vector analysis.

The exterior vectors are drawn to scale so that we may graphically sum their magnitudes. Vectors AB, BC, and CD are drawn head-to-tail, and resultants DE and EA are drawn head-to-tail in the opposite direction. Note that the sum of the two resultants is equal in magnitude to the summation of downward loads, but in an opposite sense. This load line began at point A and ended at the same point, thus closing the straight-line "polygon."

The structural analysis begins at the joint through which reaction EA acts. A free-body diagram is drawn to isolate this joint for easier analysis. The two unknowns are members A–1 and 1–E. These vectors are drawn parallel to their direction in the truss in step 1 of Fig. 9–15, with A–1 beginning at point A and 1–E beginning at point E. These directions are extended to a point of intersection, which locates point 1. Since this joint is in equilibrium, as are all joints of a system in equilibrium, the vectors must be drawn head-to-tail. Because resultant EA has an upward sense, vector A–1 must have its tail at A, giving it a sense toward point 1. By relating this sense to the free-body diagram, we can see that the sense is toward the point of application, which means that A–1 is a compres-

FIGURE 9–15.   TRUSS ANALYSIS

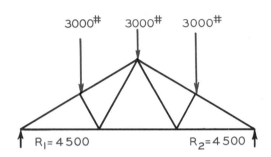

3000#   3000#   3000#

$R_1 = 4500$ $R_2 = 4500$

Given: A Fink truss loaded as shown.
Required: Find the forces in each member of the truss and indicate whether each member is in compression or tension.
Reference: Article 9–12.

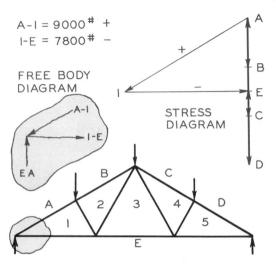

A–I = 9000# +
I–E = 7800# –

FREE BODY DIAGRAM

STRESS DIAGRAM

Step 1: Label the portions of supports between the outer forces of the truss with letters and the internal portions with numbers, using Bow's notation. Add the given load vectors graphically in a stress diagram, and sketch a free-body diagram of the first joint to be analyzed. Using vectors *EA*, *A–1*, and 1–*E* drawn head-to-tail, draw a vector diagram to find their magnitudes. Vector *A–1* is in compression (+) because its sense is toward the joint, and 1–*E* is in tension (−) because its sense is away from the joint.

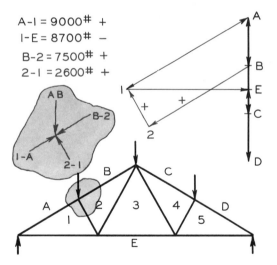

A–I = 9000# +
I–E = 8700# –
B–2 = 7500# +
2–I = 2600# +

Step 2: Draw a sketch of the next joint to be analyzed. Since *AB* and *A–1* are known, we have to determine only two unknowns, 2–1 and *B–2*. Draw these parallel to their direction, head-to-tail, in the stress diagram using the existing vectors found in step 1. Vectors *B–2* and 2–1 are in compression since each has a sense toward the joint. Note that vector *A–1* becomes 1–*A* when read in a clockwise direction.

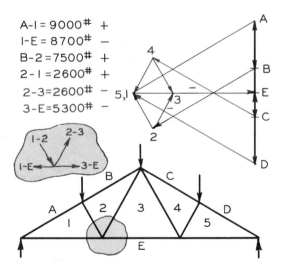

A–I = 9000# +
I–E = 8700# –
B–2 = 7500# +
2–I = 2600# +
2–3 = 2600# –
3–E = 5300# –

Step 3: Sketch a free-body diagram of the next joint to be analyzed. The unknowns in this case are 2–3 and 3–*E*. Determine the true length of these members in the stress diagram by drawing vectors parallel to given members to find point 3. Vectors 2–3 and 3–*E* are in tension because they act away from the joint. This same process is repeated to find the stress of the members on the opposite side.

sion member. Vector 1–E has a sense away from the joint, which means that it is a tension member. Determination of sense can be made by referring to the free-body diagram or to the original structural system, but the stress diagram alone is not sufficient for this analysis. The vectors are coplanar and can be scaled to determine their stresses as tabulated.

In step 2 we select the next adjacent joint to take advantage of the stress found in vector A–1. Vectors A–1 and AB are known, while vectors B–2 and 2–1 are unknown. Since there are only two unknowns it is possible to solve for them. A free-body diagram showing the joint to be analyzed is sketched. Vector B–2 is drawn parallel to the structural member through point B in the stress diagram and the line of vector 2–1 is extended through point 1 until it intersects with B–2, where point 2 is located. The sense of each vector is found by laying off each vector head-to-tail. Both vectors B–2 and 2–1 have a sense toward the joint in the free-body diagram; therefore, they produce compression. Their magnitudes are scaled and tabulated.

The next joint is analyzed in sequence to find the stresses in 2–3 and 3–E. This construction is shown in the stress diagram in step 3. The truss will have equal stresses on each side, since it is symmetrical and is loaded symmetrically. The total stress diagram is drawn to illustrate the completed work in step 3. If all the polygons in the series do not close at every point with perfect symmetry, there is an error in construction. If the error of closure is very slight, it can be disregarded, since safety factors are generally applied in derivation of working stresses of structural systems to assure safe construction.

The analytical solution to this problem could be found by applying algebraic and trigonometric methods, as discussed in Article 9–11. Besides being a more tedious process, there are many possibilities for carrying an error through the series of joint analyses that would nullify all subsequent solutions. The graphical method gives a visible indication of error in projection when the polygons do not close. Both methods of solution should be used in combination for the most satisfactory approach.

Fig. 9–16. The structural members of these stiff-leg cranes can be analyzed graphically to determine design stresses. (Courtesy of Bethlehem Steel Corp.)

9–13 NONCOPLANAR STRUCTURAL ANALYSIS —SPECIAL CASE

Structural systems that are three-dimensional require the use of descriptive geometry, since it is necessary to analyze the system in more than one plane. The crane in Fig. 9–16 can be analyzed to determine the stresses that exist in the support members when the members are positioned as shown in Fig. 9–17. It is found that when the crane is loaded with weight W, the stress in cable T is equal to 10,000 lb, as shown. We wish to determine the stresses in the noncoplanar tripod composed of members 0–3, 0–2, and 0–1. This is a special case that will serve as an introduction to the general noncoplanar problem. Since members 0–1 and 0–2 lie in the same plane and appear as an edge in the front view, we need to determine only two unknowns; that is what makes this a special case.

A vector polygon is constructed in the front view in step 1 of Fig. 9–17 by drawing force T as a vector and using the other vectors as the other sides of the polygon. One of these vectors is actually a summation of vectors 0–2 and 0–1.

FIGURE 9–17.   NONCOPLANAR STRUCTURAL ANALYSIS—SPECIAL CASE

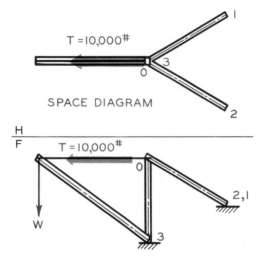

SPACE DIAGRAM

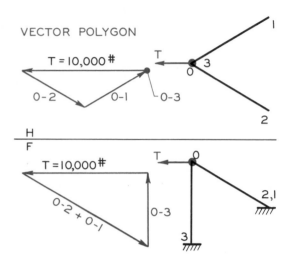

VECTOR POLYGON

Given: The top and front views of a structural crane upon which a known force of 10,000 lb is applied in the direction shown at point 0.

Required: Find the forces in each of the structural members, 0–3, 0–2, and 0–1.

Reference: Article 9–13.

Step 1: Construct a vector polygon in the front view by drawing force *T* and the other forces as vectors. Note that one side of the polygon represents the summation of two vectors, 0–2 and 0–1. Construct the top view of the polygon orthographically by drawing vectors 0–2 and 0–1 parallel to their top view. Vector 0–3 appears as a point in the top view.

$$0\text{-}1 = 6500^\# -$$
$$0\text{-}2 = 6500^\# -$$
$$0\text{-}3 = 5800^\# +$$

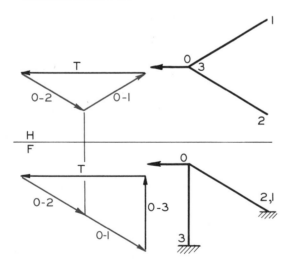

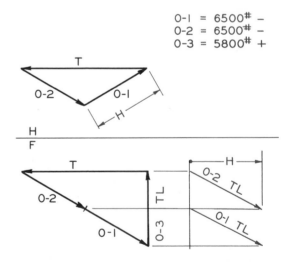

Step 2: Project the point of intersection of 0–2 and 0–1 in the top view to the front view to separate these vectors. Draw all vectors head-to-tail. Note the sense of a vector in the vector polygon and relate it with its point of application at 0 in the space diagram. Vectors 0–2 and 0–1 are in tension because their vectors are acting away from joint 0, while 0–3 is in compression.

Step 3: The completed top and front views found in step 2 do not give the true lengths of vectors 0–2 and 0–1 since they are oblique. Determine the true lengths of these lines by revolving the lines and drawing a true-length diagram. Then scale these lines to find the forces in each number. Refer to Article 4–6 to review TL diagrams.

FIGURE 9–18. NONCOPLANAR STRUCTURAL ANALYSIS—GENERAL CASE

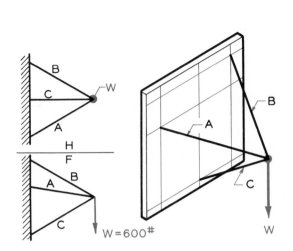

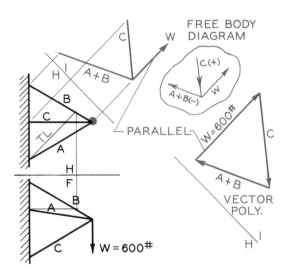

Given: The top and front views of a three-member frame which is attached to a vertical wall in such a way that it can support a maximum weight of 600 lb.
Required: Find the forces in the structural members.
References: Articles 9–12, 9–14.

Step 1: To limit the unknowns to two, construct an auxiliary view to find two vectors lying in the edge view of a plane. Use the auxiliary view and top view in the remainder of the problem. Draw a vector polygon parallel to the members in the auxiliary view in which $W = 600$ lb is the only known vector. Sketch a free-body diagram for preliminary analysis.

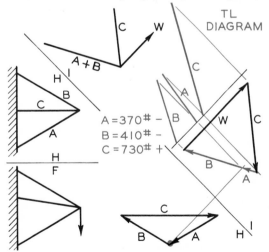

Step 2: Construct an orthographic projection of the view of the vector polygon found in step 1 so that its vectors are parallel to the members in the top view. The reference plane between the two views is parallel to the H–1 plane. This portion of the problem is closely related to the problem in Fig. 9–17.

Step 3: Project the intersection of vectors A and B in the horizontal view of the vector polygon to the auxiliary view polygon to establish the lengths of vectors A and B. Determine the true lengths of all vectors in a true-length diagram and measure them to determine their forces. Analyze for tension or compression, as covered in Article 9–12.

The top view is drawn using the vectors 0–2 and 0–1 to close the polygon from each end of vector T. In step 2, the point of intersection between the vectors in the top view is projected to the front view, where the magnitudes of vectors 0–1 and 0–2 are found. The stresses are drawn to scale in the top and front views of the vector polygon, but they cannot be measured since they are oblique and foreshortened.

The true lengths of the vectors are found by revolution in a true-length diagram in step 3. (Refer to Article 4–6 if necessary, to review construction of true-length diagrams.) The vectors are measured to determine their stresses. Vector 0–3 is found to be in compression because its sense is toward the point of concurrency, point 0. Vectors 0–1 and 0–2 are in tension.

9-14 NONCOPLANAR STRUCTURAL ANALYSIS —GENERAL CASE

The structural frame shown in Fig. 9–18 is attached to a vertical wall to support a load of $W = 600$ lb. The stresses in each member must be determined prior to the selection of the structural shapes. Since there are three unknowns in each of the views, we are required to construct an auxiliary view that will give the edge view of a plane containing two of the vectors, thereby reducing the number of unknowns to two (step 1). Once the top and primary auxiliary views are constructed by following the general steps as illustrated in the special case in Fig. 9–17, we no longer need to refer to the front view. A vector polygon is drawn by constructing vectors parallel to the members in the auxiliary view (step 1). An adjacent orthographic view of the vector polygon is also drawn by constructing its vectors parallel to the members in the top view (step 2). These two views of the vector polygon give the spatial orientation of the vectors; however, they are foreshortened in both views. A true-length diagram is used in step 3 to find the true length of the vectors so they can be scaled to determine their magnitudes.

The cranes on the huge construction barges shown in Fig. 9–19 are examples of nonco-

Fig. 9–19. The cranes on huge construction barges represent force systems whose member stresses can be solved for by vectors. (Courtesy of Humble Oil and Refining Company.)

Fig. 9–20. Tractor sidebooms represent noncoplanar, concurrent systems of forces that can be solved graphically. (Courtesy of Trunkline Gas Company.)

planar, concurrent structural systems that can be solved by application of the previously covered principles. The stresses in each of these members will vary as the position of each member changes.

Other examples of a three-dimensional system are the side-boom tractors used for lowering pipe into a ditch during pipeline construction

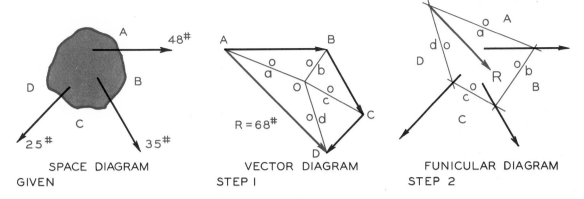

| SPACE DIAGRAM | VECTOR DIAGRAM | FUNICULAR DIAGRAM |
| GIVEN | STEP I | STEP 2 |

Fig. 9–21. The determination of nonconcurrent, coplanar vectors.

(Fig. 9–20). Stresses can be found in each member, as illustrated in Articles 9–13 and 9–14.

9–15 NONCONCURRENT, COPLANAR VECTORS

Forces *may* be applied in such a manner that they are not concurrent, as illustrated in Fig. 9–21. Bow's notation can be used to locate the resultant of this type of nonconcurrent system.

Step 1. The vectors are laid off to form a vector diagram in which the closing vector is the resultant, $R = 68$ lb. Each vector is resolved into two components by randomly locating point O on the interior or exterior of the polygon and connecting point O with the end of each vector. The components, or strings, from point O are equal and opposite components of adjacent vectors. For example, component o–b is common to vectors AB and BC. Since the strings from point O are equal and opposite, the system has not changed statically.

Step 2. Each string is transferred to the space diagram of the vectors where it is drawn between the respective vectors to which it applies. (The figure thus produced is called a funicular diagram.) For instance, string o–b is drawn in the area between vectors AB and BC. String o–c is drawn in the C-area to connect at the inter-

section of o–b and vector BC. The point of intersection of the last two strings, o–a and o–d, locates a point through which the resultant R will pass. The resultant has now been determined with respect to magnitude, sense, direction, and point of application, thus completing the solution of the problem.

9–16 NONCONCURRENT SYSTEMS RESULTING IN COUPLES

A *couple* is the descriptive name given to two parallel and equal but opposite forces which are separated by a distance and applied to a member in such a manner that they cause the member to rotate. The handwheels in Fig. 9–22 are examples of mechanical systems which take advantage of this method of force application.

An important quantity associated with a couple is its *moment*. The moment of any force is a measure of its rotational effect. An example is shown in Fig. 9–23, in which two equal and opposite forces are applied to a wheel. The forces are separated by the distance D. The moment of the couple is found by multiplying one of the forces by the perpendicular distance between it and a point on the line of action of the other: $F \times D$. If the force is 20 lb and the distance is 3 ft, the moment of the couple would be given as 60 ft-lb.

Fig. 9–22. Handwheels are designed for operation by the application of forces in the form of couples. (Courtesy of Standard Oil Company.)

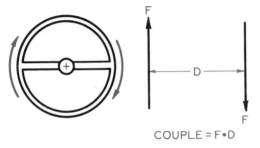

COUPLE = F•D

Fig. 9–23. Representation of a couple or moment.

A series of parallel forces is applied to a beam in Fig. 9–24. The spaces between the vectors are labeled with letters which follow Bow's notation. We are required to determine the resultant.

Step 1. After constructing a vector diagram, we have a straight line which is parallel to the direction of the forces and which closes at point *A* in such a way that the forces are equal in both directions. We then locate pole point *O* and draw the strings of a funicular diagram.

Step 2. The strings are transferred to the space diagram, where they are drawn in their respective spaces. For example, *o–c* is drawn in the *C*-space between vectors *BC* and *CD*. The last two strings, *o–d* and *o–a* do not close at a common point, but are found to be parallel; the result is therefore a couple. The distance between the forces of the couple is the perpendicular distance, *E*, between strings *o–a* and *o–d* in the space diagram, using the scale of the space diagram. The magnitude of the force is the scaled distance from point *O* to *A* and *D* in the vector diagram, using the scale of the vector diagram. The moment of the couple is equal to 7.5 lb × *E* in a counterclockwise direction.

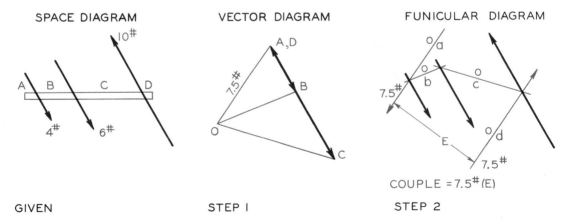

SPACE DIAGRAM   VECTOR DIAGRAM   FUNICULAR DIAGRAM

COUPLE = 7.5# (E)

GIVEN   STEP I   STEP 2

Fig. 9–24. The determination of nonconcurrent systems that result in couples.

9-17 RESULTANT OF PARALLEL, NONCONCURRENT FORCES

Forces applied to beams, such as those shown in Fig. 9–25, are parallel and nonconcurrent in many instances, and they may have the effect of a couple, tending to cause a rotational motion. When the loads exerted on the beams are known, the magnitude and location of the total resultant or equilibrant can be found. This will provide the designer with a better understanding of where supports should be placed.

The beam in Fig. 9–26 is on a rotational crane that is used to move building materials in a limited area. The magnitude of the weight W is unknown, but the counterbalance weight is known to be 2000 lb; column R supports the beam as shown. Assuming that the support cables have been omitted, we desire to find the weight W that would balance the beam.

This problem can be solved by the application of the law of moments, i.e., the force is multiplied by the perpendicular distance to its line of action from a given point, or $F \times A$. If the beam is to be in balance, the total effect of the moments must be equal to zero, or $F \times A = W \times B$. Since W is the only unknown, we may solve for it algebraically. This equation is an inverse proportion that can also be solved graphically.

The graphical solution (Fig. 9–26B) is found by constructing a line to represent the total distance between the forces F and W. Point O is projected from the space diagram to this line. Point O is the point of balance where the summation of the moments will be equal to zero. Vectors F and W are drawn to scale at each end of the line by transposing them to the opposite ends of the beam. A line is drawn from the end of vector F through point O and extended to intersect the direction of vector W. This point represents the end of vector W, which can be scaled, resulting in a magnitude of 1000 lb. This method of construction could also be used to locate the position of a resultant and to determine its magnitude if only the applied forces, F and W, were known.

Fig. 9–25. The boom of this crane can be analyzed for its resultant as a parallel, nonconcurrent system of forces when the cables have been disregarded.

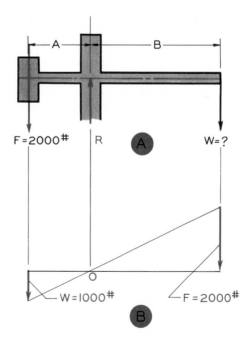

Fig. 9–26. Determining the resultant of parallel, nonconcurrent forces.

9–18 RESULTANT OF PARALLEL, NONCONCURRENT FORCES ON A BEAM

When two or more forces are applied to a beam that is supported at more than one point, such as the overhead beam in the aerospace research facility shown in Fig. 9–27, a somewhat different approach is taken to locate the resultant of the system. However, we shall use both a funicular diagram and Bow's notation to aid in the solution.

The beam given in Fig. 9–28 is supported at each end and must in turn support three given loads. We are required to determine the magnitude of each support, R_1 and R_2, along with the resultant of the loads and its location. The spaces between all vectors are labeled in a clockwise direction with Bow's notation in the space diagram in step 1. The given load vectors are added graphically by laying them head-to-tail in a single line, since the forces are parallel. Each end of the vectors is labeled using the letters of Bow's notation. Point O is located at a convenient position, and strings are drawn to the ends of each vector.

In step 2 the lines of force in the space diagram are extended and the strings from the vector diagram are drawn in their respective spaces, parallel to their original direction. *Example:* String *oa* is drawn parallel to string *OA* in space

FIGURE 9–28. BEAM ANALYSIS WITH PARALLEL LOADS

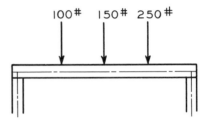

Given: A beam that is loaded with three parallel, unequal loads.
Required: Find the reactions R_1 and R_2 and the total resultant that will replace the parallel loads.
Reference: Article 9–18.

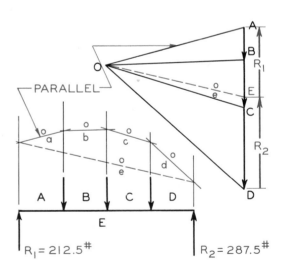

Step 2: Extend the lines of force in the space diagram, and draw a funicular diagram with string *oa* in the A-space, *ob* in the B-space, *oc* in the C-space, etc. The last string, which is drawn to close the diagram, is *oe*. Transfer this string to the vector polygon and use it to locate point E, thus establishing the lengths of R_1 and R_2 which are EA and DE, respectively.

AEROSPACE RESEARCH CHAMBER(7V)

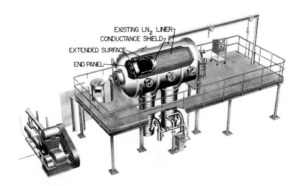

Fig. 9–27. The forces applied to the overhead beam can be analyzed graphically. (Courtesy of Arnold Air Force Station, ARO Inc.)

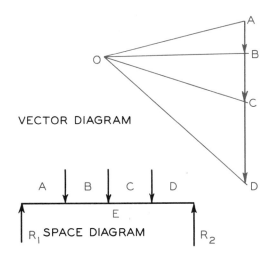

VECTOR DIAGRAM

SPACE DIAGRAM

Step 1: Letter the spaces between the loads with Bow's notation. Find the graphical summation of the vectors by drawing them head-to-tail in a vector diagram at a convenient scale. Locate pole O at a convenient location and draw strings from point O to each end of the vectors.

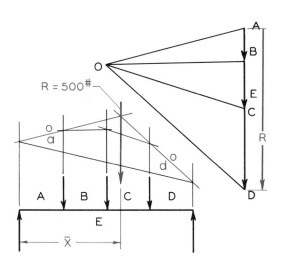

Step 3: The resultant of the three downward forces will be equal to their graphical summation, line AD. Locate the resultant by extending strings oa and od in the funicular diagram to a point of intersection. The resultant $R = 500$ lb, will act through this point in a downward direction. $\overline{X}$ is a locating dimension.

A between forces EA and AB, and string ob is drawn in space B beginning at the intersection of oa with vector AB. The last string, oe, is drawn to close the funicular diagram. The direction of string oe is transferred to the force diagram, where it is laid off through point O to intersect the load line at point E. Vector DE represents support R_2 (refer to Bow's notation as it was applied in step 1). Vector EA represents support R_1. This is the method for finding the resultants at each end of the beam.

The magnitude of the resultant of the loads (step 3) is the summation of the vertical downward forces, or the distance from A to D, or 500 lb. The location of the resultant is found by extending the extreme outside strings in the funicular diagram, oa and od, to their point of intersection. The resultant is discovered to have a magnitude of 500 lb, a vertical direction, a downward sense, and a point of application established by $\overline{X}$. This location would be important to an engineer if he intended to locate a third support under the beam.

Figure 9–29 shows a number of beams that had to be analyzed to determine their resultants and reactions. In a structure of this type, most of the forces applied are in a vertical direction, and the support members are also vertical.

Fig. 9–29. Structural beams are examples of parallel, nonconcurrently loaded beams. (Courtesy of Jones and Laughlin Steel Corporation.)

9-19 PRODUCT DESIGN—ANALYSIS

A product design example is used here to illustrate the application of graphical principles to its analysis. The problem is stated below.

Hunting seat problem. Many hunters, especially deer hunters, hunt from trees to obtain a better vantage point. Sitting in a tree for several hours can be uncomfortable and hazardous to the hunter, thus indicating a need for a hunting seat that could be used to improve this situation. Design a seat that would provide the hunter with comfort and safety while he is hunting from a tree and that would meet the general requirements of economy and limitations of hunting.

The refinement of the design was discussed in Chapter 2 to illustrate how graphical methods apply to that stage of the design process. The dimensions that were determined during refinement are now used as a basis for the vector analysis. These dimensions have been used on the work sheet in Fig. 9–30 to construct a space diagram from which a vector analysis of the seat's support system will be made. Only line representations are needed at this stage, since the structural system was determined in preliminary form in the refinement step. Lines will represent the center lines of the support members, which will be converted to vectors in the manner illustrated in this chapter.

It is assumed that a hunter weighing 210 lb, including hunting gear, is to be supported in the seat suspended from a tree by a cable attached at point O. This means that an opposite and equal force of 210 lb must be exerted at point O in an upward direction. This force is scaled as a vector, which is drawn adjacent to the front view. Since all support members lie in two planes that appear as edges in the front view, it is possible to determine the portion of the total load that will be supported by the left and right sides as shown in the vector diagram. It can be seen that the left side carries a greater load than the right side, since point O is off center and to the left. The vector which represents the load to be supported by the left side of the support system is not equal to the force

in any single member, but is a frontal vector that will be divided into components, as shown in the vector diagram in the center of the work sheet. The top and front views of the vector polygon give the components of the resultant force, which are measured to be 96 lb in the true-length diagram. This is the stress in both members O–4 and O–3. Using vector O–4, it is possible to determine, by a third vector polygon, the two unknown vectors that are concurrent at point 4 in the top view of the space diagram. Members 4–6 and 3–4 are found, thus completing the analysis of stresses on the heavier-loaded side.

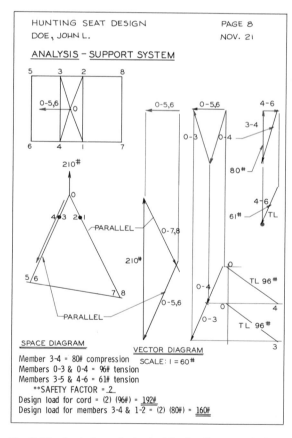

Fig. 9–30. Analysis work sheet of the hunting seat design.

This is a special problem since the forces are symmetrical about a frontal plane, through point O, which appears as an edge in the top view of the space diagram. A safety factor of 2 is used to ensure that adequate strength is provided to support the seat. The greatest load in single members, with a safety factor of 2, is in members O–3 and O–4, which have a design load of 192 lb. The load of the single cable supporting the system is 210 lb, or 420 lb when a factor of 2 is applied. The intermediate cords should be selected to withstand 192 lb. The stiffener, 3–4, should be selected to withstand 160 lb of compression.

Other analyses of this type can be applied to other components of the seat's structural system. Only this work sheet is shown as an example of the application of graphical methods. It would be beneficial to check this problem by the mathematical method to compare the results of each approach.

PROBLEMS

Problems should be presented *in instrument drawings* on $8\frac{1}{2}'' \times 11''$ paper, grid or plain, using the format introduced in Article 1–12. Each grid square represents $\frac{1}{4}''$. All notes, sketches, drawings, and graphical work should be neatly prepared in keeping with good practices. Written matter should be legibly lettered using $\frac{1}{8}''$ guide lines.

1. In Fig. 9–31(A), determine the resultant of the force system by the parallelogram method at the left of the sheet. Solve the same system using the vector polygon method at the right of the sheet. Scale: $1'' = 100$ lb (note that each gird square equals $\frac{1}{4}''$). (B) In part B of the figure, determine the resultant of the concurrent, coplanar force system shown at the left of the sheet by the parallelogram method. Solve the same system using the polygon method at the right of the sheet. Scale $1'' = 100$ lb.

9-20 SUMMARY

The analysis of forces is a prominent part of engineering and technology. It can be seen from the examples in this chapter that graphical methods have many applications in this area of analysis. In fact, the graphical method frequently has advantages over the conventional mathematical approach to the analysis of forces. The graphical method is much faster and presents fewer chances for errors that accumulate, as in the analytical method.

A number of more sophisticated graphical methods are available for solving advanced problems; however, these solutions are based almost entirely on the fundamental problems covered in this chapter. A mastery of the fundamentals will provide a broad background for grasping the principles of complex problems which will be encountered in more advanced courses.

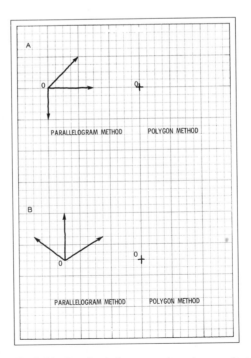

Fig. 9–31. Resultant of concurrent, coplanar vectors.

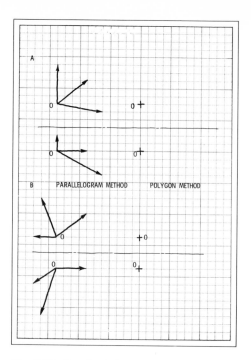

Fig. 9–32. Resultant of concurrent, noncoplanar vectors.

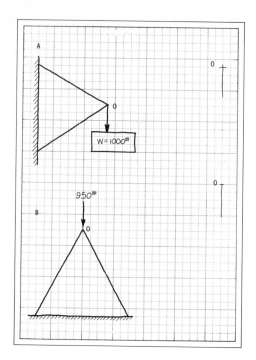

Fig. 9–33. Coplanar, concurrent forces in equilibrium.

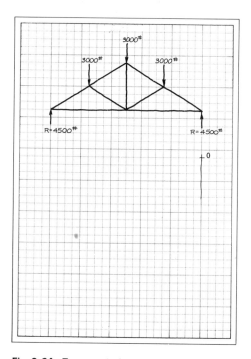

Fig. 9–34. Truss analysis.

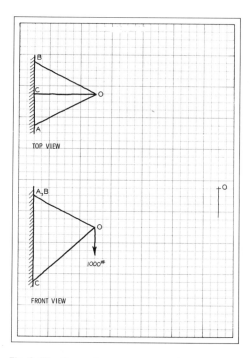

Fig. 9–35. Noncoplanar, concurrent forces in equilibrium.

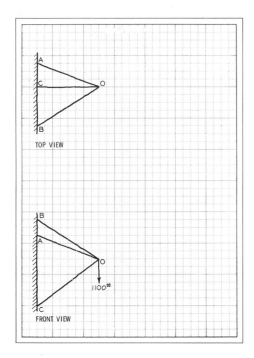

Fig. 9–36. Noncoplanar, concurrent forces in equilibrium.

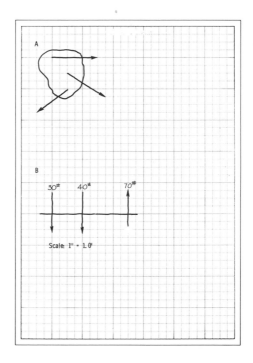

Fig. 9–37. Coplanar, nonconcurrent forces.

2. (A and B) In Fig. 9–32, solve for the resultant of each of the concurrent, noncoplanar force systems by the parallelogram method at the left of the sheet. Solve for the resultant of the same systems by the vector polygon method at the right of the sheet. Find the true length of the resultant in both problems. Letter all construction. Scale: $1'' = 600$ lb.

3. (A and B) In Fig. 9–33, the concurrent, coplanar force systems are in equilibrium. Find the stresses in each structural member. Use a scale of $1'' = 300$ lb in part A and a scale of $1'' = 200$ lb in part B. Show and label all construction.

4. In Fig. 9–34, solve for the stresses in the structural members of the truss. Vector polygon scale: $1'' = 2000$ lb. Label all construction.

5. In Fig. 9–35, solve for the stresses in the structural members of the concurrent, noncoplanar force system. Find the true length of all vectors. Scale: $1'' = 300$ lb.

6. In Fig. 9–36, solve for the stresses in the structural members of the concurrent, noncoplanar force system. Find the true length of all vectors. Scale: $1'' = 400$ lb.

7. (A) In Fig. 9–37, find the resultant of the coplanar, nonconcurrent force system. The vectors are drawn to a scale of $1'' = 100$ lb. (B) In part B of the figure, solve for the resultant of the coplanar, nonconcurrent force system. The vectors are given in their true positions and at the true distances from each other. The space diagram is drawn to scale of $1'' = 1.0'$. Draw the vectors to a scale of $1'' = 30$ lb. Show all construction.

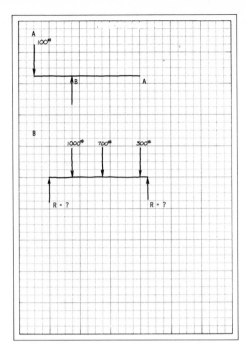

Fig. 9–38. Beam analysis.

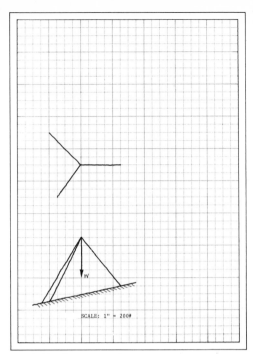

Fig. 9–39. Beam analysis.

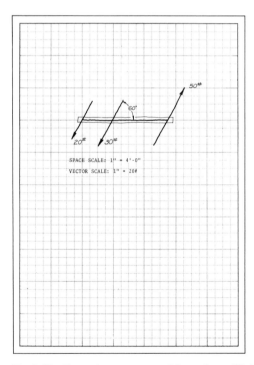

Fig. 9–40. Noncoplanar, concurrent forces in equilibrium.

8. (A) In Fig. 9–38, determine the force that must be applied at *A* to balance the horizontal member supported at *B*. Scale $1'' = 100$ lb. (B) In part B of the figure, find the resultants at each end of the horizontal beam. Find the resultant of the downward loads and determine where it would be positioned. Scale: $1'' = 600$ lb.

9. Determine the forces in the three members of the tripod in Fig. 9–39. The tripod supports a load of $W = 250$ lb. Find the true lengths of all vectors.

10. The vectors in Fig. 9–40 each make an angle of 60° with the structural member on which they are applied. Find the resultant of this force system. Refer to Article 9–16.

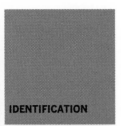

IDENTIFICATION

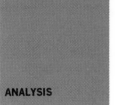

PRELIMINARY IDEAS

REFINEMENT

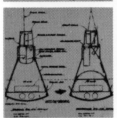

ANALYSIS

DECISION

IMPLEMENTATION

10
ANALYSIS OF DESIGN DATA

10-1 INTRODUCTION

Before a proposed design is accepted, it must be subjected to a careful analysis. During this process, data provided in many forms must be evaluated and interpreted. Most frequently, data are submitted in numerical form whose interpretation is often a lengthy and difficult procedure. Thus, to ensure that each member of the design team understands all aspects of the project (Fig. 10–1), it is customary to convert numerical data to a more convenient form which permits ready understanding.

Design information may be presented in a variety of forms. The more fundamental ones are: (1) graphs, (2) empirical equations, (3) mechanisms, (4) graphical calculus, and (5) nomograms. We shall discuss these areas of analysis to determine whether the presentation of data can be made easier through the use of graphics, since the graphic portrayal of tabular data allows a review of a large amount of data at a glance. Many data that are obtained from laboratory experiments or physical relationships can be expressed in terms of mathematical equations. This approach is helpful in that it establishes mathematical relationships that might not be apparent in the initial data. Graphical techniques can be used to advantage in determining the equation form of empirical data when such an equation exists. Using mathematical and analytical procedures (Fig. 10–2), mechanisms can be analyzed graphically for motion, function, clearance, and interference. Calculus problems can be solved graphically within the limits of reasonable accuracy. Thus the designer has at his disposal a variety of graphical procedures to supplement his analytical approach to studying a design.

10–1

10–2

10–3

10–4

Fig. 10–1. Engineering aspects of a toy engine are discussed by an industrial team. All aspects of the design and its analysis must be considered in detail before the design can be accepted for mass production. (Courtesy of Mattel, Inc.)

Fig. 10–2. Most products are tested extensively as a means of gathering data for analysis of the design; this testing is also important to effective quality control. (Courtesy of Mattel, Inc.)

Fig. 10–3. A prototype of a Dial-In-Handset telephone is tested with special sound equipment to determine its transmission qualities. (Courtesy of Bell Telephone Laboratories.)

Fig. 10–4. A Touch-Tone dial button tester is used to test the operational effectiveness of a telephone unit. (Courtesy of Bell Telephone Laboratories.)

10–2 INTRODUCTION TO GRAPHS

Any design can be evaluated to a considerable degree by reviewing the data that pertain to it. These data may fall into many different categories. Some of the basic ones are: (1) field data, (2) market data, (3) design-performance data and (4) comparative data.

Field data may affect a design directly or indirectly. A traffic engineer must gather information about traffic flow, driving habits, peak periods of volume, and traffic speed before he can prepare a new design for a traffic system at a given location. On-the-site observations and counts are made during representative periods and tabulated. It is also advisable to gather data on current designs that are believed to be satisfactory, to verify whether or not they are indeed as functional as they appear. Often, field data can be obtained from existing agencies. For instance, average temperatures, rainfall, and other weather records are usually maintained by local weather departments.

Market data are evaluated to determine the probable acceptance of an engineering project whether it is a supersonic aircraft or a household appliance; they serve as a guide in arriving at decisions concerning the market of a product. It is necessary to obtain information about the characteristics of the prospective users of the design, such as numbers, needs, average incomes, etc. Data about existing competition in the field are also of considerable value. No company will wish to produce a product for the general market that is too expensive for the typical consumer. Likewise, it would be poor planning to invest engineering funds in a public project that would not serve enough people. Data concerning populations, incomes, areas of population density, and statistical information are available from the Department of Labor and the U. S. Census Bureau, as well as state and local agencies. However, market data are meaningless unless they are presented in an understandable form which clarifies trends and existing situations.

Design performance must be studied to determine the effectiveness of a finished design. Frequently, a prototype is constructed specifically for testing the operation of the design prior to all-out production (Fig. 10–3). Most products are continuously evaluated through the process of quality control, and improvements are made in the basic design to eliminate weaknesses. Exhaustive tests are run from which data are gathered that are used as a source for further development. Failure of certain components under imposed conditions calls for modifications to improve existing designs (Fig. 10–4). Extreme conditions that a design is likely to be exposed to must be simulated prior to actual exposure, since it may not be possible to test the product under actual conditions without considerable danger and expense. The space program presents many examples of this requirement, since prior to actual flights many simulated tests have to be conducted and many data gathered to permit a sound evaluation of the limitations under which space exploration operates. The organization of these data into graphical form permits efficient analysis and evaluation.

Comparative data are used to establish relationships between two or more variables to improve the chances for making a correct decision. For example, to choose between two machines that will be used to produce the same product, one will compare the operational expenses required by each and their relative outputs, as well as the predicted life of each machine and its estimated maintenance expense. For specific applications, one may compare the advantages of one material versus those of another or the effectiveness of one fuel versus that of another.

10–3 TYPES OF GRAPHS

The nature of the data to be presented will determine the type of graph that will give the clearest picture of the information. The types of graphs emphasized in this chapter are primarily those used to analyze data that will aid in the final decision on a design. Although graphs do not make decisions or solve problems, they give the designer a picture of the background information and thus help him to familiarize himself with all aspects of the problem.

The basic types of graphs are:

1) linear (including rectangular, logarithmic, and semilogarithmic grids),
2) bar graphs,
3) pie or circular graphs,
4) polar graphs,
5) schematics and graphical diagrams,
6) computation graphs and nomograms.

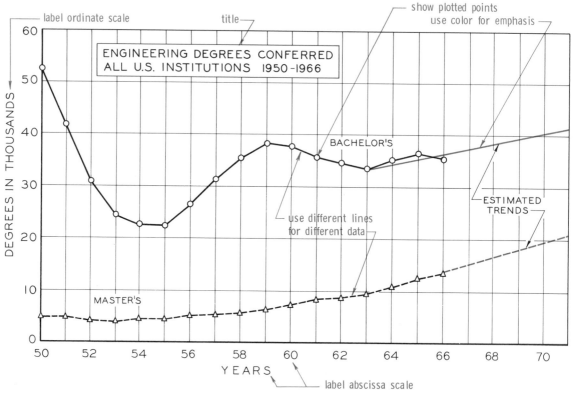

Fig. 10–5. The typical layout of a rectangular graph.

10-4 LINEAR GRAPHS—RECTANGULAR GRIDS

The linear graph is the one most commonly used to present information either to the general public or to a group of technically oriented people. Graphs of this kind may be drawn in their entirety, including the grid, or the data may be plotted on commercially prepared graph paper. A typical graph is shown in Fig. 10-5; the more important parts are properly labeled. A graph should be prepared with the same care and precision that would be exercised in any other portion of the design. The steps required to draw a graph are discussed in the following article.

10-5 DRAWING THE GRAPH

Refer to Fig. 10-5 in the following instructions for constructing a graph.

A. Selection of the Proper Grid. A graph that is to be presented in an engineering report can usually be plotted on commercially prepared graph paper. However, if the graph is to be used for publication, i.e. if it is to be reproduced in considerable quantities, then it should be traced in ink to ensure good reproduction. Only the important grid lines need be shown to permit easy analysis with a minimum of clutter. Note that the vertical scale in Fig. 10-5 was elongated to permit a noticeable variation in the data to be shown. Judgment must be used in selecting the scales to be assigned along the horizontal axis (abscissa) and the vertical axis (ordinate). Variation in either of these scales can exaggerate or minimize fluctuations. The relationship of the scales can best be interpreted by a person familiar with the information being presented.

B. Labeling the Axes. The independent variable is customarily plotted along the horizontal axis (the abscissa), and the dependent variable along the vertical axis (the ordinate). The dependent variable is best evaluated if its initial point is zero, i.e. if it is at the origin where the two axes intersect. When a vertical scale does not begin at zero, one loses the true comparison of basic trends that are advantageously shown by graphs. Although it is unnecessary to label each increment on the scale, it is preferable to label enough to permit easy interpolation. Consequently, the division, or grid, lines can be spaced according to the degree of interpolation that will be applied to the graph. If many small readings are to be made from the graph, many division lines are needed; however, if a graph will be used to portray general trends, grid lines are needed only at intervals. All scales should be labeled to be read from the bottom or the right side of the sheet. The intervals on each scale should be labeled, and a general legend should identify the units used in each scale. For example, the scales in Fig. 10–5 have been labeled "years" and "degrees in thousands."

C. Plotting the Data. The data should be plotted on the graph with symbols such as circles, triangles, rectangles, or crosses to indicate the actual data readings that were used to establish the location. The more points plotted on a graph from actual data, the more accurate will be the results. In Fig. 10–5, triangles and circles were used to indicate the plotted points. To ensure uniformity, these symbols should be drawn with a template.

D. Drawing the Curve. All data presented on a linear graph will be in one of two forms—*discrete* or *continuous*. The points representing discrete data are connected by straight lines; the resulting curve therefore often gives a broken-line appearance. The data shown in Fig. 10–5 are discrete, since there is no uniform rate of change between the data values. For example, no assumption can be made as to the number of degrees awarded at any point *between* 1953 and 1954; the data given refer only to the end of either of these years. On the other hand, the variation in speed plotted in Fig. 10–7 is continuous, since it is understood that there are an infinite number of speeds between 30 mph and 31 mph, for example, 31.01 mph, 31.02 mph, 31.03 mph, etc. To obtain a speed of 30 mph, every speed from 0 mph to 30 mph must be obtained in a continuous order; therefore a smooth curve is used to connect the points. Whether a straight-line curve or a smooth curve is drawn, the line should not continue through the symbols used to indicate the plotted points (see Fig. 10–5).

The line used to present data is commonly called a curve whether it is smooth or broken. The weight of the line is usually rather heavy to contrast with the grid on which it is drawn. When several lines appear on the same graph, symbols are used to distinguish one curve from another. Where possible, color should be added to distinguish between the data. Each curve is labeled or noted by a legend or a note near the curve. Note in Fig. 10–5 that the last four recorded years were used to estimate future trends. These trends are based on past history, and since they are general averages, they do not necessarily go through each plotted point. A different color or line symbol should be used to differentiate between actual and predicted data.

E. Title. All graphs should have a title (or caption) that will clearly identify the graph and give its general description. The importance of a title cannot be overemphasized, since a graph improperly labeled is meaningless. Data are often reviewed several months or years after they were presented graphically; hence a complete title will conserve valuable research time that might otherwise be necessary to regather data that have been poorly labeled.

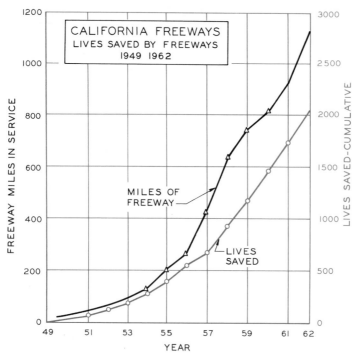

Fig. 10–6. A typical rectangular graph with composite scales to compare discrete data. (Courtesy of the California Highway Department.)

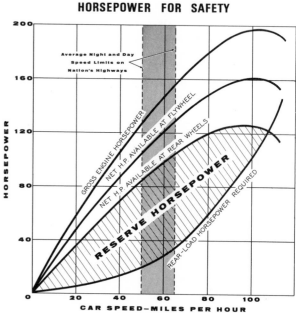

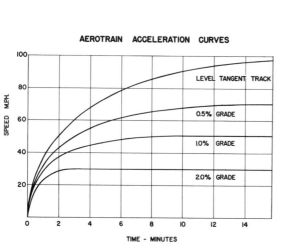

Fig. 10–7. A rectangular graph for presenting continuous data is connected with a smooth curve. (From *General Motors Engineering Journal*, **3**, No. 4, 1956, p. 15.)

Fig. 10–8. A rectangular graph used to analyze data affecting the design of an automobile's power system. (Courtesy of General Motors Corporation.)

The title can usually be placed within the grid of the graph to conserve space and to give a more pleasing appearance. Where space does not permit this, the title should be located prominently at the top or the bottom of the graph. For emphasis, titles can be surrounded by a box, as illustrated in Fig. 10–5.

10–6 INTERPRETATION OF LINEAR GRAPHS —RECTANGULAR GRIDS

In Fig. 10–6, construction of freeways in California is compared to the estimated number of lives that have been saved as a result of the freeways. Note that this graph has separate scales of different units on each ordinate—distance of freeways in miles and number of lives saved. Although the units are different, it is possible to compare the relationships between the two factors. It can be seen that approximately the same direct relationship exists between freeway miles and the number of lives saved, lending strong support to the effectiveness of freeways. These data are represented by a broken line, since roads are opened one section at a time rather than in a continuous manner.

The graph in Fig. 10–7 is an example of continuous data plotting. It compares the speed obtained during given time intervals by a vehicle on grades of four different levels. A higher rate of speed can be obtained on a level grade at a given time than on the steeper grades. The design of an automobile's power system is easily analyzed by referring to Fig. 10–8. Four types of data are compared to indicate the usable horsepower available at various velocities. The horsepower *available* at the rear wheels versus the horsepower *required* at the rear wheels is the critical information that must receive first study, since this factor will determine the performance of the automobile. The optimum speed is between 50 and 65 mph, which is the average driving speed. This provides the driver with a reserve of horsepower for quick acceleration and maneuverability to afford safety when most needed. This margin of horsepower reduces sharply after 80 mph and approaches zero at 110 mph where deceleration is the only possibility for change in speed in case of an emergency.

A simplified form of a rectilinear graph is shown in Fig. 10–9, in which the grid has been omitted. When only a visual impression is required rather than a graph from which actual computations can be made, the grid lines can be omitted. This graph compares the temperature increase in an automobile when only the front heater is used and the temperature increase when both the front and rear heaters are used.

Figure 10–10 is an example of computerized data translated into graphical form for visual interpretation. Data can be projected onto the face of a computer display tube at a rate of 30,000 characters per second.

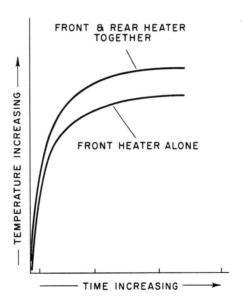

PERFORMANCE OF FRONT HEATER VS.
FRONT & REAR HEATER

Fig. 10–9. A rectangular graph comparing the speed of operation of two heater systems. (Courtesy of General Motors Corporation.)

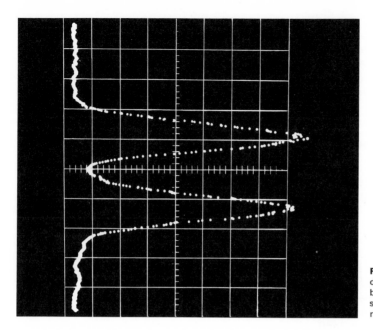

Fig. 10–10. Computer data output is translated directly into words, numbers, graphs, and symbols at speeds up to 30,000 characters per second on the tube face of data display equipment. (Courtesy of General Dynamics.)

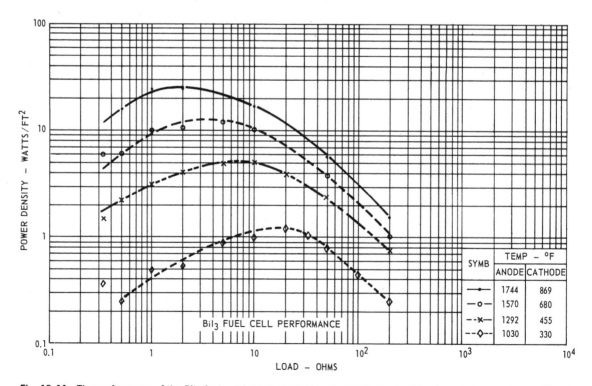

SYMB	TEMP – °F	
	ANODE	CATHODE
—•—	1744	869
—o—	1570	680
--×--	1292	455
--◇--	1030	330

BiI_3 FUEL CELL PERFORMANCE

POWER DENSITY – WATTS/FT^2

LOAD – OHMS

Fig. 10–11. The performance of the BiI_3 fuel cell is plotted on this logarithmic graph. (Courtesy of AeroJet-General Corp.)

10–7   LOGARITHMIC GRAPHS

The logarithmic graph is a type of rectangular graph in which the scales are graduated with logarithmic divisions along the ordinate and the abscissa. Commercially prepared logarithmic graphs are available in many forms and cycles to fulfill most needs. These graphs have definite uses in the analysis of empirical data (see Article 10–13).

Data that vary from small to very large numbers can be presented on logarithmic graphs in less space than would be required by a conventional rectangular grid. Note that there is no zero point on this type of graph, just as there is no zero on a slide rule scale. Each cycle is raised by a factor of ten. For example, in Fig. 10–11, the ordinate begins at 0.1 and ends at 1.0 for the first cycle. The second cycle is from 1.0 to 10 and the third cycle from 10 to 100. The abscissa is a five-cycle grid. The curves plotted in this graph are derived from experimental tests yielding variables that cannot be controlled; consequently, the plotted points suggest the trend of the curve rather than absolute points through which the curve must be drawn. The curve represents the average of the points, i.e. points are equally spaced on either side of the curve.

10–8   SEMILOGARITHMIC CHARTS

The semilogarithmic graph is referred to as a ratio graph or a rate-of-change graph, because one scale, usually the vertical scale, is logarithmic, while the other, usually the horizontal scale, is arithmetic (divided into equal divisions). Whereas the arithmetic graph gives a picture of absolute amounts of change, the semilogarithmic graph shows the relative rate of change. These two types of graphs are shown in Fig. 10–12, where the same data are plotted on each type of grid. The rate of change on the arithmetic graph can be computed from a common base point, but not from point to point as in the case of the semilogarithmic graph. Note that curve A in Fig. 10–12A appears to be increasing at a greater rate than curve B; however, the true comparison between the rates of changes of the two curves is shown in part B of the figure.

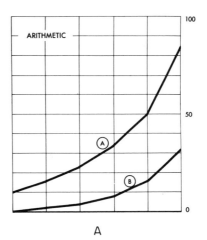

A

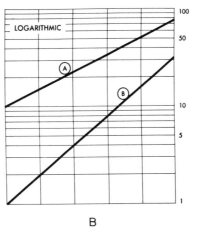

B

Fig. 10–12. Comparison of data plotted on an arithmetic scale and on a semilogarithmic scale. (Courtesy of USASI; Y15.2-1960.)

Curve A increases 50 percent each increment marked on the X-axis and 125 percent each double period. Curve B increases 100 percent each period, 300 percent each double period.

The relationship between the arithmetic scale used on the conventional rectilinear graph and the logarithmic scale used on the semilogarithmic graph can be seen in Fig. 10–13. Note that the equal amounts along the arithmetic scale have unequal ratios, and that the unequal amounts along the logarithmic scale have equal ratios. For data with a considerable variance from small numbers to relatively large numbers, commercially printed semilogarithmic

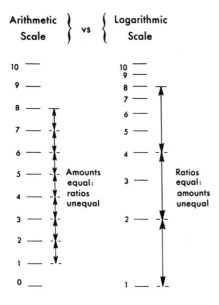

Arithmetic Scale } vs { Logarithmic Scale

Amounts equal: ratios unequal

Ratios equal: amounts unequal

Fig. 10–13. Relationship of the arithmetic scale to the logarithmic scale. (Courtesy of USASI; Y15.2-1960.)

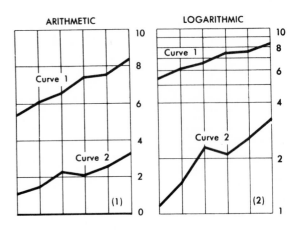

Fig. 10–15. A logarithmic scale shows a true picture of relative growth regardless of the magnitude of the data. (Courtesy of USASI; Y15.2-1960.)

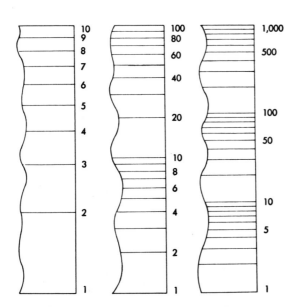

Fig. 10–14. Examples of one-cycle, two-cycle, and three-cycle logarithmic scales. Any number of cycles may be used, but three will accommodate most time-series data. (Courtesy of USASI; Y15.2-1960.)

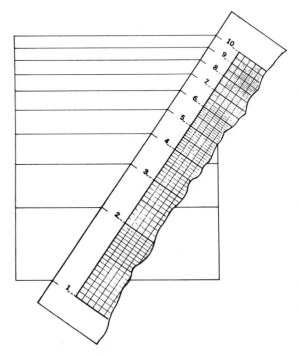

Fig. 10–16. The diagonal method of constructing a semilog grid from a printed grid. (Courtesy of USASI; Y15.2-1960.)

grid paper is available in several cycles. Examples of one-cycle, two-cycle, and three-cycle grids are shown in Fig. 10–14. Each cycle increases in magnitude by a factor of ten.

The important feature of the semilogarithmic graph is the angle of the change of the curve, since this represents the rate of change. An example of this principle can be seen in Fig. 10–15, in which the same data are presented on an arithmetic grid and a semilogarithmic grid. The relative growth of the data can be seen in the semilogarithmic graph regardless of the magnitude of the data, but is not as readily apparent in the arithmetic plot.

The semilogarithmic graph has certain fundamental advantages and disadvantages that must be considered before the type of grid best suited to the purpose is chosen. The advantages are:*

1) The semilogarithmic graph presents a picture that cannot be shown on an arithmetic scale chart;
2) it converts absolute data into a relative comparison, without computing;
3) it shows the relative change from any point to any succeeding point in a series;
4) it retains the actual units of measurement of the absolute data;
5) it reveals whether or not the data follow a consistent relative-change pattern.

The disadvantages must also be considered:*

1) The semilogarithmic graph presents a picture that many people misunderstand and mistakenly read as an arithmetic graph;
2) it cannot be used for data that include a zero or a negative value;
3) it does not provide a scale from which percentage changes can be read directly;
4) it requires a comparison of angles of change, which are difficult to compare by eye;
5) it gives a percentage decrease at a different angle of change than the same percentage increase.

* Extracted from USASI Time-Series Charts (USASI Y15.2-1960).

The same general methods that are used to construct a rectilinear arithmetic graph are applied to a semilogarithmic graph. The principles can be reviewed by referring to Article 10–5. Plotted points should be indicated on the graph by circles or other geometric symbols to provide a visual impression of the actual data. A logarithmic scale can be constructed to fit any space limitation by dividing the cycle length into equal parts and then projecting from a sheet of printed logarithmic paper, as shown in Fig. 10–16. Semilogarithmic graphs will be covered in Article 10–16, in which we shall show how they can be used to set up equations from empirically derived data.

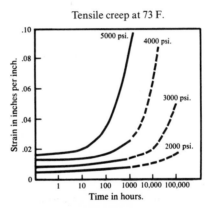

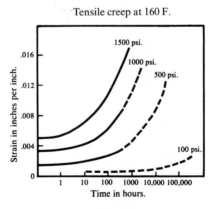

Fig. 10–17. A comparison of the deformation of a new material, Kralastic, under various loads at given temperatures. The logarithmic scale is along the horizontal axis. (Courtesy of U. S. Rubber Corporation.)

DC Curves

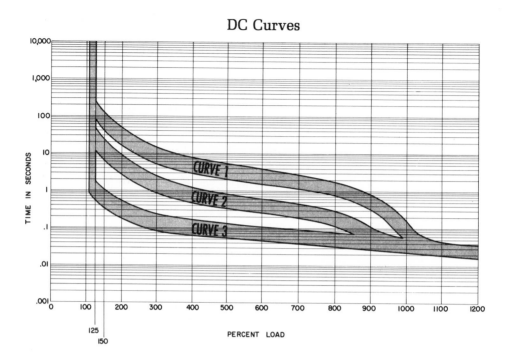

Fig. 10–18. The magnitude and duration of an overload that will be tolerated before tripping the circuit breaker. The logarithmic scale is along the vertical axis. (Courtesy of Heinemann Electric Company.)

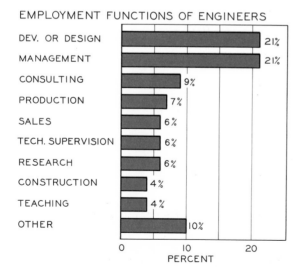

Fig. 10–19. The employment functions of engineers are shown in a bar graph. (Courtesy of the U. S. Department of Labor.)

Examples of semilogarithmic graphs are given in Figs. 10–17 and 10–18. Note that the logarithmic scale can be placed along either the vertical or the horizontal axis, depending on whichever is considered most appropriate for the data being plotted. Experience and knowledge of the data will dictate the construction and layout of the graph in specific applications.

10-9   BAR GRAPHS

Bar graphs are commonly used to compare a wide variety of variables, since they are readily understood by the general public. The bars may be vertical or horizontal (Fig. 10–19). Bar graphs are easier to interpret if the bars are arranged either in descending or ascending order according to their lengths or in chronological order. Often the amounts represented by the bars are also given numerically to pro-

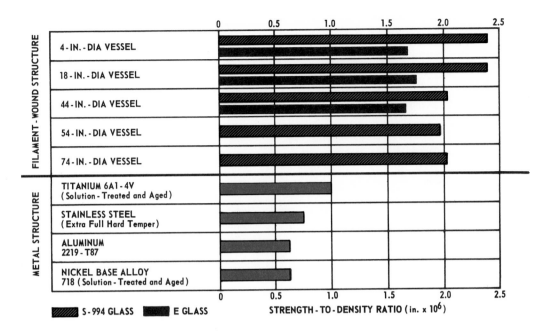

Fig. 10–20. The strength-to-density ratio of two basic types of structures is presented as a bar graph. (Courtesy of AeroJet-General Corporation.)

vide exact information. Figure 10–20 is an application of a bar graph to performance levels of pressure vessels of different sizes and materials. The bars are crosshatched or shaded differently to distinguish between different materials. A legend explains the meaning of each type of crosshatching used. The space between the bars and the widths of the bars should *not* be the same, so that the bars can easily be distinguished.

10–10 PIE GRAPHS

Pie graphs are used to compare the relationship of parts to a whole when there are not too many parts. Figure 10–21 shows the distribution of skilled workers employed in industry. The sectors are found by determining the percentage each part is of the whole and multiplying by 360°. For example, 25 percent of 360° is

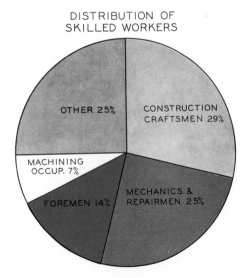

Fig. 10–21. The distribution of skilled workers presented in a pie graph. (Courtesy of U. S. Department of Labor.)

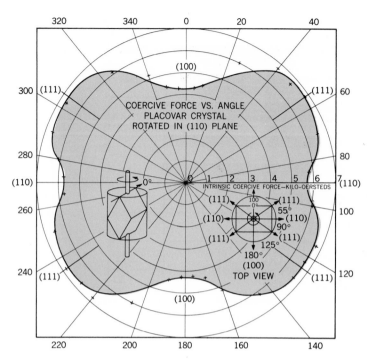

Fig. 10–22. A polar graph showing the magnitude of the intrinsic coercive force of a crystal as a function of crystallographic orientation. (Courtesy of Hamilton Watch Company.)

90°, which is the size of the sector for mechanics and repairmen. To facilitate lettering within narrow spaces, the narrow sectors should be placed in a horizontal position. Where there is not enough space, labels may be placed outside the sector. The actual percentages should be given in all cases, and, depending on the use of the graph, it may be desirable to give the actual numbers involved. Pie graphs are often used to present the expenditure of budgeted funds and other information to the general public.

10–11 POLAR GRAPHS

Polar graphs are composed of a series of concentric circles with the origin at the center. Lines are drawn from the center toward the perimeter of the graph where data can be plotted through 360° by measuring quantities from the origin. The coercive force of a Placovar crystal as it is rotated 360° is shown in Fig. 10–22. The maximum force is shown to be approximately at 55, 125, 235, and 305 degrees. This form of

graph is often used to plot the areas of illumination of lighting fixtures. Polar graph paper is available commercially.

10–12 SCHEMATICS

Designs and complicated systems may be more easily analyzed if schematics are used to separate major components. Figure 10–23 is a block diagram schematic that is useful in describing the components in a receiver. The diagram in Fig. 10–24 illustrates the layout of a reactor. Note that neither of these diagrams is drawn to scale or with any great degree of detail. Instead, they are kept simple and symbolic in order to emphasize the relationship of the components of the system. Similar schematics can be used to present more detailed components within each major section of the schematic. Diagrams of this type are used to illustrate various steps in production, or personnel organization, or any related sequence of components or activities.

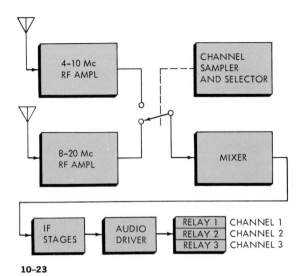

10-23

Fig. 10-23. A schematic diagram which shows the relationship between components of a dual-frequency command receiver. (Courtesy of Zenith Radio Corporation.)

Fig. 10-24. This schematic diagram of a reactor system effectively gives a simplified layout of its system. (Courtesy of the Atomic Energy Commission.)

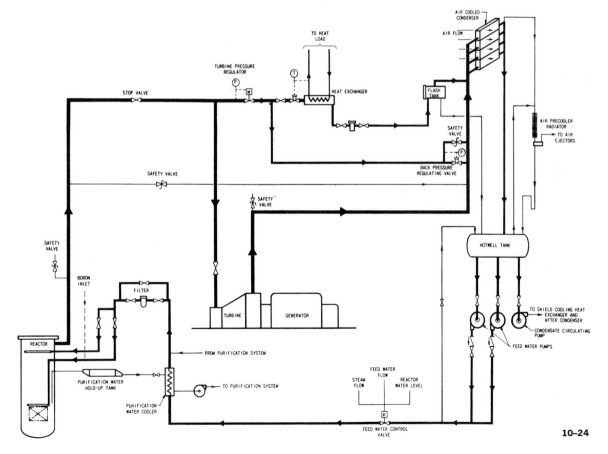

10-24

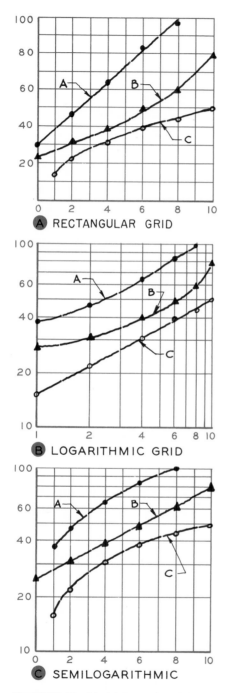

Fig. 10–25. Empirical data are plotted on each of these types of grids to determine which will render a straight-line plot. If the data can be plotted as a straight line on one of these grids, their equation can be found.

10–13 EMPIRICAL DATA

Data gathered from laboratory experiments and tests of prototypes or from actual field tests are called empirical data. Although in some instances there is no advance knowledge as to whether or not specific scientific relationships exist, in many cases the nature of the data makes it possible to set up equations that can be used to mathematically evaluate the data characteristics. Empirical data can be transformed to equation form by means of one of three types of equations to be covered here.

The analysis of empirical data begins with the plotting of the data on rectangular grids, logarithmic grids, and semilogarithmic grids. Curves are then sketched through each point to determine which of the grids renders a straight-line relationship (Fig. 10–25). We wish to determine a straight-line relationship so that we may find an equation for the data. Note that in the figure three sets of empirical data are plotted and that curves are sketched to connect them. Each curve appears as a straight line in one of the graphs. We use this straight-line curve to write an equation for the data.

10–14 LINEAR EQUATIONS

The curve fitting the experimental data plotted in Fig. 10–26 is a straight line; therefore, we may assume that these data are linear, meaning that each measurement along the Y-axis is directly proportional to X-axis units. We shall use the slope-intercept form to illustrate one method of writing the equation for the data.

Two known points are selected along the curve. The vertical and horizontal differences between the coordinates of each of these points are determined to establish the right triangle shown in part B of the figure. In the slope-intercept equation, $Y = MX + B$, M is the tangent of the angle between the curve and the horizontal, B is the intercept of the curve with the Y-axis, and X and Y are variables. In this example $M = \frac{30}{5} = 6$ and the intercept is 20, By substituting this information into the slope-intercept equation, we obtain $Y = 6X + 20$, from which we can determine values of Y by substituting any value of X into the equation.

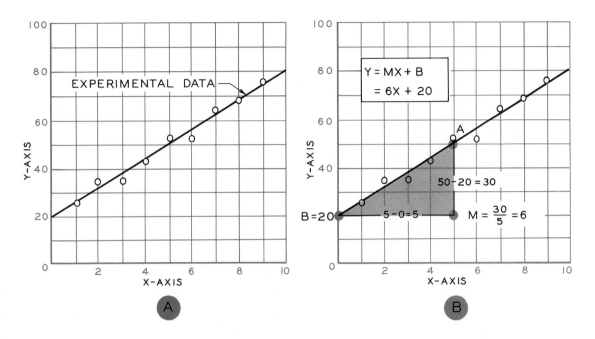

Fig. 10–26. Data that can be plotted as a straight line on an arithmetic grid have an equation of the linear form.

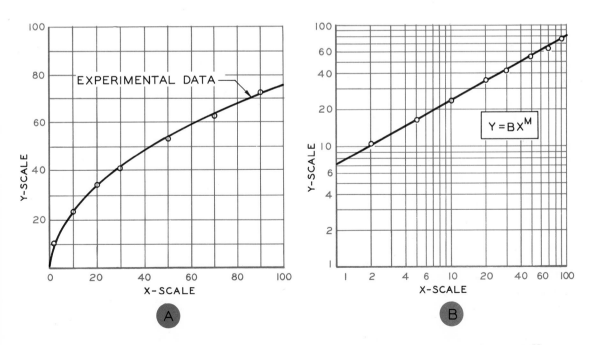

Fig. 10–27. Experimental data that project as a straight line on a logarithmic grid have a power equation, $Y = BX^M$.

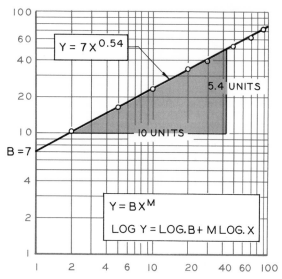

Fig. 10–28. The determination of the equation of a straight-line plot on a logarithmic grid.

10–15 THE POWER EQUATION $Y = BX^M$

Since the data shown plotted on a rectangular grid in Fig. 10–27A do not form a straight line, they cannot be expressed in the form of a linear equation. However, when the data are plotted on a logarithmic grid, they are found to form a straight line (Fig. 10–27B). Therefore, we express the data in the form of a power equation in which Y is a function of X raised to a given power or $Y = BX^M$. The equation of the data is obtained from Fig. 10–28 in much the same manner as was the linear equation, using the point where the curve intersects the Y-axis, and letting M equal the slope of the curve. Two known points are selected on the curve. Any linear scale in decimal units, such as the 20-scale on the engineers' scale, can be used, when the cycles along the X- and Y-axes are equal, to measure the vertical and horizontal differences between the coordinates of the two points. In determining the curve, no attention is paid to the units used along the X- and Y-axes, since these units may not be satisfactory. If the horizontal distance of the right triangle is drawn to be 1 or 10 or a multiple of 10, the vertical distance can be read off directly. In Fig. 10–28, the slope M (tangent of the triangle) is

found to be 0.54. The intercept B is 7; thus the equation is $Y = 7X^{0.54}$, which can be evaluated for each value of Y by converting this power equation into the logarithmic form of log Y:

$$\log Y = \log B + M \log X,$$

$$\log Y = \log 7 + 0.54 \log X.$$

10–16 THE EXPONENTIAL EQUATION $Y = BM^X$

The experimental data plotted in Fig. 10–29A form a curve, indicating that they are not linear. When the data are plotted on a semilogarithmic grid, as has been done in part B of the figure, they approximate a straight line for which we can write the equation $Y = BM^X$, where B is the Y-intercept of the curve and M is the slope of the curve. The procedure for deriving the equation is shown in Fig. 10–30, in which two points are selected along the curve so that a right triangle can be drawn to represent the differences between the coordinates of the points selected. The slope of the curve is found to be

$$\log M = \frac{\log 40 - \log 6}{8 - 3} = 0.1648$$

or

$$M = 1.46.$$

The value of M can be substituted in the equation in the following manner:

$$Y = BM^X \quad \text{or} \quad Y = 2(1.46)^X,$$

where X is a variable that can be substituted into the equation to give an infinite number of values for Y. We can write this equation in its logarithmic form, which enables us to solve it readily for the unknown value of Y for any given value of X. The equation can be written as

$$\log Y = \log B + X \log M$$

or

$$= \log 2 + X \log 1.46.$$

10–17 EXAMPLES OF EMPIRICAL DATA

Figure 10–31 is an example of how empirical data can be plotted to compare the specific weight (pounds per horsepower) of generators

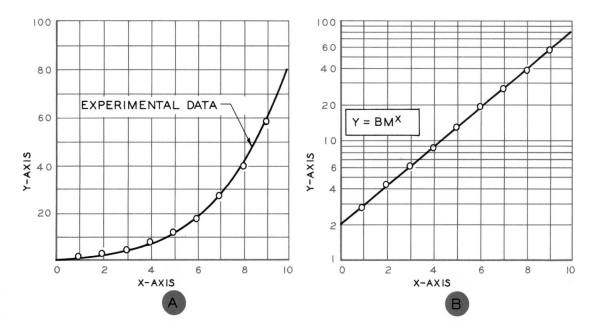

Fig. 10–29. Experimental data that can be plotted as a straight line on a semilogarithmic grid will have an equation of the exponential form, $Y = BM^X$.

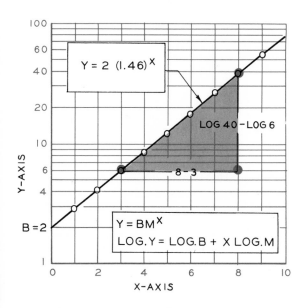

Fig. 10–30. The determination of the equation of a straight-line plot on a semilogarithmic grid.

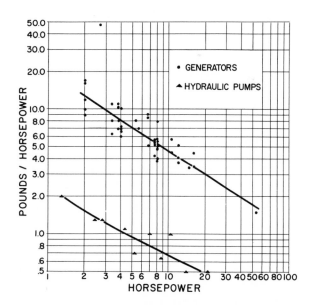

Fig. 10–31. Empirical data plotted on a logarithmic grid, showing the specific weight versus the horsepower of electric generators and hydraulic pumps. The curve is the average of points plotted. (Courtesy of General Motors Engineering Journal.)

DUCT VELOCITY/ PRESSURE RELATIONSHIPS

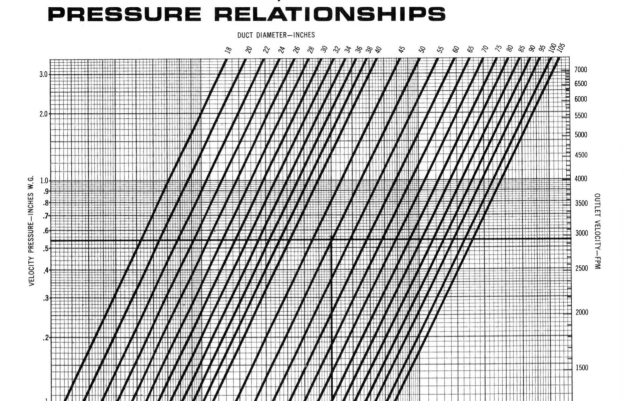

Fig. 10–32. Empirical data are used to determine two unknowns when two variables are given. Example: 40,000 cfm in a 50″ diameter duct. (a) Read directly upward from 40,000 cfm to the 50″ diameter line. (b) Read across to the right to obtain a velocity of 2940 fpm. (c) Read across to the left to obtain a 0.54″ W.G. velocity pressure. (Courtesy of Joy Manufacturing Corporation.)

and hydraulic pumps versus horsepower. Note that the weight of these units decreases as linearly as the horsepower increases. Therefore, these data can be written in the form of the power equation

$$Y = BX^M.$$

We obtain the equation of these data by applying the procedures covered in Article 10–14 and thus mathematically analyze these relationships.

Figure 10–32 is a logarithmic graph that is based on empirical data and can be used to

determine two unknowns when two variables are given. This type of graph is used for computations involving many repetitive operations dealing with the same data. For example, given that a flow of 40,000 cfm (cubic feet per minute) is desired in a 50″ diameter duct, we can find the velocity pressure and outlet pressure by reading directly up from the point labeled 40,000 cfm on the bottom horizontal to the diagonal labeled 50″ on the top horizontal giving the duct diameter. We read across to the right, and to the left from the point of intersection and find a velocity of 2940 fpm and a velocity pressure of 0.54″ W.G. These data can also be expressed in the form of the power equation, since the curves are straight lines plotted on a logarithmic grid.

10-18 INTRODUCTION TO MECHANISMS AND LINKAGES

Mechanisms are used to produce force or motion through a series of interrelated components. A mechanism is a combination of components based on rotation, leverage, or the inclined plane. A linkage is a type of mechanism relying primarily on leverage. An alternative system could be operated electronically with a minimum of mechanical links. Linkages and mechanisms are universally used in machinery (Fig. 10-33), jigs and fixtures, and, to some extent, in practically all designs. The analysis of mechanisms is often referred to as mechanics and is undertaken to determine the effects of forces upon the mechanisms.

The following definitions are fundamental to the study of linkages and mechanisms involved in a design:

Statics. The study of the effect of forces upon bodies or parts which are at rest or moving at uniform velocity.

Dynamics. The study of the effect of forces that cause a change in the motion of machine components or material bodies. Includes *Kinematics* and *Kinetics.*

Kinetics. The study of the effect of forces that cause a change in the motion of machine components or other bodies.

Kinematics. The study of motion without regard to forces.

These areas of analysis are very critical to the final analysis of a design. Complex analytical methods are employed to arrive at the final design configuration that will produce the most effective performance of a mechanism. However, as a supplement to the usual analytical

Fig. 10-33. This metal-forming machine illustrates the many linkages and mechanisms used in standard equipment. (Courtesy of A. H. Nilson Company.)

procedures, graphical methods can be used as a basis for initial steps toward analyzing a design. This chapter will be confined to graphical applications that can be used advantageously in this phase of analysis; no attempt will be made to cover the whole area of mechanics.

The mechanisms that are graphically analyzed in this chapter are cams and linkages. Several examples are given that are closely related to variations of rotary motion coupled with linkages. This motion is plotted on rectangular graphs to permit analysis.

10-19 CAMS

Cams (grooved cams, plate cams, or cylindrical cams) are components that produce motion in a single plane (usually up and down). A plate cam with a knife-edge follower is illustrated in Fig. 10-36. The cam revolving about an eccentric center produces a rise and fall in the follower during rotation. The configuration of the cam is analyzed graphically prior to the preparation of the specifications for its manufacture. Only plate cams are covered in the brief review of this mechanism. Cams utilize the principle of the inclined wedge, with the surface of the cam causing a change in the slope of the plane, thereby producing the desired motion.

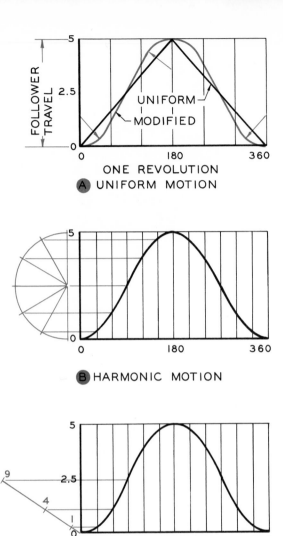

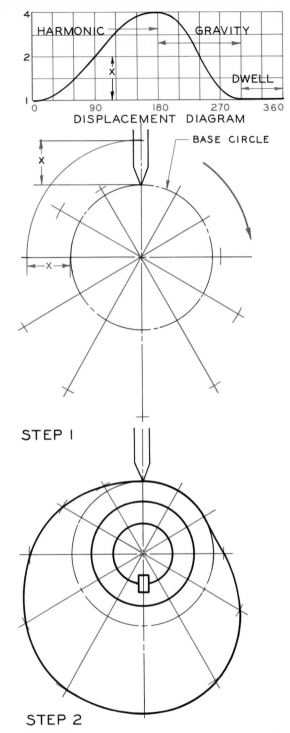

Fig. 10–34. The methods of plotting the three basic motions of cams—uniform, harmonic, and gravity.

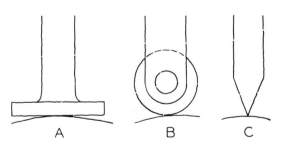

Fig. 10–35. Three basic types of cam followers—the flat surface, the roller, and the knife edge.

Fig. 10–36. The construction of a plate cam with a knife-edge follower.

10-20   TYPES OF CAM MOTION

Cams are designed primarily to produce (a) uniform or linear motion, (b) harmonic motion, (c) gravity motion, or (d) combinations of these. Some cams are designed to fit special needs that do not fit these patterns, but are instead based on particular design requirements.

Displacement diagrams are used to represent the travel of the follower relative to the rotation of the cam. Construction of a displacement diagram is the first step in cam design.

Uniform motion is shown in the displacement diagram in Fig. 10–34A. Displacement diagrams represent the motion of the cam follower as the cam rotates through 360°. It can be seen that the uniform motion curve has sharp corners, indicating abrupt changes of velocity at two points; this is impractical and inefficient, since it causes the follower to bounce. Hence this motion is usually modified with arcs that tend to smooth this change and thus the operation. The radius of the modifying arc can vary up to a radius of one-half the total displacement of the follower, depending upon the speed of operation. Usually a radius of about one-third to one-fourth total displacement is best.

Harmonic motion, plotted in part B of the figure, is a smooth continuous motion based on the change of position of the points on the circumference of a circle. At moderate speeds, this displacement results in a smooth operation. Note the method of drawing a semicircle to establish points on the displacement diagram.

Gravity motion, plotted in part C, is commonly used for high-speed operation. The variation of displacement is analogous to the force of gravity exerted on a falling body, with the difference in displacement being 1;3;5;5;3;1, based on the square of the number. For instance $1^2 = 1$; $2^2 = 4$; $3^2 = 9$. This same motion is repeated in reverse order for the remaining half of the movement of the follower. Intermediate points can be found by squaring fractional increments, such as $(2.5)^2$. The gravity fall of the follower is designed to conform to the shape of the cam, so that its contact with the surface will provide smooth operation.

10-21   CAM FOLLOWERS

Three basic types of cam followers are (A) the flat surface, (B) the roller, and (C) the knife edge, as shown in Fig. 10–35. The flat-surface and knife-edge followers are limited to use with slow moving cams where the minimum of force will be exerted by the friction that is caused during rotation. The roller is the most often used form of follower since it can withstand higher speeds and transmit greater forces.

10-22   CONSTRUCTION OF A CAM

A knife-edge follower is used with a plate cam to produce harmonic motion from 0° to 180°; gravity motion from 180° to 300°, and dwell (temporary stoppage of motion) from 300° to 360°. We are to draw from the given base circle the shape a cam will require. A displacement diagram is drawn in Fig. 10–36, in which the total displacement is drawn at the same scale as that to be used for the design of the cam. Uniform intervals are laid out along the horizontal scale, 30° in this case. The scale along the horizontal axis is not critical and can vary within a reasonable range.

Step 1. The harmonic portion of the displacement diagram is constructed by drawing a semicircle whose circumference is divided into the same number of equal parts as there are horizontal increments on the displacement diagram between 0° and 180°—six in this case. Refer to Fig. 10–34B. The gravity fall (4 increments in Fig. 10–36) of the follower is found by dividing the number of horizontal increments by 2; that is 4 : 2 = 2. Then 1^2 would give a travel of 1 during the first 30°, and 2^2 would give a travel of 4 from the peak, or a fall of 3 units in the increment between 210° and 240°. The units are laid out as shown in Fig. 10–34C. From 300 to 360 degrees, in which a dwell condition exists, the follower does not move; consequently, this portion of the curve is a straight line along the horizontal axis.

Radial lines are drawn from the center of the base circle to correspond to the intervals used

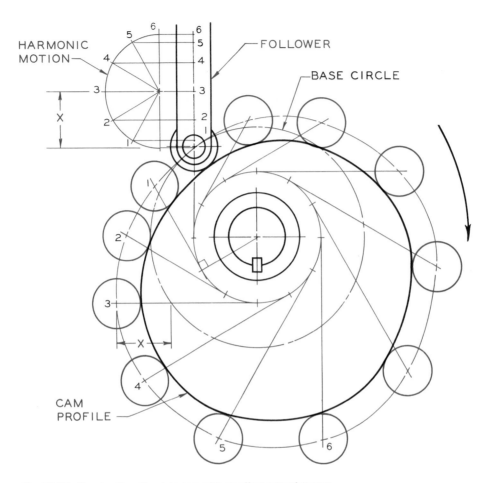

Fig. 10–37. Construction of a plate cam with an offset roller follower.

on the horizontal scale of the displacement diagram. The displacement is transferred with
dividers from the displacement diagram to appropriate radial lines measured from the base
circle. Distance *X* is located in Fig. 10–36 as an
example. Note that the initial measurements
are laid out on the side of the follower that is
opposite to the direction of rotation.

Step 2. All the points on the radial lines are
connected with a smooth curve to form the cam
profile that will produce the specified motion.
The hub and shaft key are drawn to indicate the
finished cam.

10–23 CONSTRUCTION OF A CAM WITH AN OFFSET ROLLER FOLLOWER

The cam in Fig. 10–37 is required to produce
harmonic motion through 360°. This motion
can be plotted directly from the follower rather
than on a displacement diagram, since there are
no combinations of motion involved. A semicircle is drawn with its diameter equal to the
total motion desired in the follower. In this case,
the base circle is the center of the roller of the
follower. The center line of the follower is extended down, and a circle is drawn with its
center at the center of the base circle so that it

Fig. 10–38. Examples of machined cams. (Courtesy of Ferguson Machine Company.)

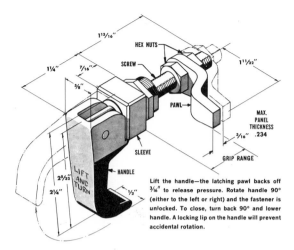

Lift the handle—the latching pawl backs off 3/16″ to release pressure. Rotate handle 90° (either to the left or right) and the fastener is unlocked. To close, turn back 90° and lower handle. A locking lip on the handle will prevent accidental rotation.

Fig. 10–39. An application of a cam to a latching pawl which secures a door. (Courtesy of South Chester Corporation.)

is tangent to the extension of the follower center line. This circle is divided into 30° intervals to establish points of tangency for all positions of the follower as it revolves through 360°. These tangent lines can be accurately constructed by drawing them perpendicular to the 30° interval lines extended from the center of the circle to the points on the circumference. The distances are transferred from the harmonic motion diagram to each subsequent tangent line. Distance *X* is located as an example of this procedure. The circular roller is drawn in all views and the profile of the cam is constructed to be tangent to the rollers at all positions, as shown.

Several examples of cams are shown in Fig. 10–38. Some cams give a follower motion in more than one plane, but most cams give a motion in a single plane. Cam blanks, from which cams are machined, are available from manufacturers who specialize in cams for general purposes.

10–24   OTHER APPLICATIONS OF CAMS

The latching pawl shown in Fig. 10–39 is an example of a cam used to apply pressure to secure a door that has been latched. This design could probably use an arc of a circle to serve the same purpose. However, as leverage becomes more critical, it is necessary to apply the principles of cam motion to provide the most efficient application of force and operation.

An application closely related to the principle of cam motion is shown in Fig. 10–40, which

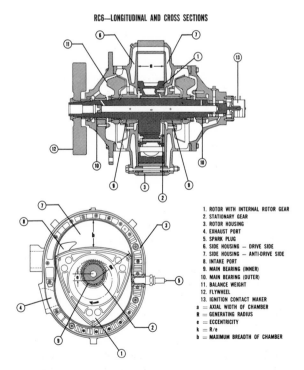

RC6—LONGITUDINAL AND CROSS SECTIONS

1. ROTOR WITH INTERNAL ROTOR GEAR
2. STATIONARY GEAR
3. ROTOR HOUSING
4. EXHAUST PORT
5. SPARK PLUG
6. SIDE HOUSING – DRIVE SIDE
7. SIDE HOUSING – ANTI-DRIVE SIDE
8. INTAKE PORT
9. MAIN BEARING (INNER)
10. MAIN BEARING (OUTER)
11. BALANCE WEIGHT
12. FLYWHEEL
13. IGNITION CONTACT MAKER
a = AXIAL WIDTH OF CHAMBER
R = GENERATING RADIUS
e = ECCENTRICITY
k = R/e
b = MAXIMUM BREADTH OF CHAMBER

Fig. 10–40. The cam principle as applied to an experimental engine, RC6. (Courtesy of Curtiss-Wright Corporation.)

Rotating Combustion Engine
COMBUSTION CYCLE

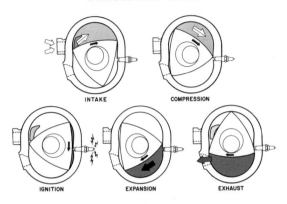

INTAKE   COMPRESSION

IGNITION   EXPANSION   EXHAUST

Fig. 10–41. The combustion cycle of the experimental engine, RC6. (Courtesy of Curtiss-Wright Corporation.)

illustrates the rotary mechanism of a combustion engine that utilizes an eccentrically mounted rotor that performs the same function as the piston in a conventional four-stroke combustion engine. The combustion cycle of this revolutionary engine is illustrated in Fig. 10–41 in a sequence of revolutions. Graphics is an important tool for developing a design of this type.

10–25   LINKAGES

The spacecraft shown in Fig. 10–42 employs a unique linkage system which is used to position the long-range earth sensor and the solar panels after the vehicle is in space. These linkages must be designed so that the components can be withdrawn into a position that will require minimum space during launching. The portable taper shown in Fig. 10–43 is a combination of gears, cams, and linkages. The hydraulic pusher in Fig. 10–44 which was designed to force pipe under roadways, is based on a linkage system utilizing hydraulic power. Linkages are universally used in mechanisms of all sizes. The initial analysis of a linkage system can be approached graphically, prior to the final mathematical analysis.

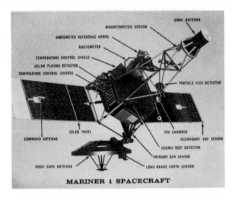

MARINER 1 SPACECRAFT

Fig. 10–42. The Mariner I Spacecraft uses a linkage system that allows the craft to be collapsed into a minimum of space during its flight through the earth's atmosphere. (Courtesy of the National Aeronautics and Space Administration.)

Fig. 10–43. This portable taper is composed of a combination of mechanisms and linkages. (Courtesy of the 3M-Company.)

Fig. 10–44. This pusher, which is used to force pipes under roadways, is a linkage system that uses hydraulic power. (Courtesy of Arnold Engineering Development Center.)

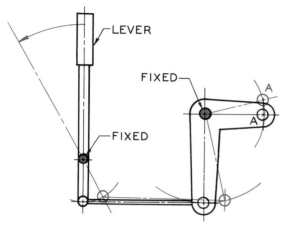

Fig. 10–45. A basic three bar linkage.

10-26 A BASIC LINKAGE SYSTEM

The simple linkage system shown in Fig. 10–45 illustrates the graphical analysis of a linkage, in which fixed points are given from which the components must pivot. The motion in this case is transmitted through levers to produce motion of point A. To locate the linkage components, all measurements are made by swinging arcs from the fixed pivot points. This is a three-bar linkage composed of three moving parts. An application of this type of system is shown in Fig. 10–46, which illustrates the linkage control system for a helicopter. To ensure proper power transmission and correct motion at the output, the designer must not only graphically analyze but also apply principles of mechanics to a linkage design of this type. Another application of a linkage system of this type is shown in Fig. 10–47.

10-27 LINKAGE APPLICATIONS

The revolution of a crankshaft is shown in Fig. 10–48, in which a connecting rod and a piston are analyzed for motion in a displacement diagram. This displacement can be found graphically with a high degree of accuracy if a sufficiently large scale is used. The graphical analysis assists the engineer in applying prin-

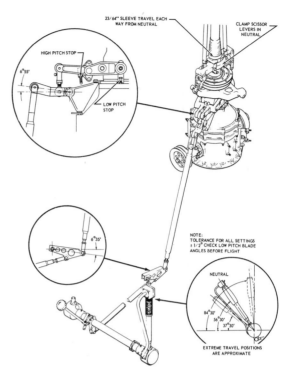

Fig. 10–46. An example of a linkage system used to control the blade pitch on helicopters. (Courtesy of Bell Helicopter Corporation.)

Fig. 10–47. This gate lock utilizes a combination of linkages and cams. (Courtesy of General American Transportation Corporation.)

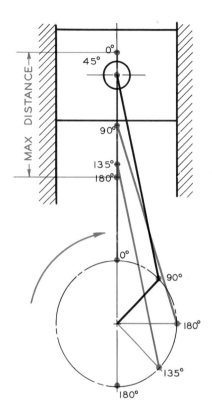

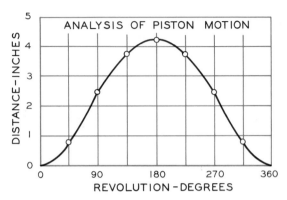

Fig. 10–48. The displacement of the travel of a piston caused by a crankshaft linkage. This is called a slider-crank mechanism.

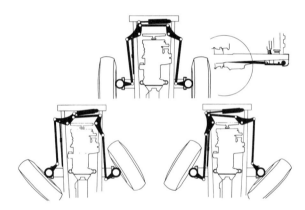

Fig. 10–49. A typical steering linkage system used on heavy-duty trucks. (Courtesy of LeTourneau-Westinghouse Company.)

ciples of mechanics to the analytical solution. A typical steering linkage system used on earth-moving trucks is shown in Fig. 10–49. Steering systems can be analyzed graphically to determine the motion of the components during the turning process.

The clearance requirements for a shuttle car to be used to convey coal or ore in limited spaces and on uneven surfaces is illustrated schematically in Fig. 10–50. It can be seen that the hinged shuttle car in part A is more efficient and has a larger capacity than the vehicle in part B. The general design of the required hinging motion was analyzed graphically to determine limits in Fig. 10–51. Clearances were a major consideration in arriving at the final dimensions of the vehicle, which is shown in operation in Fig. 10–52. The hinged body also required the study of power transmission linkage systems within the vehicle.

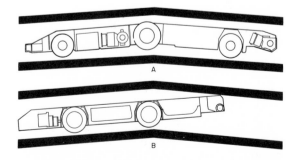

Fig. 10–50. Comparison of possible shuttle cars to be used in coal mining, in which one vehicle has been designed as a linkage system rather than in the conventional form. (Courtesy of Joy Manufacturing Corporation.)

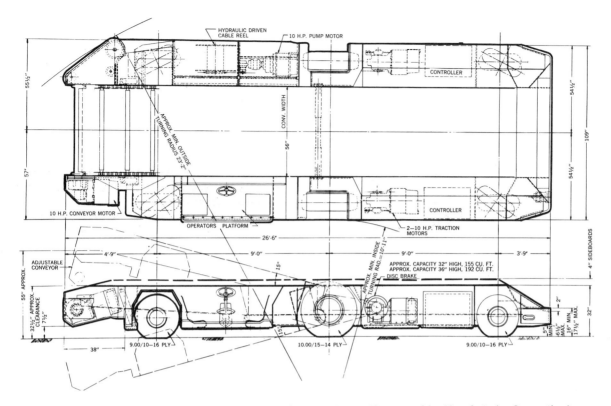

Fig. 10–51. The graphical analysis of the linkage system of the shuttle car. (Courtesy of Joy Manufacturing Corporation.)

Fig. 10–52. The shuttle car in use in a coal mine. (Courtesy of Joy Manufacturing Corporation.)

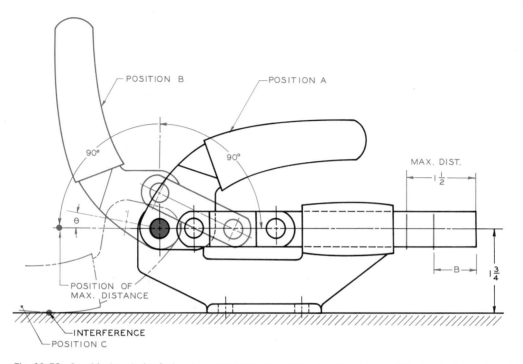

Fig. 10–53. Graphical analysis of a hand-operated clamping device that incorporates linkage principles. (Courtesy of Universal Engineering Corporation.)

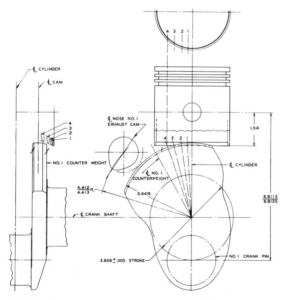

Fig. 10–54. Graphical determination of the clearance between a counterweight and a piston skirt. (Courtesy of Chrysler Corporation.)

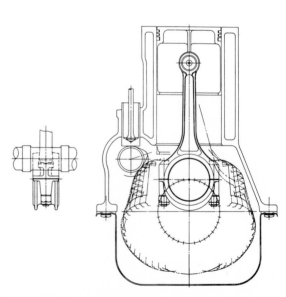

Fig. 10–55. Graphical clearances between the path of a connecting rod and the interior of a crankcase. (Courtesy of Chrysler Corporation.)

10-28 ANALYSIS OF A CLAMPING DEVICE

Many linkage systems are used in the design of clamping mechanisms which, as components of jigs and fixtures, are necessary for holding parts being machined. An example of such a device is shown in Fig. 10-53. The handle is shown in its closed position, position A, and in its revolved position, position B. A partial view of the handle is shown in position C, where the handle makes contact with the working surface. The graphical analysis of the linkage indicates that the plunger will be in its most withdrawn position at position C, where the handle is revolved θ degrees from the horizontal. If utilization of the maximum travel of the plunger were critical, the handle would have to be modified to permit full operation and hand clearance.

The advantage of the graphical method of analysis of a linkage system of this type is rather obvious. With a minimum of effort, the designer can determine the effects of the dimensions of each link with respect to the motion produced and the available clearance. The design of the handle must consider the position of the operator and the comfort of operation provided by its configuration. Within this framework other linkage systems can be developed that would enable the same clamping action with less movement of the handle if this were necessary.

10-29 ANALYSIS FOR CLEARANCE

A counterweight for an engine is shown in Fig. 10-54. For optimum operation, the counterweight should be as large as possible. The maximum radius of the counterweight is determined primarily by the path of the nose of exhaust cam 1. It is permissible to have a close clearance between the nose of the cam and the counterweight, since the centers of each are held closely, and the surfaces are finished to an acceptable tolerance. However, the clearance between the piston skirt and the counterweight should be questioned.

The determination of the clearance between these parts can be solved graphically. A series of sections, 1, 2, 3, and 4, are constructed from the center of the counterweight. The points are projected to the top and then to the side view, where the radial sections of the piston skirt can be seen. This view indicates that the application of a chamfer to the counterweight will provide the necessary clearance without interfering with effectiveness.

The path described by the connecting rod in Fig. 10-55 must be analyzed, since this path will influence the location of the camshaft, the crankcase walls, the width of oil pans, and other limiting factors. The clearance between the camshaft and the connecting rod bolt head can be close because these are finished surfaces whose centers are closely held. On the other hand, the clearance between the connecting rod and the walls and the oilpan must be somewhat greater to allow for imperfections in the rough forgings and rough crankcase walls. The designer can position the camshaft and establish the size of the crankcase by plotting the extreme path of the connecting rod. The graphical method lends itself to this form of analysis more than any other technique.

Clearances of electrical conductors within their available right-of-way can easily be evaluated by graphical techniques, as shown in Fig. 10-56. The method of supporting the conductors in part B of the figure requires a total right-of-way width of 183' to accommodate the maximum distance that the wind would blow the conductors at their lowest points between the two towers. By varying the method of support (part A) the same clearance of 12' can be maintained between the support towers but the right-of-way requirements drop: a width of only 122' is required, which is a savings of 61' or $7\frac{1}{2}$ acres per mile for an average savings of $225,000 for each 100 miles of line. The designer can employ graphical methods (sketches and scale drawings) to help him develop ideas of this type. His scale drawings serve to simplify the application of trigonometric calculations that will be made subsequently to check his graphical layout.

In Fig. 10-57, the operating positions for a backhoe are plotted in graphical form to permit visual analysis of its linkage system. The graph-

Fig. 10–56. Graphical design of a support for electrical conductors to reduce right-of-way requirements. (Courtesy of Ohio Brass Company.)

Fig. 10–57. A graphical analysis of the limits of operation of a 3141 Backhoe plotted on graph paper. (Courtesy of the International Harvester Company.)

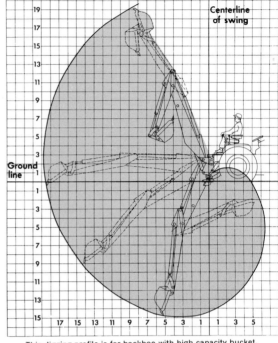

This digging profile is for backhoe with high capacity bucket. For digging profile with standard bucket, deduct 4½ inches.

10–57

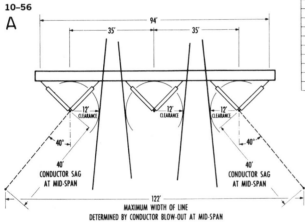

10–56

ical presentation of these positions can be used to communicate its operating characteristics and its limits of efficiency.

10-30 EMPIRICAL ANALYSIS OF A LINKAGE

Linkage systems are often designed to be movable so that the equipment may assume a variety of positions. An example of such a design can be seen in the vacuum booms for unloading barges shown in Fig. 10-58. These booms can be positioned to provide the most effective access to the cargo that is to be moved. When the booms are raised or lowered in different positions, the stresses in them and in the support cables will change. The maximum loads that will be supported by the boom, the strength of the cable, and the boom position will affect the limiting positions of the boom within which it can be safely operated. The boom is analyzed graphically in Fig. 10-59 to establish the stress in the cable when the boom is in a number of positions. The data thus obtained can be used to determine the safe operating area.

The boom is shown in seven positions in the space diagram loaded with the maximum load of 1000 lb, which will be a vertical force. Stress diagrams are drawn for each of the seven positions. For example, when the boom is at 15°, the stress in the cable is 360 lb. The stress in the cable versus the position of the boom is plotted in a graph. These points are connected with a smooth curve since the change in stress is continuous. Given that the cable is designed for an 1800-lb load, the critical point is found to be at 110°. If the boom is lowered beyond this point, the cable is subject to failure. Inspection of this graph will help the designer select a cable strong enough to withstand the stress imposed if the boom must be designed for lowering beneath the 110° zone. These data are empirical since only selected points were used. It is also customary to use a safety factor with data of this type to avoid variations or defects in the materials used.

10-31 INTRODUCTION TO GRAPHICAL CALCULUS

The engineer, designer, or technician must often deal with relationships between variables that must be solved using the principles of calculus. Data that can be dealt with by calculus and plotted on a graph can be approached graphically. If the equation of the curve is known, traditional methods of calculus will solve the problem. However, many engineering data cannot be converted to standard equations. In these cases, it is desirable to use the graphical method of calculus which provides relatively accurate solutions to irregular problems.

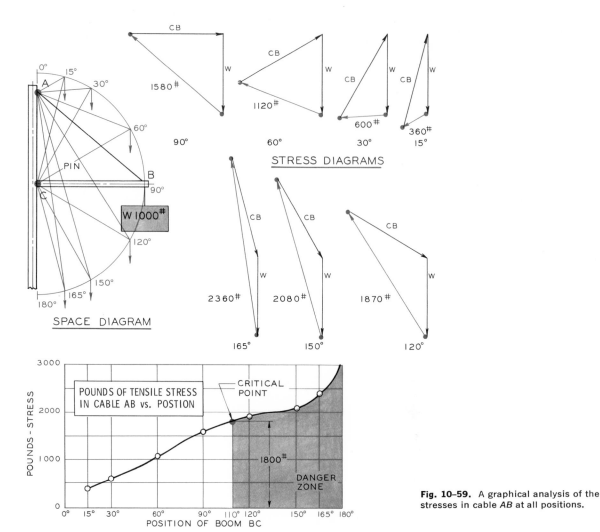

Fig. 10–59. A graphical analysis of the stresses in cable *AB* at all positions.

The two basic forms of calculus are (1) differential calculus, and (2) integral calculus. Differential calculus is used to determine the rate of change of one variable with respect to another. For example, the curve plotted in Fig. 10–60 represents the relationship between two variables. Note that the *Y*-variable is increasing as the *X*-variable increases. The rate of change of *Y* relative to *X* is an important characteristic that may influence the design of a mechanism. The rate of change at any instant along the curve is the slope of a line that is tangent to the curve

at that particular point. This exact slope is often difficult to determine graphically; consequently, it can be approximated by constructing a chord at a given interval, as shown in Fig. 10–60. The slope of this chord can be measured by finding the tangent of $\Delta Y/\Delta X$. These measurements give a general estimate of the slope of the line through this interval if the intervals are selected to be sufficiently small to minimize error. This slope can represent miles per hour, weight versus length, or a number of other meaningful rates that are important to the analysis of data.

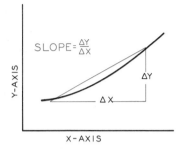

Fig. 10–60. The derivative of a curve is its rate of change at any point, which is the slope of curve, $\Delta Y/\Delta X$.

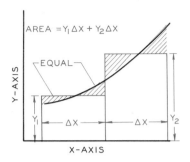

Fig. 10–61. The integral of a curve is the cumulative area enclosed by the curve, which is the product of the two variables.

Integral calculus is the reverse of differential calculus. Integration is the process of finding the area under a given curve, which can be thought of generally as the product of the two variables plotted on the X- and Y-axes. If one of the variables is area and the other is linear distance, the resulting integral is a volume. The area under a curve is approximated by dividing one of the variables into a number of very small intervals, which become small rectangular areas at a particular zone under the curve, as shown in Fig. 10–61. The bars are extended so that as much of the square end of the bar is under the curve as above the curve and the average height of the bar is therefore near its midpoint. Although this description of integration is the graphical method that will be used, it presents a general idea of the principles of calculus.

10-32 GRAPHICAL DIFFERENTIATION

Graphical differentiation is defined as the determination of the rate of change of two variables with respect to each other at any given point. Figure 10–62 illustrates the preliminary construction of the derivative scale that would be used to plot a continuous derivative curve from the given data.

Step 1. The original data are plotted graphically and the axes are labeled with the proper units of measurement. These grids need not be square, however; the nature of the data will influence the relationship of the X- and Y-units. The maximum scale required for the ordinate on

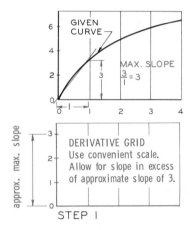

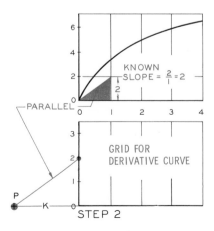

Fig. 10–62. The construction of scales for graphical differentiation.

FIGURE 10–63. GRAPHICAL DIFFERENTIATION

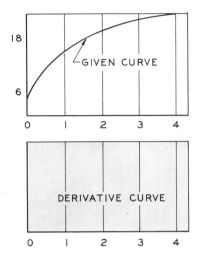

Given: The data plotted in the graph.
Required: Find the derivative curve of the given data.
Reference: Article 10–32.

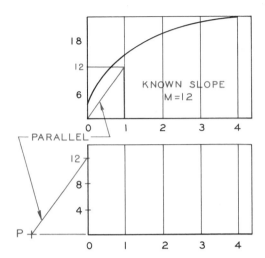

Step 1: Determine the pole distance in the derivative scale by applying the principles covered in Fig. 10–62. Find the known slope of 12 on the given scale, and draw an ordinate scale to provide for slope in excess of 12 on the derivative curve, the maximum estimated slope. Determine point P by drawing a slope from the 12 unit mark on the ordinate parallel to the known slope.

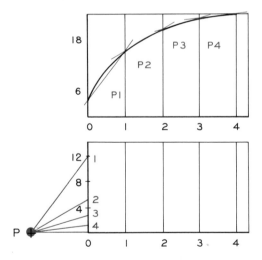

Step 2: Construct a series of chords between selected intervals on the given data curve and draw lines parallel to these chords through point P on the derivative grid. Locate points on the ordinate scale where these lines intersect. Shorter chords should be used for greater accuracy where the curve changes sharply.

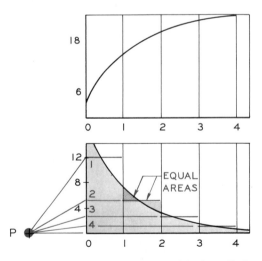

Step 3: Project points 1, 2, 3, and 4 horizontally from the ordinate scale to the intervals through which the chords were drawn. Carefully draw the derivative curve through these intervals near their midpoints. Note that the curve is constructed to have equal areas under and over the horizontal division of the bars. This curve represents the derivatives of the given data.

the derivative grid will be equal to the maximum slope of the original data. A series of chords can be constructed, so that it is possible to estimate the maximum slope by inspection. In the given curve, the maximum slope is estimated to be 3. A vertical scale is constructed in excess of 3 to provide for the plotting of slopes that may exceed the estimate. This ordinate scale is drawn to a convenient scale to facilitate measurement. It should be understood that the ordinate of the derivative scale at any point will be equal to the slope of the given curve, or its rate of change at that point.

Step 2. A known slope is plotted on the given data grid. This slope need not be related to the curve in any way. Construction is simpler if the horizontal interval used in the slope triangle is chosen to be 1, 10, or a multiple of 10, since this will simplify the arithmetic. In this case, the slope can be read directly as 2, since the abscissa spacing is 1 unit. The pole distance K can be found by drawing a triangle from the ordinate of 2 (the known slope) on the derivative scale so that its hypotenuse is parallel to the slope line. These similar triangles are used to obtain the pole distance K, which will be used in determining the derivative curve.

The steps in completing the graphical differentiation are given in Fig. 10–63. Note that the same horizontal intervals used in the given curve are projected directly beneath on the derivative scale. The procedure employed to determine the pole point P (discussed above) is applied in step 1. A known slope of 12 is found on the given grid. The maximum slope of the data curve is estimated to be slightly greater than 12. A scale is selected that will provide an ordinate that will accommodate the maximum slope. A line is drawn from point 12 on the ordinate axis of the derivative that is parallel to the known slope in the given curve grid. The point of intersection of this line and the extension of the X-axis is point P.

A series of chords are constructed on the given curve. These can be varied in length or interval to best approximate the curve. Lines are constructed parallel to these chords through point P and extended to the Y-axis of the derivative

grid to locate points 1, 2, 3, and 4. In step 3, these points are projected horizontally across to their respective intervals to give a series of vertical bars. A smooth curve is constructed through the top of these bars in such a manner that the area above the horizontal top of the bar is the same as that below it. This curve represents the derivative of the given data. The rate of change, Y/X, can be found at any interval of the variable X by reading directly from the graph at the value of X in question.

This system of graphical differentiation can be used to find the derivative curve of irregular and empirical data that cannot be expressed by a standard equation. Graphical differentiation is important, since many engineering data do not fit algebraic forms.

10–33   APPLICATIONS OF GRAPHICAL DIFFERENTIATION

The mechanical handling shuttle shown in Fig. 10–64 is used to convert rotational motion into a controlled linear motion. The linkage system for this operation is shown in Fig. 10–65 in pictorial form. A scale drawing of the linkage components is given in an orthographic view in Fig. 10–66, so that graphical analysis can be applied to determine the motion resulting from this system.

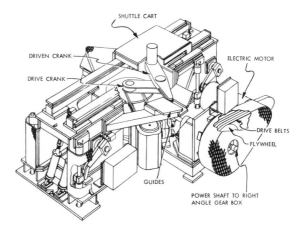

Fig. 10–64. An electrically powered mechanical handling shuttle used to move automobile parts on an assembly line. (Courtesy of General Motors Corporation.)

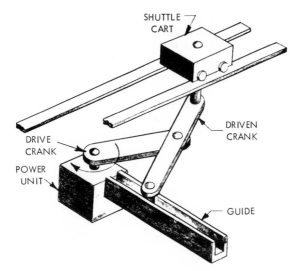

Fig. 10–65. The basic linkage system of the mechanical handling shuttle. (Courtesy of General Motors Corporation.)

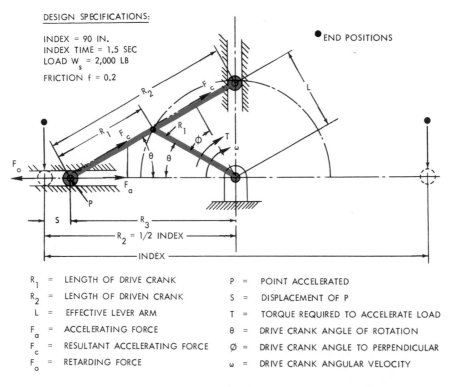

DESIGN SPECIFICATIONS:

INDEX = 90 IN.
INDEX TIME = 1.5 SEC
LOAD W_s = 2,000 LB
FRICTION f = 0.2

R_2 = 1/2 INDEX

INDEX

R_1	=	LENGTH OF DRIVE CRANK
R_2	=	LENGTH OF DRIVEN CRANK
L	=	EFFECTIVE LEVER ARM
F_a	=	ACCELERATING FORCE
F_c	=	RESULTANT ACCELERATING FORCE
F_o	=	RETARDING FORCE

P	=	POINT ACCELERATED
S	=	DISPLACEMENT OF P
T	=	TORQUE REQUIRED TO ACCELERATE LOAD
θ	=	DRIVE CRANK ANGLE OF ROTATION
$\emptyset$	=	DRIVE CRANK ANGLE TO PERPENDICULAR
ω	=	DRIVE CRANK ANGULAR VELOCITY

Fig. 10–66. A scale drawing of the linkage system of the mechanical handling shuttle which is used to graphically analyze its motion. (Courtesy of General Motors Corporation.)

The linkage is drawn to show the end positions of point P, which will be used as the zero point for plotting the travel versus the degrees of revolution. Since rotation is constant at one revolution per three seconds, the degrees of revolution can be converted to time, as shown in the data curve given at the top of Fig. 10–67. The drive crank, R_1, is revolved at 30° intervals, and the distance that point P travels from its end position is plotted on the graph, as shown in the given data. This gives the distance-vs.-time relationship. It is desirable to know the velocity and acceleration of the shuttle at various intervals, since these factors will influence the design of the unit. The rate of change of distance vs. time will give velocity, which is in units of inches per second. A derivative curve is needed to determine this rate of change at any instant.

We determine the ordinate scale of the derivative grid by estimating the maximum slope of the given data curve, which is found to be a little less than 100 in./sec. A convenient scale is chosen that will be used for the derivative curve; the maximum limit is 100 units. A slope of 40 is drawn on the given data curve; this will be used in determining the location of pole P in the derivative grid. From point 40 on the derivative ordinate scale, we draw a line parallel to the known slope, which is found on the given grid. Point P is the point where this line intersects the extension of the X-axis. The procedure of determining the pole distance and locating point P can be reviewed by referring to Fig. 10–62.

A series of chords are drawn on the given curve to approximate the slope at various points. In this example, the chords are drawn through the 30° intervals; however, these chords could be drawn through any interval. The intervals need not be equal, but should be spaced so as to give the best approximation to significant rate changes. Lines are constructed through point P of the derivative scale parallel to the chord lines of the given curve and extended to the ordinate scale. The points thus obtained are then projected across to their respective intervals to form vertical bars. A smooth curve is drawn through the top of each of the bars to give an average

of the bars (refer to Fig. 10–63). This curve can be used to find the velocity of the shuttle in inches per second at any time interval.

Analysis can also be used to determine the acceleration of the shuttle at various times. The construction of the second derivative curve is very similar to that of the first derivative. By inspecting the first derivative, we estimate the maximum slope to be 200 in./sec/sec. An easily measured scale is established for the ordinate scale of the second derivative curve. Point P is found by constructing a line of a known slope of 60 in the first derivative curve and locating the point where 60 is measured on the second derivative ordinate. From this point a line is drawn parallel to the known slope of 60 to intersect the X-axis; the point of intersection is P.

Chords are drawn at intervals on the first derivative curve. Lines are drawn parallel to these chords from point P in the second derivative curve to the Y-axis, where they are projected horizontally to their respective intervals to form a series of bars. A smooth curve is drawn through the tops of the bars to give a close approximation of the average areas of the bars. Note that a minus scale is given for the acceleration curve to indicate deceleration.

The maximum acceleration is found to be at the extreme endpoints and the minimum acceleration is at 90°, where the velocity is the maximum. It can be seen from the velocity and acceleration plots that the parts being handled by the shuttle are accelerated at a rapid rate until the maximum velocity is attained at 90°, at which time deceleration begins and continues until the parts come to rest. Note that unless there exists a proper relationship between velocity and acceleration, parts will be thrown from the carriage.

Cam displacement diagrams can be analyzed to determine the velocity and acceleration of the follower at any instant during the cam's revolution. The velocity and acceleration of the connecting rod in Fig. 10–48 can be found by graphical differentiation. The process of integration, which is discussed in the following article, can be applied to convert derivative curves to the original data and to find areas and volumes.

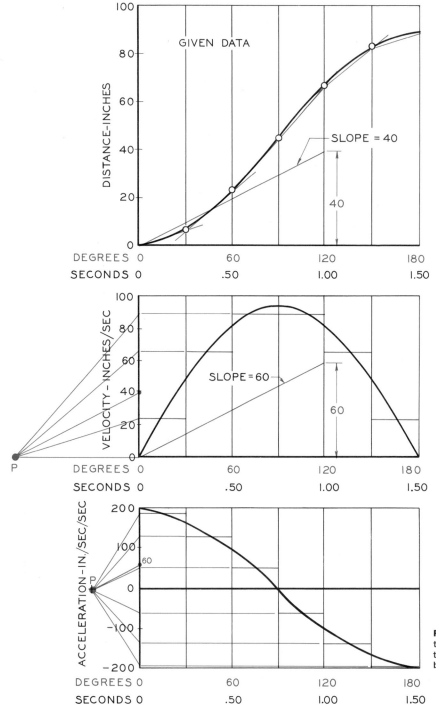

Fig. 10–67. Graphical determination of velocity and acceleration of the mechanical handling shuttle by differential calculus.

10-34 GRAPHICAL INTEGRATION

Integration is the process of determining the area (product of two variables) under a given curve. For example, if the Y-axis were pounds and the X-axis were feet, the integral curve would give the product of the variables, foot-pounds, at any interval of feet along the X-axis. Figure 10–68 depicts the method of constructing scales for graphical integration.

Step 1. The pole distance, K, is found in the given data grid by similar triangles. It is customary to locate the integral curve above the given data curve, since the integral will be an equation raised to a higher power. However, this arrangement is not necessary. A line is drawn through the given data curve to approximate the total area under the curve. This line is estimated to go through point 5 on the ordinate Y-axis to give approximately equal areas above and below the curve. The approximate area is 4 × 5 or 20 square units of area. The ordinate scale is drawn on the integral curve in excess of 20 units to provide a margin for any overage. The horizontal scale intervals are projected from the given curve to the integral grid. A convenient scale is used for the ordinate axis that will accommodate the size of the graph desired.

Step 2. The ordinate at any point on the integral scale will have the same numerical value as the area under the curve as measured from the origin to that point on the given data grid. A rectangular area is established on the given grid. The ordinate at point 2 on the X-axis directly above the rectangle must be equal to its area of 8. A slope is drawn from the origin to the ordinate of 8. Point P is found by drawing a line from point 4 on the given grid parallel to the slope established in the integral grid. This line intersects the extension of the X-axis at point P. This point will be used to find the integral curve. The procedure is opposite to that used in differentiation.

The technique illustrated in Fig. 10–69 can be applied to most integration problems. The equation of the given curve is $Y = 2X^2$, which

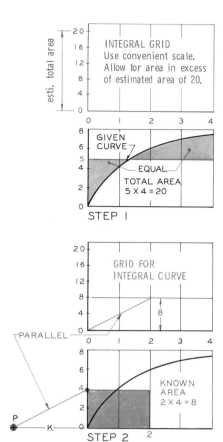

Fig. 10–68. Construction of scales for graphical integration.

can also be integrated mathematically as a check.

From the given grid, the total area under the curve can be estimated to be 40 units. This value becomes the maximum height of the Y-axis on the integral curve. A convenient scale is selected and units are assigned to the ordinate. The pole point, P, is found by constructing a rectangle of known area in the given grid and finding an ordinate in the integral curve above this area to represent the area. A line is drawn from the ordinate, MN, to the origin to give the slope of the line that will be drawn from point R to the extension of the X-axis, where point P is located. This procedure is explained in Fig. 10–68.

FIGURE 10–69. GRAPHICAL INTEGRATION

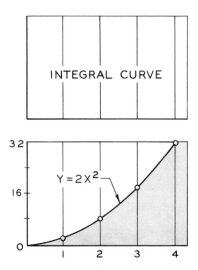

Given: The equation $Y = 2X^2$ plotted in graphical form.
Required: The integral curve of the given data.
Reference: Article 10–34.

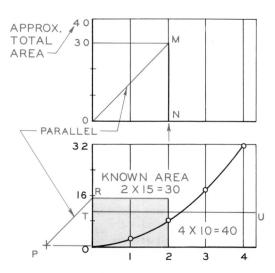

Step 1: The total area under the given curve is estimated to be 40 units by constructing line *TU*. Scale the ordinate on the integral grid to include a maximum of 40 units using a convenient scale. Find a known area of 30 on the given grid. Point *M* is the 30-unit point on the integral curve. Locate point *P* by applying the principles covered in Fig. 10–68.

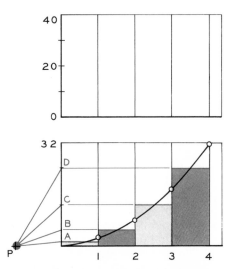

Step 2: Divide the given curve into a series of vertical bars that approximate the area under the curve at given intervals. These intervals need not be equal. Project the heights of the bars to points *A*, *B*, *C*, and *D* on the *Y*-axis and draw rays from these points to point *P*.

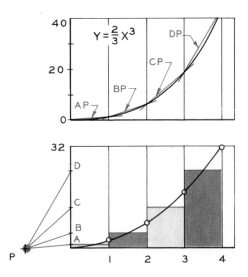

Step 3: Draw lines parallel to these rays in the integral grid at their respective intervals in succession. These sloping lines are drawn to represent the chords of the integral curve. Draw the curve through the chord intersections as shown. The total area under the integral curve from zero to three units can be measured as 18 on the integral graph.

A series of vertical bars are constructed at intervals to approximate the areas under the curve at these intervals. The narrower the bars, the more accurate will be the resulting calculations. The top lines of the bars are extended horizontally to the ordinate Y-axis, where the points are then connected by lines to point P. Lines are drawn parallel to AP, BP, CP and DP in the integral grid to correspond to the respective intervals in the given grid. The intersection points of the chords are connected by a smooth curve—the integral curve. This curve gives the cumulative product of the X- and Y-variables at any value along the X-axis. For example, the area under the curve at $X = 3$ can be read directly as 18.

Mathematical integration gives the following result for the area under the curve from 0 to 3:

$$\text{Area } A = \int_0^3 Y \, dX, \quad \text{where} \quad Y = 2X^2;$$

$$A = \int_0^3 2X^2 \, dX = \tfrac{2}{3}X^3\big]_0^3 = 18.$$

10–35 APPLICATIONS OF GRAPHICAL INTEGRATION

Integration is commonly used in the study of the strength of materials to determine shear, moments, and deflections of beams. An example problem of this type is shown in Fig. 10–70, in which a truck exerts a total force of 36,000 lb on a beam that is used to span a portion of a bridge. The first step is to determine the resultants supporting each end of the beam.

A scale drawing of the beam is made with the loads concentrated at their respective positions. A force diagram is drawn, using Bow's notational system for laying out the vectors in sequence. This process can be reviewed by referring to Article 9–12. Pole point O is located, and rays are drawn from the ends of each vector to O. The lines of force in the load diagram at the top of the figure are extended to the funicular diagram. Then lines are drawn parallel to the rays between the corresponding lines of force. For example, ray OA is drawn in the A-interval in the funicular diagram. The closing ray of the

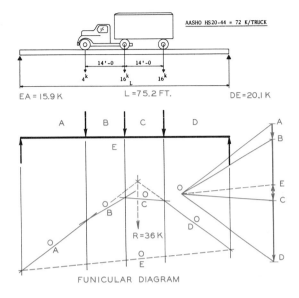

Fig. 10–70. The determination of the forces on a beam of a bridge and its total resultant.

funicular diagram, OE, is transferred to the vector diagram by drawing a parallel through point O to locate point E. Vector DE is the right-end resultant of 20.1 kips (one kip equals 1000 lb) and EA is the left-end resultant of 15.9 kips. The origin of the resultant force of 36 kips is found by extending OA and OD in the funicular diagram to their point of intersection.

From the load diagram shown in Fig. 10–71 we can, by integration, find the shear diagram, which indicates the points in the beam where failure due to crushing is most critical. Since the applied loads are concentrated rather than uniformly applied, the shear diagram will be composed of straight-line segments. In the shear diagram the left-hand resultant of 15.9 kips is drawn to scale from the axis. The first load of 4 kips, acting in a downward direction, is subtracted from this value directly over its point of application, which is projected from the load diagram. The second load of 16 kips also exerts a downward force and so is subtracted from the 11.9 kips (15.9 − 4). The third load of 16 kips is also subtracted, and the right-hand resultant will bring the shear diagram back to

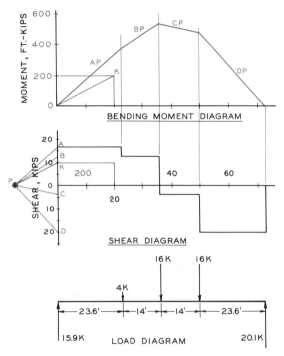

Fig. 10–71. The determination of shear and bending moment by graphical integration.

the X-axis. It can be seen that the beam must be designed to withstand maximum shear at each support and minimum shear at the center.

The moment diagram is used to evaluate the bending characteristics of the applied loads in foot-pounds at any interval along the beam. The ordinate of any X-value in the moment diagram must represent the cumulative foot-pounds in the shear diagram as measured from either end of the beam.

Pole point P is located in the shear diagram by applying the method described in Fig. 10–68. A rectangular area of 200 ft-kips is found in the shear diagram. We estimate the total area to be less than 600 ft-kips; so we select a convenient scale that will allow an ordinate scale of 600 units for the moment diagram. We locate the area of 200 ft-kips in the moment diagram by projecting the 20-ft mark on the X-axis until it intersects with a 200-unit projection from the

Y-axis, locating point K. The diagonal, OK, is transferred to the shear diagram, where it is drawn from the ordinate of the given rectangle to point P on the extension of the X-axis. Rays AP, BP, CP, and DP are found in the shear diagram by projecting horizontally from the various values of shear. In the moment diagram, these rays are then drawn in their respective intervals to form a straight-line curve that represents the cumulative area of the shear diagram, which is in units of ft-kips. Maximum bending will occur at the center of the beam, where the shear is zero. The bending is scaled to be about 560 ft-kips. The beam selected for this span must be capable of withstanding a shear of 20.1 kips and a bending moment of 560 ft-kips.

10–36   NOMOGRAPHY*

An additional aid in analyzing data is a graphical computer called a *nomogram* or *nomograph*. Basically, a nomogram or "number chart," is any graphical arrangement of calibrated scales and lines which may be used to facilitate calculations, usually those of a repetitive nature. The most frequently used nomograms are the common line graphs previously discussed in this chapter.

The term "nomogram" is frequently used to denote a specific type of scale arrangement called an alignment chart. Typical examples of alignment charts are shown in Fig. 10–72. Many other types are also used which have curved scales or other scale arrangements, for more complex problems. The discussion of nomograms in this chapter will be limited to the simpler conversion, parallel-scale, and N-type charts and their variations.

Using an Alignment Chart. An alignment chart is usually constructed to help solve for one or more unknowns in a formula or empirical relationship between two or more quantities, for example, to convert degrees centigrade to de-

---

* Articles 10–36 through 10–42 were written by Michael P. Guerard, Engineering Graphics, Texas A & M University.

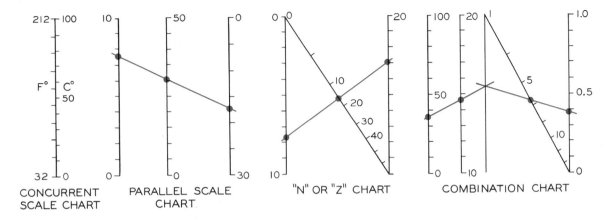

Fig. 10–72. Typical examples of types of alignment charts.

grees fahrenheit, to find the size of a structural member to sustain a certain load, etc. An alignment chart is read by placing a straightedge, or by drawing a line called an *isopleth,* across the scales of the chart, and reading corresponding values from the scales on this line. The example in Fig. 10–73 shows readings for the formula $U + V = W$.

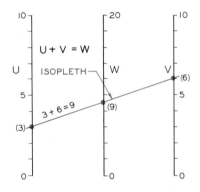

Fig. 10–73. The use of an isopleth to solve graphically for unknowns in the given equation.

10–37   ALIGNMENT CHART SCALES

To construct any alignment chart, we must first determine the graduations of the scales that will be used to give the desired relationships. Alignment-chart scales are called *functional scales*. A functional scale is one that is graduated according to values of some *function* of a variable, but *calibrated* with values of the variable. A functional scale for $F(U) = U^2$ is illustrated in Fig. 10–74. It can be seen in this example that if a value of $U = 2$ was substituted into the equation, the position of U on the functional scale would be 4 units from zero or $2^2 = 4$. This procedure can be repeated with all values of U by substitution.

The Scale Modulus. Since the graduations on a functional scale are spaced in proportion to values of the function, a proportionality, or scaling factor is needed. This constant of proportionality is called the *scale modulus* and it is

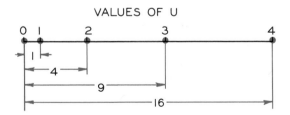

Fig. 10–74. A functional scale for units of measurement that are proportional to $F(U) = U^2$.

Table 10-1

U	0°	5°	10°	15°	20°	25°	30°	35°	40°	45°
X	0	0.74	1.47	2.19	2.90	3.58	4.24	4.86	5.45	6.00

given by the equation

$$m = \frac{L}{F(U_2) - F(U_1)}, \qquad (1)$$

where

  m = scale modulus, in inches per functional unit,

  L = desired length of scale, in inches,

$F(U_2)$ = function value at end of the scale,

$F(U_1)$ = function value at start of the scale.

For example, suppose that we are to construct a functional scale for $F(U) = \sin U$, with $0° \le U \le 45°$ and a scale 6″ in length. Thus $L = 6″$, $F(U_2) = \sin 45° = 0.707$, $F(U_1) = \sin 0° = 0$. Therefore Eq. (1) can be written in the following form by substitution:

$$m = \frac{6}{0.707 - 0} = 8.49 \text{ inches per (sine) unit.}$$

The Scale Equation. Graduation and calibration of a functional scale are made possible by a *scale equation.* The general form of this equation may be written as a variation of Eq. (1) in the following form:

$$X = m[F(U) - F(U_1)], \qquad (2)$$

where

  X = distance from the measuring point of the scale to any graduation point,

  m = scale modulus,

$F(U)$ = functional value at the graduation point,

$F(U_1)$ = functional value at the measuring point of the scale.

For example, a functional scale is constructed for the previous equation, $F(U) = \sin U$ ($0° \le U \le 45°$). It has been determined that $m = 8.49$, $F(U) = \sin U$, and $F(U_1) = \sin 0° = 0$. Thus by substitution the scale equation, (2), becomes

$$X = 8.49 (\sin U - 0) = 8.49 \sin U.$$

Using this equation, we can substitute values of U and construct a table of positions. In this case, the scale is calibrated at 5° intervals, as reflected in Table 10-1.

The values of X from the table give the positions, in inches, for the corresponding graduations, measured from the start of the scale ($U = 0°$); see Fig. 10-75. It should be noted that the measuring point does *not* need to be at one end of the scale, but it is usually the most convenient point, especially if the functional value is zero at that point.

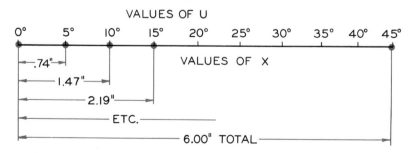

Fig. 10-75. Construction of a functional scale using values from Table 10-1, which were derived from the scale equation.

Table 10-2

r	1	2	3	4	5	6	7	8	9	10
X_r	0	0.15	0.40	0.76	1.21	1.77	2.42	3.18	4.04	5.00

Table 10-3

A	(3.14)	50	100	150	200	250	300	(314)
X_A	0	0.76	1.56	2.36	3.16	3.96	4.76	5.00

10-38 CONCURRENT SCALE CHARTS

Concurrent scale charts are useful in the rapid conversion of one value into terms of a second system of measurement. Formulas of the type $F_1 = F_2$, which relate two variables, can be adapted to the concurrent scale format. Typical examples might be the Fahrenheit-centigrade temperature relation,

$$°F = \tfrac{9}{5}°C + 32,$$

or the area of a circle,

$$A = \pi r^2.$$

Design of a concurrent-scale chart involves the construction of a functional scale for each side of the mathematical formula in such a manner that the *position* and *lengths* of each scale coincide. For example, to design a conversion chart 5″ long that will give the areas of circles whose radii range from 1 to 10, we first write $F_1(A) = A$, $F_2(r) = \pi r^2$, and $r_1 = 1$, $r_2 = 10$. The scale modulus for r is

$$m_r = \frac{L}{F_2(r_2) - F_2(r_1)}$$

$$= \frac{5}{\pi(10)^2 - \pi(1)^2} = 0.0161.$$

Thus the scale equation for r becomes

$$X_r = m_r[F_2(r) - F_2(r_1)]$$
$$= 0.0161[\pi r^2 - \pi(1)^2]$$
$$= 0.0161\pi(r^2 - 1)$$
$$= 0.0505(r^2 - 1).$$

A table of values for X_r and r may now be completed as shown in Table 10-2. The r-scale can be drawn from this table, as shown in Fig. 10-76. From the original formula, $A = \pi r^2$, the limits of A are found to be $A_1 = \pi = 3.14$ and $A_2 = 100\pi = 314$. The scale modulus for concurrent scales is always the same for equal-length scales; therefore $m_A = m_r = 0.0161$, and the scale equation for A becomes

$$X_A = m_A[F_1(A) - F_1(A_1)]$$
$$= 0.0161(A - 3.14).$$

The corresponding table of values is then computed for selected values of A, as shown in Table 10-3.

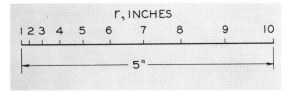

Fig. 10-76. The calibration of one scale of a concurrent scale chart using values from Table 10-2.

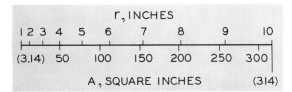

Fig. 10-77. The completed concurrent scale chart for the formula, $A = \pi r^2$. Values for the A-scale are taken from Table 10-3.

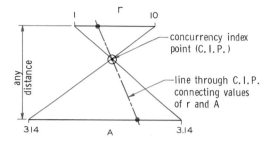

Fig. 10–78. A concurrent scale chart with unequal scales.

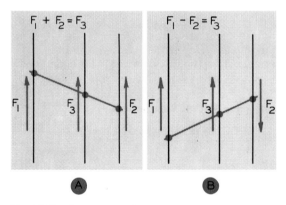

Fig. 10–79. Two common forms of parallel-scale alignment charts.

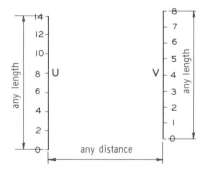

Fig. 10–80. Calibration of the outer scales for the formula $U + 2V = 3W$, where $0 \le U \le 14$ and $0 \le V \le 8$.

The *A*-scale is now superimposed on the *r*-scale; its calibrations have been placed on the other side of the line to facilitate reading (Fig. 10–77). It may be desired to expand or contract one of the scales, in which case an alternative arrangement may be used, as shown in Fig. 10–78. The two scales are drawn parallel at any convenient distance, and calibrated in *opposite* directions. A different scale modulus and corresponding scale equation must be calculated for each scale if they are *not* the same length.

10–39 CONSTRUCTION OF ALIGNMENT CHARTS WITH THREE VARIABLES

For a formula of three functions (of one variable each), the general approach is to select the lengths and positions of *two* scales according to the range of variables and size of the chart desired. These are then calibrated by means of the scale equations, as shown in the preceding section. The position and calibration of the third scale will then depend upon these initial constructions. Although definite mathematical relationships exist which may be used to locate the third scale, graphical constructions are simpler and usually less subject to error. Examples of the various forms are presented in the following articles.

10–40 PARALLEL-SCALE CHARTS

Many engineering relationships involve three variables that can be computed graphically on a repetitive basis. Any formula of the type $F_1 + F_2 = F_3$ may be represented as a parallel-scale alignment chart, as shown in Fig. 10–79A. Note that all scales increase (functionally) in the same direction and that the function of the middle scale represents the *sum* of the other two. Reversing the direction of any scale changes the sign of its function in the formula, as for $F_1 - F_2 = F_3$ in Fig. 10–79B.

To illustrate this type of alignment chart, we shall use the formula $U + 2V = 3W$, where $0 \le U \le 14$ and $0 \le V \le 8$. First, it is necessary to determine and calibrate the two outer scales for U and V; we can make them any con-

FIGURE 10–81.   PARALLEL-SCALE CHART (LINEAR)

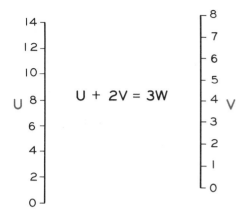

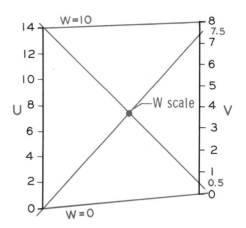

Given: The equation $U + 2V = 3W$ and the two scales constructed in Fig. 10–80.
Required: Construct a parallel-scale chart for determining various solutions of the given formula.
References: Articles 10–36 through 10–40.

Step 1: Substitute the end values of the U- and V-scales into the formula to establish the extreme values of the W-scale. These values are found to be $W = 10$ and $W = 0$. Select two sets of corresponding values of U and V that will give the same value of W. For example, when $U = 0$ and $V = 7.5$, W will equal 5, and when $U = 14$ and $V = 0.5$, W will equal 5. Connect these sets of values; the intersection of their lines locates the position of the W-scale.

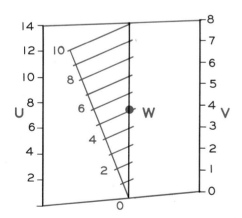

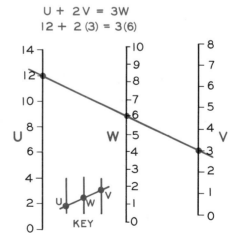

Step 2: Draw the W-scale parallel to the outer scales; its length is controlled by the previously established lines of $W = 10$ and $W = 0$. Since this scale is 10 linear divisions long, divide it graphically into ten units as shown. This will be a linear scale.

Step 3: The completed nomogram can be used as illustrated by selecting any two known variables and connecting them with an isopleth to determine the third unknown. A key is always included to illustrate how the nomogram is intended to be used. An example of $U = 12$ and $V = 3$ is shown to verify the accuracy of the graph.

venient length, and position them any convenient distance apart, as shown in Fig. 10–80. These scales are used as the basis for the step-by-step construction shown in Fig. 10–81.

The limits of calibration for the middle scale are found by connecting the endpoints of the outer scales and substituting these values into the formula. Here, W is found to be 0 and 10 at the extreme ends (step 1). Two pairs of corresponding values of U and V are selected that will give the *same* value of W. For example, values of $U = 0$ and $V = 7.5$ give a value of 5 for W. We also find that $W = 5$ when $U = 14$ and $V = 0.5$. This should be verified by substitution before continuing with construction. We connect these corresponding pairs of values with isopleths to locate their intersection, which establishes the position of the W-scale.

Since the W-scale is linear ($3W$ is a linear function), it may be subdivided into uniform intervals by the methods commonly used to divide a line into equal parts (step 2). For a nonlinear scale, the scale modulus (and the scale equation) may be found in step 2 by substituting its length and its two end values into Eq. (1) of Article 10–37. The scales can be used to determine an infinite number of problem solutions when sets of two variables are known, as illustrated in step 3.

Parallel-Scale Graph with Logarithmic Scales. Problems involving formulas of the type $F_1 \times F_2 = F_3$ can be solved in a manner very similar to the example given in Fig. 10–81 when logarithmic scales are used. An example of this type of problem is the formula $R = S\sqrt{T}$, for $0.1 \le S \le 1.0$ and $1 \le T \le 100$. Assume the scales to be 6″ long. These scales need not be equal except for convenience. This formula may be converted into the required form by taking common logarithms of both sides, which gives

$$\log R = \log S + \tfrac{1}{2} \log T.$$

Thus we have $F_1(S) + F_2(T) = F_3(R)$, where

$$F_1(S) = \log S,$$
$$F_2(T) = \tfrac{1}{2} \log T,$$
$$F_3(R) = \log R.$$

The scale modulus for $F_1(S)$ is, from Eq. (1),

$$m_s = \frac{6}{\log 1.0 - \log 0.1} = \frac{6}{0 - (-1)} = 6.$$

Choosing the scale measuring point from $S = 0.1$, we find from Eq. (2) that the scale equation for $F_1(S)$ is

$$X_S = 6(\log S - \log 0.1) = 6(\log S + 1).$$

Similarly, the scale modulus for $F_2(T)$ is

$$m_T = \frac{6}{\tfrac{1}{2} \log 100 - \tfrac{1}{2} \log 1} = \frac{6}{\tfrac{1}{2}(2) - \tfrac{1}{2}(0)} = 6.$$

Thus, the scale equation, measuring from $T = 1$, is:

$$X_T = 6(\tfrac{1}{2} \log T - \tfrac{1}{2} \log 1) = 3 \log T.$$

The corresponding tables for the two scale equations may be computed as shown in Tables 10–4 and 10–5. We shall position the two scales 5 in. apart, as shown in Fig. 10–82. The logarithmic scales are graduated using the values in Tables 10–4 and 10–5. The step-by-step procedure for constructing the remainder of the nomogram is given in Fig. 10–83 using the two outer scales determined here.

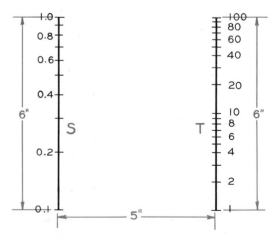

Fig. 10–82. Calibration of the outer scales for the formula, $R = S\sqrt{T}$, where $0.1 \le S \le 1.0$ and $1 \le T \le 100$.

Table 10–4

S	0.1	0.2	0.3	0.4	0.5	0.6	0.7	0.8	0.9	1.0
X_S	0	1.80	2.88	3.61	4.19	4.67	5.07	5.42	5.72	6.00

Table 10–5

T	1	2	4	6	8	10	20	40	60	80	100
X_T	0	0.91	1.80	2.33	2.71	3.00	3.91	4.81	5.33	5.77	6.00

Table 10–6

R	0.1	0.2	0.4	0.6	0.8	1.0	2.0	4.0	6.0	8.0	10.0
X_R	0	0.91	1.80	2.33	2.71	3.00	3.91	4.81	5.33	5.71	6.00

The end values of the middle (R) scale are found from the formula $R = S\sqrt{T}$ to be $R = 1.0\sqrt{100} = 10$ and $R = 0.1\sqrt{1} = 0.1$. Choosing a value of $R = 1.0$, we find that corresponding value pairs of S and T might be $S = 0.1$, $T = 100$ and $S = 1.0$, $T = 1.0$. We connect these pairs with isopleths in step 1 and position the middle scale at the intersection of the lines connecting the corresponding values. The R-scale is drawn parallel to the outer scales and is calibrated by deriving its scale modulus:

$$m_R = \frac{6}{\log 10 - \log 0.1} = \frac{6}{1 - (-1)} = 3.$$

Thus its scale equation (measuring from $R = 0.1$) is

$$X_R = 3(\log R - \log 0.1) = 3(\log R + 1.0).$$

Table 10–6 is computed to give the values for the scale. These values are applied to the R-scale as shown in step 2. The finished nomogram can be used as illustrated in step 3 to compute the unknown variables when two variables are given.

Note that this example illustrates a general method of creating a parallel-scale graph for all formulas of the type $F_1 + F_2 = F_3$ through the use of a table of values computed from the scale equation. As an alternative method, this center scale may be found graphically once the end values of the scales have been determined. An example of the graphical method is illustrated in Fig. 10–84, in which the scale is calibrated by graphical enlargement or reduction of the desired portions of printed logarithmic scales as found in common logarithmic graph paper.

10–41   N- OR Z-CHARTS

Whenever F_2 and F_3 are linear functions, we can partially avoid using logarithmic scales for formulas of the type

$$F_1 = \frac{F_2}{F_3} ;$$

instead, we use an N-chart, as shown in Fig. 10–85. The outer scales, or "legs" of the N are

FIGURE 10–83. PARALLEL-SCALE CHART (LOGARITHMIC)

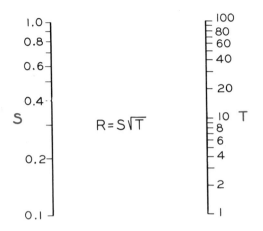

Given: The outer scales of a parallel-scale alignment graph determined in Fig. 10–82.
Required: Construct a parallel alignment chart for solving the equation $R = S\sqrt{T}$.
Reference: Article 10–40.

Step 1: Connect the end values of the outer scales to determine the extreme values of the R-scale, $R = 10$ and $R = 0.1$. Select corresponding values of S and T that will give the same value of R. Values of $S = 0.1$, $T = 100$ and $S = 1.0$, $T = 1.0$ give a value of $R = 1.0$. Connect the pairs to locate the position of the R-scale.

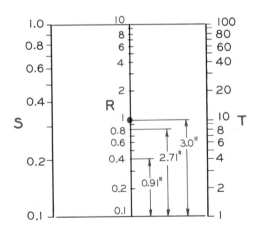

Step 2: Draw the R-scale to extend from 0.1 to 10. Calibrate it by substituting values determined from its scale equation. These values have been computed and tabulated in Table 10–6. The resulting tabulation is a logarithmic, two-cycle scale.

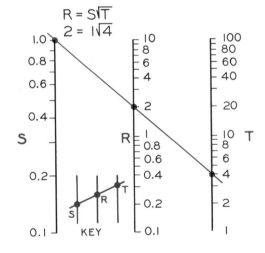

Step 3: Add labels to the finished nomogram and draw a key to indicate how it is to be used. An isopleth has been used to determine R when $S = 1.0$ and $T = 4$. The result of 2 is the same as that obtained mathematically, thus verifying the accuracy of the chart. Other combinations can be solved in this same manner.

functional scales and will therefore be linear if F_2 and F_3 are linear, whereas if the same formula were drawn as a parallel-scale chart, all scales would have to be logarithmic.

Some main features of the N-chart are:

1. The outer scales are parallel functional scales of F_2 and F_3.

2. They increase (functionally) in *opposite* directions.

3. The diagonal scale connects the (functional) *zeros* of the outer scale.

4. In general, the diagonal scale is not a functional scale for the function F_1 and is generally nonlinear.

Construction of an N-chart is simplified by the fact that locating the middle (diagonal) scale is usually less of a problem than it is for a parallel-scale chart. Calibration of the diagonal scale is most easily accomplished by graphical methods. To illustrate, an N-chart is constructed for the equation

$$A = \frac{B+2}{C+5},$$

where $0 \leq B \leq 8$ and $0 \leq C \leq 15$. This equation follows the form of

$$F_1 = \frac{F_2}{F_3},$$

where $F_1(A) = A$, $F_2(B) = B+2$, and $F_3(C) = C+5$. Thus the outer scales will be for $B+2$ and $C+5$, and the diagonal scale will be for A.

The construction is begun in the same manner as for a parallel-scale chart by selecting the layout of the outer scales (Fig. 10–86). As before, the limits of the diagonal scale are determined by connecting the endpoints on the outer scales, giving $A = 0.1$ for $B = 0$, $C = 15$ and $A = 2.0$ for $B = 8$, $C = 0$, as shown in the given portion of Fig. 10–87. The remainder of the construction is given in step form in the figure.

The diagonal scale is located by finding the *functional* zeros of the outer scales, i.e., the points where $B+2 = 0$, or $B = -2$, and $C+5 = 0$, or $C = -5$. The diagonal scale may

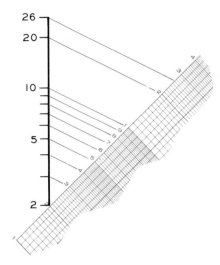

Fig. 10–84. Graphical calibration of a scale using logarithmic paper.

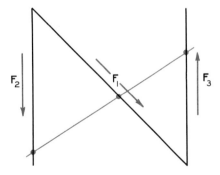

Fig. 10–85. An N-chart for solving an equation of the form $F_1 = F_2/F_3$.

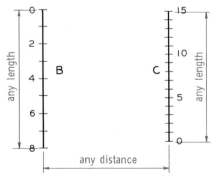

Fig. 10–86. Calibration of the outer scales of an N-chart for the equation $A = (B+2)/(C+5)$.

FIGURE 10–87.   CONSTRUCTION OF AN N-CHART

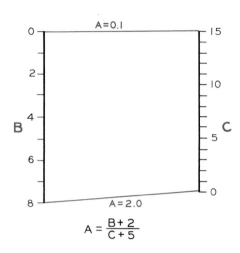

$$A = \frac{B+2}{C+5}$$

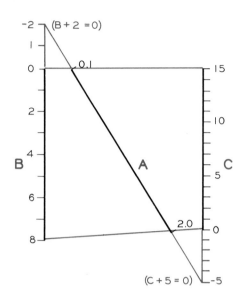

Given: The outer scales of an N-chart as determined in Fig. 10–86.
Required: Complete the N-chart for the formula $A = (B + 2)/(C + 5)$.
Reference: Article 10–41.

Step 1: Locate the diagonal scale by finding the functional zeros of the outer scales. This is done by setting $B + 2 = 0$ and $C + 5 = 0$, which gives a zero value for A when $B = -2$ and $C = -5$. Connect these points with diagonal scale A.

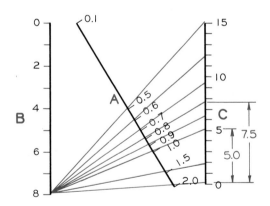

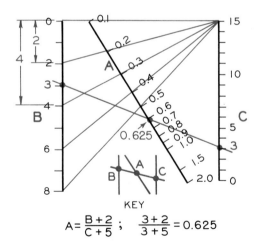

$$A = \frac{B+2}{C+5}; \quad \frac{3+2}{3+5} = 0.625$$

Step 2: Select the upper limit of one of the outer scales, $B = 8$ in this case, and substitute it into the given equation to find a series of values of C for the desired values of A, as shown in Table 10–7. Draw isopleths from $B = 8$ to the values of C to calibrate the A-scale.

Step 3: Calibrate the remainder of the A-scale in the same manner by substituting the upper limit of the other outer scale ($C = 15$) into the equation to determine a series of values on the B-scale for desired values on the A-scale, as listed in Table 10–8. Draw isopleths from $C = 15$ to calibrate the A-scale as shown. Draw a key to indicate how the nomogram is to be used. Solve an example problem to verify its accuracy.

Table 10-7

A	2.0	1.5	1.0	0.9	0.8	0.7	0.6	0.5
C	0	1.67	5.0	6.11	7.50	9.28	11.7	15.0

then be drawn by connecting these points as shown in step 1. Calibration of the diagonal scale is most easily accomplished by substituting into the formula. Select the upper limit of an outer scale, for example, $B = 8$. This gives the formula

$$A = \frac{10}{C + 5}.$$

Solve this equation for the other outer scale variable,

$$C = \frac{10}{A} - 5.$$

Using this as a "scale equation," make a table of values for the desired values of A and corresponding values of C (up to the limit of C in the chart), as shown in Table 10-7. Connect isopleths from $B = 8$ to the tabulated values of C. Their intersections with the diagonal scale give the required calibrations for approximately half the diagonal scale, as shown in step 2 of Fig. 10-87.

The remainder of the diagonal scale is calibrated by substituting the end value of the other outer scale ($C = 15$) into the formula, giving

$$A = \frac{B + 2}{20}.$$

Solving this for B yields

$$B = 20A - 2.$$

A table for the desired values of A can be constructed as shown in Table 10-8. Isopleths connecting $C = 15$ with the tabulated values of B will locate the remaining calibrations on the A-scale, as shown in step 3.

10-42 COMBINATION FORMS OF ALIGNMENT CHARTS

The types of charts discussed above may be used in combination to handle different types of formulas. For example, formulas of the type $F_1/F_2 = F_3/F_4$ (four variables) may be represented as *two* N-charts by the insertion of a "dummy" function. To do this, let

$$\frac{F_1}{F_2} = S \quad \text{and then} \quad S = \frac{F_3}{F_4}.$$

Each of these may be represented as shown in part A of Fig. 10-88, where one N-chart is inverted and rotated 90°. In this way the charts may be superimposed as shown in part B, if the S-scales are of equal length. The S-scale, being a "dummy" scale, does not need to be calibrated; it is merely a "turning" scale for intermediate values of S which do not actually enter into the formula itself. The chart is read with *two* isopleths which connect the four variable values and cross on the S-scale as shown in part C. Charts of this form are commonly called *ratio charts*.

Formulas of the type $F_1 + F_2 = F_3F_4$ are handled similarly. As in the preceding example, a "dummy" function is used: $F_1 + F_2 = S$, and $S = F_3F_4$. In order to apply the superimposition principle, a more equitable arrangement is obtained by rewriting the equations as $F_2 = S - F_1$ and $F_3 = S/F_4$. These two equations then take the form of a parallel-scale chart and

Table 10-8

A	0.5	0.4	0.3	0.2	0.1
B	8.0	6.0	4.0	2.0	0

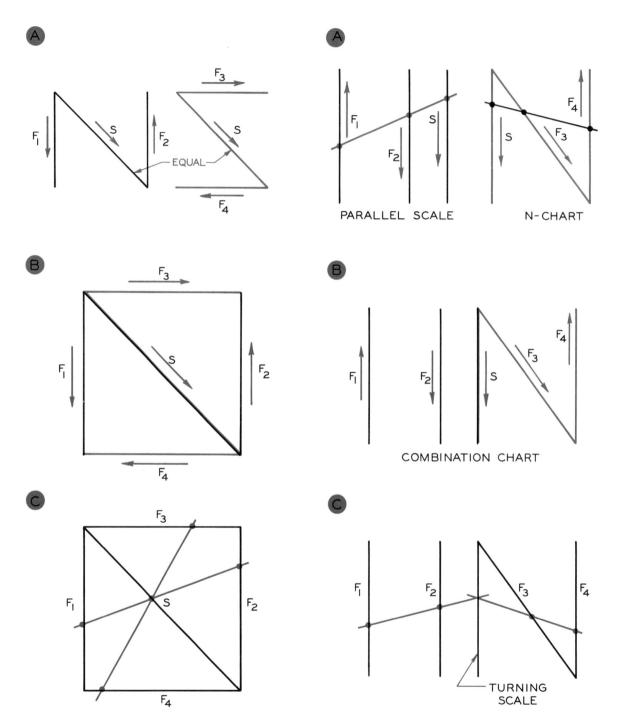

Fig. 10–88. A method of combining two N-charts with identical dummy scales, S. $F_1/F_2 = F_3/F_4$.

Fig. 10–89. A method of combining a parallel-scale chart and an N-chart with identical dummy scales, S.

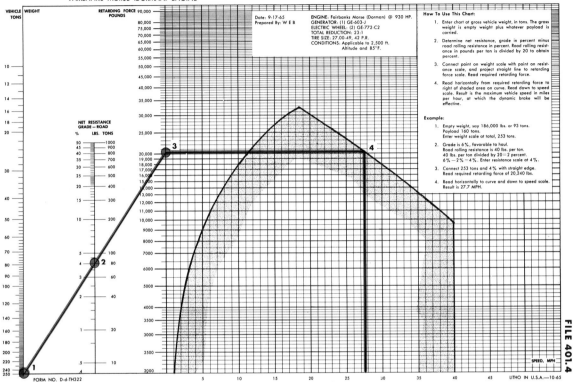

Fig. 10–90. A combination chart used to determine the allowable speed for a particular braking system. (Courtesy of LeTourneau-Westinghouse Company.)

an N-chart, respectively, as shown in part A of Fig. 10–89. Again, the *S*-scales must be identical but need not be calibrated. The charts are superimposed in part B. The *S*-scale is used as a "turning" scale for the two isopleths, as shown in part C. Many other combinations are possible, limited only by the ingenuity of the nomographer in adapting formulas and scale arrangements to his needs. A rather advanced example of a combination nomograph is given in Fig. 10–90. This nomogram is used to determine the maximum speed a truck carrying a given load may reach while maintaining the effective-

ness of the truck's dynamic brakes. Other graphs of this type are used extensively in industrial applications.

10–43 SUMMARY

Throughout the design process, graphics has been the primary agent of creativity. Sketches, graphs, and diagrams were used to identify the problem; freehand sketches were made to determine preliminary ideas; the ideas were refined graphically; and the designs were then analyzed for feasibility prior to selection of the best solution. The development process would be virtually impossible without the thinking process being recorded, and even stimulated, by the applications of graphics. Throughout this process, the designer is guided by his knowledge of physical properties, engineering fundamentals, and manufacturing limitations. However, he does not let these limitations confine his thinking or imagination during the creative development stage. The real confrontation with the physical, mathematical, and scientific principles is in the analysis stage of the design process. Many of the data derived from experiments with prototypes and laboratory experiments will be in a numerical form that must be analyzed to provide a total picture of the proposed design.

Various aspects of graphical analysis of data and components were covered in this chapter, including graphs, empirical data, linkages and mechanisms, graphical calculus, and nomography. Each of these areas can be evaluated using formal mathematical and analytical approaches; however, graphical methods are applicable to many problems. In some cases, the graphical technique will offer the best method of solution.

Although conventional engineering methods are probably used more in the analysis phase of the design process than any other, graphical methods can be applied to good advantage in this phase also. The engineer or technician should be sufficiently aware of the applications of graphics to utilize this valuable method of problem solution.

PROBLEMS

The following problems are to be solved on $8\frac{1}{2}'' \times 11''$ or on $11'' \times 15''$ paper. The graph problems may be solved on commercially prepared paper or the grid may be constructed by the student. Problems involving geometric construction and mathematical calculations should show the construction and calculations as part of the problem for future reference. If the mathematical calculations are extensive, it may be desirable to include these on a separate sheet. Legible lettering practices and principles of good layout should be followed in these problems, and all notes and constructions should be provided to explain fully the method of solution.

2. Using the data given in Table 10–10, prepare a rectangular graph to compare the supply and demand of water in the United States from 1890 to 1980. Supply and demand are given in units of billions of gallons of water per day.

3. Analyze the data given in Table 10–11 to decide which lamps should be selected to provide economical lighting for an industrial plant. You are to decide whether to use single 1000-watt bulbs or twin 400-watt bulbs. The empirical data below give the candlepower directly under the lamps (0°) and at the various angles from the vertical when the lamps are mounted at a height of 25′, as shown in Fig. 10–91.

Graphs

1. Using the data given in Table 10–9, prepare a rectangular graph to compare the number of Master's and Doctor's degrees granted in the United States from 1920 to 1965. Use these data as a basis for predicting the trend for the period from 1965 to 1980.

Table 10–9

	Master's	Doctor's
1920	5,100	1,700
1930	14,700	3,100
1940	24,500	4,500
1950	64,000	7,800
1960	73,000	9,700
1965	102,000	15,200

Table 10–10

	1890	1900	1910	1920	1930	1940	1950	1960	1970	1980
Supply	80	80	110	135	155	240	270	315	380	450
Demand	35	35	60	80	110	125	200	320	410	550

Table 10–11

Angle with vertical	0	10	20	30	40	50	60	70	80	90
Candlepower (thous.) 2–400W	37	34	25	12	5.5	2.5	2	0.5	0.5	0.5
Candlepower (thous.) 1–1000W	22	21	19	16	12.3	7	3	2	0.5	0.5

Table 10–12

F	100	200	500	1000	2000	5000	10,000
$A(1)$	0.0028	0.002	0.0015	0.001	0.0006	0.0003	0.00013
$A(2)$	0.06	0.05	0.04	0.03	0.018	0.004	0.001

4. Using the data given in Table 10–12, construct a logarithmic graph where the vibration amplitude (A) is plotted as the ordinate and vibration frequency (F) as the abscissa. The data for curve 1 represent the maximum limits of machinery in good condition with no danger from vibration. The data for curve 2 are the lower limits of machinery that is being vibrated excessively to the danger point. The vertical scale should be three cycles and the horizontal scale two cycles.

5. Using the data from a 1967 survey (Table 10–13), construct a rectangular graph to reflect the salaries of engineers during successive years after graduation with a bachelor's degree. These salaries are given in averages for deciles (10% intervals) and quartiles (25% intervals). Plot each of these as a separate curve.

6. Construct a semilogarithmic graph of the data in problem 5, using the median values to determine the ratios of increase during this time period.

7. Construct a semilogarithmic graph to compare the relative ratios of the Master's and Doctor's degrees granted, as given in problem 1.

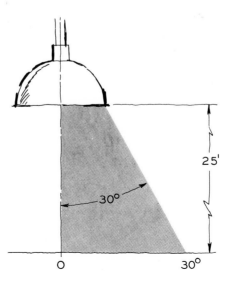

Fig. 10–91. The angular measurement of illumination under a lamp (problem 3).

Table 10–13

Years after graduation	0	5	10	15	20	25	30
Upper decile	9,800	13,000	17,500	20,500	22,500	23,800	25,000
Upper quartile	8,700	11,900	15,000	17,000	19,000	19,200	18,700
Median	8,000	10,500	13,000	14,500	15,800	15,200	15,000
Lower quartile	7,500	9,750	11,500	12,800	13,000	12,700	12,200
Lower decile	7,000	8,900	10,000	11,000	11,400	11,000	10,500

Table 10–14

S	2.1	1.05	0.85	0.5	0.45	0.18	0.14
HP	1	5	10	50	100	500	1000

Table 10–15

Ages	Percent of labor force	
	Graduates, %	Dropouts, %
16–17	18	22
18–19	12.5	17.5
20–21	8	13
22–24	5	9

Table 10–16

A	X	0	40	80	120	160	200	240	280		
	Y	4.0	7.0	9.8	12.5	15.3	17.2	21.0	24.0		
B	X	1	2	5	10	20	50	100	200	500	1000
	Y	1.5	2.4	3.3	6.0	9.2	15.0	23.0	24.0	60.0	85.0
C	X	1	5	10	50	100	500	1000			
	Y	3	10	19	70	110	400	700			
D	X	2	4	6	8	10	12	14			
	Y	6.5	14.0	32.0	75.0	115.0	320	710			
E	X	0	2	4	6	8	10	12	14		
	Y	20	34	53	96	115	270	430	730		
F	X	0	1	2	3	4	5	6	7	8	9	10
	Y	1.8	2.1	2.2	2.5	2.7	3.0	3.4	3.7	4.1	4.5	5.0

8. Using the data given in Table 10–14, construct a logarithmic graph to establish the curve that will give the maximum allowable number of starts per minute for 1800 rpm induction motors. The ordinate is the allowable number of starts per minute (S) and the abscissa is the motor horsepower rating (HP).

9. Construct a bar graph to depict the unemployment rate of high-school graduates and dropouts in various age categories. The age groups and the percent of unemployment of each group are given in Table 10–15.

10. Prepare a bar graph to compare the number of skilled workers employed in various occupations. Arrange the graph for ease of interpretation and comparison of occupations. Use the following data: carpenters, 82,000; all-round machinists, 310,000; plumbers, 350,000; bricklayers, 200,000; appliance service men, 185,000; automotive mechanics, 760,000; electricians, 380,000; painters, 400,000.

11. Prepare a pie chart to compare the areas of employment of male youth between the ages of 16 and 21 as tabulated in 1964: operatives, 25%; craftsmen, 9%; professions, technicals, and managers, 6%; clerical and sales, 17%; service, 11%; farm workers, 11%; laborers, 19%.

12. Make a pie graph to give the relationship between the following members of the scientific and technical team, as listed in 1965: engineers, 985,000; technicians, 932,000; scientists, 410,000.

Empirical Data

13. The data shown in Table 10–16, A through F, have been tabulated from experimental laboratory tests. Plot these data on rectangular, logarithmic, and semilogarithmic graphs and determine the empirical equations of the data. Select the proper graph needed for each set of data.

14. The following empirical data compare input voltage V with the input current I to a heat pump. Find the equation of the data given in Table 10–17.

Table 10-17

I	20	30	40	45
V	0.8	1.3	1.75	1.85

Table 10-18

I	2000	1840	1640	1480	1300	1120	10,000
C	1	2	5	10	20	50	100

Table 10-19

rms	7500	5200	4400	3400	2300	1700
pdc	3	6	9	15	30	60

Table 10-20

F	60	100	200	600	2000	3000
C	1.8	0.36	1.1	6.3	42	81

15. Table 10–18 lists empirical data giving the relationship between the peak allowable current in amperes (I) versus the overload operating time in cycles at 60 cycles per second (C). Place I on the Y-axis and C on the X-axis. Determine the equation for these data.

16. The empirical data given in Table 10–19 for a low-voltage circuit breaker used on a welding machine give the maximum loading during weld in amperes (rms) for the percent of duty cycle (pdc). Determine the equation for these data. Place rms along the Y-axis and pdc along the X-axis.

17. Empirical data of core loss in watts per pound (C) and frequency in cycles per second (F) are given in Table 10–20 for an electrical transformer. Place C on the Y-axis and F on the X-axis. Determine the equation for these data.

Table 10–21

Pressure drop	1.1	4.2	9.0	17.0	26.0	100.0
Valve flow		200	400	600	800	1000	2000

Table 10–22

S	2.1	1.05	0.85	0.5	0.45	0.18	0.14
HP	1	5	10	50	100	500	1000

18. Laboratory tests have resulted in the data given in Table 10–21 that compare valve pressure drop (feet of liquid) versus valve flow (gallons per minute of liquid, through a 4″ valve. Place the pressure drop on the *Y*-axis and the valve flow on the *X*-axis. Determine the equation of these data.

19. Determine the equation for the empirical data listed in Table 10–22, which give the allowable number of starts per minute for an 1800 rpm induction motor. The ordinate is the allowable number of starts per minute (*S*) and the abscissa is the motor horsepower rating (HP).

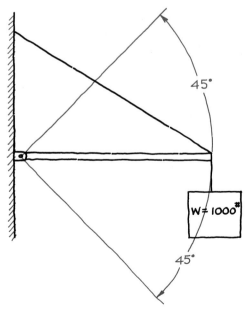

Fig. 10–92. Empirical analysis of stresses (problem 20).

20. By determining stresses in the cable at intervals, construct an empirical curve that shows the stresses in relationship to the position of the loading boom (Fig. 10–92). This problem is very similar to the one illustrated in Fig. 10–59. Construct stress diagrams to arrive at the stresses in a number of positions. The boom must permit upward and downward movement of 45° with the horizontal.

Mechanisms

21. Design and analyze the linkage system for the internal safety valve shown in Fig. 10–93. Use the dimensions given in the table for the particular problem assigned. Determine the *other dimensions* that will permit the operation for the limits given. Show all graphical analysis and the design of the linkage system on 11″ × 15″ tracing paper.

22. Determine the location of the pivot points and the lengths of the linkage members in the clamping device shown in Fig. 10–94 that will raise the bar 90° when the handle is raised 60°. Show all graphical construction and analysis on 11″ × 15″ tracing paper. Disregard the details of the specific shapes of the members; be concerned with center-to-center dimensions.

23. Analyze the motion of the piston shown in Fig. 10–48 using the following dimensions: radius of driver, 3.5″; length of piston rod, 9.7″. Plot the distance of travel of the piston for each degree of rotation. The driver is turning at a rate of one revolution per second. Show all construction on a 11″ × 15″ tracing paper.

24. Design a cam with a 3″ base circle, a knife-edge follower, and a $\frac{5}{8}$″ plate thickness that will have the following clockwise motion: Rise 1″ in 90° with harmonic motion. Draw a displacement diagram and design the cam. Select a scale that would be appropriate for an $8\frac{1}{2}$″ × 11″ sheet. Solve this same problem using a $\frac{3}{4}$″ diameter roller follower and a $1\frac{1}{2}$″ flat follower.

25. Design a cam with the same specifications as the cam in problem 24, but use a $\frac{3}{4}$″ diameter roller which is offset 1″ to the right.

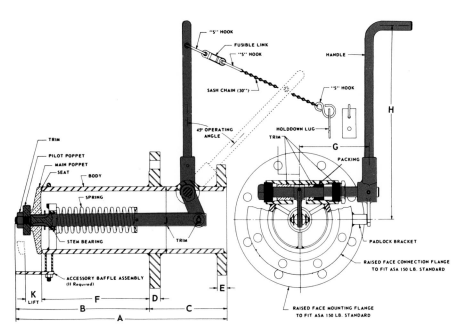

Fig. 10–93. The linkage system of an internal safety valve (problem 21). (Courtesy of General Precision Systems, Inc.)

VALVE SIZE	CONN. FLANGE SIZE	MOUNTING FLANGE SIZE		A	B	C	D	E	F	G	H	J	K	NET WT. LBS.	SHPG. WT. LBS.	BOX SIZE INCHES
		STANDARD	OVERSIZE													
4"	4"	6"	8"	17	$11\frac{5}{8}$	$5\frac{3}{8}$	1	$\frac{15}{16}$	10	$6\frac{1}{8}$	$12\frac{1}{4}$	$4\frac{1}{2}$	$1\frac{7}{16}$	78	82	16x17x19
6"	6"	8"	10"	$21\frac{3}{4}$	$13\frac{3}{4}$	8	$1\frac{1}{8}$	1	11	$7\frac{1}{4}$	$19\frac{1}{4}$	$6\frac{5}{8}$	$1\frac{3}{4}$	130	136	18x16x23
8"	8"	10"	12"	$23\frac{3}{4}$	$14\frac{3}{4}$	9	$1\frac{3}{16}$	$1\frac{1}{8}$	12	$8\frac{5}{8}$	$31\frac{3}{4}$	$8\frac{5}{8}$	$2\frac{1}{8}$	173	208	20x17x32
10"	10"	12"	16"	$24\frac{3}{4}$	$14\frac{3}{4}$	10	$1\frac{1}{4}$	$1\frac{3}{16}$	12	$10\frac{1}{8}$	$32\frac{3}{4}$	$10\frac{3}{4}$	$3\frac{1}{2}$	255	297	24x20x32
12"	12"	14"	18"	$24\frac{1}{4}$	$14\frac{7}{8}$	$9\frac{3}{8}$	$1\frac{3}{8}$	$1\frac{1}{4}$	12	$11\frac{1}{8}$	37	$12\frac{3}{4}$	$4\frac{3}{8}$	350	402	26x22x32

26. Design a cam with the following specifications: base circle, 2.5″; roller follower, $\frac{3}{4}$″ diameter; plate thickness, $\frac{3}{4}$″. The cam is to have the following motion: Rise 2″ in 180° with a modified uniform motion, then fall 2″ in 180° with a modified uniform motion. Solve this same problem using a 2″ diameter flat follower and a knife-edge follower also.

27. Design a cam with the specifications given in problem 26, except use a knife-edge follower offset 0.75″ to the right of the center of the cam.

28. Design a cam with a 3″ base circle of $\frac{5}{8}$″ thick plate with a knife-edge follower. The cam is to have the following motion: rise 2″ in 180° with harmonic motion, then fall 2″ in 180° with harmonic motion.

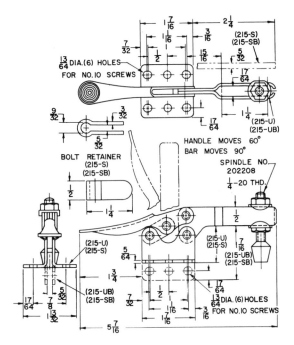

Fig. 10–94. A clamping device linkage (problem 22). (Courtesy of De-Sta-Co Corporation.)

29. Design a cam with the same specifications as in problem 28, but use a roller follower with a 1″ diameter offset 0.9″ to the left. Revolution is clockwise.

30. Design a cam which has a base circle of 3.5″ and is made from $\frac{3}{4}$″ plate stock. Use a flat follower that is 2″ in diameter. The cam is to have the following clockwise motion: rise 2″ in 180° with gravity motion, then fall 2″ in 180° with gravity motion.

31. Design a cam with the same specifications as those in problem 30; however, offset the follower 1″ to the right of center.

32. A preliminary sketch and a pictorial of a linkage system to control the pitch of a helicopter blade are shown in Fig. 10–95. The variation in pitch is to be controlled by moving the vertical stick between the vertical and the left.

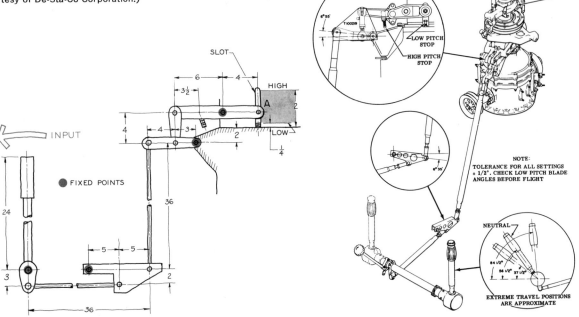

Fig. 10–95. A preliminary sketch and a pictorial of the linkage system to control the pitch on a helicopter (problem 32). (Courtesy of Bell Helicopter Corporation.)

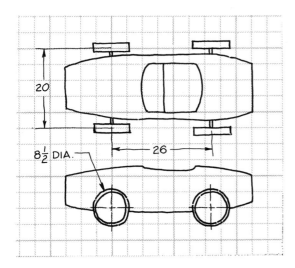

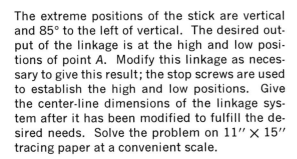

Fig. 10–96. Overall dimensions of a toy racer (problem 33).

Fig. 10–97. Photograph of the toy car in problems 33 and 34.

The extreme positions of the stick are vertical and 85° to the left of vertical. The desired output of the linkage is at the high and low positions of point A. Modify this linkage as necessary to give this result; the stop screws are used to establish the high and low positions. Give the center-line dimensions of the linkage system after it has been modified to fulfill the desired needs. Solve the problem on 11″ × 15″ tracing paper at a convenient scale.

33. Design a steering linkage for the toy racer shown in Fig. 10–96 that will be steered by a child. The wheels are 8.5″ in diameter and are 20″ apart. The linkage should be as simple and economical as possible to provide a system that could be mass-produced and assembled cheaply. Show your construction on a 11″ × 15″ sheet of tracing paper.

34. Design a linkage system for the child's racer shown in Fig. 10–97 that will enable the child to pedal the car. The front wheels are separated from the rear wheels by 26″. Estimate other dimensions to complete the linkage. Show your analysis and construction on an 11″ × 15″ sheet of tracing paper.

35. Construct a graph giving the travel of point P in Fig. 10–66 versus time in seconds. Use the following dimensions: $R_1 - 20''$, $R_2 - 40''$. Show all construction and analysis on a 11″ × 15″ sheet of tracing paper.

Calculus

36. Plot the equation $Y = X + 2$ on a rectangular graph. Graphically integrate this curve to determine the first and second integrals. Find the area under the curve between $X = 1$ and $X = 7$.

37. Plot the equation $Y = X^3/6$ as a rectangular graph. Graphically differentiate the curve to determine the first and second derivatives.

38. Analyze the motion of any of the cams designed in problems 24 through 30. Determine the velocity and acceleration at all points by graphical differentiation.

39. Analyze the motion of the piston discussed in Problem 23. Assume that the crankshaft is turning at a rate of one revolution per second. The piston rod is 9.7″ long, the radius of the input crank is 3.5″. Determine the velocity and acceleration at all intervals.

40. Analyze the motion of the shuttle plotted in problem 35. Using the rate of revolution as one revolution per three seconds, determine the velocity and acceleration by graphical differentiation.

41. Using graphical calculus, analyze a vertical strip 12″ wide on the inside face of the dam in

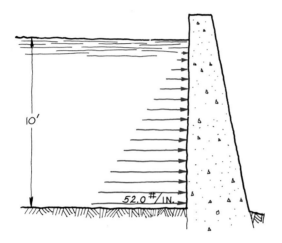

Fig. 10–98. Pressure on a 12″ wide section of a dam (problem 41).

Fig. 10–98. The force on this strip will be 52.0 lb/in at the bottom of the dam. The first graph will be pounds per inch (ordinate) vs. height in inches (abscissa). The second graph will be the integral of the first to give shear in pounds (ordinate) vs. height in inches (abscissa). The third will be the integral of the second graph to give the moment in inch-pounds (ordinate) vs. height in inches (abscissa). Convert these scales to give feet instead of inches.

42. A plot plan shows that a tract of land is bounded by a lake front (Fig. 10–99). By graphical integration, determine a graph that will represent the cumulative area of the land from point *A* to *E*. What is the total area? What is the area of each lot?

Nomography

The following problems are to be solved on an $8\frac{1}{2}″ \times 11″$ sheet with the scales selected to be most appropriate for the particular construction. Show all calculations and construction as part of the problems.

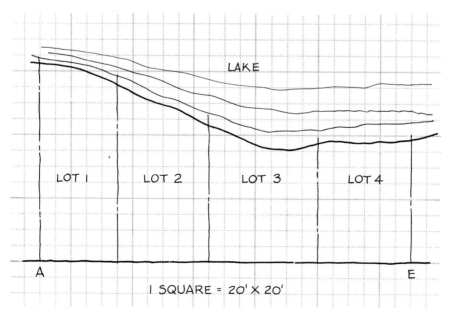

Fig. 10–99. A plot plan of a tract bounded by a lake front (problem 42).

Conversion Charts

43. Construct a chart that will convert inches to centimeters from 0 to 100 cm given that $1'' = 2.54$ cm.

44. Construct a chart for converting degrees in fahrenheit to degrees in centigrade from 32°F to 212°F using the formula, $°C = \frac{4}{9}(°F - 32)$.

45. Construct a chart that will give the period of a simple pendulum for various lengths from $0'$ to $5'$. The equation of the period is $D = 2\pi\sqrt{L/g}$, where $L = 0$ to 5 and $g = 32.2$ fps^2.

46. Construct a conversion chart that will convert weight into mass using the equation, Mass = Weight/32.2 ft/sec ($M = W/g$). Weight varies from 0 to 200 lb.

Parallel-Scale Charts

47. Construct a parallel-scale chart that will give solutions for the equation $A^2 + B^2 = C^2$ where values of A and B range from 0 to 20.

48. Construct a parallel-scale chart that will give the volume of cones varying in radius r from $1''$ to $10''$ and in height from $1''$ to $30''$. The equation for volume of a cone is $V = (\pi/3)r^2h$.

49. Construct a logarithmic parallel-scale chart to compute the areas of a series of rectangular plots using the equation, Area = $L \times W$; L and W range from 0 to 100 ft.

50. Construct a logarithmic parallel-scale chart to compute the various movements (M, in foot-pounds) for various forces (F, in pounds) and distances (D, in feet). Use the equation $M = F(D)$; D ranges from 0 to 10 ft and F from 10 to 200 lb.

N-Charts

51. Using the equations $\sigma = P/A$, where P ranges from 0 to 1000 psi and A ranges from 0 to 15 in.^{2}, construct an N-chart to determine the stresses on a load-carrying member.

52. Construct an N-chart to determine the flow velocity in a pipe, using the equation $V = 4Q/\pi D^2$, where Q varies from 0 to 5 ft^3/sec and D varies from $0.5''$ to $2.0''$ (change to feet to construct the chart, but label the calibrations in inches).

53. Construct an N-Chart to determine the values of electrical current (I, in amperes) for varying values of voltage (E, in volts) and resistance (R, in ohms). The formula for this relationship is $I = E/R$; E ranges from 0 to 110 volts and R from 0 to 50 ohms.

Combination Charts

54. Construct a combination chart to express the law of sines as expressed in the equation $a/\sin A = b/\sin B$. Assume that a and b vary from 0 to 10, and that A and B vary from 0° to 90°.

55. Construct a combination chart to determine the velocity of sound in a solid, using the formula

$$C = \sqrt{\frac{E + 4\mu/3}{\rho}},$$

where E varies from 10^6 to 10^7 psi, μ varies from 1×10^6 to 2×10^6 psi, and C varies from 1000 to 1500 fps. [*Hint:* Rewrite the formula as $C^2\rho = E + \frac{4}{3}\mu$.]

BIBLIOGRAPHY AND SUGGESTED READING

1. Chambers, S. D., and V. M. Faires, *Analytic Mechanics*. New York: Macmillan, 1949.

2. Hammond, R. H., C. P. Buck, W. B. Rogers, G. W. Walsh, Jr., and H. P. Ackert, *Engineering Graphics for Design and Analysis*. New York: Ronald, 1964.

3. Luzadder, W. J., *Basic Graphics*. Englewood Cliffs, N. J.: Prentice-Hall, 1968.

4. Wellman, B. L., *Introduction to Graphical Analysis and Design*. New York: McGraw-Hill, 1966.

5. Woodward, Forrest, *Graphical Simulation*. Scranton, Pa.: International Textbook, 1967.

APPENDIXES

CONTENTS

APPENDIX 1. LOGARITHMS OF NUMBERS

N	0	1	2	3	4	5	6	7	8	9
1.0	.0000	.0043	.0086	.0128	.0170	.0212	.0253	.0294	.0334	.0374
1.1	.0414	.0453	.0492	.0531	.0569	.0607	.0645	.0682	.0719	.0755
1.2	.0792	.0828	.0864	.0899	.0934	.0969	.1004	.1038	.1072	.1106
1.3	.1139	.1173	.1206	.1239	.1271	.1303	.1335	.1367	.1399	.1430
1.4	.1461	.1492	.1523	.1553	.1584	.1614	.1644	.1673	.1703	.1732
1.5	.1761	.1790	.1818	.1847	.1875	.1903	.1931	.1959	.1987	.2014
1.6	.2041	.2068	.2095	.2122	.2148	.2175	.2201	.2227	.2253	.2279
1.7	.2304	.2330	.2355	.2380	.2405	.2430	.2455	.2480	.2504	.2529
1.8	.2553	.2577	.2601	.2625	.2648	.2672	.2695	.2718	.2742	.2765
1.9	.2788	.2810	.2833	.2856	.2878	.2900	.2923	.2945	.2967	.2989
2.0	.3010	.3032	.3054	.3075	.3096	.3118	.3139	.3160	.3181	.3201
2.1	.3222	.3243	.3263	.3284	.3304	.3324	.3345	.3365	.3385	.3404
2.2	.3424	.3444	.3464	.3483	.3502	.3522	.3541	.3560	.3579	.3598
2.3	.3617	.3636	.3655	.3674	.3692	.3711	.3729	.3747	.3766	.3784
2.4	.3802	.3820	.3838	.3856	.3874	.3892	.3909	.3927	.3945	.3962
2.5	.3979	.3997	.4014	.4031	.4048	.4065	.4082	.4099	.4116	.4133
2.6	.4150	.4166	.4183	.4200	.4216	.4232	.4249	.4265	.4281	.4298
2.7	.4314	.4330	.4346	.4362	.4378	.4393	.4409	.4425	.4440	.4456
2.8	.4472	.4487	.4502	.4518	.4533	.4548	.4564	.4579	.4594	.4609
2.9	.4624	.4639	.4654	.4669	.4683	.4698	.4713	.4728	.4742	.4757
3.0	.4771	.4786	.4800	.4814	.4829	.4843	.4857	.4871	.4886	.4900
3.1	.4914	.4928	.4942	.4955	.4969	.4983	.4997	.5011	.5024	.5038
3.2	.5051	.5065	.5079	.5092	.5105	.5119	.5132	.5145	.5159	.5172
3.3	.5185	.5198	.5211	.5224	.5237	.5250	.5263	.5276	.5289	.5302
3.4	.5315	.5328	.5340	.5353	.5366	.5378	.5391	.5403	.5416	.5428
3.5	.5441	.5453	.5465	.5478	.5490	.5502	.5514	.5527	.5539	.5551
3.6	.5563	.5575	.5587	.5599	.5611	.5623	.5635	.5647	.5658	.5670
3.7	.5682	.5694	.5705	.5717	.5729	.5740	.5752	.5763	.5775	.5786
3.8	.5798	.5809	.5821	.5832	.5843	.5855	.5866	.5877	.5888	.5899
3.9	.5911	.5922	.5933	.5944	.5955	.5966	.5977	.5988	.5999	.6010
4.0	.6021	.6031	.6042	.6053	.6064	.6075	.6085	.6096	.6107	.6117
4.1	.6128	.6138	.6149	.6160	.6170	.6180	.6191	.6201	.6212	.6222
4.2	.6232	.6243	.6253	.6263	.6274	.6284	.6294	.6304	.6314	.6325
4.3	.6335	.6345	.6355	.6365	.6375	.6385	.6395	.6405	.6415	.6425
4.4	.6435	.6444	.6454	.6464	.6474	.6484	.6493	.6503	.6513	.6522
4.5	.6532	.6542	.6551	.6561	.6571	.6580	.6590	.6599	.6609	.6618
4.6	.6628	.6637	.6646	.6656	.6665	.6675	.6684	.6693	.6702	.6712
4.7	.6721	.6730	.6739	.6749	.6758	.6767	.6776	.6785	.6794	.6803
4.8	.6812	.6821	.6830	.6839	.6848	.6857	.6866	.6875	.6884	.6893
4.9	.6902	.6911	.6920	.6928	.6937	.6946	.6955	.6964	.6972	.6981
5.0	.6990	.6998	.7007	.7016	.7024	.7033	.7042	.7050	.7059	.7067
5.1	.7076	.7084	.7093	.7101	.7110	.7118	.7126	.7135	.7143	.7152
5.2	.7160	.7168	.7177	.7185	.7193	.7202	.7210	.7218	.7226	.7235
5.3	.7243	.7251	.7259	.7267	.7275	.7284	.7292	.7300	.7308	.7316
5.4	.7324	.7332	.7340	.7348	.7356	.7364	.7372	.7380	.7388	.7396
N	**0**	**1**	**2**	**3**	**4**	**5**	**6**	**7**	**8**	**9**

APPENDIX 1. LOGARITHMS OF NUMBERS (Cont.)

N	0	1	2	3	4	5	6	7	8	9
5.5	.7404	.7412	.7419	.7427	.7435	.7443	.7451	.7459	.7466	.7474
5.6	.7482	.7490	.7497	.7505	.7513	.7520	.7528	.7536	.7543	.7551
5.7	.7559	.7566	.7574	.7582	.7589	.7597	.7604	.7612	.7619	.7627
5.8	.7634	.7642	.7649	.7657	.7664	.7672	.7679	.7686	.7694	.7701
5.9	.7709	.7716	.7723	.7731	.7738	.7745	.7752	.7760	.7767	.7774
6.0	.7782	.7789	.7796	.7803	.7810	.7818	.7825	.7832	.7839	.7846
6.1	.7853	.7860	.7868	.7875	.7882	.7889	.7896	.7903	.7910	.7917
6.2	.7924	.7931	.7938	.7945	.7952	.7959	.7966	.7973	.7980	.7987
6.3	.7993	.8000	.8007	.8014	.8021	.8028	.8035	.8041	.8048	.8055
6.4	.8062	.8069	.8075	.8082	.8089	.8096	.8102	.8109	.8116	.8122
6.5	.8129	.8136	.8142	.8149	.8156	.8162	.8169	.8176	.8182	.8189
6.6	.8195	.8202	.8209	.8215	.8222	.8228	.8235	.8241	.8248	.8254
6.7	.8261	.8267	.8274	.8280	.8287	.8293	.8299	.8306	.8312	.8319
6.8	.8325	.8331	.8338	.8344	.8351	.8357	.8363	.8370	.8376	.8382
6.9	.8388	.8395	.8401	.8407	.8414	.8420	.8426	.8432	.8439	.8445
7.0	.8451	.8457	.8463	.8470	.8476	.8482	.8488	.8494	.8500	.8506
7.1	.8513	.8519	.8525	.8531	.8537	.8543	.8549	.8555	.8561	.8567
7.2	.8573	.8579	.8585	.8591	.8597	.8603	.8609	.8615	.8621	.8627
7.3	.8633	.8639	.8645	.8651	.8657	.8663	.8669	.8675	.8681	.8686
7.4	.8692	.8698	.8704	.8710	.8716	.8722	.8727	.8733	.8739	.8745
7.5	.8751	.8756	.8762	.8768	.8774	.8779	.8785	.8791	.8797	.8802
7.6	.8808	.8814	.8820	.8825	.8831	.8837	.8842	.8848	.8854	.8859
7.7	.8865	.8871	.8876	.8882	.8887	.8893	.8899	.8904	.8910	.8915
7.8	.8921	.8927	.8932	.8938	.8943	.8949	.8954	.8960	.8965	.8971
7.9	.8976	.8982	.8987	.8993	.8998	.9004	.9009	.9015	.9020	.9025
8.0	.9031	.9036	.9042	.9047	.9053	.9058	.9063	.9069	.9074	.9079
8.1	.9085	.9090	.9096	.9101	.9106	.9112	.9117	.9122	.9128	.9133
8.2	.9138	.9143	.9149	.9154	.9159	.9165	.9170	.9175	.9180	.9186
8.3	.9191	.9196	.9201	.9206	.9212	.9217	.9222	.9227	.9232	.9238
8.4	.9243	.9248	.9253	.9258	.9263	.9269	.9274	.9279	.9284	.9289
8.5	.9294	.9299	.9304	.9309	.9315	.9320	.9325	.9330	.9335	.9340
8.6	.9345	.9350	.9355	.9360	.9365	.9370	.9375	.9380	.9385	.9390
8.7	.9395	.9400	.9405	.9410	.9415	.9420	.9425	.9430	.9435	.9440
8.8	.9445	.9450	.9455	.9460	.9465	.9469	.9474	.9479	.9484	.9489
8.9	.9494	.9499	.9504	.9509	.9513	.9518	.9523	.9528	.9533	.9538
9.0	.9542	.9547	.9552	.9557	.9562	.9566	.9571	.9576	.9581	.9586
9.1	.9590	.9595	.9600	.9605	.9609	.9614	.9619	.9624	.9628	.9633
9.2	.9638	.9643	.9647	.9652	.9657	.9661	.9666	.9671	.9675	.9680
9.3	.9685	.9689	.9694	.9699	.9703	.9708	.9713	.9717	.9722	.9727
9.4	.9731	.9736	.9741	.9745	.9750	.9754	.9759	.9763	.9768	.9773
9.5	.9777	.9782	.9786	.9791	.9795	.9800	.9805	.9809	.9814	.9818
9.6	.9823	.9827	.9832	.9836	.9841	.9845	.9850	.9854	.9859	.9863
9.7	.9868	.9872	.9877	.9881	.9886	.9890	.9894	.9899	.9903	.9908
9.8	.9912	.9917	.9921	.9926	.9930	.9934	.9939	.9943	.9948	.9952
9.9	.9956	.9961	.9965	.9969	.9974	.9978	.9983	.9987	.9991	.9996
N	0	1	2	3	4	5	6	7	8	9

APPENDIX 2. VALUES OF TRIGONOMETRIC FUNCTIONS

Degrees	Radians	Sine	Tangent	Cotangent	Cosine		
0° 00′	.0000	.0000	.0000		1.0000	1.5708	90° 00′
10′	.0029	.0029	.0029	343.77	1.0000	1.5679	50′
20′	.0058	.0058	.0058	171.89	1.0000	1.5650	40′
30′	.0087	.0087	.0087	114.59	1.0000	1.5621	30′
40′	.0116	.0116	.0116	85.940	.9999	1.5592	20′
50′	.0145	.0145	.0145	68.750	.9999	1.5563	10′
1° 00′	.0175	.0175	.0175	57.290	.9998	1.5533	89° 00′
10′	.0204	.0204	.0204	49.104	.9998	1.5504	50′
20′	.0233	.0233	.0233	42.964	.9997	1.5475	40′
30′	.0262	.0262	.0262	38.188	.9997	1.5446	30′
40′	.0291	.0291	.0291	34.368	.9996	1.5417	20′
50′	.0320	.0320	.0320	31.242	.9995	1.5388	10′
2° 00′	.0349	.0349	.0349	28.636	.9994	1.5359	88° 00′
10′	.0378	.0378	.0378	26.432	.9993	1.5330	50′
20′	.0407	.0407	.0407	24.542	.9992	1.5301	40′
30′	.0436	.0436	.0437	22.904	.9990	1.5272	30′
40′	.0465	.0465	.0466	21.470	.9989	1.5243	20′
50′	.0495	.0494	.0495	20.206	.9988	1.5213	10′
3° 00′	.0524	.0523	.0524	19.081	.9986	1.5184	87° 00′
10′	.0553	.0552	.0553	18.075	.9985	1.5155	50′
20′	.0582	.0581	.0582	17.169	.9983	1.5126	40′
30′	.0611	.0610	.0612	16.350	.9981	1.5097	30′
40′	.0640	.0640	.0641	15.605	.9980	1.5068	20′
50′	.0669	.0669	.0670	14.924	.9978	1.5039	10′
4° 00′	.0698	.0698	.0699	14.301	.9976	1.5010	86° 00′
10′	.0727	.0727	.0729	13.727	.9974	1.4981	50′
20′	.0756	.0756	.0758	13.197	.9971	1.4952	40′
30′	.0785	.0785	.0787	12.706	.9969	1.4923	30′
40′	.0814	.0814	.0816	12.251	.9967	1.4893	20′
50′	.0844	.0843	.0846	11.826	.9964	1.4864	10′
5° 00′	.0873	.0872	.0875	11.430	.9962	1.4835	85° 00′
10′	.0902	.0901	.0904	11.059	.9959	1.4806	50′
20′	.0931	.0929	.0934	10.712	.9957	1.4777	40′
30′	.0960	.0958	.0963	10.385	.9954	1.4748	30′
40′	.0989	.0987	.0992	10.078	.9951	1.4719	20′
50′	.1018	.1016	.1022	9.7882	.9948	1.4690	10′
6° 00′	.1047	.1045	.1051	9.5144	.9945	1.4661	84° 00′
10′	.1076	.1074	.1080	9.2553	.9942	1.4632	50′
20′	.1105	.1103	.1110	9.0098	.9939	1.4603	40′
30′	.1134	.1132	.1139	8.7769	.9936	1.4573	30′
40′	.1164	.1161	.1169	8.5555	.9932	1.4544	20′
50′	.1193	.1190	.1198	8.3450	.9929	1.4515	10′
7° 00′	.1222	.1219	.1228	8.1443	.9925	1.4486	83° 00′
10′	.1251	.1248	.1257	7.9530	.9922	1.4457	50′
20′	.1280	.1276	.1287	7.7704	.9918	1.4428	40′
30′	.1309	.1305	.1317	7.5958	.9914	1.4399	30′
40′	.1338	.1334	.1346	7.4287	.9911	1.4370	20′
50′	.1367	.1363	.1376	7.2687	.9907	1.4341	10′
8° 00′	.1396	.1392	.1405	7.1154	.9903	1.4312	82° 00′
10′	.1425	.1421	.1435	6.9682	.9899	1.4283	50′
20′	.1454	.1449	.1465	6.8269	.9894	1.4254	40′
30′	.1484	.1478	.1495	6.6912	.9890	1.4224	30′
40′	.1513	.1507	.1524	6.5606	.9886	1.4195	20′
50′	.1542	.1536	.1554	6.4348	.9881	1.4166	10′
9° 00′	.1571	.1564	.1584	6.3138	.9877	1.4137	81° 00′
		Cosine	Cotangent	Tangent	Sine	Radians	Degrees

APPENDIX 2. VALUES OF TRIGONOMETRIC FUNCTIONS (Cont.)

Degrees	Radians	Sine	Tangent	Cotangent	Cosine		
9° 00′	.1571	.1564	.1584	6.3138	.9877	1.4137	81° 00′
10′	.1600	.1593	.1614	6.1970	.9872	1.4108	50′
20′	.1629	.1622	.1644	6.0844	.9868	1.4079	40′
30′	.1658	.1650	.1673	5.9758	.9863	1.4050	30′
40′	.1687	.1679	.1703	5.8708	.9858	1.4021	20′
50′	.1716	.1708	.1733	5.7694	.9853	1.3992	10′
10° 00′	.1745	.1736	.1763	5.6713	.9848	1.3963	80° 00′
10′	.1774	.1765	.1793	5.5764	.9843	1.3934	50′
20′	.1804	.1794	.1823	5.4845	.9838	1.3904	40′
30′	.1833	.1822	.1853	5.3955	.9833	1.3875	30′
40′	.1862	.1851	.1883	5.3093	.9827	1.3846	20′
50′	.1891	.1880	.1914	5.2257	.9822	1.3817	10′
11° 00′	.1920	.1908	.1944	5.1446	.9816	1.3788	79° 00′
10′	.1949	.1937	.1974	5.0658	.9811	1.3759	50′
20′	.1978	.1965	.2004	4.9894	.9805	1.3730	40′
30′	.2007	.1994	.2035	4.9152	.9799	1.3701	30′
40′	.2036	.2022	.2065	4.8430	.9793	1.3672	20′
50′	.2065	.2051	.2095	4.7729	.9787	1.3643	10′
12° 00′	.2094	.2079	.2126	4.7046	.9781	1.3614	78° 00′
10′	.2123	.2108	.2156	4.6382	.9775	1.3584	50′
20′	.2153	.2136	.2186	4.5736	.9769	1.3555	40′
30′	.2182	.2164	.2217	4.5107	.9763	1.3526	30′
40′	.2211	.2193	.2247	4.4494	.9757	1.3497	20′
50′	.2240	.2221	.2278	4.3897	.9750	1.3468	10′
13° 00′	.2269	.2250	.2309	4.3315	.9744	1.3439	77° 00′
10′	.2298	.2278	.2339	4.2747	.9737	1.3410	50′
20′	.2327	.2306	.2370	4.2193	.9730	1.3381	40′
30′	.2356	.2334	.2401	4.1653	.9724	1.3352	30′
40′	.2385	.2363	.2432	4.1126	.9717	1.3323	20′
50′	.2414	.2391	.2462	4.0611	.9710	1.3294	10′
14° 00′	.2443	.2419	.2493	4.0108	.9703	1.3265	76° 00′
10′	.2473	.2447	.2524	3.9617	.9696	1.3235	50′
20′	.2502	.2476	.2555	3.9136	.9689	1.3206	40′
30′	.2531	.2504	.2586	3.8667	.9681	1.3177	30′
40′	.2560	.2532	.2617	3.8208	.9674	1.3148	20′
50′	.2589	.2560	.2648	3.7760	.9667	1.3119	10′
15° 00′	.2618	.2588	.2679	3.7321	.9659	1.3090	75° 00′
10′	.2647	.2616	.2711	3.6891	.9652	1.3061	50′
20′	.2676	.2644	.2742	3.6470	.9644	1.3032	40′
30′	.2705	.2672	.2773	3.6059	.9636	1.3003	30′
40′	.2734	.2700	.2805	3.5656	.9628	1.2974	20′
50′	.2763	.2728	.2836	3.5261	.9621	1.2945	10′
16° 00′	.2793	.2756	.2867	3.4874	.9613	1.2915	74° 00′
10′	.2822	.2784	.2899	3.4495	.9605	1.2886	50′
20′	.2851	.2812	.2931	3.4124	.9596	1.2857	40′
30′	.2880	.2840	.2962	3.3759	.9588	1.2828	30′
40′	.2909	.2868	.2994	3.3402	.9580	1.2799	20′
50′	.2938	.2896	.3026	3.3052	.9572	1.2770	10′
17° 00′	.2967	.2924	.3057	3.2709	.9563	1.2741	73° 00′
10′	.2996	.2952	.3089	3.2371	.9555	1.2712	50′
20′	.3025	.2979	.3121	3.2041	.9546	1.2683	40′
30′	.3054	.3007	.3153	3.1716	.9537	1.2654	30′
40′	.3083	.3035	.3185	3.1397	.9528	1.2625	20′
50′	.3113	.3062	.3217	3.1084	.9520	1.2595	10′
18° 00′	.3142	.3090	.3249	3.0777	.9511	1.2566	72° 00′
		Cosine	Cotangent	Tangent	Sine	Radians	Degrees

(Cont.)

APPENDIX 2. VALUES OF TRIGONOMETRIC FUNCTIONS (Cont.)

Degrees	Radians	Sine	Tangent	Cotangent	Cosine		
18° 00′	.3142	.3090	.3249	3.0777	.9511	1.2566	72° 00′
10′	.3171	.3118	.3281	3.0475	.9502	1.2537	50′
20′	.3200	.3145	.3314	3.0178	.9492	1.2508	40′
30′	.3229	.3173	.3346	2.9887	.9483	1.2479	30′
40′	.3258	.3201	.3378	2.9600	.9474	1.2450	20′
50′	.3287	.3228	.3411	2.9319	.9465	1.2421	10′
19° 00′	.3316	.3256	.3443	2.9042	.9455	1.2392	71° 00′
10′	.3345	.3283	.3476	2.8770	.9446	1.2363	50′
20′	.3374	.3311	.3508	2.8502	.9436	1.2334	40′
30′	.3403	.3338	.3541	2.8239	.9426	1.2305	30′
40′	.3432	.3365	.3574	2.7980	.9417	1.2275	20′
50′	.3462	.3393	.3607	2.7725	.9407	1.2246	10′
20° 00′	.3491	.3420	.3640	2.7475	.9397	1.2217	70° 00′
10′	.3520	.3448	.3673	2.7228	.9387	1.2188	50′
20′	.3549	.3475	.3706	2.6985	.9377	1.2159	40′
30′	.3578	.3502	.3739	2.6746	.9367	1.2130	30′
40′	.3607	.3529	.3772	2.6511	.9356	1.2101	20′
50′	.3636	.3557	.3805	2.6279	.9346	1.2072	10′
21° 00′	.3665	.3584	.3839	2.6051	.9336	1.2043	69° 00′
10′	.3694	.3611	.3872	2.5826	.9325	1.2014	50′
20′	.3723	.3638	.3906	2.5605	.9315	1.1985	40′
30′	.3752	.3665	.3939	2.5386	.9304	1.1956	30′
40′	.3782	.3692	.3973	2.5172	.9293	1.1926	20′
50′	.3811	.3719	.4006	2.4960	.9283	1.1897	10′
22° 00′	.3840	.3746	.4040	2.4751	.9272	1.1868	68° 00′
10′	.3869	.3773	.4074	2.4545	.9261	1.1839	50′
20′	.3898	.3800	.4108	2.4342	.9250	1.1810	40′
30′	.3927	.3827	.4142	2.4142	.9239	1.1781	30′
40′	.3956	.3854	.4176	2.3945	.9228	1.1752	20′
50′	.3985	.3881	.4210	2.3750	.9216	1.1723	10′
23° 00′	.4014	.3907	.4245	2.3559	.9205	1.1694	67° 00′
10′	.4043	.3934	.4279	2.3369	.9194	1.1665	50′
20′	.4072	.3961	.4314	2.3183	.9182	1.1636	40′
30′	.4102	.3987	.4348	2.2998	.9171	1.1606	30′
40′	.4131	.4014	.4383	2.2817	.9159	1.1577	20′
50′	.4160	.4041	.4417	2.2637	.9147	1.1548	10′
24° 00′	.4189	.4067	.4452	2.2460	.9135	1.1519	66° 00′
10′	.4218	.4094	.4487	2.2286	.9124	1.1490	50′
20′	.4247	.4120	.4522	2.2113	.9112	1.1461	40′
30′	.4276	.4147	.4557	2.1943	.9100	1.1432	30′
40′	.4305	.4173	.4592	2.1775	.9088	1.1403	20′
50′	.4334	.4200	.4628	2.1609	.9075	1.1374	10′
25° 00′	.4363	.4226	.4663	2.1445	.9063	1.1345	65° 00′
10′	.4392	.4253	.4699	2.1283	.9051	1.1316	50′
20′	.4422	.4279	.4734	2.1123	.9038	1.1286	40′
30′	.4451	.4305	.4770	2.0965	.9026	1.1257	30′
40′	.4480	.4331	.4806	2.0809	.9013	1.1228	20′
50′	.4509	.4358	.4841	2.0655	.9001	1.1199	10′
26° 00′	.4538	.4384	.4877	2.0503	.8988	1.1170	64° 00′
10′	.4567	.4410	.4913	2.0353	.8975	1.1141	50′
20′	.4596	.4436	.4950	2.0204	.8962	1.1112	40′
30′	4625	.4462	.4986	2.0057	.8949	1.1083	30′
40′	.4654	.4488	.5022	1.9912	.8936	1.1054	20′
50′	.4683	.4514	.5059	1.9768	.8923	1.1025	10′
27° 00′	.4712	.4540	.5095	1.9626	.8910	1.0996	63° 00′
		Cosine	Cotangent	Tangent	Sine	Radians	Degrees

APPENDIX 2. VALUES OF TRIGONOMETRIC FUNCTIONS (Cont.)

Degrees	Radians	Sine	Tangent	Cotangent	Cosine		
27° 00'	.4712	.4540	.5095	1.9626	.8910	1.0996	63° 00'
10'	.4741	.4566	.5132	1.9486	.8897	1.0966	50'
20'	.4771	.4592	.5169	1.9347	.8884	1.0937	40'
30'	.4800	.4617	.5206	1.9210	.8870	1.0908	30'
40'	.4829	.4643	.5243	1.9074	.8857	1.0879	20'
50'	.4858	.4669	.5280	1.8940	.8843	1.0850	10'
28° 00'	.4887	.4695	.5317	1.8807	.8829	1.0821	62° 00'
10'	.4916	.4720	.5354	1.8676	.8816	1.0792	50'
20'	.4945	.4746	.5392	1.8546	.8802	1.0763	40'
30'	.4974	.4772	.5430	1.8418	.8788	1.0734	30'
40'	.5003	.4797	.5467	1.8291	.8774	1.0705	20'
50'	.5032	.4823	.5505	1.8165	.8760	1.0676	10'
29° 00'	.5061	.4848	.5543	1.8040	.8746	1.0647	61° 00'
10'	.5091	.4874	.5581	1.7917	.8732	1.0617	50'
20'	.5120	.4899	.5619	1.7796	.8718	1.0588	40'
30'	.5149	.4924	.5658	1.7675	.8704	1.0559	30'
40'	.5178	.4950	.5696	1.7556	.8689	1.0530	20'
50'	.5207	.4975	.5735	1.7437	.8675	1.0501	10'
30° 00'	.5236	.5000	.5774	1.7321	.8660	1.0472	60° 00'
10'	.5265	.5025	.5812	1.7205	.8646	1.0443	50'
20'	.5294	.5050	.5851	1.7090	.8631	1.0414	40'
30'	.5323	.5075	.5890	1.6977	.8616	1.0385	30'
40'	.5352	.5100	.5930	1.6864	.8601	1.0356	20'
50'	.5381	.5125	.5969	1.6753	.8587	1.0327	10'
31° 00'	.5411	.5150	.6009	1.6643	.8572	1.0297	59° 00'
10'	.5440	.5175	.6048	1.6534	.8557	1.0268	50'
20'	.5469	.5200	.6088	1.6426	.8542	1.0239	40'
30'	.5498	.5225	.6128	1.6319	.8526	1.0210	30'
40'	.5527	.5250	.6168	1.6212	.8511	1.0181	20'
50'	.5556	.5275	.6208	1.6107	.8496	1.0152	10'
32° 00'	.5585	.5299	.6249	1.6003	.8480	1.0123	58° 00'
10'	.5614	.5324	.6289	1.5900	.8465	1.0094	50'
20'	.5643	.5348	.6330	1.5798	.8450	1.0065	40'
30'	.5672	.5373	.6371	1.5697	.8434	1.0036	30'
40'	.5701	.5398	.6412	1.5597	.8418	1.0007	20'
50'	.5730	.5422	.6453	1.5497	.8403	.9977	10'
33° 00'	.5760	.5446	.6494	1.5399	.8387	.9948	57° 00'
10'	.5789	.5471	.6536	1.5301	.8371	.9919	50'
20'	.5818	.5495	.6577	1.5204	.8355	.9890	40'
30'	.5847	.5519	.6619	1.5108	.8339	.9861	30'
40'	.5876	.5544	.6661	1.5013	.8323	.9832	20'
50'	.5905	.5568	.6703	1.4919	.8307	.9803	10'
34° 00'	.5934	.5592	.6745	1.4826	.8290	.9774	56° 00'
10'	.5963	.5616	.6787	1.4733	.8274	.9745	50'
20'	.5992	.5640	.6830	1.4641	.8258	.9716	40'
30'	.6021	.5664	.6873	1.4550	.8241	.9687	30'
40'	.6050	.5688	.6916	1.4460	.8225	.9657	20'
50'	.6080	.5712	.6959	1.4370	.8208	.9628	10'
35° 00'	.6109	.5736	.7002	1.4281	.8192	.9599	55° 00'
10'	.6138	.5760	.7046	1.4193	.8175	.9570	50'
20'	.6167	.5783	.7089	1.4106	.8158	.9541	40'
30'	.6196	.5807	.7133	1.4019	.8141	.9512	30'
40'	.6225	.5831	.7177	1.3934	.8124	.9483	20'
50'	.6254	.5854	.7221	1.3848	.8107	.9454	10'
36° 00'	.6283	.5878	.7265	1.3764	.8090	.9425	54° 00'
		Cosine	Cotangent	Tangent	Sine	Radians	Degrees

(Cont.)

APPENDIX 2. VALUES OF TRIGONOMETRIC FUNCTIONS (Cont.)

Degrees	Radians	Sine	Tangent	Cotangent	Cosine		
36° 00′	.6283	.5878	.7265	1.3764	.8090	.9425	54° 00′
10′	.6312	.5901	.7310	1.3680	.8073	.9396	50′
20′	.6341	.5925	.7355	1.3597	.8056	.9367	40′
30′	.6370	.5948	.7400	1.3514	.8039	.9338	30′
40′	.6400	.5972	.7445	1.3432	.8021	.9308	20′
50′	.6429	.5995	.7490	1.3351	.8004	.9279	10′
37° 00′	.6458	.6018	.7536	1.3270	.7986	.9250	53° 00′
10′	.6487	.6041	.7581	1.3190	.7969	.9221	50′
20′	.6516	.6065	.7627	1.3111	.7951	.9192	40′
30′	.6545	.6088	.7673	1.3032	.7934	.9163	30′
40′	.6574	.6111	.7720	1.2954	.7916	.9134	20′
50′	.6603	.6134	.7766	1.2876	.7898	.9105	10′
38° 00′	.6632	.6157	.7813	1.2799	.7880	.9076	52° 00′
10′	.6661	.6180	.7860	1.2723	.7862	.9047	50′
20′	.6690	.6202	.7907	1.2647	.7844	.9018	40′
30′	.6720	.6225	.7954	1.2572	.7826	.8988	30′
40′	.6749	.6248	.8002	1.2497	.7808	.8959	20′
50′	.6778	.6271	.8050	1.2423	.7790	.8930	10′
39° 00′	.6807	.6293	.8098	1.2349	.7771	.8901	51° 00′
10′	.6836	.6316	.8146	1.2276	.7753	.8872	50′
20′	.6865	.6338	.8195	1.2203	.7735	.8843	40′
30′	.6894	.6361	.8243	1.2131	.7716	.8814	30′
40′	.6923	.6383	.8292	1.2059	.7698	.8785	20′
50′	.6952	.6406	.8342	1.1988	.7679	.8756	10′
40° 00′	.6981	.6428	.8391	1.1918	.7660	.8727	50° 00′
10′	.7010	.6450	.8441	1.1847	.7642	.8698	50′
20′	.7039	.6472	.8491	1.1778	.7623	.8668	40′
30′	.7069	.6494	.8541	1.1708	.7604	.8639	30′
40′	.7098	.6517	.8591	1.1640	.7585	.8610	20′
50′	.7127	.6539	.8642	1.1571	.7566	.8581	10′
41° 00′	.7156	.6561	.8693	1.1504	.7547	.8552	49° 00′
10′	.7185	.6583	.8744	1.1436	.7528	.8523	50′
20′	.7214	.6604	.8796	1.1369	.7509	.8494	40′
30′	.7243	.6626	.8847	1.1303	.7490	.8465	30′
40′	.7272	.6648	.8899	1.1237	.7470	.8436	20′
50′	.7301	.6670	.8952	1.1171	.7451	.8407	10′
42° 00′	.7330	.6691	.9004	1.1106	.7431	.8378	48° 00′
10′	.7359	.6713	.9057	1.1041	.7412	.8348	50′
20′	.7389	.6734	.9110	1.0977	.7392	.8319	40′
30′	.7418	.6756	.9163	1.0913	.7373	.8290	30′
40′	.7447	.6777	.9217	1.0850	.7353	.8261	20′
50′	.7476	.6799	.9271	1.0786	.7333	.8232	10′
43° 00′	.7505	.6820	.9325	1.0724	.7314	.8203	47° 00′
10′	.7534	.6841	.9380	1.0661	.7294	.8174	50′
20′	.7563	.6862	.9435	1.0599	.7274	.8145	40′
30′	.7592	.6884	.9490	1.0538	.7254	.8116	30′
40′	.7621	.6905	.9545	1.0477	.7234	.8087	20′
50′	.7650	.6926	.9601	1.0416	.7214	.8058	10′
44° 00′	.7679	.6947	.9657	1.0355	.7193	.8029	46° 00′
10′	.7709	.6967	.9713	1.0295	.7173	.7999	50′
20′	.7738	.6988	.9770	1.0235	.7153	.7970	40′
30′	.7767	.7009	.9827	1.0176	.7133	.7941	30′
40′	.7796	.7030	.9884	1.0117	.7112	.7912	20′
50′	.7825	.7050	.9942	1.0058	.7092	.7883	10′
45° 00′	.7854	.7071	1.0000	1.0000	.7071	.7854	45° 00′
		Cosine	Cotangent	Tangent	Sine	Radians	Degrees

APPENDIX 3. WEIGHTS AND MEASURES

UNITED STATES SYSTEM

LINEAR MEASURE

Inches	Feet	Yards	Rods	Furlongs	Miles
1.0 =	.08333 =	.02778 =	.0050505 =	.00012626 =	.00001578
12.0 =	1.0 =	.33333 =	.0606061 =	.00151515 =	.00018939
36.0 =	3.0 =	1.0 =	.1818182 =	.00454545 =	.00056818
198.0 =	16.5 =	5.5 =	1.0 =	.025 =	.003125
7920.0 =	660.0 =	220.0 =	40.0 =	1.0 =	.125
63360.0 =	5280.0 =	1760.0 =	320.0 =	8.0 =	1.0

SQUARE AND LAND MEASURE

Sq. Inches	Square Feet	Square Yards	Sq. Rods	Acres	Sq. Miles
1.0 =	.006944 =	.000772			
144.0 =	1.0 =	.111111			
1296.0 =	9.0 =	1.0 =	.03306 =	.000207	
39204.0 =	272.25 =	30.25 =	1.0 =	.00625 =	.0000098
	43560.0 =	4840.0 =	160.0 =	1.0 =	.0015625
		3097600.0 =	102400.0 =	640.0 =	1.0

AVOIRDUPOIS WEIGHTS

Grains	Drams	Ounces	Pounds	Tons
1.0 =	.03657 =	.002286 =	.000143 =	.0000000714
27.34375 =	1.0 =	.0625 =	.003906 =	.00000195
437.5 =	16.0 =	1.0 =	.0625 =	.00003125
7000.0 =	256.0 =	16.0 =	1.0 =	.0005
14000000.0 =	512000.0 =	32000.0 =	2000.0 =	1.0

DRY MEASURE

Pints	Quarts	Pecks	Cubic Feet	Bushels
1.0 =	.5 =	.0625 =	.01945 =	.01563
2.0 =	1.0 =	.125 =	.03891 =	.03125
16.0 =	8.0 =	1.0 =	.31112 =	.25
51.42627 =	25.71314 =	3.21414 =	1.0 =	.80354
64.0 =	32.0 =	4.0 =	1.2445 =	1.0

LIQUID MEASURE

Gills	Pints	Quarts	U. S. Gallons	Cubic Feet
1.0 =	.25 =	.125 =	.03125 =	.00418
4.0 =	1.0 =	.5 =	.125 =	.01671
8.0 =	2.0 =	1.0 =	.250 =	.03342
32.0 =	8.0 =	4.0 =	1.0 =	.1337
			7.48052 =	1.0

METRIC SYSTEM

UNITS

Length—Meter : Mass—Gram : Capacity—Liter

for pure water at 4°C. (39.2°F.)

1 cubic decimeter or 1 liter = 1 kilogram

1000 Milli $\begin{cases} meters\ (mm) \\ grams\ (mg) \\ liters\ (ml) \end{cases}$ = 100 Centi $\begin{cases} meters\ (cm) \\ grams\ (cg) \\ liters\ (cl) \end{cases}$ = 10 Deci $\begin{cases} meters\ (dm) \\ grams\ (dg) \\ liters\ (dl) \end{cases}$ = 1 $\begin{cases} meter \\ gram \\ liter \end{cases}$

1000 $\begin{cases} meters \\ grams \\ liters \end{cases}$ = 100 Deka $\begin{cases} meters\ (dkm) \\ grams\ (dkg) \\ liters\ (dkl) \end{cases}$ = 10 Hecto $\begin{cases} meters\ (hm) \\ grams\ (hg) \\ liters\ (hl) \end{cases}$ = 1 Kilo $\begin{cases} meter\ (km) \\ gram\ (kg) \\ liter\ (kl) \end{cases}$

1 Metric Ton	= 1000 Kilograms
100 Square Meters	= 1 Are
100 Ares	= 1 Hectare
100 Hectares	= 1 Square Kilometer

(Courtesy of the American Institute of Steel Construction.)

APPENDIX 4. DECIMAL EQUIVALENTS AND TEMPERATURE CONVERSION

DECIMAL EQUIVALENTS—INCH-MILLIMETER CONVERSION TABLE

1/2	1/4	1/8	1/16	1/32	1/64	Decimals	Millimeters
				1	1	.015625	.396875
				1		.031250	.793750
					3	.046875	1.190625
			1			.062500	1.587500
					5	.078125	1.984375
				3		.093750	2.381250
					7	.109375	2.778125
		1				.125000	3.175000
					9	.140625	3.571875
				5		.156250	3.968750
					11	.171875	4.365625
			3			.187500	4.762500
					13	.203125	5.159375
				7		.218750	5.556250
					15	.234375	5.953125
	1					.250000	6.350000
					17	.265625	6.746875
				9		.281250	7.143750
					19	.296875	7.540625
			5			.312500	7.937500
					21	.328125	8.334375
				11		.343750	8.731250
					23	.359375	9.128125
		3				.375000	9.525000
					25	.390625	9.921875
				13		.406250	10.318750
					27	.421875	10.715625
			7			.437500	11.112500
					29	.453125	11.509375
				15		.468750	11.906250
					31	.484375	12.303125
1						.500000	12.700000

1/2	1/4	1/8	1/16	1/32	1/64	Decimals	Millimeters
					33	.515625	13.096875
				17		.531250	13.493750
					35	.546875	13.890625
			9			.562500	14.287500
					37	.578125	14.684375
				19		.593750	15.081250
					39	.609375	15.478125
		5				.625000	15.875000
					41	.640625	16.271875
				21		.656250	16.668750
					43	.671875	17.065625
			11			.687500	17.462500
					45	.703125	17.859375
				23		.718750	18.256250
					47	.734375	18.653125
	3					.750000	19.050000
					49	.765625	19.446875
				25		.781250	19.843750
					51	.796875	20.240625
			13			.812500	20.637500
					53	.828125	21.034375
				27		.843750	21.431250
					55	.859375	21.828125
		7				.875000	22.225000
					57	.890625	22.621875
				29		.906250	23.018750
					59	.921875	23.415625
			15			.937500	23.812500
					61	.953125	24.209375
				31		.968750	24.606250
					63	.984375	25.003125
2	4	8	16	32	64	1.000000	25.400000

TEMPERATURE CONVERSION

-210 to 0

C.	C. or F.	F.
-134	-210	-346
-129	-200	-328
-123	-190	-310
-118	-180	-292
-112	-170	-274
-107	-160	-256
-101	-150	-238
-95.6	-140	-220
-90.0	-130	-202
-84.4	-120	-184
-78.9	-110	-166
-73.3	-100	-148
-67.8	-90	-130
-62.2	-80	-112
-56.7	-70	-94
-51.1	-60	-76
-45.6	-50	-58
-40.0	-40	-40
-34.4	-30	-22
-28.9	-20	-4
-23.3	-10	14
-17.8	0	32

1 to 25

C.	C. or F.	F.
-17.2	1	33.8
-16.7	2	35.6
-16.1	3	37.4
-15.6	4	39.2
-15.0	5	41.0
-14.4	6	42.8
-13.9	7	44.6
-13.3	8	46.4
-12.8	9	48.2
-12.2	10	50.0
-11.7	11	51.8
-11.1	12	53.6
-10.6	13	55.4
-10.0	14	57.2
-9.44	15	59.0
-8.89	16	60.8
-8.33	17	62.6
-7.78	18	64.4
-7.22	19	66.2
-6.67	20	68.0
-6.11	21	69.8
-5.56	22	71.6
-5.00	23	73.4
-4.44	24	75.2
-3.89	25	77.0

26 to 50

C.	C. or F.	F.
-3.33	26	78.8
-2.78	27	80.6
-2.22	28	82.4
-1.67	29	84.2
-1.11	30	86.0
-0.56	31	87.8
0	32	89.6
0.56	33	91.4
1.11	34	93.2
1.67	35	95.0
2.22	36	96.8
2.78	37	98.6
3.33	38	100.4
3.89	39	102.2
4.44	40	104.0
5.00	41	105.8
5.56	42	107.6
6.11	43	109.4
6.67	44	111.2
7.22	45	113.0
7.78	46	114.8
8.33	47	116.6
8.89	48	118.4
9.44	49	120.2
10.0	50	122.0

51 to 75

C.	C. or F.	F.
10.6	51	123.8
11.1	52	125.6
11.7	53	127.4
12.2	54	129.2
12.8	55	131.0
13.3	56	132.8
13.9	57	134.6
14.4	58	136.4
15.0	59	138.2
15.6	60	140.0
16.1	61	141.8
16.7	62	143.6
17.2	63	145.4
17.8	64	147.2
18.3	65	149.0
18.9	66	150.8
19.4	67	152.6
20.0	68	154.4
20.6	69	156.2
21.1	70	158.0
21.7	71	159.8
22.2	72	161.6
22.8	73	163.4
23.3	74	165.2
23.9	75	167.0

76 to 100

C.	C. or F.	F.
24.4	76	168.8
25.0	77	170.6
25.6	78	172.4
26.1	79	174.2
26.7	80	176.0
27.2	81	177.8
27.8	82	179.6
28.3	83	181.4
28.9	84	183.2
29.4	85	185.0
30.0	86	186.8
30.6	87	188.6
31.1	88	190.4
31.7	89	192.2
32.2	90	194.0
32.8	91	195.8
33.3	92	197.6
33.9	93	199.4
34.4	94	201.2
35.0	95	203.0
35.6	96	204.8
36.1	97	206.6
36.7	98	208.4
37.2	99	210.2
37.8	100	212.0

101 to 340

C.	C. or F.	F.
43	110	230
49	120	248
54	130	266
60	140	284
66	150	302
71	160	320
77	170	338
82	180	356
88	190	374
93	200	392
99	210	410
100	212	413
104	220	428
110	230	446
116	240	464
121	250	482
127	260	500
132	270	518
138	280	536
143	290	554
149	300	572
154	310	590
160	320	608
166	330	626
171	340	644

341 to 490

C.	C. or F.	F.
177	350	662
182	360	680
188	370	698
193	380	716
199	390	734
204	400	752
210	410	770
216	420	788
221	430	806
227	440	824
232	450	842
238	460	860
243	470	878
249	480	896
254	490	914

491 to 750

C.	C. or F.	F.
260	500	932
266	510	950
271	520	968
277	530	986
282	540	1004
288	550	1022
293	560	1040
299	570	1058
304	580	1076
310	590	1094
316	600	1112
321	610	1130
327	620	1148
332	630	1166
338	640	1184
343	650	1202
349	660	1220
354	670	1238
360	680	1256
366	690	1274
371	700	1292
377	710	1310
382	720	1328
388	730	1346
393	740	1364
399	750	1382

INTERPOLATION FACTORS

C.	F.	F.	C.	F.	F.
0.56	1	1.8	3.33	6	10.8
1.11	2	3.6	3.89	7	12.6
1.67	3	5.4	4.44	8	14.4
2.22	4	7.2	5.00	9	16.2
2.78	5	9.0	5.56	10	18.0

NOTE:—The numbers in bold face type refer to the temperature either in degrees Centigrade or Fahrenheit which it is desired to convert into the other scale. If converting from Fahrenheit degrees to Centigrade degrees the equivalent temperature will be found in the left column, while if converting from degrees Centigrade to degrees Fahrenheit, the answer will be found in the column on the right.

$$°F = \frac{9}{5}(°C) + 32$$

$$°C = \frac{5}{9}(°F - 32)$$

(Courtesy of Stephens–Adamson Manufacturing Co.)

APPENDIX 5. WEIGHTS AND SPECIFIC GRAVITIES

Substance	Weight Lb. per Cu. Ft.	Specific Gravity	Substance	Weight Lb. per Cu. Ft.	Specific Gravity
METALS, ALLOYS, ORES			**TIMBER, U. S. SEASONED**		
Aluminum, cast, hammered	165	2.55-2.75	Moisture Content by Weight:		
Brass, cast, rolled	534	8.4-8.7	Seasoned timber 15 to 20%		
Bronze, 7.9 to 14% Sn	509	7.4-8.9	Green timber up to 50%		
Bronze, aluminum	481	7.7	Ash, white, red	40	0.62-0.65
Copper, cast, rolled	556	8.8-9.0	Cedar, white, red	22	0.32-0.38
Copper ore, pyrites	262	4.1-4.3	Chestnut	41	0.66
Gold, cast, hammered	1205	19.25-19.3	Cypress	30	0.48
Iron, cast, pig	450	7.2	Fir, Douglas spruce	32	0.51
Iron, wrought	485	7.6-7.9	Fir, eastern	25	0.40
Iron, spiegel-eisen	468	7.5	Elm, white	45	0.72
Iron, ferro-silicon	437	6.7-7.3	Hemlock	29	0.42-0.52
Iron ore, hematite	325	5.2	Hickory	49	0.74-0.84
Iron ore, hematite in bank	160-180	....	Locust	46	0.73
Iron ore, hematite loose	130-160	....	Maple, hard	43	0.68
Iron ore, limonite	237	3.6-4.0	Maple, white	33	0.53
Iron ore, magnetite	315	4.9-5.2	Oak, chestnut	54	0.86
Iron slag	172	2.5-3.0	Oak, live	59	0.95
Lead	710	11.37	Oak, red, black	41	0.65
Lead ore, galena	465	7.3-7.6	Oak, white	46	0.74
Magnesium, alloys	112	1.74-1.83	Pine, Oregon	32	0.51
Manganese	475	7.2-8.0	Pine, red	30	0.48
Manganese ore, pyrolusite	259	3.7-4.6	Pine, white	26	0.41
Mercury	849	13.6	Pine, yellow, long-leaf	44	0.70
Monel Metal	556	8.8-9.0	Pine, yellow, short-leaf	38	0.61
Nickel	565	8.9-9.2	Poplar	30	0.48
Platinum, cast, hammered	1330	21.1-21.5	Redwood, California	26	0.42
Silver, cast, hammered	656	10.4-10.6	Spruce, white, black	27	0.40-0.46
Steel, rolled	490	7.85	Walnut, black	38	0.61
Tin, cast, hammered	459	7.2-7.5			
Tin ore, cassiterite	418	6.4-7.0			
Zinc, cast, rolled	440	6.9-7.2			
Zinc ore, blende	253	3.9-4.2	**VARIOUS LIQUIDS**		
			Alcohol, 100%	49	0.79
			Acids, muriatic 40%	75	1.20
VARIOUS SOLIDS			Acids, nitric 91%	94	1.50
			Acids, sulphuric 87%	112	1.80
Cereals, oats .... bulk	32	....	Lye, soda 66%	106	1.70
Cereals, barley .... bulk	39	....	Oils, vegetable	58	0.91-0.94
Cereals, corn, rye .... bulk	48	....	Oils, mineral, lubricants	57	0.90-0.93
Cereals, wheat .... bulk	48	....	Water, 4°C. max. density	62.428	1.0
Hay and Straw .... bales	20		Water, 100°C	59.830	0.9584
Cotton, Flax, Hemp	93	1.47-1.50	Water, ice	56	0.88-0.92
Fats	58	0.90-0.97	Water, snow, fresh fallen	8	.125
Flour, loose	28	0.40-0.50	Water, sea water	64	1.02-1.03
Flour, pressed	47	0.70-0.80			
Glass, common	156	2.40-2.60			
Glass, plate or crown	161	2.45-2.72	**GASES**		
Glass, crystal	184	2.90-3.00			
Leather	59	0.86-1.02	Air, 0°C. 760 mm.	.08071	1.0
Paper	58	0.70-1.15	Ammonia	.0478	0.5920
Potatoes, piled	42	....	Carbon dioxide	.1234	1.5291
Rubber, caoutchouc	59	0.92-0.96	Carbon monoxide	.0781	0.9673
Rubber goods	94	1.0-2.0	Gas, illuminating	.028-.036	0.35-0.45
Salt, granulated, piled	48	....	Gas, natural	.038-.039	0.47-0.48
Saltpeter	67	....	Hydrogen	.00559	0.0693
Starch	96	1.53	Nitrogen	.0784	0.9714
Sulphur	125	1.93-2.07	Oxygen	.0892	1.1056
Wool	82	1.32			

The specific gravities of solids and liquids refer to water at 4°C., those of gases to air at 0°C. and 760 mm. pressure. The weights per cubic foot are derived from average specific gravities, except where stated that weights are for bulk, heaped or loose material, etc.

(Courtesy of the American Institute of Steel Construction.)

APPENDIX 5. WEIGHTS AND SPECIFIC GRAVITIES (CONT.)

Substance	Weight Lb. per Cu. Ft.	Specific Gravity	Substance	Weight Lb. per Cu. Ft.	Specific Gravity
ASHLAR MASONRY			**MINERALS**		
Granite, syenite, gneiss......	165	2.3-3.0	Asbestos.................	153	2.1-2.8
Limestone, marble............	160	2.3-2.8	Barytes..................	281	4.50
Sandstone, bluestone........	140	2.1-2.4	Basalt...................	184	2.7-3.2
			Bauxite..................	159	2.55
MORTAR RUBBLE MASONRY			Borax...................	109	1.7-1.8
			Chalk...................	137	1.8-2.6
Granite, syenite, gneiss......	155	2.2-2.8	Clay, marl...............	137	1.8-2.6
Limestone, marble............	150	2.2-2.6	Dolomite................	181	2.9
Sandstone, bluestone........	130	2.0-2.2	Feldspar, orthoclase......	159	2.5-2.6
			Gneiss, serpentine........	159	2.4-2.7
DRY RUBBLE MASONRY			Granite, syenite.........	175	2.5-3.1
Granite, syenite, gneiss......	130	1.9-2.3	Greenstone, trap.........	187	2.8-3.2
Limestone, marble............	125	1.9-2.1	Gypsum, alabaster........	159	2.3-2.8
Sandstone, bluestone........	110	1.8-1.9	Hornblende..............	187	3.0
			Limestone, marble........	165	2.5-2.8
BRICK MASONRY			Magnesite...............	187	3.0
Pressed brick...............	140	2.2-2.3	Phosphate rock, apatite....	200	3.2
Common brick...............	120	1.8-2.0	Porphyry................	172	2.6-2.9
Soft brick..................	100	1.5-1.7	Pumice, natural..........	40	0.37-0.90
			Quartz, flint............	165	2.5-2.8
CONCRETE MASONRY			Sandstone, bluestone........	147	2.2-2.5
Cement, stone, sand...........	144	2.2-2.4	Shale, slate.............	175	2.7-2.9
Cement, slag, etc.............	130	1.9-2.3	Soapstone, talc..........	169	2.6-2.8
Cement, cinder, etc...........	100	1.5-1.7			
			STONE, QUARRIED, PILED		
VARIOUS BUILDING MATERIALS			Basalt, granite, gneiss........	96	....
Ashes, cinders................	40-45	....	Limestone, marble, quartz	95	....
Cement, portland, loose.....	90	....	Sandstone...............	82	....
Cement, portland, set........	183	2.7-3.2	Shale..................	92	....
Lime, gypsum, loose..........	53-64	....	Greenstone, hornblende......	107	....
Mortar, set..................	103	1.4-1.9			
Slags, bank slag..............	67-72	....			
Slags, bank screenings........	98-117	....			
Slags, machine slag...........	96	....	**BITUMINOUS SUBSTANCES**		
Slags, slag sand..............	49-55	....	Asphaltum...............	81	1.1-1.5
			Coal, anthracite.........	97	1.4-1.7
EARTH, ETC., EXCAVATED			Coal, bituminous.........	84	1.2-1.5
Clay, dry....................	63	....	Coal, lignite............	78	1.1-1.4
Clay, damp, plastic...........	110	....	Coal, peat, turf, dry........	47	0.65-0.85
Clay and gravel, dry..........	100	....	Coal, charcoal, pine........	23	0.28-0.44
Earth, dry, loose.............	76	....	Coal, charcoal, oak........	33	0.47-0.57
Earth, dry, packed............	95	....	Coal, coke..............	75	1.0-1.4
Earth, moist, loose...........	78	....	Graphite................	131	1.9-2.3
Earth, moist, packed..........	96	....	Paraffine...............	56	0.87-0.91
Earth, mud, flowing...........	108	....	Petroleum...............	54	0.87
Earth, mud, packed...........	115	....	Petroleum, refined........	50	0.79-0.82
Riprap, limestone............	80-85	....	Petroleum, benzine.......	46	0.73-0.75
Riprap, sandstone............	90	....	Petroleum, gasoline.......	42	0.66-0.69
Riprap, shale................	105	....	Pitch...................	69	1.07-1.15
Sand, gravel, dry, loose......	90-105	....	Tar, bituminous..........	75	1.20
Sand, gravel, dry, packed...	100-120	....			
Sand, gravel, dry, wet........	118-120	....			
EXCAVATIONS IN WATER			**COAL AND COKE, PILED**		
Sand or gravel...............	60	....	Coal, anthracite.........	47-58	....
Sand or gravel and clay......	65	....	Coal, bituminous, lignite..	40-54	....
Clay.......................	80	....	Coal, peat, turf.........	20-26	....
River mud...................	90	....	Coal, charcoal..........	10-14	....
Soil........................	70	....	Coal, coke..............	23-32	....
Stone riprap................	65	....			

The specific gravities of solids and liquids refer to water at 4°C., those of gases to air at 0°C. and 760 mm. pressure. The weights per cubic foot are derived from average specific gravities, except where stated that weights are for bulk, heaped or loose material, etc.

WIRE AND SHEET METAL GAGES
IN DECIMALS OF AN INCH

Name of Gage	United States Standard Gage*		The United States Steel Wire Gage	American or Brown & Sharpe Wire Gage	New Birmingham Standard Sheet & Hoop Gage	British Imperial or English Legal Standard Wire Gage	Birmingham or Stubs Iron Wire Gage	Name of Gage
Principal Use	Uncoated Steel Sheets and Light Plates		Steel Wire except Music Wire	Non-Ferrous Sheets and Wire	Iron and Steel Sheets and Hoops	Wire	Strips, Bands, Hoops and Wire	Principal Use
Gage No.	Weight Oz. per Sq. Ft.	Approx. Thickness Inches	Thickness, Inches					Gage No.
7/0's			.4900		.6666	.500		7/0's
6/0's			.4615	.5800	.625	.464		6/0's
5/0's			.4305	.5165	.5883	.432	.500	5/0's
4/0's			.3938	.4600	.5416	.400	.454	4/0's
3/0's			.3625	.4096	.500	.372	.425	3/0's
2/0's			.3310	.3648	.4452	.348	.380	2/0's
0			.3065	.3249	.3964	.324	.340	0
1			.2830	.2893	.3532	.300	.300	1
2			.2625	.2576	.3147	.276	.284	2
3	160	.2391	.2437	.2294	.2804	.252	.259	3
4	150	.2242	.2253	.2043	.250	.232	.238	4
5	140	.2092	.2070	.1819	.2225	.212	.220	5
6	130	.1943	.1920	.1620	.1981	.192	.203	6
7	120	.1793	.1770	.1443	.1764	.176	.180	7
8	110	.1644	.1620	.1285	.1570	.160	.165	8
9	100	.1495	.1483	.1144	.1398	.144	.148	9
10	90	.1345	.1350	.1019	.1250	.128	.134	10
11	80	.1196	.1205	.0907	.1113	.116	.120	11
12	70	.1046	.1055	.0808	.0991	.104	.109	12
13	60	.0897	.0915	.0720	.0882	.092	.095	13
14	50	0747	.0800	.0641	.0785	.080	.083	14
15	45	.0673	.0720	.0571	.0699	.072	.072	15
16	40	.0598	.0625	.0508	.0625	.064	.065	16
17	36	.0538	.0540	.0453	.0556	.056	.058	17
18	32	.0478	.0475	.0403	.0495	.048	.049	18
19	28	.0418	.0410	.0359	.0440	.040	.042	19
20	24	.0359	.0348	.0320	.0392	.036	.035	20
21	22	.0329	.0318	.0285	.0349	.032	.032	21
22	20	.0299	.0286	.0253	.0313	.028	.028	22
23	18	.0269	.0258	.0226	.0278	.024	.025	23
24	16	.0239	.0230	.0201	.0248	.022	.022	24
25	14	.0209	.0204	.0179	.0220	.020	.020	25
26	12	.0179	.0181	.0159	.0196	.018	.018	26
27	11	.0164	.0173	.0142	.0175	.0164	.016	27
28	10	.0149	:0162	.0126	.0156	.0148	.014	28
29	9	.0135	.0150	.0113	.0139	.0136	.013	29
30	8	.0120	.0140	.0100	.0123	.0124	.012	30
31	7	.0105	.0132	.0089	.0110	.0116	.010	31
32	6.5	.0097	.0128	.0080	.0098	.0108	.009	32
33	6	.0090	.0118	.0071	.0087	.0100	.008	33
34	5.5	.0082	.0104	.0063	.0077	.0092	.007	34
35	5	.0075	.0095	.0056	.0069	.0084	.005	35
36	4.5	.0067	.0090	.0050	.0061	.0076	.004	36
37	4.25	.0064	.0085	.0045	.0054	.0068		37
38	4	.0060	.0080	.0040	.0048	.0060		38
39			.0075	.0035	.0043	.0052		39
40			.0070	.0031	.0039	.0048		40

* U. S. Standard Gage is officially a weight gage, in oz. per sq. ft. as tabulated. The Approx. Thickness shown is the "Manufacturers' Standard" of the American Iron and Steel Institute, based on steel as weighing 501.81 lbs. per cu. ft. (489.6 true weight plus 2.5 percent for average over-run in area and thickness). The A.I.S.I. standard nomenclature for flat rolled carbon steel is as follows:

Widths, Inches	Thicknesses, Inch							
	0.2500 and thicker	0.2499 to 0.2031	0.2030 to 0.1875	0.1874 to 0.0568	0.0567 to 0.0344	0.0343 to 0.0255	0.0254 to 0.0142	0.0141 and thinner
To 3½ incl.	Bar	Bar	Strip	Strip	Strip	Strip	Sheet	Sheet
Over 3½ to 6 incl.	Bar	Bar	Strip	Strip	Strip	Sheet	Sheet	Sheet
" 6 to 12 "	Plate	Strip	Strip	Strip	Sheet	Sheet	Sheet	Sheet
" 12 to 32 "	Plate	Sheet	Sheet	Sheet	Sheet	Sheet	Sheet	Black Plate
" 32 to 48 "	Plate	Sheet	Sheet	Sheet	Sheet	Sheet	Sheet	Sheet
" 48 "	Plate	Plate	Plate	Sheet	Sheet	Sheet	Sheet	———

(Courtesy of the American Institute of Steel Construction.)

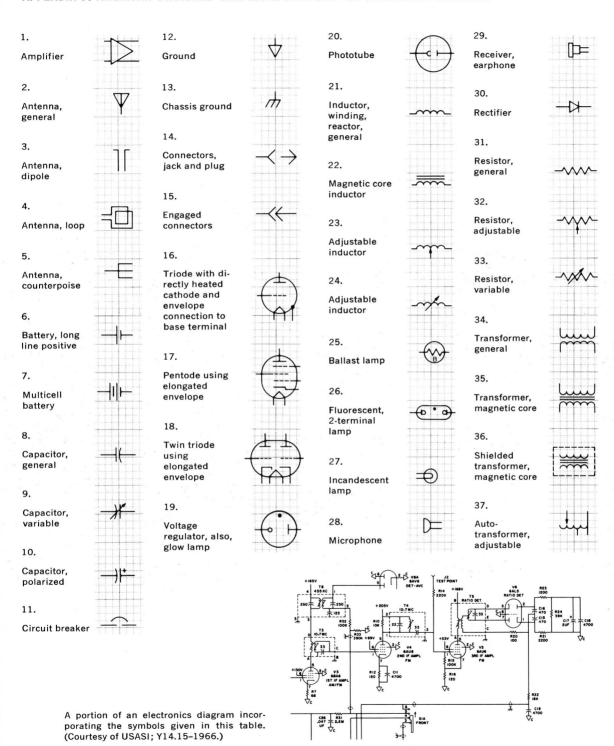

1. Amplifier

2. Antenna, general

3. Antenna, dipole

4. Antenna, loop

5. Antenna, counterpoise

6. Battery, long line positive

7. Multicell battery

8. Capacitor, general

9. Capacitor, variable

10. Capacitor, polarized

11. Circuit breaker

12. Ground

13. Chassis ground

14. Connectors, jack and plug

15. Engaged connectors

16. Triode with directly heated cathode and envelope connection to base terminal

17. Pentode using elongated envelope

18. Twin triode using elongated envelope

19. Voltage regulator, also, glow lamp

20. Phototube

21. Inductor, winding, reactor, general

22. Magnetic core inductor

23. Adjustable inductor

24. Adjustable inductor

25. Ballast lamp

26. Fluorescent, 2-terminal lamp

27. Incandescent lamp

28. Microphone

29. Receiver, earphone

30. Rectifier

31. Resistor, general

32. Resistor, adjustable

33. Resistor, variable

34. Transformer, general

35. Transformer, magnetic core

36. Shielded transformer, magnetic core

37. Auto-transformer, adjustable

A portion of an electronics diagram incorporating the symbols given in this table. (Courtesy of USASI; Y14.15–1966.)

GRAPHICAL SYMBOLS FOR PIPE FITTINGS & VALVES

	FLANGED	SCREWED	BELL & SPIGOT	WELDED	SOLDERED
1 BUSHING					
2 CAP					
3 CROSS					
3.1 STRAIGHT SIZE					
4 CROSSOVER					
5 ELBOW					
5.1 45-DEGREE					
5.2 90-DEGREE					
5.3 TURNED DOWN					
5.4 TURNED UP					
5.5 LONG RADIUS					
5.6 REDUCING					

(Courtesy of USASI; Z32.2.3–1949.)

	FLANGED	SCREWED	BELL & SPIGOT	WELDED	SOLDERED
6 JOINT					
6.1 CONNECTING PIPE					
6.2 EXPANSION					
7 LATERAL					
8 REDUCER					
8.1 CONCENTRIC					
8.2 ECCENTRIC					
9 SLEEVE					
10 TEE					
10.1 (STRAIGHT SIZE)					
10.2 (OUTLET UP)					
10.3 (OUTLET DOWN)					
11 UNION					
12 CHECK VALVE					
12.1 (STRAIGHT WAY)					

APPENDIX 8. AMERICAN STANDARD PIPING, HEATING, AND PLUMBING GRAPHICAL SYMBOLS (Cont.)

	FLANGED	SCREWED	BELL & SPIGOT	WELDED	SOLDERED
13 COCK					
14 GATE VALVE					
15 GLOBE VALVE					
16 SAFETY VALVE					
17 STOP VALVE	SAME AS	SYMBOLS	14		

GRAPHICAL SYMBOLS FOR PIPING

COMPRESSED AIR	———————A———————
COLD WATER	— - — - — - — -
GAS	——G———G——
SOIL, WASTE OR LEADER (ABOVE GRADE)	———————
SOIL, WASTE OR LEADER (BELOW GRADE)	— — — — —

APPENDIX 9. AMERICAN WELDING SOCIETY STANDARD WELDING SYMBOLS

AWS A2.1-68

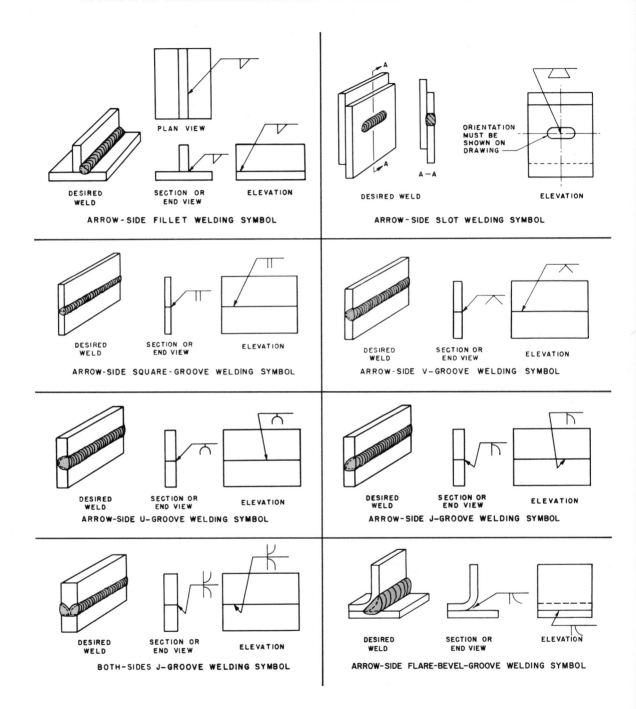

(Courtesy of USASI; Y32.3–1959.)

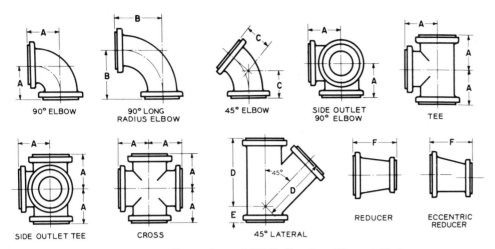

90° ELBOW   90° LONG RADIUS ELBOW   45° ELBOW   SIDE OUTLET 90° ELBOW   TEE

SIDE OUTLET TEE   CROSS   45° LATERAL   REDUCER   ECCENTRIC REDUCER

Dimensions of 250-lb Cast Iron Flanged Fittings

Nominal Pipe Size	Flanges			Fittings		Straight					
	Dia of Flange	Thickness of Flange (Min)	Dia of Raised Face	Inside Dia of Fittings (Min)	Wall Thickness	Center to Face 90 Deg Elbow Tees, Crosses and True "Y"	Center to Face 90 Deg Long Radius Elbow	Center to Face 45 Deg Elbow	Center to Face Lateral	Short Center to Face True "Y" and Lateral	Face to Face Reducer
						A	B	C	D	E	F
1	$4\frac{7}{8}$	$\frac{11}{16}$	$2\frac{11}{16}$	1	$\frac{7}{16}$	4	5	2	$6\frac{1}{2}$	2	....
$1\frac{1}{4}$	$5\frac{1}{4}$	$\frac{3}{4}$	$3\frac{1}{16}$	$1\frac{1}{4}$	$\frac{7}{16}$	$4\frac{1}{4}$	$5\frac{1}{2}$	$2\frac{1}{2}$	$7\frac{1}{4}$	$2\frac{1}{4}$	....
$1\frac{1}{2}$	$6\frac{1}{8}$	$\frac{13}{16}$	$3\frac{9}{16}$	$1\frac{1}{2}$	$\frac{7}{16}$	$4\frac{1}{2}$	6	$2\frac{3}{4}$	$8\frac{1}{2}$	$2\frac{1}{2}$	....
2	$6\frac{1}{2}$	$\frac{7}{8}$	$4\frac{3}{16}$	2	$\frac{7}{16}$	5	$6\frac{1}{2}$	3	9	$2\frac{1}{2}$	5
$2\frac{1}{2}$	$7\frac{1}{2}$	1	$4\frac{15}{16}$	$2\frac{1}{2}$	$\frac{1}{2}$	$5\frac{1}{2}$	7	$3\frac{1}{2}$	$10\frac{1}{2}$	$2\frac{1}{2}$	$5\frac{1}{2}$
3	$8\frac{1}{4}$	$1\frac{1}{8}$	$5\frac{11}{16}$	3	$\frac{9}{16}$	6	$7\frac{3}{4}$	$3\frac{1}{2}$	11	3	6
$3\frac{1}{2}$	9	$1\frac{3}{16}$	$6\frac{5}{16}$	$3\frac{1}{2}$	$\frac{9}{16}$	$6\frac{1}{2}$	$8\frac{1}{2}$	4	$12\frac{1}{2}$	3	$6\frac{1}{2}$
4	10	$1\frac{1}{4}$	$6\frac{15}{16}$	4	$\frac{5}{8}$	7	9	$4\frac{1}{2}$	$13\frac{1}{2}$	3	7
5	11	$1\frac{3}{8}$	$8\frac{5}{16}$	5	$\frac{11}{16}$	8	$10\frac{1}{4}$	5	15	$3\frac{1}{2}$	8
6	$12\frac{1}{2}$	$1\frac{7}{16}$	$9\frac{11}{16}$	6	$\frac{3}{4}$	$8\frac{1}{2}$	$11\frac{1}{2}$	$5\frac{1}{2}$	$17\frac{1}{2}$	4	9
8	15	$1\frac{5}{8}$	$11\frac{15}{16}$	8	$\frac{13}{16}$	10	14	6	$20\frac{1}{2}$	5	11
10	$17\frac{1}{2}$	$1\frac{7}{8}$	$14\frac{1}{16}$	10	$\frac{15}{16}$	$11\frac{1}{2}$	$16\frac{1}{2}$	7	24	$5\frac{1}{2}$	12
12	$20\frac{1}{2}$	2	$16\frac{7}{16}$	12	1	13	19	8	$27\frac{1}{2}$	6	14
14	23	$2\frac{1}{8}$	$18\frac{15}{16}$	$13\frac{1}{4}$	$1\frac{1}{8}$	15	$21\frac{1}{2}$	$8\frac{1}{2}$	31	$6\frac{1}{2}$	16
16	$25\frac{1}{2}$	$2\frac{1}{4}$	$21\frac{1}{16}$	$15\frac{1}{4}$	$1\frac{1}{4}$	$16\frac{1}{2}$	24	$9\frac{1}{2}$	$34\frac{1}{2}$	$7\frac{1}{2}$	18
18	28	$2\frac{3}{8}$	$23\frac{5}{16}$	17	$1\frac{3}{8}$	18	$26\frac{1}{2}$	10	$37\frac{1}{2}$	8	19
20	$30\frac{1}{2}$	$2\frac{1}{2}$	$25\frac{9}{16}$	19	$1\frac{1}{2}$	$19\frac{1}{2}$	29	$10\frac{1}{2}$	$40\frac{1}{2}$	$8\frac{1}{2}$	20
24	36	$2\frac{3}{4}$	$30\frac{5}{16}$	23	$1\frac{5}{8}$	$22\frac{1}{2}$	34	12	$47\frac{1}{2}$	10	24
30	43	3	$37\frac{3}{16}$	29	2	$27\frac{1}{2}$	$41\frac{1}{2}$	15	....	....	30

All dimensions given in inches.

(Courtesy of USASI; B16.1–1967.)

APPENDIX 12. ENGINEERING FORMULAS

Motion

S = distance (inches, feet, miles)
t = time (seconds, minutes, hours)
v = average velocity (feet per second, miles per hour, etc.)
v_1 = initial velocity
v_2 = final velocity
a = acceleration (feet per second per second)

(1) $S = vt$

(2) $V(\text{avg.}) = \dfrac{v_2 + v_1}{2}$

(3) $S = \left(\dfrac{v_1 + v_2}{2}\right) \dfrac{\text{ft}}{\text{sec}} \ (t \text{ sec})$

(4) $a = \dfrac{v_2 - v_1}{t}$

(5) $S = V_1 t + \frac{1}{2}at^2$

Angular Motion

V = linear velocity
N = number of revolutions per min
θ = angular distance in radians
1 radian = $360°/2\pi = 57.3°$
ω (omega) = average angular velocity
$\qquad = \theta/t$ (rad per sec, rev per min)
ω_1 = initial velocity
ω_2 = final velocity
α (alpha) = angular acceleration = rad per sec^2
S = length of arc
r = radius of arc
D = diameter

(6) $\theta = (\text{avg. } \omega)t$

(7) $\omega(\text{avg}) = \dfrac{\omega_2 + \omega_1}{2}$

(8) $\alpha = \dfrac{\omega_2 - \omega_1}{t}$

(9) $\omega_2 = \omega_1 + \alpha t$

(10) $\theta = \omega_1 t + \dfrac{\alpha t^2}{2}$

(11) $V = \pi DN$ or $V = r\omega$ (ft per sec, ft per min, etc.)

(12) $\omega = \dfrac{2\pi rn}{r} = 2\pi N$

Force and Acceleration

F = force (pounds)
M = mass
a = acceleration (ft per sec^2)
g = gravitational acceleration = 32.2 ft/sec^2
W = weight (pounds)
$M = F/a = W/g$ (units of mass in slugs)

Work

W = work (ft·lb)
F = force (lb)
d = distance
$W = Fd$

Power

W = work
t = time
1 horsepower = $550 \ \dfrac{\text{ft·lb}}{\text{sec}}$

Avg. power = $\dfrac{W}{t} = \dfrac{\text{ft·lb}}{\text{sec}}$ or $\dfrac{\text{ft·lb}}{\text{min}}$ etc.

Kinetic Energy

W = weight
V = velocity
g = 32.2 ft per sec^2
K.E. = $WV^2/2g$

APPENDIX 13. Lettering Instruments

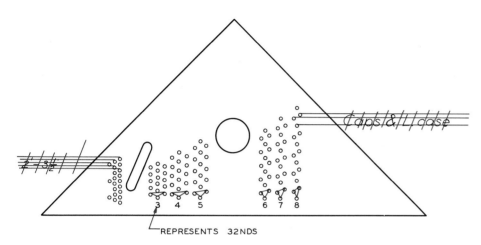

The *Braddock-Rowe triangle* serves a dual role as a 45° triangle and a lettering instrument. Guidelines are drawn lightly by inserting the pencil point in the guide holes and sliding the triangle along a stationary edge of a drafting machine or T-square. The numbers under the holes represent 32nds of an inch. *Example:* 4 represents $\frac{4}{32}''$ or $\frac{1}{8}''$. A slot is provided for constructing guide lines for slanted lettering. (Courtesy of Braddock Instrument Company.)

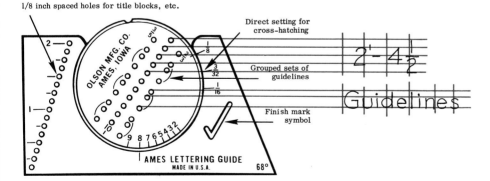

The *Ames lettering instrument* can be used for the construction of guidelines in much the same manner as the Braddock-Rowe triangle. An adjustable disc can be set on the letter height desired as seen at the bottom of the disc, where the numbers given represent 32nds of an inch. The disc is shown set at $\frac{8}{32}''$ or $\frac{1}{4}''$. (Courtesy of Olson Manufacturing Co.)

INDEX

339

ABCDE7987654321

Harnessing the world's surging rivers for irrigation and power—a challenge met by engineers and construction men with many notable achievements. The first great masonry dam—the first Aswan—was constructed on the Nile, and completed in 1902. The Hoover Dam (726.4 feet high, 1200 feet long) was started in 1928, dedicated in 1935 and became one of the largest hydroelectric suppliers in the world.

Probing and observing, engineers begin to chart the course of a fabulous voyage—the penetration of outer space. To accomplish it, engineering on a massive scale, to unprecedented degrees of accuracy and reliability, produced the first manned satellites (1961), Telstar (1962), the first photographs of the moon and Mars. Giant radio telescopes now "see" to the outer edges of the universe.